HARDPRESS

ISBN: 978129016286

Published by:
HardPress Publishing
8345 NW 66TH ST #2561
MIAMI FL 33166-2626

Email: info@hardpress.net
Web: http://www.hardpress.net

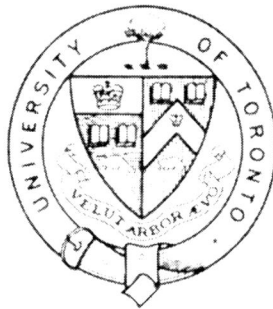

A STRANGE WORLD

BY

MISS M. E. BRADDON

AUTHOR OF "LADY AUDLEY'S SECRET," "AURORA FLOYD," ETC.

———

DONOHUE, HENNEBERRY & CO.
407 TO 425 DEARBORN ST.,
CHICAGO.

A STRANGE WORLD.

BY MISS M. E. BRADDON.

CHAPTER I.

POOR PLAYERS.

A FAIR slope of land in buttercup-time, just when May, the capricious, melts into tender June—a slope of fertile pasture within two miles of the city of Eborsham, whose cathedral towers rise tall in the blue, dim distance—a wealth of hedgerow flowers on every side, and all the air full of their faint, sweet perfume, mixed with the odorous breath of the fast-perishing hawthorn. Two figures are grouped in a corner of the meadow, beneath the umbrage of an ancient thorn, not Arcadian or pastoral figures by any means—not Phillis, the milkmaid, with sun-browned brow and carnation cheeks, nor Corydon fluting sweetly on his tuneful pipe as he reclines at her feet—but two figures which carry the unmistakable stamp of city life in every feature and every garment. One is a tall, lanky girl of seventeen, with a pale, tired face, and a look of having out-grown her strength, shot up too swiftly from childhood to girlhood, like a fast-growing weed. The other is a man who may be any age from forty to sixty—a man with sparse gray hair crowning a high forehead, bluish-gray eyes under thick dark brows, a red nose, a resolute mouth, a square jaw, and stalwart figure.

The girl's eyes are large and clear and changeful, of that dark blue-gray which often looks like black; eyes which are the chief beauty of a face that possesses no other strong claim to be admired—a scarcely noticeable countenance, indeed, save for those gray eyes.

The raiment of both man and girl is of the shabbiest. His threadbare coat has become luminous with much friction, a kind of phosphorescent brightness pervades the sleeves, like the oleaginous scum that shines upon sea waves; the tall hat which lies beside him in the deep grass has a look of having been soaped. His boots have obviously been soled and heeled, and have arrived at that debatable period in boot life when they must either be soled again or hie them straight to the dust-hole. The girl's gown is faded and too short for her long legs, her mantle a flimsy silken thing of an almost forgotten fashion, her hat a fabric of tawdry net and ribbon patched together by her own unskilled hands.

She sits with her lap full of bluebells and hawthorn, looking absently at the landscape, with those solemn towers rising out of the valley.

"How grand they are, father!"

The father is agreeably occupied in filling a cutty pipe embrowned by much smoking, which he handles fondly, as if it were a sentient thing.

"What's grand?"

"The cathedral towers. I could look at them for hours together, with that wide blue sky above them, and the streets and houses clustering at their feet. There's a bird's nest in one of them, oh! so high up, squeezed behind a horrid grinning face. Do you know, father, I've stood and looked at it sometimes till I've strained my eyes with looking. And I've wished I was a bird in that nest, to live up there in the cool shadow of the stone; no care, no trouble, no work, and all that blue sky above me forever and ever."

"The sky isn't always blue, stupid," answered the father, contemptuously. "Your bird's nest would be a nice place in stormy weather. You talk like a fool, Justina, with your towers and nests and blue skies; and you're getting a young woman now, and ought to have some sense. As for cathedral towns, for my part, I've never believed in 'em. Never saw good business for a fortnight on end in a cathedral town. It's all very well for a race week, or you may pull up with a military bespeak, if there's a garrison. But, in a general way, as far as the profession goes, your cathedral town is a dead failure."

"I wasn't thinking of the theater, father," said the girl, with a contemptuous shrug of her thin shoulders. "I hate the theater, and everything belonging to it!"

"There's a nice young woman, to quarrel with your bread and butter."

"Bread and ashes, I think, father," she said, looking downward at the flowers, with a moody face. "It tastes bitter enough for that."

"Did ever any one hear of such discontent?" ejaculated the father, lifting his eyes toward the heavens, as if invoking Jove himself as a witness of his child's depravity. "To go and run down the Pro.! Hasn't the Pro. nourished you, and brought you up, and maintained you since you were no higher than that?"

He spread his dingy hand a foot or so above the buttercups to illustrate his remarks.

The Pro. of which he spoke with so fond an air was the calling of an actor, and this elderly gentleman in threadbare raiment was Mr. Mathew Elgood, a performer of that particular line of dramatic business known in his own circle as "the first heavies," or in more familiar parlance, Mr. Elgood was the heavy man—the king in "Hamlet," Iago, Friar Lawrence, the robber chief of melodrama, the relentless father of the ponderous top-booted and pigtailed comedy. And Justina Elgood, his seventeen-year-old daughter, commonly called Judy. Was she Juliet or Desdemona, Ophelia or Imogen? No. Miss Elgood had not yet soared above the humblest drudgery. Her line was general utility, in which she worked with the unrequited patience of an East End shirt-maker.

"Hasn't the Pro. supported you from the cradle?" growled Mr. Elgood, between short, thoughtful puffs at his pipe.

"Had I ever a cradle, father?" the girl demanded, wonderingly. "If you were always moving about then as you are now, a cradle must have been a great inconvenience."

"I've a sort of recollection of seeing you in one, for all that," replied Mr. Elgood, shutting his eyes with a meditating air, as if he were casting his gaze back into the past—"a clumsy edifice of straw, bulky, and awkward of shape. It might have held properties pretty well, but I don't remember traveling with it. I dare say your mother borrowed the thing of her landlady. You were born at Seacomb, you know, in Cornwall, and Seacomb people are uncommonly friendly. I make no doubt your mother borrowed it."

"I dare say, father. We are great people for borrowing!"

"Why not?" asked Mr. Elgood, lightly. "give and take, you know, Judy, that's a Christian sentiment."

"Yes, father, but we always take."

"Man is the slave of circumstances, my dear. 'Give to him that asketh thee, and from him that would borrow of thee turn not away.' That's the Gospel, Justina. If I have been rather in the position of the borrower than the lender, that has been my misfortune, and not my fault. Had I been the possessor of ten thousand per annum, I would have been the last of men to refuse to take a box ticket for a fellow-creature's benefit."

The girl gave a faint sigh, and began to arrange her bluebells and hawthorn into a nosegay, somewhat listlessly, as if even her natural joy in these things were clouded by a settled gloom within her breast.

"You're in the first piece, aren't you, Judy?" inquired Mathew Elgood, after indulging himself with a snatch of slumber, his elbow deep in the buttercups, and his head resting on his hand.

"Yes, father," with a sigh—"the countess, you know."

"The countess in the 'Stranger,' a most profitable part. Don't put on that hat and feather you wore last time we played the piece. It made the gallery laugh. I wonder whether you'll ever be fit for the juvenile lead, Judy," he went on, meditatively. "Do you know, sometimes I am afraid you never will, you're so gawky and so listless. The gawkiness would be nothing—you'll get over that when you've done growing. I dare say—but your heart is not in your profession, Justina. There's the rub."

"My heart in it!" echoed the girl, with a dreary laugh, "why, I hate it, father; you must know that. Hasn't it kept me ignorant and shabby, and looked down upon all the days of my life, since I was two years old, and went on as the child in 'Pizarro?' Hasn't it kept me hanging about the wings till midnight, from year's end to year's end, when other children were in bed, with a mother to look after them? Haven't I been told often enough that I've no talents, and no good looks to help me, and that I must be a drudge all my life?"

" No good looks! Well, I'm not so sure about that," said the father, thoughtfully. " Talent, I admit, you are deficient of, Judy; but your looks even now are by no means despicable, and will improve with time. You have a fine pair of eyes, and a complexion that lights up uncommonly well. I have seen leading ladies earning their three or four guineas a week with less personal advantages."

" I wish I could earn a good salary, father, for your sake: but I should never be fond of acting. I've seen too much of the theater. If I'd been a young lady, now, shut up in a drawing-room all my life, and brought to the theater for the first time to see ' Romeo and Juliet,' I could fancy myself wanting to play Juliet; but I've seen too much of the ladder Juliet stands on in the balcony scene, and the dirty looking man that holds it steady for her, and the way she quarrels with Mrs. Wappers, the nurse, between the acts. I've read the play often, father, since you've told me to study Juliet, and I've tried to fancy her a real living woman in Verona, under a cloudless sky as blue as these flowers; but I can't; I can only think of Miss Villeroy in her white-brown satin, and Mrs. Wappers in her old green and yellow brocade, and the battered old garden scene, and the palace flats we use so often, and the scene-shifters in their dirty shirt sleeves. All the poetry has been taken out of it for me, father."

"That's because yours is a commonplace mind, child," answered Mr. Elgood, with a superior air. " Look at me, now! If I feel as dull as ditch-water when I go on the stage, the first hearty round of applause kindles the poetic fire, and the second fans it into a blaze. The divine afflatus, Judy, that's what you want—the afflatus!"

"I suppose you mean applause, father. I know I don't get much of that."

" No, Justina, I mean the breath of the gods—the sacred wind which breathes from the nostrils of genius, which gives life and shape to the imaginings of the dramatic poet, which inspires a Kean—and, occasionally, an Elgood. I suppose you didn't hear of their encoring my exit in Iago on Tuesday night?"

" Yes, father, I heard of it."

" Come, Judy, we must be going," said Mr. Elgood, raising himself from his luxurious repose among the buttercups, after looking at a battered silver watch, " it's past four, and we've a good two miles to walk before we get our teas."

" Oh, how I wish we could stay here just as long as we like, and then go quietly home in the starlight to some cottage among those trees over there."

" Cottages among trees are proverbially damp, and the kind of existence you talk of—mooning about a meadow and going home to a cottage—would be intolerably dull for a man with any pretension to intellect."

" Oh, father, we might have books, and music, and flowers, and birds, and animals, and a few friends, perhaps, who woul/

like and respect us—if we were not on the stage. I don't think we need be dull."

"The varied pages of the busy world comprise the only book I care to study, Justina. As for birds, flowers, and animals, I consider them alike messy and unprofitable. I never knew a man who had a pet dog come to much good. It's a sign of a weak mind."

They were both standing by this time looking across the verdant undulating landscape to the valley where nestled the city of Eborsham. The roofs and pinnacles did not seem far off, but there was that intervening sea of meadow land, about the navigation of which these wanderers began to feel somewhat uncertain.

"Do you know your way home, Judy?"

The girl looked across the meadows doubtfully.

"I'm not quite sure, father; but I fancy we came across that field over there, where there's such a lot of sorrel."

"Fancy be hanged!" exclaimed Mr. Elgood, impatiently; "I've got to be on the stage at half-past seven o'clock, and you lead me astray in this confounded solitary place to suit your childish whims, and don't know how to get me back. It would be a nice thing if I were to lose a week's salary through your tomfoolery."

"No fear of that, father. We shall find our way back somehow, depend upon it. Why, we can't go very far astray when we can see the cathedral towers."

"Yes, and we might wander about in sight of them from now till midnight without getting any nearer to 'em. You ought to have known better, Justina."

Justina hung her head, abashed by this stern reproof.

"I dare say somebody will come by presently, father, and we can ask——"

"Do you dare say? then I don't dare say anything of the sort. Here we've been sitting in this blessed meadow full two hours without seeing a mortal except one plow-boy, who went across with a can of something half an hour ago—beer most likely; I know the sight of it made me abominably thirsty—and according to the doctrine of averages, there's no chance of another human being for the next hour. Never you ask me to come for a walk with you again, Justina, after being trapped in this manner."

"Look, father! there's some one," cried Justina.

"Some two," said Mr. Elgood; "swells, by the cut of their jibs. Down for the races, I dare say."

Eborsham was a city which had its two brief seasons of glory every year. The "Eborsham spring" and the "Eborsham summer" were meetings famous in the sporting world; but the spring to the summer was as Omega to Alpha in the sideral heavens—or, taking a more earthly standard of magnitude, while beds for the accommodation of visitors were freely offered at half a crown during the spring meeting, the poorest pallet on hire in Eborsham was worth half a guinea in the summer.

The strangers approached at a leisurely pace. Two men in

the spring-time of their youth, clothed in gray.   One tall, strong
of limb, broad of chest, somewhat slovenly in attire; loose
cravat, gray felt hat, stout, sportsman-like boots, fishing-rod
under his arm.   The other shorter, slighter, smaller, dressed
with a certain girlish prettiness and neatness that smacked of
Eton.

Both were smoking as they came slowly strolling along the
field path, on the other side of the irregular hawthorn hedge,
the younger and smaller held a paper cigarette between his
girlish lips.   The other smoked a black-muzzled clay, which
would not have been out of keeping with the costume and bearing of an Irish navvy.

They came to a gap in the hedge, which brought them close
to the strollers.

"Gentlemen, can you enlighten me as to the nearest way to
Eborsham?" said Mr. Elgood, with a grandiose air, which the
prolonged exercise of his avocation had made second nature.

The elder of the strangers stared at him blankly, with that
unseeing gaze of the deep thinker, and went on sucking his
blackened pipe.   The younger smiled kindly, and made haste to
answer, with a shy eagerness—just a little stammer in his
speech at first—which was not unpleasing.

"I really am at a loss to direct you," he said.   "We are
strangers here ourselves—only came to Eborsham last night."

"For the races. I opine," interrupted Mr. Elgood.

"Not exactly for the races," replied the young man, doubtfully.

"You came for the races, Jim," said the taller stranger, looking down at his companion as from an altitude of wisdom and
experience.   "I came to see that you were not fleeced.   There
are no rogues like the rogues that haunt a race-course."

This with a dark glance at the actor.

"He looks the image of a tout," thought the tall stranger.
His fancies had been up aloft in his own particular cloud-land
when the wayfarers accosted him, and he was slowly coming
down to the level of work-a-day life.   Only this instant had he
become conscious of the girl's presence.

Justina stood in the background of her father's bulky figure,
making herself as narrow as she possibly could.   Her detract-
ors in the theater found fault with that narrowness of Justina's.
She had been disadvantageously likened to gas-pipes, May-poles,
and other unsubstantial objects, and was considered a mere profile of a girl, an outline sketch, only worth half the salary that
might have been given to a plumper damsel.

"Good heavens. Elgood!" the manager had exclaimed once
when Justina played a page, "when will your daughter begin
to have legs?"

The tall stranger's slow gaze had now descended upon Justina.
To that bashful maiden, conscious of her gawkiness, the darkly
bright eyes seemed awful as the front of Jove himself.   She
shrank behind her father, dazzled as if by a sunburst.   There
was such power in Humphrey Clissold's face.

"We came here anyhow, following the windings of yonder

trout-stream," said Clissold, with a backward glance at the valley. "I haven't the faintest notion how we are to get back, except by turning our noses to the cathedral, and then following them religiously. We can hardly fail to get there sooner or later, if we are true to our noses."

Justina began to laugh, as if it had been a green-room jokelet, and then checked herself, blushing vehemently. She felt it was taking a liberty to be amused by this tall stranger.

"Perhaps time is no object to you, sir," said Mr. Elgood.

"Not the slightest. I don't think time ever has been any object to me, except when I was gated at Oxford," replied Clissold.

"To me, sir, it is vital. If I do not reach yon city before the clock strikes seven, the prospects of a struggling commonwealth are blighted."

"Father." remonstrated the girl, plucking his sleeve, "what do these gentlemen know about commonwealths?"

"I have studied the subject but superficially in the pages of our friend Cicero," said Clissold, lightly. "Modern scholars call him Kikero, but your elder erudition might hardly accept the Kappa."

"The commonwealth to which I allude. sir, is a company of actors, now performing on their own hook at the Theater Royal, Eborsham. If I am not on the stage before eight o'clock to-night, our chances in that town are gone. The provincial public, having paid its shillings and sixpences, will not brook disappointment. You will hardly credit the fact, perhaps, sir, but there are seven places taken in the dress circle, paid in advance, sir, further secured by a donation to the box-keeper, for this evening's performance. Conceive the feelings of those seven dress circles, sir, if Mathew Elgood is conspicuous by his absence."

"That must not be, sir." returned Humphrey Clissold, gravely. "Pedestrian wanderings have somewhat developed my organ of locality, and if you like to trust yourself to my guidance I will do my best to navigate you in the desired direction. Is that young lady also required by the British public?"

"Yes," responded Elgood, indifferently; "she's in the first piece. But we might send a ballet-girl on for her part, if "—as an after-thought—"we had any ballet."

"The numerical strength of your commonwealth is limited, I infer from your remark," remarked Clissold, as the stroller stepped through the gap in the hedge, and joined those other strollers in the lane.

"Well, sir·—'lead on. I follow thee'—when a manager puts it to his company roundly that he must either make it a commonwealth or shut up shop altogether, the little people are generally the first to fall away."

"The little people?"

"Yes, sir—second walking gentleman, ditto lady; second chamber-maid, general utility; second old man, proverbially duffing, and ballet. The little people lack that confidence in their own genius which sustains a man under the fluctuations of a commonwealth. They want the afflatus, and when the ghost walks not——"

"The ghost?"

"In vulgar English, when there is no treasury, no reliable weekly stipend, the little people collapse. The second walking lady and chambermaid go home to their mothers; the second old man opens a sweet-stuff shop. They fade and evanish from a profession they did nothing to adorn."

"What is a commonwealth?" asked the younger gentleman, interested by this glimpse of a strange world.

"In a theatrical sense," added Clissold.

"A theatrical commonwealth is a body without a head. There is no responsible lessee. The weekly funds are divided into so many shares, each share representing half a sovereign. The actor whose nominal salary is two pound ten takes five shares. The actor whose ordinary pay is fifteen shillings claims but a share and a half, and has his claim allowed. I have known the shares to rise to fourteen and ninepence half-penny; I have seen them dwindle to one and seven-pence."

"Thanks for the explanation. Does prosperity attend you in Eborsham?"

"Sir, our receipts heretofore have been but middling. Our anchor of hope is the spring meeting, which begins, as you are doubtless aware, to-morrow."

"Do you remain here long?" asked Mr. Penwyn, the younger pedestrian.

"A fortnight, at most. Our next engagement is Duffield, thence we proceed to Humberston, then Slingerford, after which we separate to seek 'fresh woods and pastures new.'"

Mr. Penwyn looked at the vagabond wonderingly. The man spoke so lightly of his fortuitous life. James Penwyn, of Penwyn Manor, Cornwall, had been brought up like the Danish princess who discovered the presence of the pea under seven feather-beds and seven mattresses. He had never been inconvenienced in his life; and this encounter with a fellow-creature who anatomically resembled himself, and yet belonged to a world so wide apart from his world, at once interested and amused him. He pitied the stroller with a serio-comic pity, as he might have compassionated an octopus in an uncomfortable position.

Perhaps there was never in this world a better-natured youth than this James Penwyn. He had not the knack of sending his thoughts far afield, never lost himself in a tangle of speculative fancies, like his dark-eyed, wide-browed friend and master, Humphrey Clissold, but within its somewhat narrow limit his mind was clear as a crystal streamlet. His first thought in every relation of life was to do a kindness. He was a man whom sponges of every order and college scouts and cabmen and tavern waiters adore, and for whom the wise and prudent apprehend a youth of waste and riot and an after-life of ruin.

"I'll tell you what," said he, with a friendly air, "we'll come to the theater to-night and see you act—and the young lady," with a critical glance at Justina, who walked close beside her

father, and did her best to extinguish herself in the shadow of
Mr. Elgood's bulky form. It was as much as James Penwyn
could do to get a glimpse of the girl's face, which had a pale,
tired look just now. "Humph," thought James, "fine eyes,
but not particularly pretty—rather a washed-out look."

"Sir," said Mr. Elgood, "you will confer at once honor and
substantial benefit upon us poor players. And if you like to
take a peep at life behind the scenes, my position in the theater
warrants my admitting you to that esoteric region."

"I should like it of all things, and we can sup together afterward. They've a decent cook at the inn where my friend and
I are staying, though it's only a roadside tavern. You know it
perhaps—the Waterfowl, half a mile out of the town. It's my
friend's fancy that we should stop there."

"It's your friend's necessity that he should avoid costly hotels." said Humphrey, lightly.

They had crossed a couple of meadows, where young lambs
scuttled off at the sight of them, bleating vehemently. and now
came to a green lane, a long grassy gully between tall hedges,
where the earliest of the dog-roses were budding, creamy white
amidst tender green leaves. Mr. Penwyn took advantage of the
change to slip behind Mr. Elgood, and place himself beside
Justina. Humphrey looked after him darkly. A too generous
worship of the fair sex was one of James Penwyn's foibles.

No, decidedly she was not pretty, thought James, after a
closer inspection of the pale young face, with its somewhat pensive mouth and grayish-blue eyes. She blushed a little as he
looked at her, and the delicate rose-tint became the oval cheek.
All the lines of her face were too sharp, for want of that filling
out and rounding of angles which is the ripening of beauty. She
was like a pale greenish-hued peach on a wall in early June, to
which July and August will bring roundness, velvety texture,
and richest bloom.

"I hope you are not very tired," said James, gently.

"Not very," answered Justina, with an involuntary sigh.
"We had a long rehearsal this morning."

"Yes, there always must be long rehearsals while there are
stupid people in a theater," interjected Mr. Elgood, with a
sharpness that made the remark sound personal.

"We are getting up a burlésque for the race nights, gentlemen," continued the actor—"'Faust and Marguerite'—the last
popular thing in London, and my daughter knows as much
about burlesque business as an eating-house waiter knows of a
holiday."

"Are you fond of acting?" asked James, confidentially, ignoring Mr. Elgood's remarks.

"I hate it," answered Justina, less shyly than she had spoken
before. There was something friendly in the young man's voice
and manner which invited to confidence; and then he was so
pleasant to look at, with his small, clearly cut features, light
auburn mustache, crisp auburn hair, cut close to the well-shaped
head, garments of rough gray tweed, which looked more distinguished than any clothes Justina had ever seen before; thick

cable chain and pendent locket—a large, dull gold locket, with a Gothic monogram in black enamel—tawny gloves upon the small hands—altogether a very different person from the tall man in the shabby shooting-coat, leather gaiters, and bulky boots who walked on the other side of Mr. Elgood. Justina was young enough to be impressed by externals.

"Hate it?" exclaimed Mr. Penwyn. "I thought actresses always adored the stage, and looked forward to acquiring the fame of an O'Neil or a Fawcet."

"Do they?" said Justina; "those I know are like horses in a mill, and go the same round year after year. When I think that I may have to lead that kind of life till I die of old age, I almost feel that I should like to drown myself, if it wasn't wicked; but then I haven't any talent. I suppose it would all seem different if I were clever."

"Aren't you clever?" asked James, smiling at her simplicity. Although not pretty she was far from unpleasing. He was amused—interested even. But then he was always ready to interest himself in any tolerably attractive young woman.

Humphrey Clissold fell away from the actor, and walked beside his friend, overlooking James and Justina from his superior height. There was plenty of space in the wide green lane for four to walk abreast.

"No," said Justina, confidentially, not wishing her father to hear ungrateful murmurs against the art he respected, "I believe I'm very stupid. If there is a point to be made, I generally miss it—speak too fast or too slow, or drop my voice at the end of a speech, or raise it too soon. Even in Francois I didn't get a round the other night. You know Francois?"

"Haven't the honor of his acquaintance."

"The page in 'Richelieu.' He has a grand speech. One is bound to get a tremendous round of applause; but somehow I missed it. Father said he should like to have boxed my ears."

"He didn't do it, I hope?"

"No, but it was almost as bad; he said it before everybody in the green-room."

"I understand—like a fellow saying something unpleasant of one at one's club."

They came to the end of the green lane at last. It opened upon a level sweep of land, across which they saw the city, all its roofs and walls steeped in the declining light. The ground was marshy, and between low rush-grown banks gently flowed the Ebor, a narrow river that wound its sinuous course around the outskirts of Eborsham, without entering the city.

"I have not led you astray, you see, sir," said Humphrey. "behold the cathedral! Yonder path by the water's edge will bring us to the lower end of the town."

"We have to thank you for extrication from a difficulty, sir," replied Mr. Elgood, with dignity. "You have brought us a shorter way than that which my daughter and I traversed when we came out this afternoon."

They followed the river path—a tow-path along which slow,

clumsy horses were wont to drag the lingering chain of a heavily-laden barge. The dark green rushes shivered in the west wind, the slow river was gently rippled; the city had a look of unspeakable stillness, like a city in a picture.

Half-way along the tow-path they encountered some stragglers—a man laden with oakum mats, who walked wide of his companions on the marshy ground outside the path; a boy running here and there at random, chasing the small yellow butterflies and shouting at them in the ardor of the chase; an elderly woman, of the gypsy race, carrying a string of light fancy baskets across her shoulder.

"That's the worst of a race meeting." said James Penwyn, with reference to those nomads; "it brings together such a lot of rabble."

One of the rabble stopped and blocked his pathway. It was the elderly gypsy woman.

"Let me tell you your fortune, my pretty gentleman," she said, pouncing on Mr. Penwyn, as if she had discovered his superior wealth at a glance. "Cross the poor gypsy's hand with a bit of silver—half a crown won't hurt you, my pretty gentleman. You've riches in your face—you've never known what it is to want a sovereign, and never will. The world was made for such as you."

"Avaunt, harridan!" cried the tragedian, "and suffer us to proceed."

"What, you'd like to spoil my market, would you?" cried the sibyl, vindictively. "No one was ever a penny the richer for your generosity, and no one will be a penny the worse off when you're dead and gone, except yourself. Let me tell your fortune, pretty gentleman," she went on, laying a persuasive hand on James Penwyn's gray sleeve, and keeping up with the pedestrians as they strove to pass her. "There's plenty of pleasant things the old gypsy woman can tell you. You're a gentleman that likes a dark blue eye, and there's an eye that looks kindly upon you now; and though there's crosses for true lovers, all will come out happy in the end, if you listen to the old gypsy."

James laughed, and flung the prophetess a florin.

"Show me your hand, kind gentleman," she urged, after a string of thanks and benedictions; "your left hand. Yes, there's the Mount of Venus, and not an ugly line across it, and you've a long thumb, my pretty gentleman, long between the first joint and the second; that means strength of will, for the thumb is Jupiter, and rules the house of life. Don't take your hand away, pretty gentleman. Let's see the line——"

"What's the matter, mother?" asked James, as the woman stopped in the middle of a sentence, and still holding his hand, and staring at the palm steadfastly with a scared look.

"What's that?" she asked, pointing to a short, indented line across the palm.

"Why, what keen eyes you have, old lady! That's the mark of a hole I dug in my palm two years ago, cutting a tough bit of cavendish. My scout told me I was bound to have lock-jaw, but I didn't realize his expectations. I suppose lock-jaw doesn't run in our family."

"Right across the line of life!" muttered the gypsy, still examining the seam left by the knife upon the pinkish, womanish palm.

"Does that mean anything bad—that I am to die young, for instance?"

"The scar of a knife can't overrule the planets," replied the sibyl, sententiously.

CHAPTER II.

BEHIND THE SCENES.

James Penwyn and Humphrey Clissold went to the Eborsham Theater as soon as they had eaten their dinner and smoked a single cigar apiece, lounging by the open window in the gloaming, talking over their afternoon's adventure.

"What a fellow you are, Jim!" cried Humphrey, with a half-contemptuous, half-compassionate air, as for the foolishness of a child. "To hear you go on about that scarecrow of a girl one would suppose you had never seen a pretty woman in your life."

"I never saw prettier eyes," said James; "and she has a manner that a fellow might easily fall in love with—so simple, so childish, so confiding."

"Which means that she gazed with undisguised admiration upon the magnificent Squire Penwyn, of Penwyn Manor. A woman need only flatter you, Jim, for you to think her a Venus."

"That poor little thing didn't flatter me. She's a great deal too innocent."

"No, she only admired you innocently; opening those big blue eyes of hers to their widest in a gaze of rapture. Was it the locket, or the studs, or the mustache, I wonder, that struck her most?"

"Don't be a fool, Clissold. If we are to go to the theater, we'd better not waste any more time. I want to see what kind of an actor our friend is."

"Student of humanity," jeered Humphrey; "even a provincial player is not beneath your notice. Cuvier was profound upon spiders. Penwyn has a mind of a wider range."

"What is his name, by the bye?" mused James, thinking of Mr. Elgood. "We don't even know his name, and we've asked him to supper. That's rather awkward, isn't it?"

"Be sure he will come. No doubt he has already speculated on the possibility of borrowing five pounds from you."

Mr. Penwyn rang the bell, and gave his orders with that easy air of a man unaccustomed to count the cost. The best supper the Waterfowl could provide at half-past eleven.

They walked along the lonely country road into Eborsham. The Waterfowl Inn was upon one of the quietest, most obscure roads out of the city; not the great coach road to London, bordered for a mile beyond the town by snug villas and bandboxical detached cottages—orderly homes of retired traders—but a byroad leading to a village or two.

This road followed the wind of the river which traversed the lower end of Eborsham, and it was for its vicinity to the river, and a something picturesque in its aspect, that the two friends had chosen the Waterfowl as their resting-place. There was a small garden behind the inn, which sloped to the edge of the stream, and a rustic summer-house, where the young men smoked their pipes after dinner.

Between the Waterfowl and Eborsham the landscape was low and flat; on one side a narrow slip of marshy ground between road and river, with a scrubby brush here and there marking the boundary; on the other a tall neglected hedge-row at the top of a steep bank, divided from the road by a wide weedy ditch.

The two friends entered Eborsham through a Gothic archway called Lowgate. It had been a strongly fortified city, famous for its walls, and there were several of these stone gateways. The theater stood in the angle of a small square, almost overshadowed by the mighty towers of the cathedral, as if the stage had gone to the church for sanctuary and protection from the intolerance of bigots.

Here Mr. Penwyn and Mr. Clissold placed themselves among the select few of the dress circle, a cool and airy range of seats, whose sparsely scattered occupants listened with rapt attention to the gloomy prosings of the Stranger. James Penwyn was not ravished by that Germanic drama. Even Mrs. Haller bored him. She dropped her h's, and expressed the emotions of grief and remorse by spasmodic chokings and catchings of her breath. Mr. Penwyn lighted up a little when the countess appeared, for the countess had the large, melancholy blue eyes of the girl he had met in the meadow.

Miss Elgood did not look her best on the stage. Tall, slim, and willow-waisted, sharp of elbow, and angular of shoulder, dressed in cheap finery, soiled satin, tarnished silver-lace, murky marabouts, badly painted with two dabs of rouge that were painfully visible upon the pure pale of her young cheeks—artistically Justina was a failure, and feeling herself a failure, suffered from an inability to dispose of her arms, and a lurking conviction that the audience regarded her with loathing.

Mr. Clissold exchanged his front seat for a place on the hindmost bench before the stranger was half-way through his troubles, and here, secure in the shade, slept comfortably. James Penwyn endured two acts and a half, and then, remembering Mr. Elgood's offer to show him life behind the scenes, slipped quietly out of the dress circle, and asked the box-keeper how he was to get to the side scenes.

That official, sweetened by a liberal donation, unlocked a little door behind the proscenium box—a door sacred to the manager—and let Mr. Penwyn through into the mystic world of behind the scenes. He would hardly have done such a thing under a responsible lessee, but in a commonwealth morals become relaxed.

The mystic world looked dark and dusty, and smelled of gas and dirt, to the unaccustomed senses of Mr. Penwyn.

The voices on the stage sounded loud and harsh now that they were so near his ear: There was hardly room for him to move between the side scenes and the wall—indeed, it was only by screwing himself against this whitewashed wall that he made his way in the direction which a scene-shifter had indicated as the way to the green-room.

Mr. Penwyn's experience of life had never before led him behind the scenes. He had a vague idea that a green-room was a dazzling saloon, lighted by crystal chandeliers, lined with mirrors, furnished with divans of ruby velvet, an idealized copy of a club-house smoking-room. He found himself in a small dingy chamber, carpetless, curtainless, uncleanly, furnished with narrow baize-covered benches, garnished with one cloudy looking-glass, on either side whereof flared an unscreened gas-jet.

Here over the narrow wooden mantel-shelf hung casts of pieces in preparation. "Jack Sheppard," "Delicate Ground," "Courier of Lyons," "Box and Cox," a wide range of dramatic art, calls for next day's rehearsal. Here, in divers attitudes of weariness, lounged various members of the dramatic commonwealth, among them Mr. Elgood, in the frogged coat, crimson worsted pantaloons, and Hessian boots of the baron, and Justina, seated disconsolately, with her limp satin trailing over the narrow bench beside her, conning her part in the piece for to-morrow night.

"My dear sir!" exclaimed Mathew Elgood, shaking hands with enthusiasm, "this is kind! Dempson"—this to a gentleman in mufti, small, sallow, close-cropped, and smelling of stale tobacco—"this is my pioneer of to-day. Mr. Dempson, Mr.—— Stay, we did not exchange cards."

"Penwyn," said James, smiling.

Mr. Elgood stared at the speaker curiously, as if he hardly believed his own ears, as if this name of Penwyn had some strange significance for him.

"Penwyn!" he repeated; "that's a Cornish name, isn't it?"

"By Tre, Pol, and Pen, you may know the Cornish men. There is nothing more Cornish. I was born and brought up near London, but my race belongs to the Cornish soil. We were indigenous at Penwyn, I believe, the founders and earliest inhabitants of the settlement. Do you know Cornwall?"

"Not intimately; merely as a traveler."

"Were you ever at Penwyn?"

"I don't think so; I have no recollection."

"Well, it's a place you might easily forget; not a promising locality for the exercise of your art. But you seemed struck by my name just now, as if you had heard it before."

"I think I must have heard it somewhere, but I can't recall the occasion. Let that pass!" And with a majestic wave of the hand Mr. Elgood performed the ceremony of introduction.

"Mr. Dempson, Mr. Penwyn. Mr. Dempson is our sometime manager, now a brother professional. He has resigned the round and top of sovereignty, and the carking cares of Saturday's treasury."

Mr. Dempson assented to this statement with a plaintive sigh. "A harassing profession, the drama, Mr. Penwyn," he said. "The many-headed is a monster of huge ingratitudes."

James bowed assent.

"The provincial stage is in its decline, sir. Time was when this very theater could be kept open for ten consecutive months in every year, to the profit of the manager, and when the good old comedies and the Shakespearean drama were acted week after week to an intelligent and approving audience. Nowadays a man must rack his brains in order to cater for a frivolous and insatiable.public, which has been taught to consider a house on fire or a railway smash the end and aim of dramatic composition. I speak from bitter experience. My grandfather was manager of the Eborsham circuit, and retired with a competency. My father inherited the competency, and lost it in the Eborsham circuit. I have been cradled in the profession, and have failed as manager, with credit to my head and heart, as my friends have been good enough to observe, some three or four times, and now hang on to dramatic art, quite out of fashion, like a rusty nail in monumental armor. That's what I call the decline of the drama, Mr. Penwyn."

James assented, and was not sorry that Mr. Dempson, having vented his woe, went off to dress for the afterpiece.

" What a melancholy person!" said James.

" An excellent low comedian," replied Mr. Elgood. " You'll hear the people screaming at him in the 'Spitalfields Weaver' by and by. His business with the tea and bread and butter is the finest thing I ever saw, not second to Wright's. Indeed "—as an afterthought—" I believe it is Wright's business."

" Then it can hardly claim the merit of originality."

" Genius, Mr. Penwyn, finds its material where it can."

" Baron!" screamed a small boy, putting his head in at the door.

" My scene!" exclaimed Mr. Elwood, and vanished.

James seated himself on the narrow bench beside Justina.

" I have been in the boxes to see you act," he said, in that gentle winning voice which had made him a favorite among women. To Justina it sounded fresh as a voice from another world. No one in her world spoke like that, in tones so deferential, with accents so pure.

" I am very sorry for it," said Justina.

" Sorry! but why?"

" Because you must hate me. The audience always do hate me. I feel it in their looks—feel it freezing me directly I go on the stage. 'Oh, there *she* is again!' they say to themselves. 'Can't they manage to get through the piece without sending *her* on?'"

" What a curious notion! I thought actresses were conceited people."

" Yes, when they are favorites."

" I don't know about the rest of the audience, Miss Elgood,"

said James, almost tenderly, " but I know I did not hate you—
my feelings leaned too much the other way."

Justina blushed through those two dabs of rouge; compliments were so new to her, and a compliment from this elegant
stranger was worth all the loud praises of the vulgar herd. She
hardly envied Miss Villeroy—the leading lady—whose chokings
and sobbings in Mrs. Haller had been applauded to the echo,
while the poor countess, in her draggle-tailed sky-blue satin, had
walked on and off unnoticed.

" So this is the way you enjoy the legitimate drama, Mr.
Penwyn," said a sonorous voice—the full rich barytone of
Humphrey Clissold—and, looking up, James and Justina beheld
that gentleman watching them from the door.

" I left *you* asleep," James replied, abashed by his friend's
advent.

" Yes, sneaked off and left me to grope my way to this abominable den as best I could. I beg your pardon, Miss Elgood, but
it really is a den."

" You can't hate it worse than I do," said Justina, " or so
badly; I have to sit here every night."

" Poor child! It's a strange life—and a hard one. Seen from
the outside, there seems a not unpleasant Bohemian flavor about
it, but when one comes behind the scenes the Bohemian flavor
appears to be mainly dirt. I've inhaled enough dust and escaped
gas within the last ten minutes to last me comfortably for my
lifetime. And you breathe this atmosphere for four or five hours
every night! Poor child!"

James sighed. His benevolent heart longed to rescue the girl
from such a life—a girl with pensive violet eyes, fringed by
darkest lashes; soft brown hair, so luxuriant that it made a
crown of plaits upon the well-shaped head—altogether a girl
whom benevolence would fain benefit.

" Come, Jim," said Clissold, who had a knack of reading his
friend's thoughts, " you've seen enough of behind the scenes."

" No, I haven't," answered James, sturdily, as the countess
ran off to act her part in the close of the play. He was wont to
be plastic as wax in the hands of his guide, philosopher, and
friend, but to-night there glowed a spark of rebellion in his soul.
" I am going to stop to see Mr. Elgood, and to ask him to bring
his daughter to supper."

"Bring his daughter! To visit two young men at a roadside
inn?"

"*Honi soit*," said James. "Can a girl be safer anywhere
than with her father?"

" Look here, Penwyn," said Clissold, earnestly: " I've made it
the business of my life for the last two years to keep you in the
straight path. I won't have you kicking over the traces for any
blue-eyed chit in the universe. Remember what I promised
your poor mother, Jim?"

" That you'd act the part of an elder brother—supply the
balance of good sense wanting to my shallow brains. That's
all very well, Humphrey. I always respected my poor mother's

ideas, even when they took the shape of prejudices. But a man must enjoy his life."

" Yes, but he is bound to enjoy life with the least possible injury to other people."

" Whom am I going to injure ?" demanded Mr. Penwyn, with an impatient shrug, as he moved toward the wings.

" You are putting foolish ideas into that poor child's head."

" What nonsense! simply because I am civil to her. I mean to ask her to supper, whether you like it or not."

" I hope her father will have the sense to refuse."

" If you come to that, I'll invite the whole company," cried the spoiled child of fortune.

The curtain came down at this moment, and Mr. Elgood returned to the green-room, unbuckling his sword-belt as he came along.

" I waited to remind you of your promise to sup with us to-night, Mr. Elgood," said James.

" My dear sir, it is not an engagement to be forgotten. I shall be there."

" Will half-past eleven be too early ?"

" No; the 'Stranger' has played quick to-night, and the afterpiece is short. I shall be there."

" Miss Elgood will accompany you, I hope."

" Thanks, no. The proprieties would be outraged by her appearance at a bachelor's table. The only lady present."

" We could easily remedy that, if any other lady in the company would honor us."

" Upon my word, you are very kind, and I know the child would consider it a treat. If you put the question in such a friendly manner, I feel sure that Mr. and Mrs. Dempson would be delighted to join us."

" Pray bring them. Is Mrs. Dempson also dramatic ?"

" You have seen her to-night in one of her greatest parts—Mrs. Haller."

" I thought the lady was a Miss Villeroy."

" Her professional name merely. Joe Dempson and Miss Villeroy have been united in the sacred bonds of matrimony for some years."

" I shall be charmed to make the lady's acquaintance. You know your way to the Waterfowl ?"

" It is familiar to me as the path of my infancy."

" And you'll be sure to bring Miss Elgood ?"

" Judy shall come without fail."

" Judy ?"

" The pet name chosen by affection. She was christened Justina. Pardon me if I leave you hastily. I play in the next piece."

Mr. Elgood hurried away. James Penwyn glanced at his friend with the glance of triumph.

" Out of leading-strings, you see, Humphrey," he said.

Humphrey Clissold shrugged his shoulders and turned away with a sigh. James, more touched by silence than reproof, put his arm through his friend's with a gay laugh, and they went out of the green-room and out of the theater together, arm in arm, like brothers who loved each other.

CHAPTER III.

GLAMOUR.

THE supper at the Waterfowl was a success. Every one, except perhaps Clissold, was in the humor to be pleased with everything, and even Clissold could not find it in his heart to make himself vehemently disagreeable amidst mirth so harmless, gayety so childishly simple. To an actor supper after the play is just the one crowning delight of life—that glimpse of paradise upon earth which we all get in some shape or other—a supper at a comfortable hostelry like the Waterfowl, where the land-lord knew how to do things in good style for a customer who could pay the piper. In this northern district there was a liberal plenty, a bounteous wealth of provision hardly known elsewhere. Tea at Eborsham meant dinner and supper and break-fast rolled into one. Supper at Eborsham meant aldermanic barn-door fowls, and a smoking home-cured ham weighing five-and-twenty pounds or so, lobsters nestling among crisp green lettuce, pigeon-pie, cheese-cakes, tarts, and, lest these lighter trifles should fail to satisfy appetite, a lordly cold sirloin by way of *corps de reserve*, to come in at a critical juncture, like Blucher at Waterloo.

Mr. Dempson made himself the life of the party. The small melancholy man who had bewailed the decline of the drama vanished altogether at sight of that plenteously furnished sup-per-table, and in his place appeared a jester of the first water—so James Penwyn thought, at any rate, as he laughed, " with youth's silver-clear laughter," at the low comedian's jokes. Even Miss Villeroy was sprightly, though she had a worn look about the eyes, as if she had aged herself prematurely with the woes of Mrs. Haller and other heroines of tragedy. Justina sat next to James Penwyn, and was supremely happy, though only an hour ago she had shed tears of girlish shame at the idea of coming to a supper-party in her threadbare brown merino gown—. last winter's gown—which she was obliged to wear in the warm glad spring for want of fitter raiment. No one thought of her shabby gown, however, when the pale young face brightened and flushed with unwonted pleasure, and the large, thoughtful eyes took a new light, and darkened into a deeper gray.

James Penwyn did his uttermost to make her happy and at ease, and succeeded only too well. There is no impression so swift and so vivid as that which the first admirer makes upon a girl of seventeen. The tender words, the subdued tones, the smiles, the praises, have such a freshness. The adulation of a Cæsar in after-years would hardly seem so sweet as these first flatteries of commonplace youth to the girl on the threshold of womanhood.

Mr. Elgood saw what was going on, but was by no means alarmed by the aspect of affairs. He felt himself quite able to take care of Justina, even if Mr. Penwyn had been a hardened libertine instead of a kind-hearted youth fresh from the university. He had no desire to stifle admiration which might mean very little, but which would most likely result in liberal patronage for his own benefit and a trifling present or two for Justina, a ring, or a bracelet, or a box of gloves.

"I don't want to stand in Justina's light," mused Mr. Elgood, as he leaned back in his chair and sipped his last glass of champagne, when the pleasures of the table had given way to an agreeable sense of repletion.

"What did that gypsy woman mean by the line of life and the planets?" asked Justina. She had lost all sense of shyness by this time, and she and James were talking to each other in lowered voices, as much alone as if the rest of the party had been pictures on the wall. Humphrey marked them as he sat a little way apart from the others smoking his black-muzzled pipe.

"Pshaw! only the professional jargon. What does she know of the planets?"

"But she stared at your hand in such a curious way, and looked so awful that she frightened me. Do tell me what she meant."

James laughed, and laid his left hand in Justina's, palm upward. "Look there," he said. "You see that line, a curve from below the first finger to the base of the thumb; that is to say, it should go to the base of the thumb, but in my hand it doesn't. See where the line disappears midway, just by that seam left by my pocket-knife. You can see nothing beyond that line."

Justina closely scrutinized the strong unwrinkled palm. "What does that mean?" she asked. "I don't understand even now."

"It means a short life and a merry one."

The rare bloom faded from Justina's cheek.

"You don't believe in that," she said, anxiously.

"No more than I believe in gypsies, or spirit-rappers, or the cave of Trophonius," answered James, gayly. "What a silly child you are to look so scared."

Justina gave a little sigh, and then tried to smile. Even this first dawn of a girlish fancy, airy as a butterfly's passion for a rose, brought new anxieties along with it. The gypsy's cant was an evil omen that disturbed her like a shapeless fear. Women resemble those mediæval roysterers of whom the old chronicler wrote. They taste their pleasure sadly.

The moon was at the full. There she sailed, a silver targe, above the distant hill-tops. James looked up at her, looked into that profound world above, which draws the fancies of youth with irresistible power. The room opened on the garden by two long windows, and the one nearest to Mr. Penwyn's end of the table stood open.

"Let us get away from the smoke," he said, vexed to see Clissold's eyes upon him, fixed and gloomy. The room was tolerably full of tobacco by this time, and Mr. Elgood was urging Mr. Dempson to favor the company with his famous song, "The Ship's Carpen*teer*."

"Come into the garden, Maud," said James, gayly, flinging a
look of defiance at his monitor.

Justina blushed, hesitated, and obeyed him. They went out
into the moon-lit night together, and strolled side by side across
the rustic garden, a slope of grass on which the most ancient of
apple-trees, and pear-trees big enough to have been mistaken
for small elms, cast their crooked shadows. It was more orchard
than garden; pot-herbs grew among the rose-bushes on the
border by the boundary hedge. and on one side of the inn there
was a patch of ground that grew cabbages and broad beans, but
all the rest was grass and apple-trees.

At the edge of that grassy slope ran the river, silver-shining
under the moon. Eborsham, seen across the level landscape,
looked a glorified city in that calm and mellow light. The boy
and girl walked silently down to the river's brim, and looked at
the distant hills and woods, scattered cottages with lowly
thatched roofs and antique chimney-stacks, and here and there
the white walls of a mansion silvered by the moon, dominating
all in sublime and gloomy grandeur the mighty towers of the
cathedral, God's temple, rising like fortalice and sanctuary above
all human habitations, as of old the Acropolis.

Justina gazed, and was silent. It was one of those rare moments of exaltation which poets tell us are worth a lifetime of
sluggish feeling. The girl felt as if she had never lived till
now.

"Pretty, isn't it?" remarked James, very much in the tone of
Brummel, who, after watching a splendid sunset, was pleased
to observe, "How well he does it?"

"It is too beautiful," said Justina.

"Why too beautiful?"

"I don't know. It hurts me somehow like actual pain."

"You are like Byron's Lara:

"'But a night like this,
A night of beauty, mocked such a breast as his.

I hope it is not a case of bad conscience with you, as it was with
him."

"No, it is not my conscience. The worst I have ever done
has been to grumble at the profession, and though father says
it is wicked, the thought of my wickedness has never troubled
me. But to me there's something awful in the beauty of night
and stillness, a solemnity that chills me. I feel as if there were
some trouble hanging over me, some great sorrow. Don't
you?"

"Not the least in the world. I think moonlight awfully
jolly. Would you much mind my lighting a cigar? You'll
hardly feel the effects of the smoke out here."

"I never feel it anywhere," answered Justina, frankly.
"Father hardly ever leaves off smoking."

There was a weeping-willow at the edge of the garden, a willow whose lower branches dipped into the river, and just beside
the willow a bench, where these two seated themselves in the
full glory of the moon. A much better place than the dusky
summer-house, which might, peradventure, be a harbor for

frogs, snails, or spiders at that late hour. They sat by the river's brim and talked—talked as easily as if they had a thousand ideas in common, these two, who had never met until to-day, and whose lives lay so far apart.

They had youth and hope in common, and that bond was enough to unite them.

James asked Justina a good many questions about stage life, and was surprised to find the illusions of his boyhood vanish before stern truth.

"I thought it was such a jolly life, and the easiest in the world," he said. "I've often fancied I should like to be an actor. I think I could do it pretty well. I can imitate Buckstone and Charles Matthews."

"Pray, don't think of it," exclaimed Justina. "You'd be tired to death in a year."

"I dare say I should. I'm not much of a fellow for sticking to anything. I got ' plowed ' a year ago at Oxford, and now I've been trying to read with Clissold, walking through England and Wales, and putting up at all the quietest places we can find. Clissold is a first-rate coach, and it won't be his fault if I don't get my degree next time. How do you like him?"

"I don't know. I haven't thought about him," answered the girl, simply. This younger and fairer stranger had made her oblivious of Humphrey Clissold, with his tall, strong frame, dark, penetrating eyes, and broad brow. Too manly a man altogether to be admired by a girl of seventeen.

"He is as good a fellow as ever breathed; a little bitter, perhaps; but most wholesome things are bitter," said James. "He has his crotchets. One is that I am to be a model master of Penwyn by and by, go into Parliament, marry an heiress—set up as a fine old English gentleman, in fact. Rather a wearisome *metier*, I should think. The worst of it is he keeps it continually before my mind's eye, is always reminding me of how much I owe to Penwyn Manor and my race, and won't let me get much enjoyment out of youth's brief holiday. He's a good fellow, but I might love him better if I didn't respect him so much. He was a great favorite of my poor mother's—a romantic story, by the way. She was engaged to Humphrey's father some years before she married mine. He was a captain in the East India Company's service, and fell fighting the niggers at Gujerat. Years afterward, when my father was dead and gone, Clissold and I met at Eton. My mother burst into tears when she heard my school-fellow's name, and asked me to bring him to see her. Of course I obeyed, and from that time to the day of her death my mother had a second son in Humphrey. I think she loved him as well as she loved me."

"And you were never jealous?"

"No; I was too fond of both of them for that. And then my dear mother was all love, all tenderness. I could afford to share her affection with my adopted brother. And now tell me something about your own life."

"There is so little to tell," answered the girl, drearily. "Ever since I can remember we have lived the same kind of life—

sometimes in one town, sometimes in another. When father
could afford the money he used to send me to a day-school, so
I've been a little educated somehow, only I dare say I'm very
ignorant, because my education used to stop sometimes, and by
the time it began again I had forgotten a good deal."

" Poor child!" murmured James, compassionately. " Is your
mother still living?"

" She died three years ago. She had had so much trouble, it
wore her out at last." And Justina paid her dead mother
the tribute of a hidden tear.

" I say, Jim, do you know that it is half-past two o'clock, and
that Mr. Elgood is waiting for his daughter?" asked the voice of
common-sense, in the tones of Humphrey Clissold.

The two children started up from the bench by the willow,
scared by the sudden question. There stood Mr. Clissold, tall
and straight and severe-looking.

" I heard the cathedral clock a few minutes ago, and I am
quite aware of the time. If Mr. Elgood wants his daughter he
can come for her himself," replied James.

Mr. Penwyn was resolved to make a stand against his mentor,
and he felt that now was the time for action.

Mr. Elgood and Mr. Dempson came strolling out into the garden, cigars in their mouths. Penwyn's choicest brand had been
largely sacrificed at the altar of hospitality.

" Judy, have you forgotten the time?" asked the heavy father,
with accents that had a legato sound—one syllable gliding gently
into another—a tone that was all sweetness and affection, though
indistinct.

" Yes, father," answered the girl, innocently, " It's so beautiful out here."

" Beautiful!" echoed the father, thickly. " Look how the
floor of heaven is thick inlaid with—what's its names—of bright
gold. Come, Jessica—Judy—put on your bonnet and shawl.
Mrs. Dempson has been fast asleep for the last half hour. But
look! The moon, in russet mantle clad, walks o'er the dew of
yon high eastern hill, which reminds me that we have nearly a
mile to walk before we get home."

" I'll go with you," said James. " I want to arrange about
to-morrow. We must make up a jolly party for the races. I'll
get a roomy carriage that will hold all of us."

" I haven't seen a race in anything like comfort for the last
fifteen years," responded Mr. Elgood.

" We'll make a day of it; Clissold and I will come to the
theater in the evening."

" Make your own engagements, if you please, James, and allow me to make mine," said Mr. Clissold. " I shall not go to
the races to-morrow—or if I do, it will be by myself, and on
foot; and I shall not go to the theater in the evening."

" Please yourself," answered James, offended.

They were all ready by this time. Mrs. Dempson had been
awakened, and shaken out of the delusion that she had fallen
asleep on the sofa in her own lodgings, and somewhat harshly
reminded that she had a mile or so to walk before she could ob-

tain complete repose. Mr. Dempson had finished his cigar, and accepted another as solace during the homeward walk. Justina had put on her shabby little bonnet and mantle: every one was ready.

The players took their leave of Humphrey Clissold, who was but coldly civil. James Penwyn went out with them, and gave his arm to Justina, as if it were the most natural thing in the world. They walked on in front, the other three straggling after them—walked arm in arm along the lonely foot-path, the low murmur of the river sounding near, the stream showing silvery now and again between a break in the screen of alders.

They talked as they had talked in the garden—about each other, their thoughts and fancies, hopes, dreams, imaginings.

O youth! O glamour! Strange world, in which for the first bright years we live as in a dream! Sweet dawn of life, when nothing in this world seems so real as the hopes that are never to know fruition!

CHAPTER IV.
"LOVE'S A MIGHTY LORD."

SIR NUGENT BELLINGHAM was one of those men who are born and reared amidst pecuniary difficulties, and whose existence is spent upon the verge of ruin. Yet it seems a tolerably comfortable kind of life notwithstanding, and men of Sir Nugent's type hardly realize the meaning of the word deprivation. Sir Nugent had never known what it was to be out of debt. The Bellingham estate was mortgaged up to the hilt when he inherited it. Indeed, to be thus encumbered was the normal condition of all Bellingham property.

Of course Sir Nugent had from time to time possessed money. He hardly could have drifted on so long without some amount of specie, even in such an easy-going world as that patrician sphere in which he revolved. He had inherited a modest fortune from his mother, with which he had paid his creditors something handsome on account all round, and made them his bond-slaves for all time to come, since they cherished the hope of something more in the future. Sir Nugent had legacies from an aunt and uncle or two, and these afforded further sops for his Cerberus, and enabled the baronet's dainty little household to sail gayly down the stream of time for some years.

When the amelioration of manners brought bankruptcy within the reach of any gentleman, Sir Nugent Bellingham availed himself of the new code, and became insolvent in an easy, gentleman-like manner. And what with one little help and another, the bijou house in May Fair where Sir Nugent lived with his two motherless girls was always kept up in the same good style; the same dinners—small and *soignes*—the same lively receptions after the little dinners. The best music, the newest books, the choicest hot-house flowers, were always to be found at No. 12 Cavendish Row, May Fair. There were only a dozen houses in Cavendish Row, and Sir Nugent Bellingham's

was at the corner, squeezed into an angle made by the lofty wall
of Lord Loamshire's garden—one of those dismal, awe-inspiring
London gardens, gray and dull and blossomless, which looked
like a burial-ground without any graves.

Seen from the street, No. 12 looked a mere doll's house, but
the larger rooms were behind, giving upon Lord Loamshire's
garden. It was an irregular old house, full of corners, but, finished after the peculiar tastes of the two Misses Bellingham,
was one of the most charming houses in London. No upholsterer had been allowed to work his will—Madge Bellingham
had chosen every item: the chairs and tables, and sofas and
cabinets, were the cheapest that could be had, for they were all
of unstained light woods, made after designs from Miss Bellingham's own pencil. The cabinets were mere frames for glass
doors, behind which appeared the Bellingham collection of bric-
a-brac upon numerous shelves covered with dark green silk.
Madge's own clever hands had covered the deal shelves; and the
bronzes, the Venetian glass, the Sevres, Copenhagen, Berlin,
Vienna, and Dresden porcelains, looked all the better for so
simple a setting.

There were no draperies but chintz, the cheapest that could be
bought, but always fresh. The looking-glasses had no frame
save a natural garland of ivy. The floors were bees-waxed
only, a Persian carpet here and there offering accommodation
for the luxurious. The one costly object in the two drawing-
rooms, after that bric-a-brac upon which the Bellingham race
had squandered a small fortune, was the piano, a Broadwood
grand, in a case made by a modern workman out of veritable
Louis Seize marquetry. The old ormolu mountings, goats'
heads, festoons, and masks had been religiously preserved, and
the piano was a triumph of art. It occupied the center of the
back drawing-room, the largest room in the house, and when
Madge Bellingham sat before it, girl and piano made a cabinet-
picture of the highest school.

"People know we are out at elbows," Madge said to her father, when they began housekeeping in Cavendish Row. "If
we have expensive furniture, every one will be sure we haven't
paid for it; but if you let me carry out my ideas, the bills will
be so light that you can pay them at once."

"I can give the fellows something on account, at any rate,"
replied Sir Nugent.

Lady Bellingham died soon after the birth of Viola, the second daughter, and Sir Nugent lived the life of a bachelor, for
the most part in other people's houses, while his girls were in his
sister's nursery, or at school. When they grew to womanhood,
and a very lovely womanhood—for good looks were hereditary
in the Bellingham family—Sir Nugent found it incumbent upon
him to provide them with a home; so he took the house in Cavendish Row, and brought home the Bellingham bric-a-brac,
which had been left him by the aforesaid aunts and uncles, and
lodged at the Pantechnicon pending his settlement in life. He
began housekeeping at five-and-forty years of age, and gave his
little dinners at home henceforward, instead of at one or other

of his clubs, and cherished high hopes of seeing his daughters splendidly established by and by.

"I think you have seen enough of what it is to be tormented by a set of harpies to teach you the value of money, Madge," said Sir Nugent one morning, pointing to a small heap of letters which he had just now opened and dismissed with a glance. The harpies in question were his creditors, who expressed an unwarrantable eagerness for something more "on account."

"With your knowledge of life, you are not likely to marry a pauper," pursued Sir Nugent, dipping into a Strasburg pie.

"No, papa, not with my knowledge of life," answered Madge, with ever so slight an upward curl of the firm lip. Miss Bellingham fondly loved her father, but it is possible that respect may have been somewhat lessened by her experience of that financial scramble in which his life was spent.

Two or three evenings before the night which made James Penwyn acquainted with life behind the scenes of a small provincial theater, Sir Nugent Bellingham gave one of his snug little dinners—a dinner of eight—the guests of choicest brands, like the wines. Lady Cheshunt, one of the most exalted matrons in the great world, kept the Misses Bellingham in countenance. Madge was her pet *protegee*, whose praises she was never tired of sounding among the chosen ones of the earth. Mr. Albert Noyce, a distinguished wit and *litterateur*, supplied the salt of the banquet. He was a small, mild-looking man, with a pretty, unoffending wife, and dined out perpetually during the London season. Mr. Shinebar, the famous barrister, made a fourth; Lord George Bulrose, a West of England man, a gourmet, and, in so far as after-dinner talk went, a mighty hunter, was the fifth; and Sir Nugent and his two daughters completed the circle.

After dinner there was to be an evening party, and before the small hours of the morning a great many famous people would have dropped in at the corner house in Cavendish Row.

The ladies have retired, leaving Sir Nugent and his chosen friends to talk about law, and horses, and the last new burlesque actress, as they draw closer in to the dainty round table, where the glass sparkles and the deep-hued blossoms brighten under the cluster of wax-lights in the central chandelier.

Viola and Lady Cheshunt go up-stairs arm in arm, the girl nestling affectionately against the substantial shoulder of the portly matron. Mrs. Noyce trips lightly after these two, and Madge follows alone, with a grave brow, and that lofty air which so well becomes Sir Nugent Bellingham's elder daughter.

Rarely have sisters been less alike than these two. Viola is a blonde, complexion alabaster, hair the color of raw silk—plenteous flaxen hair—which the girl weaves into a crown of pale-gold upon the top of her small head; eyes of liquid turquois blue; figure a thought too slim, but the perfection of grace in every movement and attitude; foot and hand absolutely faultless—altogether a girl to be put under a glass case.

"I should admire the younger Miss Bellingham more if she

were a little less like Sevres china," one of the magnates of society had observed.

Madge is a brunette; hair almost black, and with a natural ripple; complexion a rich olive, through which the warm blood flushes with nature's peerless carmine; eyes darkest hazel; features the true Bellingham type, clearly-cut as a profile on an old Roman medal; figure tall and commanding—a woman born to rule, one would say, judging by externals; a woman with the stuff in her to make a general, Sir Nugent was wont to boast. But although of a loftier mold than the generality of women, there was no hardness about Madge Bellingham. In love or in anger she was alike strong. For hate she was too noble.

The rooms were deliciously cool, the light somewhat subdued, the windows open to the warm spring night. There were flowers enough in the small front drawing-room to make it an in-door garden.

The dowager seated herself upon the most comfortable sofa in this room, a capacious, square-backed sofa, in a dusky corner, fenced off and sheltered by a well-filled *jardiniere.*

"Come here, Madge," she cried, with good-natured imperiousness; "I want to talk to you. Viola, child, go and amuse yourself with Mrs. Noyce. Show her your photograph album, or *parlez chiffons.* I want Madge all to myself."

Madge obeyed without a word, and squeezed herself into the corner of the sofa, which Lady Cheshunt and Lady Cheshunt's dress almost filled.

"How big you are growing, child! there's hardly room enough for you," remarked the matron. "And now tell me the truth, Madge; what is the matter with you to-night?"

"I don't think there is anything the matter more than usual, Lady Cheshunt."

"I know better than that. You were dull and *distrait* all dinner-time. True, there was no one to talk to but two married men and that old twaddler, Bulrose; but a young lady should be always equally agreeable—that is one of the fundamental principles of good-breeding."

"If I seemed a little out of spirits you can hardly wonder. Papa's sadly involved state is enough to make me uneasy."

"My dear, your papa has been involved ever since my first season—when my waist was only eighteen inches, and Madame Devy made my gowns. He is no worse off now than he was then, and he will go on being hopelessly involved till the end of the chapter. I don't see why you should be unhappy about it. He will be able to give you and Viola a tolerable home till you marry and make better homes for yourselves, which it is actually incumbent upon you to do."

This was said with a touch of severity. Madge sighed, and the pretty little foot in the satin shoe tapped the ground with a nervous, impatient movement.

"Madge, I hope there is no truth in what I hear about you and Mr. Penwyn."

A deep tell-tale glow burned in Miss Bellingham's cheek. She fanned herself vehemently.

"I cannot imagine what you have heard, Lady Cheshunt."

"I have heard your name coupled with Mr. Penwyn—the poor Mr. Penwyn."

"I only know one Mr. Penwyn."

"So much the worse for you, my dear. You know the wrong one. There is a cousin of that young man's who has a fine estate in Cornwall—the Penwyn estate. You must have heard of that."

"Yes, I have heard Mr. Penwyn speak of his cousin's property."

"Of course. Poor penniless young man! very natural that he should talk of it. Don't suppose that I have no feeling for him. He is next heir to the property, but no doubt the other young man, James Penwyn's son, will marry and have a herd of children. I knew James Penwyn years ago. There were three brothers—George, the eldest, who was in the army, and was killed in a skirmish with some wild Indians in Canada—very sad story; James, who was in the church, and had a living somewhere near London; and Balfour, who was a lawyer, I believe, whose son you know."

"Yes," sighed Madge.

She had heard the family history from Churchill Penwyn, but the dowager liked to hear herself talk, and did not like to be interrupted.

"Now, if by any chance the present James Penwyn, who is little more than a lad, were to die unmarried, Churchill Penwyn would come into the property under his grandfather's will, which left the estate to the oldest surviving son and his children after him. George died unmarried. James left an only son. Churchill is, therefore, heir presumptive. But it's a very remote contingency, my love, and it would be madness for you to give it a thought, with your chances."

Madge shrugged her shoulders despondently.

"I don't think my chances are particularly brilliant, Lady Cheshunt."

"Nonsense, Madge. Everybody talks of the beautiful Bellinghams. And you refused a splendid offer only the other day—that Mr. Cardingham, the great manufacturer."

"Who had only seen me four times when he had the impudence to ask me to marry him. He was old and ugly, too."

"When the end is a good establishment, one must not look at the means too closely. Poor dear Cheshunt was many years my senior, and no beauty, even in his wig. You must take a more serious view of things, my dear Madge. It will not do for you and your sisters to hang fire. The handsomer girls are, the more vital it is for them to go off quickly. A plain little unobtrusive thing may creep through half a dozen seasons, and surprise everybody by making a good match at last. But a beauty who doesn't marry soon is apt to get talked about. Malicious people put it down to too much flirtation. And then, my love, consider your milliner's bills! What will they be at the end of a few seasons?"

"Not very much, Lady Cheshunt. I cut out all my own

dresses and Viola's too, and our maid runs them together. Viola and I help sometimes, when we can steal a moment from society. I couldn't bear to wear anything that wasn't paid for."

"Upon my word you are an exemplary girl, Madge," exclaimed Lady Cheshunt, astounded by such Roman virtue. "What a wife you will make!"

"Yes, I think I might make a tolerable wife for a poor man."

"Don't speak of such a thing. You were born for wealth and power. You are bound to make a great marriage—if not for your own sake, for Viola's. See what a poor helpless child she is, sadly wanting in moral stamina. If you had a good establishment she would have a haven of refuge. But if you were to marry badly, what would become of her? She would never be able to manage your papa."

Madge sighed again, and this time deeply. Love for her sister was Madge Bellingham's weakest point. She positively adored the fair fragile girl who had been given into her childish arms eighteen years ago, on that bitter day which made her an orphan. There was only four years' difference between the ages of the sisters. yet Madge's affection was almost maternal in its protecting thoughtfulness. To marry well would be to secure a home for Viola. Sir Nugent was but a feeble staff to lean upon.

"I have no objection to marrying well whenever a fair opportunity arises, Lady Cheshunt," she said, firmly; "but I will never marry a man whom I cannot respect and like."

"Of course not, my poor pet," murmured the widow, soothingly; "but fortunately there are so many men in the world one can like and respect. It is that foolish sentimental feeling called love which will only fit one person. In the meantime, Madge, take my advice, and don't let people talk about you and Mr. Penwyn."

"I don't know why they should talk about us."

"Yes, you do, Madge—in your heart of hearts. You know that you have sat together in corners, and that you have a knack of blushing when he comes into the room. It won't do, Madge; it won't do. That young fellow has nothing except what he can earn himself. I know his mother had a struggle to bring him up, and if he hadn't been an only son, could hardly have brought him up at all. He was a Bluecoat Boy, I believe, or something equally dreadful. It is not to be thought of, Madge."

"I do not think of it, Lady Cheshunt," replied Miss Bellingham, resolutely, "and I wish you would not worry yourself and me about imaginary dangers."

"Your visitors are beginning to come; go and receive them, and leave me in my corner. Mr. Penwyn is to be here, I've no doubt."

"I don't know. He knows that Saturday is our night."

"Mr. Churchill Penwyn," announced a footman at the door of the larger room,

"I thought so," said Lady Cheshunt; "and the first to arrive, too. That looks suspicious."

CHAPTER V.

CHURCHILL PENWYN.

CHURCHILL PENWYN was one of those men who are sure to obtain a certain amount of notice in whatsoever circle they appear; a man upon whom the stamp of good blood or good breeding had been set in a distinct and palpable manner; a man who had no need for self-assertion.

It would have been difficult for any one to state in what the distinction lay. He was not particularly good-looking. Intellect rather than regularity of features was the leading characteristic of his countenance. Already, though he was still on the sunward side of his thirtieth birthday, the dark brown hair grew thinly upon the broad high brow, showing signs of premature baldness. His features were sharply cut, but by no means faultless, the mouth somewhat sunken, the lips thin. His light gray eyes had a keen, cold luster—only those who saw Churchill Penwyn in some rare moment of softer feeling knew that those severe orbs could be beautiful. Mr. Penwyn was a barrister, still in the up-hill stage of his career. He got an occasional brief, went on circuit assiduously, and did a little in the literature of politics—a hard, dry kind of literature, but fairly remunerative when he got it to do. He had contributed hard-headed statistical papers to the *Edinburgh* and the *Westminster*, and knew a good deal about the condition of the operative classes. He had lectured in some of the northern manufacturing towns, and knew the Black Country by heart. People talked of him as a young man who was sure to make his mark by and by; but by and by might be a long way off. He would be fifty years of age, perhaps, before he had worked his way to the front.

Churchill Penwyn went a great deal into society, when it is considered how hard and how honestly he worked; but the houses in which he was to be found were always houses affected by the best people. He never wasted himself among second-rate circles. He was an excellent art critic; knew enough about music to talk of it cleverly, though he had hardly the faculty of distinguishing one tune from another; waltzed like a Viennese; rode like a centaur; spoke three Continental languages perfectly. It was his theory that no man should presume to enter society who could not do everything that society could require him to do. Society was worth very little in itself, according to Churchill Penwyn, but a man owed it to himself to be admired and respected.

"I see a good many men who go into the world to stare about them through eye-glasses," said Churchill. "If I couldn't do anything more than that, I should spend my evenings in my own den."

Churchill Penwyn went into the gay world with a definite

aim—some of the people he met must needs be useful to him
sooner or later.

Ohne Hast, ohne Rast—without haste, without rest—was his
motto. He had it engraved on his signet-ring instead of the
Penwyn crest. He was never in a hurry. While striving.for
success, he had the air of a man who had already succeeded.
He occupied a couple of dingy rooms in the Temple, and lived
like an anchorite, but his tailor and bootmaker were among the
best in London, and he was a member of the Traveler's and the
Garrick. He was to be seen sometimes lunching at his club.
and occasionally entertained a friend at luncheon, but he rarely
dined there, and was never seen to drink anything more costly
than a pint of La Rose or Medoc. No man had ever mastered
the art of economy more thoroughly than Churchill Penwyn,
and yet he had never laid himself open to the charge of meanness.

Miss Bellingham received him with a bright look of welcome
despite the dowager's warning, and their hands met, with a
gentle pressure on Churchill's part. Viola was discreetly occupied in showing Mrs. Noyce a new photograph, and only gave
the visitor a bow and a smile. So he had a fair excuse for seat-
ing himself next Madge on the divan by the fireplace, where
there was just room for those two.

"I did not think you would come to-night," said Madge, opening and shutting her large black fan, with a slightly nervous
movement.

"Why not?"

"I saw your name in the paper at Halifax, or somewhere,
hundreds of miles away."

"I was at Halifax the day before yesterday, but I would not
miss my Saturday evening here. You see I have come a quarter
of an hour in advance of your people, so that I might have you
to myself for a few minutes."

"It is so good of you," faltered Madge; "and you know I am
always glad."

"I should be wretched if I did not know it."

This was going further than Mr. Penwyn's usual limits. The
man was the very soul of prudence. No sweet words, no tender promises, had ever passed between these two, and yet they
knew themselves beloved. Madge knew it to her sorrow, for
she was fain to admit the wisdom of the dowager's warning. It
would never do for her to marry Churchill Penwyn.

Happily for her, up to this time Churchill had never asked her
to be his wife.

"He is too wise," she said to herself, with the faintest touch
of bitterness—"too much a man of the world."

But that this man of the world loved her she was very sure.

For just ten minutes they sat side by side, talking of indifferent things, but only as people talk who are not quite indifferent to each other. And then more visitors were announced.
Sir Nugent and his friends came up-stairs, the rooms began to
fill. Musical people arrived. A German with long rough hair,
bony wrists, and an eye-glass seated himself at the piano, and

began a performance of so strictly classical a character that he had the enjoyment of it all to himself, for nobody else listened. Minor chords chased one another backward and forward about the middle of the piano as if they were hunting for the melody and couldn't find it. Little runs and arpeggio passages went under and over each other still searching for the subject, and finally gave up the quest in utter despair, appropriately expressed by vague grumblings in the bass, which slowly faded into silence. Whereupon every one became enthusiastic in their admiration.

After this a young lady in pink sang an airy little *chanson*, with elaborate variations—using her bright soprano voice as freely as if she had been Philomel trilling her vespers in the dusky woods of June. And then Madge Bellingham sat down to the piano, and played—played as few young ladies play—as if her glad young soul were in the music.

It was only a Hungarian march that she played. There were no musical fireworks—no difficulties conquered; none of those passages which make the listeners exclaim, "Poor girl; how she must have practiced!" It was but a national melody—simple and spirit-stirring—played as if the soul of a patriot were guiding those supple fingers. The graceful figure was bent a little over the key-board, the dark eyes followed the swift flight of the hands over the keys. She seemed to caress the notes as she struck them—to play with the melody. Pride, love, hope, rage—every passion expressed itself by turns as she followed that wild strange music through the mazes of its variations, never losing the subject. It sounded like the war-cry of a free people. Even Churchill Penwyn, who in a general way cared so little for music, listened entranced to this. He could hardly have recalled the air half an hour later, but for the moment he was enchanted. He stood a little way from the instrument, watching the player, watching the beautiful head, with its dark rippling hair wound into a Greek knot at the back; the perfect throat, with its classic necklet of old Wedgwood medallions set in plainest gold; the drooping lashes, as the downcast eyes followed the flying touch. To hear Madge play was delightful, but to see her was still better. And this man's love had all the strength of a passion repressed. He had held himself in check so long, and every time he saw her he found her more and more adorable.

The evening wore on. People came in and out. Madge played the hostess divinely, always supported by Lady Cheshunt, who sat in the smaller drawing-room as in a temple, and had all the best people brought to her. Some came to Cavendish Row on their way somewhere else, and were careful to let their acquaintance know that they were "due" at some very grand entertainment, and made rather a favor of coming to Sir Nugent. The last of the guests went about half an hour after midnight, and among the last Churchill Penwyn.

"May I bring you that book after church to-morrow?" he asked. The book was a comedy of Augier's, lately produced at the Francais, which he had been telling her about.

Madge looked embarrassed. She had a particular wish to avoid a *tete-a-tete* with Mr. Penwyn, and Sunday was an awkward day. Sir Nugent would be at Hurlingham, most likely, and Viola was such a foolish little thing, almost as bad as nobody.

"If you like," she answered. "But why take the trouble to call on purpose? You might bring it next Saturday, if you come to us."

"I shall bring it you to-morrow," he said, as they shook hands.

That tiresome Viola was in a hopeless state of headache and prostration next morning, so Madge had to go to church alone. Coming out of the pretty little Anglican temple she found herself face to face with Churchill Penwyn. He had evidently been lying in wait for her.

"I was so afraid I might not find you at home," he said, half apologetically, "so I thought I might as well walk this way. I knew this was your church. I've brought you the play we were talking about."

"You're very kind, but I hope you don't think I read French comedies on Sundays."

"Of course not; only Sunday is my leisure day, and I thought you would not shut your door upon me even on Sunday."

The church was only five minutes' walk from Cavendish Row. When Sir Nugent's door was opened, Mr. Penwyn followed Miss Bellingham into the house as a matter of course. She had no help for it but to go quietly up-stairs to her fate. She almost knew what was coming. There had been something in his manner last night that told her it was very near.

"Prudence, courage," she whispered to herself, and then, "Viola!" The last word was a kind of charm.

The rooms looked bright and gay in the noontide sunlight tempered by Spanish blinds. The flowers, the feminine prettiness scattered about, struck Churchill's eye, they gave such a look of home.

"If I could afford to give her as good a home as this!" he thought.

He shut the door carefully behind him, and glanced round the room to make sure they were alone, and went close to Madge as she stood by one of the small tables, fidgeting with the clasp of her prayer-book.

"I think you know why I came to-day," he said.

"You have told me about three times—to bring me 'La Quarantaine.'"

"I have come to tell you a secret I have kept more than a year. Have you never guessed it, Madge? Have I been clever enough to hide the truth altogether? I love you, dearest. I, penniless Churchill Penwyn, dare to adore one of the belles of the season. I, who cannot for years to come offer you a house in May Fair. I, who at most must venture to begin married life in a Bloomsbury lodging, supported by the fruits of my pen. It sounds like madness, doesn't it?"

"It is madness," she answered, looking full at him with her truthful eyes.

The answer surprised and humiliated him. He fancied she loved him, would be ready to face poverty for his sake. She was so young, and would hardly have acquired the wisdom of her world yet awhile.

"I beg your pardon." he said, a curious change coming over his face, a sudden coldness, that made those definite features look as if they had been cut out of stone. "I have been deceiving myself all along, it seems. I did not think I was quite indifferent to you."

The eyelids drooped over the dark eyes for a moment, and were then lifted suddenly, and the eyes met Churchill's. That one look told all. She loved him.

"I have been learning to know the world while other girls are allowed to dream," she said. "I know what the burden of debt means. Poverty brings debt as a natural sequence. If you were a wood-cutter and we could live in a hovel and pay our way, there would be nothing appalling in marriage. But our world will not let us live like that. We must play at being fine ladies and gentlemen while our hearts are breaking and our creditors being ruined. Ever so long ago I made up my mind that I must marry a rich man. If I have ever seemed otherwise to you than a woman of the world, bent upon worldly success, I humbly beg you to forgive me."

"Madge," cried Churchill, passionately, "I will forgive anything if you will only be frank. Were my luck to turn speedily, through some unlooked-for professional success, for instance, would you have me then?"

"If I stood alone in the world, if I had not my sister to consider, I would marry you to-morrow. Yes, though you were a beggar," she answered, grandly.

He clasped her to his breast and kissed those proud lips—the first lover's kiss that had ever rested there.

"I will be rich for your sake, distinguished for your sake," he said, impetuously, "if wealth and fame are within the reach of man's effort."

CHAPTER VI.

"THERE IS NO LIFE ON EARTH BUT BEING IN LOVE."

THE first faint streak of day parted the eastern clouds when James Penwyn got back to the Waterfowl, but late as it was, and though a long day's various fatigues might have invited him to repose, Humphrey Clissold had waited up for his friend. He was walking up and down the inn parlor, where empty bottles and glasses, cigar ashes, and a broken clay pipe or two bestrewed the table, and gave a rakish look to the room. The windows stood wide open to the pale cold dawn, and the air was chill.

"Not gone to bed yet, Humphrey?" exclaimed James, surprised, and perhaps somewhat embarrassed by this unexpected encounter.

"I was in no humor for sleep. I never can sleep when I have anything on my mind. I waited up to ask you a question, Jim."

Something like defiance sparkled in Mr. Penwyn's eyes as he planted himself upon the arm of the substantial old sofa, and lighted a final cigar.

"Don't restrain your eloquence," he said; "I should hardly have considered four o'clock in the morning a time for conversation, but if you think so, I'm at your service."

"I want to know, in plain words, what you mean by this, James?"

"By what?"

"Your conduct to that girl."

"I shouldn't think anything so simple needed explanation. I meet a strolling player and his daughter. The strolling player is something of a character: the daughter—well, not pretty, perhaps, though she has lovely eyes, but interesting. I offer them the small attention of a supper, and, seeing that my friend the player is a trifle the worse for the champagne consumed, humanity urges me to escort the young lady to her own door lest her father should lead her into one of the ditches which beset the way. I believe that is the sum total of my offenses."

"It sounds simple enough, Jim," answered the other, gravely, but not unkindly; "and I dare say no harm will come of it if you let things stop exactly where they are. But I watched you and that poor child to-night—she is little more than a child at best—and I saw that you were doing your utmost, unconsciously perhaps, to turn her silly head. I saw you together in the moonlight afterward."

"If there was anything sentimental, you must blame the moon, not me," said James, lightly.

"And now you talk of spending to-morrow with these people, and taking them to the races."

"And I mean to do it. There's a freshness about them that amuses me. I've been getting rather tired of Nature and Greek—though, of course, we've had an uncommonly jolly time of it together, my dear old Humphrey—and I find a relief in a glimpse of real life. When you turn mentor, you make yourself intensely disagreeable. Do you suppose I harbor one wicked intention about this girl?"

"No, James, I don't suppose you do. If I thought you were a deliberate sinner, I should leave you to go your own road, and only try to save the girl. But I know what misery has been wrought in this world by gentlemanly trifling, and what still deeper wretchedness has been brought about by unequal marriages."

"Do you suppose I think of marrying Mr. Elgood's daughter because I say a few civil words to her?" cried James, forgetting how much earnestness there had been in those civil words only an hour ago.

"If you have no such thought, you have no right to cultivate an acquaintance that can only end in unhappiness to her, if not to yourself."

James answered with a sneer, to which Clissold replied-some-
what warmly, and there were angry words between the two
young men before they parted in the corridor outside their bedrooms. The people of the house, already thinking about morning, heard the raised voices and angry tones—heard and remembered.

It was ten o'clock when James Penwyn went down to breakfast next morning. The sun was shining in at the open windows, all traces of last night's revelry were removed, the room
was in the nicest order, the table spread for breakfast with spotless linen and shining tea-service, but only set for one. James
plucked impatiently at the bell-rope. It irked him not to see his
friend's face on the other side of the board. He had come down-
stairs prepared to make peace on the easiest terms, ready even
to own himself to blame.

"Has Mr. Clissold breakfasted?" he asked the girl who answered his summons.

"No, sir. He wouldn't stop for breakfast; he went out soon
after seven this morning with his fishing-rod. And he left a
note, please. sir."

There it was among the shells and shepherdesses on the mantelpiece—a little pencil scrawl twisted into a cocked hat.

"DEAR JIM,—Since it seems that my counsel irritates and an-
noys you, I take myself off for a day's fly-fishing. You must
please yourself about the races, only remember that it is easy
for a man to drift upon quicksands from which he can hardly
extricate himself, without the loss of honor or of happiness.
The sum total of a man's life depends very much upon what he
does with the first years of his manhood. I shall be back before night.

"Yours always, H. C."

James Penwyn read and re-read the brief epistle, musing over
it frowningly. It was rather tiresome to have a friend who took
such a serious view of trifles. Toward what quicksand was he
drifting? Was it a dishonorable thing to admire beautiful eyes,
to wish to do some kindness to a friendless girl *en passant?* As
to the races, he could not dream of disappointing the people he
had invited. Was he to treat them cavalierly because they
were poor? He rang the bell again, and ordered the largest
landau or barouche which the Waterfowl could obtain for him,
with a pair of good horses.

"And get me up a picnic basket," he said, "and plenty of
champagne."

At two-and-twenty, with the revenues of Penwyn Manor at
his command, a man would hardly do things shabbily.

He had arranged everything with his guests. The Dempsons
and the Elgoods lodged in the same house, an ancient dwelling
not far from the archway at the lower end of the city. Mr.
Penwyn was to call for them in a carriage at twelve o'clock,
and they were to drive straight to the race-course.

James breakfasted slowly, and with little appetite. He missed
the companion whose talk had been wont to enliven all their

meals. He thought it unkind of Humphrey to leave him—was at once angry with his friend, and with himself for his contemptuous speeches of last night. He left his breakfast unfin-' ished at last, and went out into the garden, and down by the narrow river, which had a different look by day. It was beautiful still—the winding stream with its sedgy banks and far-off background of low hills, and the grave old city in the middle distance—but it lacked the magic of night, the mystic charms of moonbeams and shadow.

The scene, even without the moonlight, put him painfully in mind of last night, when Justina and he had sat side by side on the beach by yonder willow.

"Why shouldn't I marry her if I love her?" he said to himself. "I am my own master. Who will ask Squire Penwyn for his wife's pedigree? It isn't as if she were vulgar or ignorant. She speaks like a lady, and she seems to know as much as most of the girls I have met."

He strolled up and down by the river-brink, smoking and musing, until the carriage was ready. It was a capacious vehicle, of the good old Baker Street Repository build, a vehicle which looked as if it had been a family traveling carriage about the period of the Bourbon restoration, and had done the tour of Europe, and been battered and bruised a good deal between the Alps and the Danube. There was a vast amount of leather in its composition, and more iron than sticklers for absolute elegance would desire, whereby it jingled considerably in its progress. But it was roomy, and for a race-course that was the main point.

James drove to the dingy old street where the players lodged, an old-fashioned street, with queer old houses, more picturesque than clean. The players' lodgings were above a small shop in the chandlery line, and as there was no private door, James had to enter the realms of Dutch cheese, kippered herrings, and dip candles—pendent from the low ceiling like stalactites—in quest of his new acquaintances.

The ladies were ready, but Mr. Elgood was still in his shirt-sleeves, and his countenance had a warm and shiny look, as if but that moment washed. Justina came running down the stairs and into the shop, where James welcomed her warmly. She was quite a transformed and glorified Justina—decked in borrowed raiment, which Mrs. Dempson had good-naturedly supplied for the occasion. "There was no knowing what would come of to-day's outing," the leading lady had remarked, significantly; "Mr. Penwyn was young and foolish, and seemed actually taken with Justina, and it would be such a blessing if she could marry well. poor child, seeing that she had not a spark of talent for the profession."

Justina wore a clean muslin dress, which hardly reached her ankles, a black silk jacket, and a blue crape bonnet, not too fresh, but quite respectable—a bonnet which had been pinned up in paper and carefully kept since last summer.

" I shall trim it up with a feather or two, and wear it for ligh🖤

comedy by and by," said Mrs. Dempson, as she pulled the bonnet into shape upon Justina's head.

The girl looked so happy that she was almost beautiful. There was a soft bloom upon her cheek, a tender depth in the dark blue eyes, a joyous, smiling look that charmed James Penwyn, who liked people to be happy and enjoy themselves, when he was in humor for festivity.

" How good of you to be ready!" cried James, taking her out to the carriage, " and how bright and fresh and gay you look!" Justina blushed, conscious of her borrowed bonnet. " I've got a nice old rattle-trap to take us to the race-course."

" Oh. beautiful!" exclaimed Justina, gazing at the patriarchal tub with respectful admiration.

" Are the others ready?"

" Father's just putting on his coat, and the Dempsons are coming down-stairs."

The Dempsons appeared as she spoke, Mrs. Dempson superb in black moire antique and the pinkest of pink bonnets, and a white lace shawl, which had been washed a good many times, and had rather too much darning in proportion to the pattern, but, as Mrs. Dempson remarked, " it always looked graceful." It was her bridal veil as Pauline Deschappelles. She wore it during that grand scene in Sheridan Knowle's " Hunchback," where the erring Julia interviews the ruined Clifford.

"Now, then," cried James, as Mr. Elgood appeared, still struggling with his coat. The carriage was packed without further delay, Mrs. Dempson and Justina in the seat of honor, Mr. Penwyn and Mr. Dempson opposite them, Mr. Elgood on the box. He had declared his preference to that seat.

Off they went, oh! so gayly, Justina thought, the landlady gazing at them from her shop door, and quite a cluster of small children cheering their departure. " As if it had been a wedding," Mrs. Dempson said, archly.

Away they went through the quaint old city, which wore its holiday look to-day. Crowds were pouring in from the station; coffee-houses and eating-houses had set forth a Rabelaisian abundance in their shining windows; taverns were decorated with flags and greenery; flies, driven by excited coachmen with ribbons on their whips, shot up and down the streets. All was life and brightness, and Justina, who had rarely ridden in a carriage, felt that just in this one brief hour she could understand how duchesses and such people must feel.

CHAPTER VII.

" LET THE WORLD SLIP; WE SHALL NE'ER BE YOUNGER."

THEY left the town behind them, and rattled along the wide high-road for half a mile or so before they turned off to the race-ground. Perhaps the Eborsham course is one of the prettiest in England—an oval basin of richest greensward set among low wooded hills, a water pool shining here and there in the valley, where the placid kine browse in pensive solitude, save during the race week, when the placid kine are wisely withdrawn from the dangerous neighborhood of tramps and gypsies and the wild excitement of the turf.

The grand stand, a permanent building of white freestone, looks very grand to Justina's eyes as the family ark blunders and jingles into a place exactly opposite—one of the best places on that privileged piece of ground. for which James pays three shining sovereigns. Temporary stands of wood-work border the course, crowded with warm humanity. Justina wonders where so many people come from, and how it is so few of them come to the theater, and sighs to think that the drama has never taken a grip upon the public mind as a thoroughly national amusement. See how the people congregate to-day, tier above tier on yonder fragile stages, pressed together with scarce breathing room, and yet there will be room to spare in the little theater to-night. Justina fears, despite immense attractions and an unparalled combination of talent, as advertised in the play-bills.

But after this one sigh for the neglected drama, Justina abandons herself to the delight of the hour, and is supremely content. James tells her all about the horses—how that one has done great things at Newmarket, how the other was winner of the Chester cup. He shows her the colors, explains everything, and the race assumes a new interest. Mr. Dempson leaves the carriage. to stretch his legs a bit, he says, and see who's on the course, but in reality because he is of a roving disposition, and soon tires of repose. Mr. Elgood devotes himself exclusively to Mrs. Dempson—"Villeroy," as he calls her, being more accustomed to her professional alias than the name she renders illustrious in domestic life. So James and Justina are left to themselves, and behave very much as if they had been plighted lovers ever so long—quite unconsciously upon Justina's part, for she knows little of real lovers and their ways.

Presently there is a sudden stir. a dispersement of pedestrians from the race course, as a policeman or two gallop up and down, and the clerk of the course, in his scarlet coat and buckskins, canters briskly over the grass; then a dog driven past with hootings and ignominy, then more ringing of bells, the preliminary canter, and then the race.

A few minutes of breathless attention, a thundering rush past all the carriages, and the eager a-tiptoe spectators, and white body with red spots has pulled off the first stakes.

"Did you see it?" asked James, turning to the girl's bright face. glowing with excitement.

"Oh, it was beautiful. I don't wonder at people coming to races now. I feel as if I had never been quite alive before. Just that one moment when the horses were tearing past. It was wonderful."

"A very fair race," said James, with a patronizing air: "but there were some wretched screws among them. You'll see a better set by and by, for the cup. Iphianassa. the Oaks winner, is first favorite. The book men call her Free-and-Easy for short. And now we'll have a bottle of cham."

"Not a bad move," said Mr. Elgood, approvingly. "That kind of thing makes a fellow dryish."

He made himself very useful in helping to open the baskets: there were two hampers, one for wine and the other for comestibles, the Waterfowl having done things handsomely. Mr. Elgood took one of the golden-necked bottles out of the rush case, found the glasses, the nippers. and opened the bottle as neatly as a waiter. He had the lion's share of the wine for his trouble.

James and Justina had only one glass between them. They could very easily have two, but they liked this mutual goblet, and sipped the bright wine gayly, Justina taking about as much as Titania might have consumed from a chalice made of a harebell.

The champagne bottle was hardly open when a gypsy appeared at the carriage door, as if attracted by the popping of the cork— an elderly gypsy, with an orange silk handkerchief tied across her black hair, among which a few silver threads were visible. She was the identical gypsy woman who had stopped James Penwyn and his companion yesterday afternoon by the river.

"Give the poor old gypsy woman a little drop of wine, kind gentlemen," she asked, insinuatingly.

Justina drew back shuddering, drew nearer her companion, till her slight form pressed against his shoulder, and he could feel that she trembled.

"Why, what's the matter, you timid bird?" he whispered, tenderly. drawing his arm round her by an instinctive movement. They were standing up in the carriage as they had stood to see the race, Mrs. Dempson with her face toward the box, whence Mr. Elgood was pointing out features of interest on the course.

"It is the same woman!" exclaimed Justina, in a half whisper.

"What woman. my pet?"

It had come to this already, and Justina at this particular moment was too absorbed to remonstrate.

"The woman who told you about the mark on your hand."

"Is it really? I didn't notice," answered James, smiling at her concern. The gypsy had gone to the next carriage, whose occupants were in the act of discussing a bottle of sherry and a packet of appetizing sandwiches, thin and daintily-trimmed sandwiches, made to provoke rather than appease appetite.

"Upon my word I didn't notice," repeated James. "All gypsies are alike to my eye, the same tawny skins, the same shiny black hair. But why should you be frightened at her, pretty one? She prophesied no evil about me."

"No, but she looked at you so curiously; and then a line across the line of life—that must mean something dreadful."

"My dearest, do you think any reasonable being believes in lines of life or any such bosh? Gypsies must have some kind of jargon, or they would get no dupes. But I think you and I are too wise to believe in their nonsense. We'll give the harridan a tumbler of fiz, and I'll warrant she'll prophesy smooth things. Hi! mistress, this way!"

The gypsy having paid unfruitful homage to the carriage of sandwich consumers came quickly at James Penwyn's bidding.

"Let me drink your health, pretty gentleman," she pleaded. "and the health of the young lady that loves you best; and I know of one that loves you well, and a beautiful young lady, and is well beloved by you. You've courted a many, young gentleman, in your time, the old gypsy knows, for you've a wicked eye and a wanton 'art; but the most fickle must fix at last, and may you never rove no more! for you've fixed upon one as can be constant to you. Thank you, sir; and here's health and happiness to you and the young lady, and a short courtship and a long fambly; and give the poor gypsy a mossel of somethink to eat, like a dear young lady," appealing to the blushing Justina, "for fear the wine should turn acid upon my inside."

The picnic basket had to be opened in order to meet this judicious demand, and this being done, the sibyl was gratified with a handsome wedge of veal pie. This partly dispatched and partly pocketed, she made the familiar request for a piece of silver to cross the young lady's palm, which charm being performed she could tell things that would please her. James complied, and Justina surrendered her hand, most unwillingly, to the gypsy's brown claw.

The sibyl told the usual story—happy wooing, prosperous wedded life; all things were to go smoothly for the blue-eyed lady and the blue-eyed gentleman.

"But beware of a dark man," said the witch, who felt it necessary to introduce some shadow in her picture—"beware of a dark-complexioned man. I won't say as he's spades; better call him clubs, perhaps. Be on your guard against a club man, my sweet young lady and gentleman, for he bears a jealous heart toward you both, and he stands to do you harm, if he has the power."

"That will do," said James: "we've had enough for our money, thank you, old lady; you can move on to the next carriage."

"Don't be offended with the poor gypsy, your honor. She's truth-spoken and plain-spoken, and she sees deeper into things than some folks would give her credit for."

And thus, after an affectionate farewell, the prophetess pursued her way. Other prophetesses followed in her wake, all begging for food and wine, and James lavished more champagne in this direction than Mr. Elgood approved. but even his good-nature wore out at last, and he grew tired of the copper-skinned medicants, some with babies in arms. for whom they begged a little drop of champagne or the claw of a lobster.

The races went on. The great race was at hand.

"Now, then, Justina, we must have something on," said James. "You don't mind me calling you Justina, do you?"

"*I* don't mind," the girl answered, simply, "if father doesn't."

"Well, you see, I can't ask him now, but I will by and by,

We can let the question stand over, and I may call you Justina meanwhile, mayn't I, Justina?" he asked, softly.

"If you like," she answered, almost in a whisper. They stood so near together that there was no need for either of them to speak loud, even amidst the noise of the race-course.

"Look here now, Justina. I'll bet you half a dozen gloves, even money, that Free-and-Easy doesn't win. That's giving you a great advantage, for they are laying three to two on the favorite."

"I don't think I can bet," said Justina, embarrassed. "If I were to lose I could not pay you."

"Ladies never pay debts. Come, if Iphianassa wins you shall have a dozen pairs of the prettiest gloves I can buy, straw-colored, pink, pearl gray—which is your favorite color?"

"I like any kind of gloves," answered the girl, remembering two wretched pairs which had been to the cleaner's so often that the insides were all over numbers like a multiplication-table.

Now came the start; breathlessness; attention strained almost to agony; a hoarse clamor yonder in and about the ring; one big man, wearing a white hat with a black hat-band, offering frantically to bet ten to one against anything, bar one; then a shout as of universal victory, for Free-and-Easy has shot sud-denly to the front, after having been tenderly nursed during the first half mile or so; and now she comes along gallantly, with a great lead, and her backers tremble; and now cold dews break out upon the foreheads of those eager backers, for another horse, almost an unknown animal, creeps up to Iphianassa, gallops shoulder to shoulder with the Oaks winner, passes her, and wins by a neck, while a suppressed groan mingles with the hurrahs of that miserable outside public which never stakes more than half a sovereign, and is ready to cheer any horse. Only among the book-men is there real rejoicing, for they have been betting against the favorite.

"You've lost your gloves, Justina. Never mind, we'll have another venture on the next race. It's a selling stake, and we can go and see the auction afterward—such fun! And now for the basket. Make yourself useful, Elgood. Mrs. Dempson, you must be famishing."

Mrs. Dempson, upon being pressed, owned to feeling a little faint. A lady of Mrs. Dempson's caliber never confesses to being hungry; with her want of food only produces a genteel faintness.

The basket was emptied, lobster, chicken, pie, set out upon a table-cloth laid on the front seat of the carriage. Then the scrambling meal began, the ladies seated with plates in their laps, the gentlemen standing. Again James and Justina shared the same glass of champagne, while Mr. Elgood obligingly held on by the bottle, and filled his own glass by installments, so that it was never empty, and never full. Mr. Dempson was mod-erate but jovial; Mrs. Dempson protested vehemently every time her glass was replenished, but contrived to drink the wine out of politeness.

James was the gayest of Amphitrions. He kept on declaring tnat he had never enjoyed himself so much—never had such a jolly day.

"I am sorry your friend is not with us," remarked Mr. El-good, with his mouth full of lobster; "he has lost a treat."

"His loss is our gain," observed Mr. Dempson. "There'd have been less champagne for the rest of us if he'd been here."

"My friend is an ass," said James, carelessly. His errant fancy, so easily caught, was quite enchained by this time. He had been growing fonder of Justina all day, and with the growth of his boyish passion his anger against Humphrey increased. He had almost made up his mind to do the very thing which Clissold had stigmatized as madness. He had al-most made up his mind to marry the actor's daughter. He was in love with her, and how else should his love end? He came of too good a stock, had too good a heart, to contemplate a dis-honorable ending. It only remained for him to discover if he really loved her—if this fancy that had but dawned upon him yesterday were indeed the beginning of his fate, or that consid-erable part of a man's destiny which is involved in his marriage. He had been very little in the society of women since his moth-er's death. His brief harmless flirtations had been chiefly with damsels of the bar-maid class; and after these meretricious charmers, Justina, with her wild-rose-tinted cheeks and inno-cent blue eyes, seemed youth and beauty personified. Perchance Proserpine, when the grim ruler of the under-world beheld her gathering wild flowers on the lea, was hardly the loveliest of earthly maidens; but to the jaded eye that had grown weary of pandemonium's lurid beauties, freshness and purity must have had an ineffable charm.

Justina looked shyly up at her admirer, happier than words could have told. Little had she ever tasted of pleasure's mad-dening cup before to-day. The flavor of the wine was not stranger to her lips than the flavor of joy to her soul. For her girlhood had meant hard work and deprivation. Since she had been young enough to play hop-scotch on the doorstep with a neighbor's children, and think it happiness, she had hardly known what it was to be glad. To-day life brimmed over with enchantment—a carriage, a picnic, races, all the glad, gay world smiling at her. She looked at James with a grateful smile when he asked her if she was enjoying herself.

"How can I help enjoying myself?" she said; "I never had such a day in my life. It will all be over to-night, and to-mor-row the world will look just as it does when one awakens from a wonderful dream. I have had dreams just like to day," she added, simply.

"Might we not lengthen the dream, find some enjoyment for to-morrow?" asked James. "We might even come to the races again, if you like."

"We couldn't come. There will be a long rehearsal to-mor-row. We play the new burlesque to-morrow night, and I thought you were going away to-morrow. Your friend said so."

"My friend would have been wiser had he spoken for himself, and not for me. I shall stay till the races are over: longer
perhaps. How long do you stay?"

"Till next Saturday week, unless the business should get too
bad."

"Then I think I shall stay till next Saturday week. I can
read a Greek play at Eborsham as well as anywhere else, and I
don't see why I should be hurried from place to place to please
Clissold?" added the young man, rebelliously.

There had been no hurrying from place to place hitherto.
They had done a good deal of Wales, and the English lakes, by
easy stages, stopping at quiet inns, and reading hard in the intervals of their pedestrianism, and James had been completely
happy with the bosom friend of his youth. It was only since
yesterday that the bosom friend had been transformed into a
tyrant. Clissold had warned and reproved before to-day; he
had spoken with the voice of wisdom when James seemed going a little too far in some village flirtation, and James had listened meekly enough. But this time James Penwyn's soul rejected counsel. He was angry with his friend for not thinking
it the most natural thing in the world that he, Squire Penwyn,
of Penwyn, should fall head over ears in love with a country
actor's daughter.

"I may come behind the scenes to-night, mayn't I, Justina?"
said James, by and by, when the last race was over, and he and
Justina had seen the winner disposed of to the highest bidder,
and the patriarchal tub was rolling swiftly—oh, too swiftly—
back to the town; back to common life and the old dull world.

"You must ask father or Mr. Dempson," Justina answered,
meekly. "Sometimes they make a fuss about any one coming
into the green-room, but I don't suppose they would about you.
It would be very ungrateful if they did."

James asked the question of Mr. Elgood, and was answered
heartily. He was to consider the Eborsham green-room an ad-
junct to his hotel, and the Eborsham Theater as open to him as
his club, without question of payment at the doors.

"Your name shall be left with the money-taker," the heavy
father said, somewhat thickly.

Mr. Dempson laughed.

"Our friend is a trifle screwed," he said, "but I dare say he'll
get through Sir Oliver pretty well."

The play was the "School for Scandal," a genteel entertainment in honor of the patrons of the races.

The roomy traveling carriage was blundering through one of
the narrow streets near the cathedral when James Penwyn stood
up suddenly and looked behind him.

"What's the matter?" asked Mr. Dempson.

"Nothing. I thought I saw a fellow I know, that's all. He's
just gone into that public-house, the quiet-looking little place
at the corner. I fancied I saw him on the course, but I don't
see how it could be the man," added James, dubiously. "What
should bring him down here? It isn't in his line?"

CHAPTER VIII..
HAVE THE HIGH GODS ANYTHING LEFT TO GIVE?

MR. PENWYN set down his guests at the chandler's door, and drove home to the Waterfowl in solitary state, the chariot in which he sat seeming a great deal too big for one medium-sized young man.

His ample meal on the course made dinner an impossibility; so he ordered a cup of coffee to be taken to him in the garden, and went out to smoke a cigar on his favorite bench by the willow. The Waterfowl was too far off the beaten tracks for any of the race people to come there, so James had the garden all to himself even this evening.

The sun was setting beyond the bend of the river, just where the shining water seemed to lose itself in a rushy basin. The ruddy light shone on the windows of the town till they looked like fiery eyes gleaming through the gray evening mist, while, grandly dominating the level landscape and the low irregular town, rose the dusky bulk of the cathedral, dwarfing the distant hills. and standing darkly out against that changeful sky.

James Penwyn was in a meditative mood, and contemplated the landscape dreamily as he smoked an excellent cigar with epicurean slowness. letting pleasure last as long as it would. Not that his soul was interpenetrated by the subtle beauties of the scene. He only thought that it was rather jolly, that solemn stillness after the riot of the race-course, that lonely landscape after the movement of the crowd.

Only last night had Justina and he stood side by side in the moonlight—only last night had their hands met for the first time—and yet she seemed a part of his life, indispensable to his happiness.

"Is it love?" he asked himself, "first love? I didn't think it was in me to be such a spoon."

He was at the age when that idea of "spooniness" is to the last degree humiliating. He had prided himself upon his manliness—thought that he had exhausted the well-spring of sentiment in those passing flirtations, the transitory loves of an under-graduate. He had talked big about marrying by and by for money and position, to add new luster to the house of Penwyn. to carry some heiress' arms on his shield upon an escutcheon of some pretense.

Was it really love?—love for a foolish girl of seventeen, with sky-blue eyes, and a look of adoration when she raised them ever so fearfully to his face? Justina had a pensiveness that charmed him more than other women's gayety. and till now sprightliness had been his highest quality in woman—a girl who would light his cigar for him and take three or four puffs daintily before she handed him the weed—a girl who was quick at retort, and could "chaff" him. This girl essayed not repartee; this girl was fresh and simple as Wordsworth's ideal woman. And he loved her. For the first time in his glad young life his heart throbbed with the love that is so near akin to pain.

"I'll marry her," he said to himself. "She shall be mistress of Penwyn Manor."

The sun went down and left the landscape gloomy. James Penwyn rose from the bench with a faint shiver.

"These early summer evenings are chilly," he thought, as he walked back to the house. He felt lonely, somehow, in spite of his fair new hope. It was so strange to him not to have Clissold at his side—to reprove or warn. But at worst the voice was a friendly one. The silence of this garden, the dusky gloom on yonder river, the solemn grandeur of the dark cathedral, chilled him.

The great clock boomed eight, and reminded him that the play had begun half an hour. It would be a relief to find himself in the lighted play-house among those rollicking actors.

He went down to the theater, and made his way straight to the green-room. There was a good house—a great house, Mr. Elgood told James—and the commonwealth's shares were already above par. Everybody was in high spirits, and most people's breath was slightly flavored with beer.

"We have been turning away money at the gallery door," said Mr. Dempson, who was dressed for Moses, "I should think to the tune of seventeen shillings. This is the right sort of thing, sir. It reminds me of my poor old governor's time, when the drama was respected in the land, and all the gentry within a twenty-mile radius used to come to his benefit."

Justina was the Maria of the piece, dressed in an ancient white satin—or rather an ancient satin which had once been white—but which by long service and frequent cleaning had mellowed to a pleasing canary-color. She had some airy puffings of muslin about her, and wore a black sash in memory of her departed parents, and her plenteous brown hair fell over her neck and shoulders in innocent ringlets.

Justina had never looked prettier than she looked to-night. She had even had a round of applause when she made her courtesy to Sir Peter. The actors told her that she was growing a deuced fine girl, after all, and that one of these days she would learn how to act. Was it the new joy in her soul that embellished and exalted her?

James thought her lovely, as he stood at the wing and talked to her. Miss Villeroy, who was esteemed a beauty by her friends, seemed to this uninitiated youth a painted sepulcher; for she had whitened her complexion to match her powdered wig, and accentuated her eyebrows and eyelids with Indian ink, and picked out her lips with a rose-pink saucer, and incarnadined her cheek-bones; by which artistic efforts she had attained that kind of beauty to which distance lends enchantment, but which, seen too near, is apt to repel. Miss Villeroy had the house with her, however. She had the audience altogether with her as Lady Teazle, and, being a virtuous matron, cared not to court James Penwyn's admiration. Indeed, she was very glad to see that the foolish young man was taken with poor Judy, Mrs. Dempson told her husband; for poor dear Judy wasn't every-

body's money, and about the worst actress the footlights ever
shone upon.

Mr. Elgood being in high spirits, and feeling himself flush of
money—his share in to-night's receipts could hardly be less than
fifteen shillings—was moved to an act of hospitality.

" I'll tell you what I'll do, Mr. Penwyn," he said: " the treating sha'n't be all on your side, though you're a rich young
swell and we are poor beggars of actors. Come home with us
to-night, after the last piece, and I'll give you a lobster. Judy
knows how to make a salad, and if you can drink bitter beer,
you shall have enough to swim in."

Mr. Penwyn expressed his ability to drink bitter beer, which
he infinitely preferred to champagne. But what would he not
have drunk for the pleasure of being in Justina's society?

" It's a poor place to ask you to come to," said Mr. Elgood.
" Dempson and I go shares in the sitting-room, and we don't
keep it altogether as tidy as we might, the womenkind say; but
I'll take care the lobster's a good one, for I'll go out and pick it
myself. I don't play in the last piece, luckily."

The afterpiece was " A Roland for an Oliver," in which
Justina enacted a walking lady who had very little to do. So
there was plenty of time for James to talk to her as she stood
at the wing, where they were quite alone, and had nobody to
overhear them except a passing scene-shifter now and then.

This seemed to James Penwyn the happiest night he had ever
spent in his life, though he was inhaling dust and escaped gas
all the time. It seemed a night that flew by on golden wings.
He thought he must have been dreaming when the curtain fell,
and the lights went out, and people told him it was midnight.

He waited amidst darkness and chaos while Justina ran away
to change her stage dress for the garments of common life. She
was not long absent, and they went out together, arm in arm.
It was only a little way from the theater to the actors' lodgings,
so James persuaded her to walk round by the cathedral, just to
see how it looked in the moonlight.

" Your father said half-past twelve for supper, you know," he
pleaded, "and it's only just the quarter."

The big bell chimed at the instant, in confirmation of this
statement, and Justina, who could not for her life have said no,
assented hesitatingly.

The cathedral had a colossal grandeur seen from so near, every
finial and water-spout clearly defined in the moonlight. Justina
looked up at it with reverent eyes.

" Isn't it grand?" she whispered. " One could fancy that God
inhabits it. If I were an ignorant creature from some savage
land, and nobody told me it was a church, I think I should know
that it was God's house."

" Should you?" said James, lightly. " I think I should as
soon take it for a corn exchange or a wild-beast show."

" Oh!"

" You see, I have no instinctive sense of the fitness of things
You would just suit Clissold. He has all those queer fancies.
I've seen him stand and talk to himself like a lunatic sometimes,

among the lakes and mountains—what you call the artistic faculty, I suppose."

They walked round the Cathedral Square arm in arm, Justina charmed to silence by the solemn splendor of the scene. All was quiet at this end of the city. Up at the subscription-rooms there might be riot and confusion; but here, in this ancient square, among these old gabled houses, almost coeval with the cathedral, silence reigned supreme.

"Justina," James began presently, "you told me yesterday that you didn't care about being an actress."

"I told you that I hated it," answered the girl, candidly. "I suppose I should like it better if I were a favorite, like Villeroy."

"I prefer your acting to Miss Villeroy's ever so much. You do it rather too quietly, perhaps, but that's better than yelling as she does."

"I'm glad you like me best," said Justina, softly. "But then you're not the British public. Yes, I hate theaters. I should like to live in a little cottage, deep, deep, deep down in the country, where there were woods and fields and a shining blue river. I could keep chickens, and live upon the money I got by the new-laid eggs."

"Don't you think it would be better to have a nice large house, with gardens and orchards and a park, in a wild hilly country not far from the Atlantic Ocean?"

"What should I do with a big house, and how should I earn money to pay for it?" she asked, laughing.

"Suppose some one else were to find the money, some one who has plenty, and only wants the girl he loves to share it with him? Justina, you and I met yesterday for the first time, but you are the only girl I ever loved, and I love you with all my heart. It may seem sudden, but it's as true as that I live and speak to you to-night."

"Sudden!" echoed Justina; "it seems like a dream; but you mustn't speak of it any more. I won't believe a word you say. I won't listen to a word. It can't be true. Let's go home immediately. Hark, there's the half hour. Take me home, please, Mr. Penwyn."

"Not till you have answered me one question."

"No, no."

"Yes, Justina. I must be answered. I have made up my mind, and I want to know yours. Do you think you care for me just a little?"

"I won't answer. It is all more foolish than a dream."

"It is the sweetest dream that was ever dreamed by me. Obstinate lips! Cannot I make them speak? No? Then the eyes shall tell me what I want to know. Look up, Justina; just one little look—and then we'll go home."

The heavy lids were lifted slowly, shyly, and the young lover looked into the depths of those dark eyes. A girl's first, purest love, that love which is so near religion, shone there like a star.

James Penwyn needed no other answer.

"You shall never act again unless you like, darling," he said.

"I'll speak to your father to-night, and we'll be married as soon as the business can be done. When you leave Eborsham it will be as mistress of Penwyn Manor. There is not a soul belonging to me who has the faintest right to question what I do. And it is my duty to marry young. The Penwyn race has been sorely dwindling of late. If I were to die unmarried my estate would go to my cousin, a fellow I don't care two straws about."

Perhaps this was said more to himself than to Justina. She understood nothing about estates and heirships, she to whom property was an unknown quantity. She only knew that life seemed changed to a delicious dream. The hard, work-a-day world, which had not been too kind to her, had melted away. and left her in paradise. Her hand trembled beneath the touch of her lover as he clasped it close upon his arm.

They walked slowly through the silent, shadowy street, so narrow that the moonlight hardly reached it, and went in by the shop door, which had been left ajar in a friendly way for their reception.

"What a time you've been, Judy!" cried Mr. Elgood, standing before the table, stirring a bowl of green stuff, with various cruets at his elbow. "I've had to make the salad myself. Sit down and make yourself at home, Penwyn. Dempson, draw the cork of that bitter. The right thing nowadays is to pour it into a jug. When I was a young man we couldn't have too much froth."

Mrs. Dempson had smartened her usual toilet with a bow or two and a black lace veil, which she wore gracefully festooned about her head to conceal the curl-papers in which she had indued her tresses for to-morrow evening's performance. She would be too tired to curl her hair by the time she got rid of this foolish young man.

The supper was even gayer than the luncheon on the race-course. There was a large dish of cold corned beef, ready sliced, from the cook's shop; a cucumber, a couple of lobsters, and a bowl of salad, crisp and oily, upon which Mr. Elgood prided himself.

"There are not many things that this child can do," he remarked, "but he flatters himself he can dress a salad."

The ale being infinitely better of its kind than the champagne provided by the Waterfowl, proved more exhilarating. James Penwyn's spirits rose to their highest point. He invited everybody to Penwyn Manor, promised Miss Villeroy a season's hunting. Mr. Dempson any amount of sport. They would all go down to Cornwall together, and have a jolly time of it. Not a word did he say about his intended marriage: even though elated by beer, he felt a restraining delicacy which kept him silent on this one subject.

Justina was the quietest of the party. She sat by her father's side, looking her prettiest, with eyes that joy had glorified, and a delicate bloom upon her cheeks. She neither ate nor drank, but listened to her lover's careless rattle, and felt more and more that life was like a dream. How handsome he was! how

good! how brave! how brilliant! Her simplicity accepted the
young man's under graduate jocosity for wit of the purest water.
She laughed her gay young laugh at his jokes.

" If you could laugh like that on the stage, Judy, you'd make
as good a company actress as Mrs. Jordan," said her father.

" As if any one could laugh naturally to a cue!" cried Justina.

They sat late, almost as late as they had sat on the previous
night, and when James rose at last to take his leave, urged
thereto by the unquiet slumbers of Villeroy, who had fallen
asleep in an uncomfortable position on the rickety old sofa, and
whose snores were too loud to be agreeable. Mr. Elgood had arrived at that condition of mind in which life wears its rosiest
hue. He was anxious to see his guest home; but this favor
James declined.

"It's an—comm'ly bad road," urged the heavy father. " Y'd
berrer let me see y' 'ome—cut thro' row;" which James interpreted to mean " a cut-throat road." " Don't like y' t' go
'lone."

Justina watched her father with a troubled look. It was
hard that he should show himself thus degraded just now, when,
but for this, life would be all sweetness. James smiled at her
reassuringly, undisturbed by the thought that such a man
might be an undesirable father in-law.

He pushed his entertainer back into his seat.

"Talk about seeing me home!" he said. laughing, " why, it
isn't half an hour's walk. Good-night, Mr. Dempson. I'm
afraid I've kept your wife up too late, after her exertions in
Lady Teazle. Will you open the door for me, Justina?"

Justina went down the narrow. crooked staircase with him—
one of those staircases of the good old times, better suited to a
belfry tower than a dwelling-house. They went into the dark
little shop together. and just at the door, amidst odors of Irish
butter and Dutch cheese, Scotch herrings and Spanish onions,
James took his betrothed in his arms and kissed her fondly,
proudly, as if he had won a princess for his helpmeet.

" Remember, darling, you are to be my wife. If I had a hundred relations to bully me, they wouldn't make me change my
mind. But I've no one to call me to account, and you are the girl
of my choice. I haven't been able to speak to your father to-
night, but I'll talk to him to-morrow morning. and settle everything. Good-night, and God bless you, my own dear love!"

One more kiss, and he was gone. She stood on the door-step
watching him as he walked up the narrow street. The moon was
gone, and only a few stars shone dimly between the-drifting
clouds. The night wind came coldly up from the water-side
yonder, and made her shiver. A man crossed the street and
walked briskly past her, going in the same direction as James
Penwyn. She noticed, absently enough, that he wore a heavy
overcoat and muffler for defense against that chill night air, no
doubt, but more clothing than people generally wear in the
early days of June,

CHAPTER IX.

"OTHER SINS ONLY SPEAK; MURDER SHRIEKS OUT."

VERY radiant were Justina's dreams during the brief hours that remained to her for slumber after that Bohemian supper-party—dreams of her sweet new life, in which all things were bright and strange. She was with her lover in a garden—the dream-garden which those sleepers know who have seen but little of earthly gardens; a garden where there were marble terraces and statues and fountains, and a placid lake lying in a valley of bloom; a vision made up of faint memories of pictures she had seen or poems she had read. They were together and happy in the noonday sunshine. And then the dream changed. They were together in the moonlight again—not outside the cathedral, but within the long solemn nave. She could see the distant altar gleaming faintly in the silver light, while a solemn strain of music, like the muffled chanting of a choir, rolled along the echoing arches overhead. Then the silvery light faded, the music changed to a harsh, dirge-like cry, and she woke to hear the rain-drops pattering against her little dormer-window —Justina's room was the worst of the three bed-chambers, and in the garret story—and a shrill-voiced hawker bawling water-cresses along the street.

She had the feeling of having overslept herself, and not being provided with a watch, had no power to ascertain the fact, but was fain to dress as quickly as she could, trusting for the cathedral clock to inform her of the hour. To be late for rehearsal involved a good deal of snubbing from the higher powers, even in a commonwealth. The stage-manager retained his authority, and knew how to make himself disagreeable.

Life seemed all reality again this morning, as Justina plaited her hair before the shabby little mirror, and looked out at the dull gray sky, the wet sloppy streets, the general aspect of poverty and damp which pervaded the prospect. She had need to ask herself if yesterday and the night before had not been all dreaming. She the chosen bride of a rich young squire—she the mistress of Penwyn Manor! It was surely too fond a fancy. She, whose shabby weather-stained under-garments — the green stuff-gown of two winters ago converted into a petticoat last year, and worn threadbare; the corset which a nurse-maid might have despised, lay yonder on the dilapidated rush-bottomed chair, like the dull reality of Cinderella's rags, after the fairy ball dress had melted into air.

She hurried on her clothes, more ashamed of their shabbiness than she had ever felt yet, and ran down to the sitting-room, which smelled of stale lobster and tobacco, the windows not having been opened on account of the rain. Breakfast was laid. A sloppy cup and saucer, the dorsal bone of a haddock on a greasy plate, indicated that some one had breakfasted. The cathedral clock chimed eleven. Justina's rehearsal only began at half-past. She had time to take her breakfast comfortably, if she liked.

Her first act was to open the window and let in the air and the rain—anything was better than stale lobster. Then she looked into the tea-pot, and wondered who had breakfasted, and if her father were up. Then she poured out a cup of tea, and sipped it slowly, wondering if James Penwyn would come to the theater while she was rehearsing. He had asked her the hour of the re- hearsal. She thought she would see him there, most likely, and the dream began again.

A jug of wild flowers stood on the table by the window—the flowers she had gathered two days ago, before she had seen *him*.

They were a little faded—wild flowers droop so early—but in no wise dead; and yet a passion had been born and attained its majority since those field flowers were plucked.

Could she believe in it, could she trust in it? Her heart sank at the thought that her lover was trifling with her—that there was nothing but foolishness in this first love dream.

Her father had not yet left his room. Justina saw his one presentable pair of boots waiting for him outside his door as she went by on her way down-stairs.

She found Mr. and Mrs. Dempson at rehearsal, both with a faded and washed-out appearance, as if the excitement of the previous day had taken all the color out of them.

The rehearsal went forward in a straggling way. That good house of last night seemed to have demoralized the common- wealth, or perhaps the scene of dissipation going on out-of- doors, the races and holiday-makers, and bustle of the town, may have had a disturbing influence. The stage-manager lost his temper, and said business was business, and he didn't want the burlesque to be a "munge"—a word borrowed from some unknown tongue, which evidently made an impression upon the actors.

Justine had been in the theater for a little more than a hour, when Mr. Elgood burst suddenly into the green-room, pale as a sheet of letter-paper, and wearing his hat anyhow.

"Has anybody heard of it?" he asked, looking round at the assembly. Mrs. Dempson was sitting in a corner covering a satin shoe. Justina stood by the window studying her part in the burlesque. Mr. Dempson, with three or four kindred spirits, was smoking on some stone steps just outside the green-room. Everybody looked round at this sudden appeal, wondering at the actor's scared expression of countenance.

"Why, what's up, mate?" asked Mr. Dempson. "Is the ca- thedral on fire? Bear up under the affliction; I dare say it is in- sured."

"Nobody has heard, then?"

"Heard what?"

"Of the murder."

"What murder? Who's murdered?" cried every one at once, except Justina. Her thoughts were slower than the rest, per- haps. She stood looking at her father, fixed as marble.

"That poor young fellow, that good-hearted young fellow, who stood treat yesterday. Did you ever know such a black- guard thing, Demps? Shot from behind a hedge on the road

between Lowgate and the Waterfowl. Only found this morning between five and six by some laborers going to their work.
Dead and cold; shot through the heart. He's lying at the Lowgate Arms, just inside the archway, and;there's to be a coroner's
inquest at two o'clock this afternoon."

"How awful!" cried Dempson. "What was the motive?
Robbery, I suppose."

"So it was thought at first, for his pockets were empty,
turned inside out. But the police searched the ditch for the
weapon, which they didn't find, but found his watch and purse
and pocket-book, half an hour ago, buried in the mud, as if
they'd been rammed down with a stick. So there must have
been revenge at the bottom of the business, unless it was that
the fellow who did it—I dare say there was more than one
—took the alarm, and hid the plunder, with the intention of
fishing it up again on the quiet afterward."

"It looks more like that," said Mr. Dempson, "The hay-
makers are beginning to be about—a bad lot. Any scoundrel
can use a scythe. Don't cry, old woman"—this to his wife,
who was sobbing hysterically over the satin shoe. "He was a
nice young fellow, and we're all very sorry for him; but crying
won't bring him back."   •

"Such a happy day as we had with him!" sobbed the leading
lady. "I never enjoyed myself so much, and to think that he
should be m—m—murdered! It's too dreadful."

Nobody noticed Justina, till the thin straight figure suddenly
swayed, like a slender young poplar in a high wind, when
Mathew Elgood darted forward and caught her in his arms
just as she was falling. Her face lay on his shoulder, white
and set.

"I'm blessed if she hasn't fainted!" cried her father. "Poor
Judy! I forgot he was rather sweet upon her."

"You didn't ought to have blurted it out like that," exclaimed
Mrs. Dempson, more sympathetical than grammatical. "Run
and get a glass of water, Dempson. Don't you fuss with her"—
to the father. "I'll bring her to, and take her home, and get her
to lie down a bit. She sha'n't go on with the rehearsal, whatever
Pyecroft says." Pyecroft was the stage-manager. "She'll be all
right at night."

Justina, after having water splashed over her poor pale face,
recovered consciousness, stared with a blank, awful look at her
father and the rest, and then went home to her lodgings meekly,
leaning on Mrs. Dempson's arm. A bleak awakening from her
dream!

Yes, it was all true. The gay, light-hearted lad, the prosperous lord of Penwyn Manor, had been taken away from the
fair, fresh world, from the life which for his unsated spirit
meant happiness. Slain by a secret assassin's hand, he lay in
the darkened club-room of the Lowgate Arms awaiting the inquest.

The Eborsham police were at work, but not alone. The case
was felt to be an important one. A gentleman of property was
not to be murdered with impunity. Had the victim been some

agricultural laborer slain in a drunken fray, some turnpike man
murdered for plunder, the Eborsham constabulary would have
felt itself able to cope with the difficulties of the case. But this
was a darker business, a crime which was likely to be heard of
throughout the length and breadth of the land, and the Eborsham constable felt that the eyes of Europe were upon him. He
knew that his own men were slow and blundering, and. doubtful of their power to get at the bottom of the mystery, telegraphed to Spinnersbury for a couple of skilled detectives, who
came swift as an express train could carry them.

"Business is business!" said the Eborsham constable. "Whatever reward may be offered by and by—there's a hundred already
by our own magistrates—we work together, as between man and
man, and share it honorably."

"That's understood," replied the gentlemen from Spinnersbury, the chief center of that northern district. And affairs
being thus established on an agreeable footing, the skilled
detectives went to work.

The watch and purse had been found by the local police before the arrival of these Spinnersbury men. The purse was
empty, so it still remained an open question whether plunder
had not been the motive. The man who took the money might
have been afraid to take the watch, as a compromising bit of
property likely to bring him into trouble. Dorkis, one of the
Spinnersbury men, went straight to the Waterfowl to hunt up
the surroundings of the dead man. Pawfoot, his companion,
remained in Eborsham, where he made a round of the low-class
public-houses, with a view to discovering what doubtful characters had been hanging about the town during the last day or
two. A race meeting is an occasion when doubtful characters
are apt to be abundant: yet it seemed a curious thing that Mr.
Penwyn, whom nobody supposed to be a winner of money,
should have been waylaid on his return from the town, rather
than one of those numerous gentlemen who had gone home from
the rooms that night with full pockets and wine-bemused
heads.

Mr. Dorkis found the Waterfowl people as communicative as
he could desire. They had done nothing but talk about the
murder all the morning with a ghoulish gusto, and could talk
of nothing else. From them Mr. Dorkis heard a good deal that
set his sapient mind working in what he considered a happy
direction.

"Pawfoot may do all he can in the town," he thought; "I'm
not sorry I came here."

The landlady. who was dolefully loquacious, took Mr. Dorkis
aside, having ascertained that he was a detective from Spinnersbury, and informed him that there were circumstances about
the case she didn't like; not that she wished to throw out anything against anybody, and it would weigh heavy on her mind
if she suspected them that were innocent; still thought was free,
and she had her thoughts.

Pressed home by the detective, she went a little further, and
said she didn't like the look of things about Mr. Clissold.

"Who is Mr. Clissold?" asked Dorkis.

"Mr. Penwyn's friend. They came here together three days ago, and seemed as comfortable as possible together, like brothers, and they went out fishing together the day before yesterday, and then in the evening they brought home some of the play-actors to supper—the best of everything—and going up to bed they had high words. Me and my good man heard them, for the loud talking wakened us, and it was all along of some girl. And they were both very much excited, and Mr. Penwyn banged his door that violent as to shake the house, being an old house, as you may see."

"A girl!" said Mr. Dorkis; "that sometimes means mischief. But there's not much in a few high words between two young gentlemen after supper, even if it's about a girl. They were all right and friendly again next morning, I suppose?"

"I dare say they would have been," replied the hostess, "only Mr. Clissold went out early next morning with his fishing-rod, leaving a bit of a note for Mr. Penwyn, and didn't come back till twelve o'clock to-day."

"Curious!" said Mr. Dorkis.

"That's what struck me. Mr. Penwyn expected him back yesterday evening, and left word to say where he'd gone, if his friend came in. Of course Mr. Clissold was awfully shocked when he came in to-day and heard of the murder. I don't think I ever saw a man turn so white. But it did strike me as strange that he should be out all night just that very night."

"Did he tell you where he had been?"

"No. He went out of the house again directly with the police. He was going to telegraph to Mr. Penwyn's lawyer and some of his relations, I think."

"Ready to make himself useful," muttered Mr. Dorkis. "I should like to have a look round these gentlemen's rooms."

Being duly armed with authority, this privilege was allowed Mr. Dorkis. He examined bed-chambers and sitting-room, looked at the few and simple belongings of the travelers, who were naturally not encumbered with much luggage. Finding little to employ him here, Mr. Dorkis took a snack of lunch in the public parlor, heard the gossip of the loungers at the bar through the half-open door, meditated, smoked a pipe, and went out into the high-road.

He met Pawfoot, who seemed dispirited.

"Nothing turned up?" asked Dorkis.

"Less than half nothing. How's yourself?"

"Well, I think I'm in the right lay, but it's rather dark at present."

They went back to the inn together, conferring in half whispers. A quarter of an hour later Humphrey Clissold returned from his mission. He looked pale and wearied, and hardly saw the two men whom he passed in the porch. He had scarcely entered the house when these two men came close up to him, one on each side.

"I arrest you on suspicion of being concerned in the murder of James Penwyn," said Dorkis.

" And bear in mind that anything you say now will be used against you by and by," remarked Pawfoot.

CHAPTER X.

"NOTHING COMES AMISS, SO MONEY COMES WITHAL."

THE inquest was held at two o'clock, and adjourned. Few facts were elicited beyond those which had been in everybody's mouth that morning, when Matbew Elgood heard of the murder at the bar of that tavern where he took his noontide dram— the three-pennorth of gin and bitters which revivified him after last night's orgies.

James Penwyn had been shot through the heart by a hidden assassin. It seemed tolerably clear that the murderer had taken aim from behind the ragged hedge which divided the low-lying land by the river from the road just at this point. There were footprints on the marshy turf—not the prints of a clod-hopper's bulky boots. The line of footsteps indicated that the murderer had entered the field by a gate a hundred yards nearer the city, and had afterward gone across the grass to the tow-path. Here, on harder ground, the footsteps ceased altogether. They were the impressions of a gentleman's sole; or so thought the detectives, who were anxious to find a correspondence between these footprints and the boots of Humphrey Clissold. Here, however, they were somewhat at fault. Humphrey's stout shooting-boot made a wider and longer print on the sward.

" He may have worn a smaller boot last night," said Pawfoot. " But they say up at the inn that he has only two pairs, one off, one on, both the same make. I looked at those he's wearing, and they are just as big as these."

This was a slight check to the chain, which had run out pretty freely till now. True that there seemed little or no motive for the crime, but the one fact of the quarrel was something to go upon, and the curious absence of Humphrey Clissold on that particular night was a circumstance that would have to be accounted for.

Who could tell how serious that quarrel might have been?— perhaps the last outbreak of a long-smoldering flame; perhaps a dispute involving deepest interests. Further evidence would come out by degrees. At any rate, they had got their man.

Humphrey was present at the inquest, very calm and quiet, and made no statement whatever, by the advice of the local solicitor, Mr. Brent, whose aid he had not rejected. He would have been more agitated, perhaps, by the fact of his friend's untimely death, but for this monstrous accusation. That made him iron.

The inquest was adjourned, the facts being so few; and Mr. Clissold was taken to Eborsham Castle—a mediæval fortress, which our modern civilization had converted into the county jail.

Here he was comfortable enough, so far as surroundings went, for he was a young man of adventurous mind, and tastes so simple that a hard bed and a carpetless room were no afflictions to him.

Mr. Brent, the solicitor, visited him in his confinement, and discussed the facts of the case.

"It's hard upon you both ways," said the lawyer; "hard to lose your friend, and still harder to find yourself exposed to this monstrous suspicion."

" I don't care two straws for the suspicion," answered Humphrey, "but I do care very much for the loss of my friend. He was one of the best fellows that ever lived—so bright, so brimming over with freshness and vitality! If I had not seen him lying in that tavern, stark and cold, I couldn't bring myself to believe in his death. It's hard to believe in it even with the memory of that poor murdered clay fresh in my mind. Poor James! I loved him like a younger brother."

" You have no knowledge of any circumstance in his life that can help us to find the murderer?" asked Mr. Brent.

" I know of nothing. He had picked up some people I didn't care about his being intimate with—strolling players, who are acting at the theater in this place. But my worst fear was that he might be trapped into some promise of marriage. I can hardly fancy these people concerned in a crime."

" No. They are for the most part harmless vagabonds," replied the lawyer. " Do you know where Mr. Penwyn spent last night?"

" With these people, no doubt—a man called Elgood and his daughter. The man ought to be called as a witness, I should think."

" Unquestionably. We'll have him before the coroner next Saturday, and we'll keep an eye upon him meanwhile."

The inquest had been adjourned for three days, to give time for new facts to be elicited.

" Your friend had no enemies, you say?"

" Not one," answered Clissold. " He was one of those men who never make an enemy. He hadn't the strength of mind to refuse a favor to the veriest blackguard. It was my knowledge of his character that made me anxious about this Elgood acquaintance. I saw that he was fascinated with the girl, and feared he might be lured into some false position. That was the sole cause of our dispute the other night."

" Why did you leave him?"

" Because I saw that my interference irritated him, and was likely to arouse a lurking obstinacy which I knew to be in his nature. He was such a spoiled child of fortune that I fancied if I left him alone to take his own way his passion would cool. Opposition fired him."

" There is only one awkward circumstance in the whole case —as regards yourself, I mean."

" What is that?" asked Clissold.

" Your objection to state where you spent last night."

" I should be sorry if I were driven to so poor a defense as an *alibi*."

"I don't think there's any fear of that. The evidence against you amounts to so little. But why not simplify matters by accounting for your time up to your return to-day? You only came back to Eborsham by the twelve o'clock train from Spinnersbury, you say."

" I came by that train."

" Do you think any of the porters or ticket collectors would remember seeing you ?"

" Not likely. The train was crowded with people coming to the races. It was as much as I could do to get a seat. I had to scramble into a third-class compartment as the train began to move."

" But why not refer to some one at Skinnersbury to prove your absence from Eborsham last night ?"

" When my neck is in danger I may do that. In the meantime you may as well let the matter drop. I have my own reasons for not saying where I was last night, unless I am very hard pushed."

Mr. Brent was obliged to be satisfied. The case against his client was one of the weakest in the world as yet: but it was curious that this young man should so resolutely refuse to give a straightforward account of himself. Mr. Brent had felt positive of his client's innocence up to this point; but this refusal disturbed him. He went home with an uncomfortable feeling that there was something wrong somewhere.

Messrs. Pawfoot and Dorkis were not idle during the interval. Dorkis lodged at the Waterfowl, and heard all the gossip of the house, where the one absorbing topic was the murder of James Penwyn.

Among other details the Spinnersbury detective heard Mrs. Marport, the landlady, speak of a certain letter which the morning's post brought Mr. Clissold the day he went away. It came by the first delivery, which was before eight o'clock. Jane, the house-maid, took it up to Mr. Clissold's room with his boots and shaving water.

"I never set eyes upon such a letter," said Mrs. Marport. "It seemed to have been all round the world for sport, as the saying is. It had been to some address in London, and to Wales, and to Cumberland, and was all over post-marks. I suppose it must have been something rather particular, to have been sent after him so."

" A bill, I dare say—or a lawyer's letter perhaps."

"Oh, no, it wasn't. It was a lady's handwriting. I took particular notice of that."

" Any cress or mornagarm ?" asked Dorkis.

" No, there was nothing on the envelope; but the paper was as thick as parchment. Whoever wrote that letter was quite the lady."

" Ah," said Dorkis, " Mr. Clissold's sweetheart, very likely."

"That's what I've been thinking, and that it was that letter, perhaps, that took him off so sudden, and that he really may have been far away from Eborsham on the night of the murder."

" If he was, he'll be able to prove it," replied Mr. Dorkis, who was not inclined to entertain the idea of Humphrey Clissold's innocence. To earn his share of the reward he must find the murderer, and it mattered very little to Mr. Dorkis where he found him.

CHAPTER XI.

" WHAT, THEN, YOU KNEW NOT THIS RED WORK INDEED ?"

IN the afternoon of the day succeeding the inquest, two persons of some importance to the case arrived at Eborsham. They came by the same train. and had traveled together from London. One was Churchill Penwyn, the inheritor of the Penwyn estate; the other was Mr. Pergament. the family solicitor, chief partner in the firm of Pergament & Pergament, New Square, Lincoln's Inn.

Churchill Penwyn and the solicitor met at King's Cross station five minutes before the starting of the five o'clock express for Eborsham. They were very well acquainted with each other; Churchill's meager portion, inherited under the will of old Mrs. Penwyn, his grandmother, who had been an heiress in a small way, having passed through Mr. Pergament's hands. Nicholas Penwyn's will, which disposed of Penwyn Manor for two generations. had been drawn up by Mr. Pergament's father, and all business connected with the Penwyn estate had been transacted in Mr. Pergament's office for the last hundred years. Pergaments had been born and died during the century. but the office was the same as in the time of Penruddock Penwyn, who, inheriting a farm of a hundred and fifty acres or so, had made a fortune in the East Indies, and extended the estate by various important additions to its present dimensions. For before the days of Penruddock the race of Penwyn had declined in splendor, though it was always known and acknowledged that the Penwyns were one of the oldest families in Cornwall.

Of course Mr. Pergament, knowing Nicholas Penwyn's will by heart, was perfectly aware of the alteration which this awful event of the murder made in Churchill's circumstances. Churchill had been a cadet of the house heretofore. though his Cousin James' senior by nearly ten years—a person of no importance whatever. Mr. Pergament had treated him with a free and easy friendliness—was always ready to do him a good turn—sent him a brief now and then, and so on. To-day Mr. Pergament was deferential. The old friendliness was toned down to a subdued respect. It seemed as if Mr. Pergament's eye. respectfully raised to Churchill's broad pale brow, in imagination beheld above it the round and top of sovereignty, the lordship of Penwyn Manor.

" Very distressing event," murmured the lawyer as they seated themselves opposite each other in the first-class carriage. This was a comfortable train to travel by, not arriving at Eborsham till three. The race traffic had been cleared off by a special at an earlier hour.

" Very," returned Churchill, gravely. " Of course I cannot be expected to be acutely grieved by an event which raises me from a workingman's career to affluence, especially as I knew so little

of my cousin; but I was profoundly shocked at the circumstances of his death. A commonplace, vulgar murder for gain,
I apprehend, committed by some rustic ruffian. I doubt if
that class of man thinks much more of murder than of sparrow
shooting."

"I hope they'll get him, whoever he is," said the lawyer.

"If the acuteness of the police can be stimulated by the hope
of reward, that motive shall not be wanting, returned Churchill.
"I shall offer a couple of hundred pounds for the conviction of
the murderer."

"Very proper," murmured Mr. Pergament, approvingly.
"No, you had seen very little of poor James, I apprehend," he
went on in a conversational tone.

"I doubt if he and I met half a dozen times. I saw him once
at Eton soon after my father's death, when I was spending a
day or two at a shooting-box near Bracknell, and walked over
to have a look at the college. He was a little curly-headed chap
playing cricket, and I remember tipping him, ill as I could
afford the half sovereign. One can't see a school-boy without
tipping him. I dare say the young rascal ran off and spent my
hard-earned shillings on strawberry ices and pound-cake as soon
as my back was turned. I saw him a few years afterward in
his mother's house, somewhere near Baker Street. She asked
me to a dinner-party, and, as she made rather a point of it, I
went. A slowish business, as women's dinners generally are—
all the delicacies that were just going out of season, and some
elderly ladies to adorn the board. I asked James to breakfast
at my club—put him up for the Garrick—and I think that's
about the last time I ever saw him.

"Poor lad!" sighed the family solicitor. "Such a promising
young fellow! But I doubt if he would have kept the property
together. There was very little of his grandfather, old Squire
Penwyn, about him. A wonderful man that, vigorous in body
and mind to the last year of his life. I spent a week at Penwyn
about seventeen years ago, just before your poor uncle was
killed by those abominable niggers in Cabool. I can see the
squire before me now, a hale old country gentleman, always
dressed in green coat with basket buttons, Bedford cords, and
vinegar tops—hunted three times a week every season after he
was seventy years of age—the Assheton Smith stamp of a man.
The rising generation will never ripen into that kind of thing,
Mr. Penwyn. The stuff isn't in 'em."

"I never saw much of my grandfather," said Churchill, in his
grave, quiet voice, which expressed so little emotion save when
deepest passion warmed his spirit to eloquence. "My father's
marriage offended him, as, I dare say, you heard at the time."

Mr. Pergament nodded assent.

"Prejudice, prejudice," he murmured, blandly. "Elderly
gentlemen who live on their estates are prone to that sort of
thing."

"He did my mother the honor to call her a shop-keeper's
daughter—her father was a brewer at Exeter, in a very fair way
of business—upon which my father, who had some self-respect,

and a great deal of respect for his wife, told the squire that he should take care not to intrude the shop-keeper's daughter upon his notice. 'If I hadn't made my will,' said my grandfather, 'it might be the worse for you. But I have made my will, as you all know. I made it six years ago, and I don't mean to budge from it. When I do a thing it's done. When I say a thing it's said. I never undo or unsay. The estate will be kept together for the next half century, I think, come what may.' "

"Just like him," said Mr. Pergament, chuckling. "The man to the life. How well you hit him off!"

"I've heard my father repeat that speech a good many times," answered Churchill.

"Then you never saw the old squire?"

"Only once. I was a day boy at Westminster, and one afternoon, when I was playing ball in the Quadrangle, a curious-looking elderly gentleman, with a drab overcoat and a broad-brimmed white hat, breeches. and top-boots, a bunch of seals at his fob, and a gold-headed riding-whip in his hand. came into the court and looked about him. He looked like a figure out of a sporting print. Yet he looked a gentleman all the same. 'Can anybody tell me where to find a boy called Penwyn?' he inquired. I ran forward. 'What, you're Churchill Penwyn, are you. youngster?' he asked, with his hands upon my shoulders, looking at me straight from under his bushy gray eyebrows. 'Yes, you're a genuine Penwyn; none of the brewer here. It's a pity your father was a younger son. You wouldn't have made a bad squire. I dare say you have heard of your grandfather?'

"'Yes. sir, very often,' I said. 'Are you he?'

"'I am. I'm up in London for a week, and I took it into my head I should like to have a look at you. It isn't likely the estate will ever come to you, but if by any chance it should come your way, I hope you'll think of the old squire sometimes when he lies under the sod, and try and keep things together in my way.' He tipped me a five pound note, shook hands, and walked out of the Quad; and that's the only time I ever saw Nicholas Penwyn."

"Curious," said Mr. Pergament.

"By the way, talking of estates, what is Penwyn worth? My inheritance seemed so remote a contingency that I have never taken the trouble to ask the question."

"The estate is a fine one," replied the lawyer, joining the tips of his fat fingers, and speaking with unction, as of a favorite and familiar subject; "but land in Cornwall, as you are doubtless aware, is not the most remunerative investment. The farm lands of Penwyn produce, on an average. a bare three per cent. on their value, that is to say about three pounds an acre. There are eleven hundred acres of farm land, and thus we have three thousand three hundred pounds. But," continued the lawyer, swelling with importance, "the more remunerative portion of the estate consists of mines, which, after lying idle for more than a quarter of a century, were reopened at the latter end of the squire's life, and are now being worked by a company who

pay a royalty upon their profits, which royalty in the aggregate
amounts to something between two and four thousand a year,
and is likely to increase, as they have lately opened a tin mine,
and come upon a promising lode."

"My grandfather risked nothing in the working of these
mines, I suppose?"

"No!" exclaimed the lawyer, with tremendous emphasis.
"Squire Penwyn was much too wise for that. He let other
people take the risks and only stood in for the profits."

They talked about the estate for some little time after this,
and then Churchill threw himself back into his corner, opened
a newspaper, and appeared to read—appeared only, for his eyes
were fixed upon one particular bit of the column before him in
that steady gaze which betokens deepest thought. In sooth he
had enough to think of. The revolution which James Penwyn's
death had wrought in his fate was a change to set most men
thinking. From a struggling man just beginning to make a little way in an arduous profession, he found himself all at once
worth something like six thousand a year, master of an estate
which would bring with it the respect of his fellow-men, position
and power—the means of climbing higher than any Penwyn had
yet risen on the ladder of life.

"I shall not bury myself alive in a stupid old manor-house,"
he thought, "like my grandfather. And yet it will be rather a
pleasant thing playing at being a country squire."

Most of all he thought of her who was to share his fortunes—
the new bright life they could lead together—of her beauty,
which would be an influence to help his aggrandizement. He
fancied himself member for Penwyn, making his mark in the
House, as he had already begun to make it at the bar. Literature and statecraft should combine to help him on. He saw
himself far away, in the fair prosperous future, leader of his
party. He thought that when he first crossed the threshold of
the old senate-house as a member he should say to himself,
almost involuntarily:

"Some day I shall enter this door as prime minister."

He was not a man whose desires were bounded by the idea of
a handsome house and gardens, a good stable, wine-cellar, and
cook. He asked Fortune for something more than these. If
not for his own sake, for his betrothed, he would wish to be
something more than a prosperous country gentleman. Madge
would expect him to be famous. Madge would be disappointed
if he failed to make his mark in the world. He fell to calculating how long it would have been in the common course of
things, plodding on at literature and his profession, before he
could have won a position to justify his marrying Madge Bellingham. Far away to the extreme point in perspective stretched
the distance.

He gave a short, bitter sigh of very weariness. "It would
have been ten or fifteen years before I could have given her as
good a home as her father's," he said to himself. "Why fatigue
one's brain by such profitless speculations? She would never
have been my wife. She is a girl who must have made a great

marriage. She might be true as steel, but everybody else would have been against me. Her father and her sister would have worried her almost to death. and some morning, while I was marching bravely on toward the distant goal, I should have received a letter, tear-blotted, remorseful, telling me that she had yielded to the persuasions of her father. and had consented to marry the millionaire stockbroker, or the wealthy lordling, as the case might be."

"Who is this Mr. Clissold?" Churchill asked, by and by, throwing aside his unread paper, and emerging from that brown-study in which he had been absorbed for the last hour or so.

"A college friend of poor James', his senior by some few years. They had been reading together in the north. You must have met Clissold in Axminster Square, I should think, when you dined with your aunt. He and James were inseparable."

"I have some recollection of a tall, dark-browed youth, who seemed one of the family."

"That was young Clissold, no doubt."

"Civil of him to telegraph to me," said Churchill; and there the subject dropped. The two gentlemen yawned a little. Churchill looked out of the window and relapsed into thoughtfulness, and so the time went on, and the journey came to an end.

Churchill and the lawyer drove straight to the police station, to inquire if the murderer had been found. There they heard what had befallen Humphrey Clissold.

"Absurd!" exclaimed the solicitor. "No possible motive."

The official in charge shook his head sagely.

"There appears to have been a quarrel," he said, in his slow, ponderous way, "between the two young gents the night previous. High words was over'eard at the hinn. and on the night of the murder Mr. Cliss'll was absent, which he is unwilling to account for his time."

Mr. Pergament looked at Churchill as much as to say, "This is serious."

"Young men do not murder each other on account of a few high words," said Mr. Penwyn. "I daresay Mr. Clissold will give a satisfactory account of himself when the proper time comes. No one in his right senses could suspect a gentleman of such a crime—a common robbery, with violence, on the high-road. In the race week, too. when a place is always running over with ruffians of every kind."

"I beg your pardon. sir," said the superintendent, "but that's the curious part of the case. The footsteps of the murderer have been traced. Mr. Penwyn was shot at from behind a hedge, you see, and the print of the sole looks like the print of a gentleman's boot. narrow, and a small heel; nothing of the clod-hopper about it. The ground's a bit of marshy clay just there, and the impression was uncommonly clear."

Churchill Penwyn looked at the man thoughtfully for a moment with that penetrating glance of his which was wont to survey an adverse witness in order to see what might be made of him—the glance of a man familiar with the study of his fellow-men.

"There are vagabonds enough in the world who wear decently made boots," he said, "especially your racing vagabonds."

He made all necessary inquiries about the inquest, and then adjourned to one of the chief hotels, all crowded with racing men, though not to suffocation, as at the summer meeting.

"You'll watch the case in the interests of the family, of course," he said to Mr. Pergament. "I should like you to do what you can for this Mr. Clissold too. There can be no ground for his arrest."

"I should suppose not, he and James were such friends."

"And then the empty purse shows that the murder was done for gain. My cousin may have won money, or have been supposed to have won, on the race-course, and may have been watched and followed by some prowling ruffian, tout, or tramp, or gypsy."

"It's odd that Mr. Clissold refused to account for his time last night."

"Yes, that is curious. But I feel pretty sure the explanation will come when he's pressed."

And then the gentlemen dined together comfortably.

A little later on Mr. Pergament got up to go out.

"There are the last melancholy details to be arranged," he said. "Have you any wish on that point, as his nearest relation?"

"Only that his own wishes should be respected"

"His father and mother are buried at Kensal Green. I dare say he would rather be there than at Penwyn."

"One would suppose so."

"Then I'll go and see about thé removal and so on," said Mr. Pergament, taking up his hat. "By the way, perhaps, before it's too late, you would like to see your cousin."

Churchill gave a little start, almost a shudder,

"No," he said, "I never went in for that kind of thing."

* * * * * * *

Justina lived through the day, and acted at night pretty much as she had been accustomed to act: but she saw her audience dimly through a heavy blinding cloud, and the glare of the footlights seemed to her hideous as the fires of pandemonium. People spoke to her in the dressing-room where she dragged on her shabby finery, and dabbed a little rouge on her pale wan face, and she answered them somehow, mechanically. She had lived that life and among the same people so long that the mere business of existence went on without any effort of her own. She felt like a clock that had been wound and must go its appointed time. She sat in a corner of the green-room, looking straight before her, and thought how her bright new world had melted away; and no one took any particular notice of her.

Mrs. Dempson had been kind and compassionate, and after Justina's fainting fit had dabbed her forehead with vinegar and water, and sat with her arm round the girl's waist, consoling her and reasoning with her, reminding her that they had only known poor Mr. Penwyn a day and a half, and that it was against nature to lament him as if he had been a near relation or an old friend. Who, in sober middle age, when the sordid cares of every-day life are paramount—who, when youth's morning is past, can comprehend the young heart's passionate mystery; the love which, like some bright tropical flower, buds and blooms in a single day; the love which is more than half fancy; the love of a lover of no common clay, but the fair incarnation of girlhood's poetic dream; love wherein the senses have no more part than the phosphor lights of a rank marsh in the clear splendor of the stars.

Justina kept the secret of her brief dream. She thought Mrs. Dempson and even her father would have laughed her to scorn had she told them that the generous young stranger had asked her to be his wife. She held her peace, and shut herself in her garret chamber, and flung her weary head face downward on the flock pillow, and thought of her murdered lover—thought of the bright, handsome face fixed in death's marble stillness, and cursed the wretch who had slain him.

Mr. Elwood and his daughter were both subpœnaed for the adjourned inquest. The actor, who rather rejoiced in the opportunity of exhibiting his powers in a new arena, and seeing his name in the papers, appeared in grand form on the morning of the examination. He had brushed his coat, sported a clean white waistcoat and a smart blue neck-tie, wore a pair of somewhat ancient buff leather gloves, and carried a cane which he was wont to flourish as the exasperated father of old-fashioned comedy.

Justina entered the room pale as a sheet, and sat by her father's side, with her large dark eyes fixed on the coroner, as if from his lips could issue the secret of her lover's doom. She had the most imperfect idea of the nature of an inquest and the coroner's power.

The jury were seated round the coroner at the upper end of the room; Mr. Pergament, the solicitor, stood at the end of the table, ready to put any questions he might desire to have answered by the witnesses.

On the right of the coroner, a little way from the jury, sat Humphrey Clissold, with a constable at his side. Nearly opposite him, and next to the lawyer, stood the new master of Penwyn Manor, ready to prompt a question if he saw the lawyer at fault. Churchill and Mr. Pergament had gone into the case thoroughly together, with the Spinnersbury detectives and the local constabulary, and had their facts pretty well in hand.

The jury answered to their names, and the inquiry began—Mr. Pergament interrogating, the coroner taking notes of the evidence. Mr. Elgood was one of the first witnesses sworn.

"I believe you were in the company of the deceased on the night, or rather morning, of the murder?" said the coroner.

"Yes, he supped at my lodging on that night."

"Alone with you?"

"No. Mr. Dempson and his wife, and my daughter, were of the party.

"At what hour did Mr. Penwyn leave you?"

The actor's countenance assumed a look of perplexity.

"It was half-past twelve before we sat down to supper," he said, "but I can't exactly say how long we sat afterward. We smoked a few cigars, and, to be candid, were somewhat convivial. I haven't any clear idea as to the time; my daughter may know."

"Why your daughter, and not you?"

"She let him out through the shop when he went away. Our apartments are respectable but humble, over a chandler's."

"And your daughter was more temperate than you, and may have some idea as to the time? We'll ask her the question presently. Do you know if Mr. Penwyn had any considerable sum of money about him at the time he left you?"

"I don't know. He had entertained us handsomely at the Waterfowl on the previous night, and he stood a carriage and any quantity of champagne to the races that day, but I did not see him pay away any money."

"Did you see him receive any money on the race-course?"

"No."

"Was he with you all day?"

"From twelve o'clock till half-past six in the evening."

"And in that time you had no knowledge of his winning or receiving any sum of money?"

"No."

"Do you know of his being associated with disreputable people of any kind—betting men, for instance?"

"I know next to nothing of his associations. There was an old gypsy woman who pretended to tell his fortune by the riverside the day before the races, when he and the rest of us happened to be walking together. He gave her money then, and he gave her money on the race-day, when she was hanging about the carriage, begging for drink."

Churchill Penwyn, who had been looking at the ground in a listening attitude hitherto, raised his eyes at this juncture, half in interrogation, half in surprise.

"Is that all you know about the deceased?" continued Mr. Pergament.

"About all. I had only enjoyed his acquaintance six-and-thirty hours at the time of the murder."

"You can sit down," said Mr. Pergament.

"Justina Elgood," cried the summoning officer; and Justina stood up in the crowded room, pale to the lips, but unfaltering.

Again Churchill Penwyn raised those thoughtful eyes of his, and looked at the girl's pallid face.

"Not a common type of girl," he said to himself.

CHAPTER XII.
" BRAVE SPIRITS ARE A BALSAM TO THEMSELVES."

HUMPHREY CLISSOLD also looked at the girl as she stood up at the end of the table in the little bit of clear space left for the witnesses. A shaft of sunshine slanted from the sky-light. The room was built out from the house, and lighted from the top—an apartment usually devoted to Masonic meetings and public dinners. In that clear radiance the girl's face was wondrously spiritualized. Easy to fancy that some being not quite of this common earth stood there, and that from those pale lips the awful truth would speak as if by the voice of revelation.

So Humphrey Clissold thought as he looked at her. Never till this moment had she appeared to him beautiful, and now it was no common beauty which he beheld in her, but a strange and spiritual charm impossible of definition.

" You were the last person who saw Mr. Penwyn alive, except his murderer ?" said Mr. Pergament, interrogatively, after the usual formula had been gone through.

" I opened the shop door for him when he went out after supper."

" At what o'clock ?"

" Half-past two."

" Was he perfectly sober at that time ?"

" Oh, yes," with an indignant look.

" Was he going back to the Waterfowl alone ?"

" Quite alone."

" Did he say anything particular to you just at last? Anything that it might be important for us to know ?"

A faint color flushed the pale face at the question.

" Nothing."

" Is that all you can tell us ?"

" There is only one thing more," the girl answered, calmly. " I stood at the door a few minutes to watch Mr. Penwyn walking up the street, and just as he turned the corner a man passed on the opposite side of the way in the same direction."

" Toward Lowgate ?"

" Yes."

" What kind of a man ?"

" He was rather tall, and wore an overcoat, and a thick scarf round his neck, as if it had been winter."

" Did you see his face ?"

" No."

" Or notice anything else about him —anything besides the overcoat and the muffler ?"

" Nothing."

" You say he was tall. Was he as tall as that gentleman, do you suppose? Stand up, for a moment, if you please, Mr. Clissold."

Clissold stood up. He was above the average height of tall men, well over six feet.

" No, he was not as tall as that."

" Are you sure of that? A man would look taller in this room than in the street. Do you allow for that difference?" inquired Mr. Pergament.

" I do not believe that the man I saw that night was as tall as Mr. Clissold, nor as broad across the shoulders."

"That will do."

The chief constable next gave evidence as to the finding of the body, the watch buried in the ditch, the empty purse. Then came the landlady of the Waterfowl, with an account of the high words between the two gentlemen, and Mr. Clissold's abrupt departure on the following morning. The Spinnersbury detectives followed, and described Mr. Clissold's arrest, the tracing of footsteps behind the hedge and down to the tow-path, and how they had compared Mr. Clissold's boot with the foot-prints without being able to arrive at any positive conclusion.

" It might very easily be the print of the same foot in a different boot," said Dorkis. " It isn't so much the difference between the size of the feet as the shape and cut of the boot. The man must have been tall, the length of his stride shows that."

There was no further evidence. The coroner addressed the jury.

After a few minutes' consultation they returned their verdict. " That the deceased had been murdered by some person or persons unknown."

Thus Humphrey Clissold found himself a free man again, but with the uncomfortable feeling of having been for a few days supposed the murderer of his bosom friend. It seemed to him that a stigma would attach to his name henceforward. He would be spoken of as the man who had been suspected, and who was in all probability guilty, but who had been let slip because the chain of evidence was not quite strong enough to hang him.

" I suppose if I had been tried in Scotland the verdict would have been 'non-proven,'" he thought.

Only one means of self-justification remained open to him, viz., to find the real murderer. He fancied that Dorkis and Pawfoot looked at him with unfriendly eyes. They were aggravated by the loss of the reward. They would turn their attention in a new direction, no doubt, but considerable time had been lost while they were on a wrong scent.

Humphrey Clissold could not quite make up his mind about those Bohemians of the Eborsham Theater—whether this vagabond heavy father might not know something more than he cared to reveal about James Penwyn's fate. He had given his evidence with a sufficiently straightforward air, and the girl was above doubt. Truth was stamped on the pale, sorrowful face—truth and a silent grief. Could that grief have its root in some fatal secret? Did she know her father guilty of this crime, and shield him with heroic falsehoods only less sublime than truth?

She stood by her father's side a little way apart from the crowd, as she had stood throughout the inquiry, intently watchful.

While Humphrey lingered, debating whether he should follow up the strolling players, Churchill Penwyn came straight across the room toward him before the undispersed assembly.

"I congratulate you on your release, Mr. Clissold," he said, offering his hand with a friendly air; "and permit me to assure you that I, for one, have been fully assured of your innocence throughout this melancholy business."

"I thank you for doing me justice, Mr. Penwyn. I was very fond of your cousin. I liked him as well as if he had been my brother, and if the question had been put to me whether harm should come to him or me, I believe I should have chosen the evil lot for myself. His mother was a second mother to me. God bless her. She asked me to take care of him a few hours before her death, and I felt from that time as if I were responsible for his future. He was little more than a boy when his poor mother died. He was little more than a boy the last time I saw him alive, the night we had our first quarrel."

"What was the quarrel about?"

Mr. Clissold shrugged his shoulders, and glanced round the room, which was clearing by degrees, but not yet empty.

"It's too long a story to enter upon here," he said.

"Come and dine with me at the castle, at eight o'clock, and tell me all about it," said Churchill.

"You're very good. No. I can't manage that. I have something to do."

"What is that?"

"To begin a business that may take a long time to finish."

"May I ask the nature of that business?"

"I want to find James Penwyn's murderer."

Churchill shrugged his shoulders and smiled—the half-compassionate smile which he might have bestowed on Don Quixote when that erratic hidalgo was setting out on his travels, had he been an acquaintance of the knight's, privy to his heroic purpose.

"My dear sir," he said, "do you think that the murderer is ever found in such a case as this?—given a delay of three days and nights—ample time for him to ship himself for any port in the known world. A low, clod-hopping assassin, no doubt, in no way distinguishable from other clod-hoppers. Find him! did you say? I can conceive no endeavor more hopeless. It is the fashion to rail at our police because they find it a little difficult to put their hands upon every delinquent who may be wanted, but it is hardly the simplest business in the world to pick the right man out of ten or fifteen millions."

Humphrey Clissold heard him with a troubled look, and short impatient sigh.

"I dare say you are right," he said. "But I shall do my best to unravel the mystery, even if I am doomed to fail."

He asked some questions about his friend's funeral. It was to be at three o'clock on the following day, and Churchill was going back to London by an early train in order to attend as chief mourner.

" I shall be there," said Humphrey Clissold, and they parted with a friendly hand-shake.

Clissold wa   touched by Mr. Penwyn's friendliness. That stigma of *non-proven* had not affected Churchill's opiuion at any rate.

He followed Mathew Elgood and his daughter into the street, and joined them as they walked slowly homeward, the girl's face half-hidden by her veil.

" I want to have a talk with you, Mr. Elgood, if you've no objection," said Humphrey—" unless you consider me tainted by the suspicion that has hung over me for the last three days, and object to hold any intercourse with me."

" No, sir, I suspect no man," answered the actor with dignity. " Although you were pleased to object to your lamented friend's inclination for my society, I bear no malice, and I do you the justice to believe you had no part in his untimely end."

" I thank you, Mr. Elgood, for your confidence. Since I have been in that abominable jail, I feel as if there were some odor of felony hanging about me. With regard to the objections of which you speak, I can assure you that they were founded upon no personal dislike, but upon prudential reasons, which I need not enlarge upon."

" Enough, Mr. Clissold; it boots not now. If you will follow to our humble abode, and share the meal our modest means provide, I will enlighten you upon this theme, so far as my scant knowledge serve withal," said the actor, unconsciously lapsing into blank verse.

Humphrey accepted the invitation. He had a curious desire to see more of that girl whose pale face had assumed a kind of sublimity just now in the crowded court. Could she really have cared for his murdered friend ? She, who had but known him two days? Or was there some dark secret which moved her thus deeply ? The man seemed frank and open enough. Hard to believe that villainy lurked beneath the Bohemian's rough kindliness.

They went straight to the lodging in the narrow street leading down to the river. Here all seemed comfortable enough. The evening meal, half tea, half dinner, was ready laid when Mr. Elgood and his visitor went in, and Mr. and Mrs. Dempson were waiting with some impatience for their refreshment. They looked somewhat surprised at the appearance of Clissold, and Mrs. Dempson returned his greeting with a certain stiffness. " It isn't the pleasantest thing in the world to sit down to the table with a suspected murderer," she remarked afterward; to which Justina replied, with a sudden flash of anger, " Do you suppose I would sit in the same room with him if I thought him guilty ?"

The low comedian took things more easily than his wife.

" Well, Mat," he said, " I thought you were never coming. I've been down at the Arms, and heard the inquest. Glad to see you at liberty again, Mr. Clissold. A most preposterous business, your arrest. I heard all the evidence. I think those Spinnersbury detectives ought to get it hot. I dare say the press will slang 'em pretty tolerably. Well done, Judy,'' he went on, with a friendly slap on Justina's shoulders; " you spoke up like a good one. If you spoke as well as that on the stage, you'd soon be fit for the juvenile lead."

Justina spoke no word, but took her place quietly at the table, where Mrs. Dempson was pouring out the tea, while Mr. Elgood dispensed a juicy rump-steak.

" I went to the butcher's for it myself," he said. " There's nothing like personal influence in these things. They wouldn't dare give me a slice off some superannuated cow. They know when they've got to deal with a judge. ' That's beef,' said the butcher, as he slapped his knife across the loin; and beef it is. Do you like it with the gravy in it, Mr. Clissold ?"

There was a dish of steaming potatoes, and a bowl of lettuces, which green stuff Mrs. Dempson champed as industriously as if she had been a blood-relation of Nebuchadnezzar's.

Never had Humphrey Clissold seen any one so silent and so self-sustained as this pale, thin, shadowy-looking girl, whom her friends called Judy. She interested him strangely, and he did sorry justice to Mr. Elgood's ideal steak while watching her. She herself hardly ate anything; but the others were too deeply absorbed in their own meal to be concerned about her. She sat by her father, and drank a little tea—sat motionless, for the most part, with her dark, thoughtful eyes looking far away, looking into some world that was not for the rest.

So soon as the pangs of hunger were appeased, and the pleasures of the table in some measure exhausted, Mr. Elgood became loquacious again. He gave a detailed description of that last day on the race-course—the supper—all that James Penwyn had said or done within his knowledge. And then came a discussion as to who could have done the deed.

"He was in the theater all the evening, you say," said Humphrey. " Is it possible that any of the scene-shifters, or workmen of any kind, may have observed him—seen him open a well-filled purse, perhaps—and followed him after he left this house? It was one of his foolish habits to carry too much money about him—from twenty to fifty pounds, for instance. He used to say it was a bore to sit down and write a check for every trifle he wanted. And of course, in our travels, ready money was a necessity. Could it have been one of your people, do you think ?"

" No, sir," replied Mr. Elgood. " The stage has contributed nothing to the records of crime. From the highest genius who has ever adorned the drama to the lowest functionary employed in the working of its machinery, there has been no such thing as a felon."

" I am glad to hear you say so, Mr. Elgood; yet it is clear to me that this crime must have been committed by some one who watched and followed my poor friend—some one who knew enough of him to know that he had money about him."

" I grant you, sir," replied the actor.

It was now time for these Thespians to repair to the theater— all but Justina, who, for a wonder, was not in the first piece.

Humphrey took notice of this fact, and after walking to the theater with Mr. Elgood, went back to that gentleman's lodgings to have a few words alone with his daughter.

He passed through the shop unchallenged, visitors for the lodgers being accustomed to pass in and out in a free and easy manner. He went quietly up-stairs. The sitting-room door stood ajar. He pushed it open and went in.

CHAPTER XIII.

"MY LOVE, MY LOVE, AND NO LOVE FOR ME."

JUSTINA was kneeling before an old easy-chair, her face buried in the faded chintz cushion, sobbing vehemently—curiously changed from the silent, impassible being Humphrey had taken leave of ten minutes earlier. The sight of her sorrow touched him. Whatever it meant, this was real grief, at any rate.

"Forgive me for this intrusion, Miss Elgood," he said, gently, remaining near the door lest he should startle her by his abrupt approach. "I am very anxious to talk to you alone, and ventured to return."

She started up, hastily wiping away her tears.

"I am sorry to see you in such deep grief," he said. "You must have a tender heart, to feel my poor friend's sad fate so acutely."

The pallid face crimsoned, as if this had been a reproof.

"I have no right to be so sorry, I dare say," faltered Justina; "but he was very kind to me—kinder than any one ever was before—and it is hard that he should be taken away so cruelly, just when life seemed to be all new and different because of his goodness."

"Poor child! You must have a grateful nature."

"I am grateful to *him*."

"I can understand that just at first you may feel his death as if it were a personal loss, but that cannot last long. You had known him so short a time. Granted that he admired you, and paid you pretty compliments and attentions which may be new to one so young, if he had lived to bid you good-bye to-morrow, and pass on his way, you would hardly have remembered him a week."

"I should have remembered him all my life," said Justina, firmly.

"He had made a deep impression upon your mind or your fancy, then, in those two days?"

"He loved me," the girl answered, with a little burst of passion, "and I gave him back love for love with all my heart, with all my strength, as they tell us we ought to love God. Why do you come here to torment me about him? You cannot bring him back to life. God will not. I would spend all my life upon my knees if he could be raised up again, like Lazarus! I meant never to have spoken of this. I have kept it even from my father. He told me that he loved me, and that I was to be his wife, and that all our lives to come were to be spent together. Think what it is to have been so happy, and to have lost all."

" Poor child!" repeated Humphrey Clissold, laying his hand gently, as priest or father might have laid it, on the soft brown hair. thrust back in a tangled mass from the hot brow. " Poor children—children both! It would have been a foolish marriage at best, my dear girl, if he had lived, and kept in the same mind, poor fellow! Unequal marriages bring remorse and misery for the most part. James Penwyn was not a hard-working wayfarer like me, who may choose my wife at any turn on the world's high road. He was the owner of a good old estate, and the happiness of his future depended on his making a suitable marriage. His wife must have been somebody before she was his wife. She must have had her own race to refer to, something to boast of on her own side, so that when their children grew up they should be able to give a satisfactory account of their maternal uncles and aunts. I dare say you think me worldly-minded, poor child; but I am only worldly-wise. If it were a question of personal merit, you might have made the best of wives."

The girl heard this long speech with an absent air, the tearful eyes fixed on vacancy, the restless hands clasped tightly, as if she would fain have restrained her grief by that muscular grip.

" I don't know whether it was wise or foolish," she said, " but I know we loved each other."

" I loved him, too, Justina," said Humphrey, using her Christian name involuntarily—she was not the kind of person to be called Miss Elgood—" as well as one man can love another. I take his death quietly enough, you see, but I would give ten years of my life to find his murderer!"

" I would give all my life,' said Justina, with a look that made him think she would verily have done it.

" You know nothing more than you told at the inquest this afternoon? Nothing that could throw any light upon his death ?"

" Nothing. You ought to know much more about it than I."

" How so ?"

" You know all that went before the time—his circumstances, his associates. I have lain awake thinking of this thing from night till morning, until I believe that every idea that could be thought about it has come into my head. There must have been some motive for his murder."

" The motive seems obvious enough—highway-robbery."

" Yet his watch was found in the ditch."

" His murderer may naturally have feared to take anything likely to lead to detection. His money was taken."

" Yes; it may have been for that. Yet it seems strange that he should have been chosen out of so many—that he should have been the only victim—murdered for the sake of a few pounds."

" Unhappily, sordid as the motive is. that is a common kind of murder," replied Humphrey.

" But might not some one have a stronger motive than that ?"

"I can imagine none. James never in his life made an enemy."

" Are you quite sure of that ?"

" As sure as I can be of anything about a young man whom I knew as well as if he had been my brother," replied Humphrey, wondering at the girl's calm, clear tone. At this moment she seemed older than her years—his equal, or more than his equal, in shrewdness and judgment.

" Is there any one who would be a gainer by his death ?" she said.

"Naturally. The next heir to the Penwyn estate is a very considerable gainer. For him James Penwyn's death means the difference between a hard working life like mine and a splendid future."

" Could he have anything to do with the crime?"

" He! Churchill Penwyn? Well, no, it would be about as hard to suspect him as it was to suspect me. Churchill Penwyn is a gentleman, and, I conclude, a man of honor. His conduct toward me to-day showed him a man of kind feeling."

" No. I suppose gentlemen do not commit such crimes," mused Justina; "and we shall never know who killed him. That seems hardest of all. That bright young life taken, and the wretch who took it left to go free."

Tears filled her eyes as she turned away from Humphrey Clissold, ashamed of her grief—tears which should have been shed in secret, but which she could not keep back when she thought of her young lover's doom.

Clissold tried to soothe her, assured her of his friendship— his help, should she ever need it.

" I shall always be interested in you," he said. " I shall think of you as my poor lad's first and last love. He had had his foolish boyish flirtations before, but I have reason to know that he never asked any other woman to be his wife; and he was too stanch and true to make such an offer unless he meant it."

Justina gave him a grateful look. It was the first time he had seen her face light up with anything like pleasure that day.

" You do believe that he loved me then?" she exclaimed eagerly. " It was not all my own foolish dream. He was not " —the next words came slowly, as if it hurt her to speak them —"amusing himself at my expense?"

" I have no doubt of his truth. I never knew him tell a lie. I do not say that his fancy would have lasted; it may have been too ardent, too sudden, to stand wear and tear. But, be assured, for the moment he was true—would have wrecked his life, perhaps, to keep true to the love of a day."

This time the girl looked at him angrily.

" Why do you tell me he must have changed if God had spared him ?" she added. " Why do you find it so hard to imagine that he might have gone on loving me? And I am so degraded a creature in your eyes ?"

" I am quite ready to believe that you are a very noble girl," answered Humphrey, " worthy a better lover than my poor

friend. But you are Miss Elwood, of the Theater Royal, Eborsham, and he was Squire Penwyn of Penwyn. Time would not
have changed those two facts, and might have altered his way
of looking at them."

" Don't tell me that he would have changed," she cried, passionately. " Let me think that I have lost all—love, happiness,
home, wealth—all that any woman ever hoped to win. It cannot add to my grief for him. It would not take away from my
love for him even to know that he was fickle, and would have
grown tired of me. Those two days were the only happy days
of my life. They will dwell in my mind forever, a changeless
memory. I shall never see the sunshine without thinking how
it shone once upon us two on Eborsham race-course. I shall
never see the moonlight without remembering how we two sat
side by side watching the willow branches dipping into the
river."

A childish love, thought Humphrey—a young heart's first
fancy, a fabric that would wear out in six months or so!

" Happy days will come again," he said, gently. " You will
go on acting, and succeed in your profession. You are just the
kind of girl to whom genius will come in a flash like inspiration. You will succeed and be famous by and by, and look
back with a sad, pitying smile at James Penwyn's love, and say
to yourself, with a half regretful sigh, ' That was youth!' You
will be loved some day by a man who will prove to you that true
love is not the growth of a few summer hours."

" I should like to be famous some day," the girl answered,
proudly, " just to show you that I might have been worthy of
your friend's love."

" I fear I have offended you by my plain speaking. Miss
Elgood," returned Humphrey; " but if ever you need a friend,
and will honor me with your confidence, you shall not find me
unworthy of your trust. I have not a very important position
in the world, but I am a gentleman of birth and education, and
not wanting in some of those commonplace qualities which help
a man on the road of life—such as patience and perseverance,
industry and strength of purpose. I have chosen literature for
my profession, for that calling gives me the privilege I should
be least inclined to forego—liberty. My income is happily just
large enough to make me independent of earning, so that I can
afford to write as the birds sing—without cutting my coat according to any other man's cloth. If ever you and your father
are in London, Miss Elgood, and inclined to test my sincerity,
you may find me at this address."

He gave Justina his card:

> " MR. HUMPHREY CLISSOLD,
>   Hogarth Place,
>   Bloomsbury."

" Not a fashionable locality by any means," he said, " but
central, and near the British Museum, where I generally spend
my mornings when I am in London."

Justina took the card listlessly enough, not as if she had any intention of taxing Mr. Clissold's friendship in the future. He saw how far her thoughts were from him, and from all common things. She rose with a startled look as the cathedral clock chimed the three-quarters after seven.

"I shall be late for the piece!" she exclaimed, with alarm. "I forget everything."

"It is my fault for detaining you," said Humphrey, concerned to see her look of distress. "Let me walk to the theater with you."

"But I've some things to carry," she answered, hurriedly rolling up some finery which had bestrewed a side-table—veil, shoes, ribbons, feathers, a dilapidated fan.

"I am not afraid of carrying a parcel."

They went out together, Justina breathless, and hurried to the stage-door.

Humphrey penetrated some dark passages and stumbled up some break-neck stairs in his anxiety to learn if his companion were really late. The band was grinding away at an overture. The second piece had not begun.

"Is it all right?" asked Humphrey, just as the light figure that had sped on before him was disappearing behind a dusky door.

"Yes," cried Justina; "I don't go on until the second scene. I shall have just time to dress."

So Humphrey groped his way to the outer air, relieved in mind.

It was a still summer evening, and this part of the city had a quiet, forgotten air, as of a spot from which busy life had drifted away. The theater did not create any circle of animation and bustle in these degenerate days, and, seen from the outside, might have been mistaken for a chapel. There were a few small boys hanging about near the stage-door as Mr. Clissold emerged, and these he perceived looked at him with interest, and spoke to one another about him. He was evidently known, even to these street boys, as the man who had been suspected of his friend's murder.

He walked round to the quiet little square in front of the theater, lighted his pipe, and took a turn up and down the empty pavement, meditating what he should do with himself for the rest of the evening.

Last night he had slept placidly enough in the mediæval jail, worn out with saddest thoughts. To-night there was nothing for him to do but go back to the Waterfowl, where the rooms would seem haunted, put his few belongings together, and get ready for going back to London. His holiday was over, and how sad the end!

He had been very fond of James Penwyn. Only now, when they two were parted forever, did he know how strong that attachment had been.

The bright young face, the fresh, gay voice, all gone!

"I am not quick at making friendships," thought Humphrey. "I feel as if his death had left me alone in the world."

His life had been unusually lonely, save for this one strong friendship. He had lost his father in childhood, and his mother a few years later. Happily Captain Clissold, although a younger son, had inherited a small estate in Devonshire from his mother. This gave his orphan son four hundred a year—an income which permitted his education at Eton and Oxford, and which made him thoroughly independent as a young man to whom the idea of matrimony and its obligations seemed far off.

His uncle, Sir Henry Clissold, was a gentleman of some standing in the political world, a county member, a man who was chairman of innumerable committees, and never had a leisure moment. This gentleman's ideas of the fitness of things were outraged by his nephew's refusal to adopt any profession.

"I could have pushed you forward in almost any career you had chosen," he said, indignantly. "I have friends I can command in all the professions; or, if you had cared to go to India, you might have been a judge in the Sudder before you were five-and-thirty.

"Thanks, my dear uncle. I shouldn't care about being broiled alive, or having to learn from twenty to thirty dialects before I could understand plaintiff or defendant," Humphrey replied, coolly. "Give me my crust of bread, and liberty."

"Fortunate for you that you have your crust of bread." growled Sir Henry, "but at the rate you are going you will never provide yourself with a slice of cheese."

To-night, perhaps for the first time, Humphrey Clissold felt that life was a mistake. His friend and comrade had been more necessary to him than he could have believed, for he had never quite accepted James as his equal in intellect. He had had his own world of thought, which the careless lad never entered. But now that the boy was gone, he felt that shadowy world darkened by his loss.

"Would to Heaven I could stand face to face with his murderer!" he said to himself. "One of us two should go down, never to rise again!"

CHAPTER XIV.

"TRUTH IS TRUTH TO THE END OF TIME."

MR. PERGAMENT went back to London by a train which left Eborsham at half-past five in the afternoon, half an hour after the termination of the inquest. Churchill went to the station with his solicitor, saw him into the railway-carriage, and only left the platform when the train had carried Mr. Pergament away on his road to London. It was an understood thing that Pergament & Pergament were to keep the Penwyn estate in their hands, and that Churchill's interests were henceforward to be their interests. To Pergament & Pergament, indeed, it was as if James Penwyn had never existed, so completely did they transfer their allegiance to his successor.

Churchill walked slowly away from the station, seemingly somewhat at a loss how to dispose of his time. He might have gone back to London with Mr. Pergament, certainly, for he had no further business in the city of Eborsham. But for some suffi-

cient reason of his own he had chosen to remain, although he
was not a little anxious to see Madge Bellingham, whom he had
not met since the change in his fortunes. He had written to her
before he left London to announce that fact—but briefly, feeling
that any expression of pleasure in the altered circumstances of
his life would show badly in black and white. He had expressed
himself properly grieved at his cousin's sad death, but had affected no exaggerated affliction. Those clear dark eyes of
Madge's seemed to be looking through him as he wrote.

"I wonder if it is possible to keep a secret from her?" he
thought. "She has a look that pierces my soul—such utter
truthfulness."

He had ordered his dinner for eight, and it was not yet six, so
he had ample leisure for loitering. He went back to Lowgate,
and out through the bar to the dull, quiet road where James
met his death. Churchill Penwyn wanted to see the spot
where the murder had been committed.

He had heard it described so often that it was easy enough for
him to find it. A ragged hedge of alder and blackberry divided the low marshy ground from the road just at this point.
From behind this hedge the murderer had taken his aim—at
least that was the theory of the police. Between the road and
the river the herbage was sour and scant, and the cattle that
browsed thereon had a solitary and dejected look, as if they
knew they were shut out from the good things of this life.
They seemed to be the odds and ends of the animal creation,
and to have come there accidentally. A misanthropical don-
key, a lean cow or two, some gaunt, ragged-looking horses, a
bony pig, scattered wide apart over the narrow track of sward
along the low bank of the river.

Mr. Penwyn contemplated the spot thoughtfully for a little
while, as if he would fain have made out something which the
police had failed to discover, and then strolled across the grass
to the river-bank. The gloomy solitude of the scene seemed to
please him, for he walked on for some distance, meditative and
even moody. Fortune brings its own responsibilities, and a
man who finds himself suddenly exalted from poverty to wealth
is not always gay.

He was strolling quietly along the bank, his eyes bent upon
the river, with that dreaming gaze which sees not the thing it
seems to contemplate, when he was startled from his reverie
by the sound of voices near at hand, and looking away from the
water, perceived that he had stumbled on a gypsy encampment.
There were the low arched tents—mere kennels under canvas,
where the dusky tribe burrowed at night or in foul weather; the
wood fire; the ever-simmering pot; the litter of ashes and dirty
straw and bones, and a broken bottle or two; the sinister-browed
vagabond lying on his stomach like the serpent, smoking his
grimy pipe, and scowling at any chance passer-by; the half-
naked children playing among the rubbish; the women sitting
on the ground plaiting rushes into a door-mat. All these
Churchill's eye took in at a glance—something more too, per-

haps, for he looked at one of the women curiously for a moment, and slackened his leisurely pace.

She put down her mat, rose, and walked beside him.

"Let me tell your fortune," pretty gentleman." she began, with the same professional sing-song, in which she had addressed James Penwyn a few days before.   It was the same woman who stopped the late Squire of Penwyn lower down on the river-bank.

"I don't want my future told, thank you.   I know what it is pretty well." replied Churchill, in his calm, cold voice.

" Don't say that, pretty gentleman. · No one can look into the urn of fate."

" And yet you and your tribe pretend to do so," said Church-ill.

"We study the stars more than others do, and learn to read 'em, my noble gentleman.   I've read something in the stars about you since the night your cousin was murdered."

"And pray what do the stars say of me ?" inquired Churchill, with a scornful laugh.

" They say that you're a kind-hearted gentleman at bottom, and will befriend a poor gypsy."

" I'm afraid they're out in their reckoning for once in a way. Perhaps it was Mercury you got the information from.   He's a notorious trickster.   And now pray, my good woman "—turn-ing to see that they were beyond the ken of the rest—" what did you mean by sending me a letter to say you could tell me some-thing about my cousin's death? If you really have any informa-tion to give, your wisest course is to carry it directly to the police; and if your information should lead to the discovery of the mur-derer, you may earn a reward that will provide for you for the rest of your life."

His eyes were on the woman's face as he spoke, with that in-tent look with which he was accustomed to read the human countenance.

"I've thought of that." answered the gypsy, "and I was very near going and telling all I knew to the police the morning after the murder, but I changed my mind about it when I heard you were here; I thought it might be better for me to see you first."

" I can't quite fathom your motive. However, as I am willing to give two hundred pounds reward for such information as may lead to the apprehension and conviction of the murderer, you may have come to the right person in coming to me; only, I tell you frankly, that, deeply as I am interested in the punishment of my cousin's assassin, I had rather not be troubled about de-tails.   I won't even ask the nature of your information.   Take my advice, my good soul, and carry it to the police.   They are the people to profit by it; they are the people to act upon it."

" Yes, and cheat me of the reward after all, and choke me off with a five-pound note, perhaps.   I know too much of the police to be over-inclined to trust 'em."

"Is your information conclusive?" asked Churchill: "certain to lead to the conviction of the murderer?"

"I won't say so much as that; but I know it's worth hearing, and worth paying for."

"You may as well tell me all about it, if you don't like to tell the police."

"What, without being paid for my secret? No, my pretty gentleman, I'm not such a fool as that."

"Come," said Churchill, with a laugh, "what does your knowledge amount to? Nothing, I dare say, that every one else in Eborsham doesn't share. You know that my cousin has been murdered, and that I am anxious to find the murderer."

"I know more than that, my noble gentleman."

"What then?"

"I know who did it."

Churchill turned his quick glance upon her again, searching, incredulous, derisive.

"Come," he said, "you don't expect to make me believe that you know the criminal, and let him slip, and lost your chance of the reward? You are not that kind of woman."

"I don't say that I've let him slip, or lost my chance of profiting by what I know. Suppose the criminal was some one I'm interested in—some one I shouldn't like to see come to harm?"

"In that case you shouldn't come to me about it. You don't imagine that I'm going to condone my cousin's murder? But I believe your story is all a fable."

"It is as true as the planets. We have been encamped here for the last week, and on the night of the murder we'd all been at the races. Folks are always kind to gypsies upon a race-course, and there was plenty to eat and drink for all of us—perhaps a little too much drink—and when the races were over I fell asleep in one of the booths, among some straw in a corner where no one took any notice of me. My son Reuben—him as you saw yonder just now—was in the town, up to very little good, I dare say, and left me to take care of myself; and when I woke it was late at night, and the place was all dark and quiet. I didn't know how late it was till I came through the town and found all the lights out and the streets empty, and heard the cathedral clock strike two. I walked slow, and the clock had struck the half hour before I got through the Bar; I was dead tired, standing and walking about the race-course all day; and as I came along this road I saw some one walking a little way ahead of me. He walked on, and I walked after him, keeping on the other side of the way, and in the shadow of the hedge about a hundred yards behind him, and all at once I heard a shot fired, and saw him drop down. There was no one to give the alarm to, and no good in giving it if he was dead. I kept on in the shadow until I came nearly opposite where he lay, and then I slipped down into the ditch. There was no water in it, nothing but mud and slime and duck-weed, and such like; and I squatted there in the shadow and watched."

"Like some toad in its hole," said Churchill. "Common humanity would have urged you to try to help the fallen man."

"He was past help, kind gentleman. He dropped without a groan, never so much as moaned as he lay there. And it was wiser for me to watch the murderer, so as to be able to bear witness against him, when the right time came, than to scare him away by skreeking out like a raven."

"Well, woman, you watched and saw—what?"

"I saw a man stooping over the murdered gentleman: a tall man in a loose overcoat with a scarf muffled round his neck. He put his hand in the other one's bosom, to feel if his heart had left off beating, I suppose, and drew it out again bloody. I could see that, even in the dim light betwixt night and morning, for I've something of a cat's eye, your honor, and am pretty well used to seeing in the dark. Candles ain't over-plentiful with our people. He held up a hand dripping with blood, and pulled a white handkerchief out of his pocket with the other hand to wipe the blood off."

Churchill turned and looked her in the face for the first time since she had begun her narrative.

"Come," he said, "you are overdoing the details. Your story would sound more like truth if it were less elaborate."

"I can't help the sound if it, sir. There's not a word I'm saying that I wouldn't swear by to-morrow in a court of justice."

"You've kept your evidence back too long, I'm afraid. You ought to have given this information at the inquest. A jury would hardly believe your story now."

"What, not if I had the proof of what I say?"

"What proof, woman?"

"The handkerchief with which the murderer wiped those blood-stains off his hands!"

"Pshaw!" exclaimed Churchill, contemptuously. "There are a hundred ways in which you might come possessed of a man's handkerchief. Your tribe lives by such petty plunder. Do you suppose that you, a gypsy and a vagabond, would ever persuade a British jury to believe your evidence against a gentleman?"

"What!" cried the woman, eagerly; "then you know it was a gentleman who murdered your cousin?"

"Didn't you say so, just this minute?"

"Not I, my noble gentleman. I told you he was tall, and wore an overcoat. That's all I told you about him."

"Well, what next?"

"He wiped the blood off his hand, then put the handkerchief back in his pocket, as he thought; but I suppose he wasn't quite used to the work he was doing, for in his confusion he missed the pocket and let the handkerchief fall into the road. I didn't give him time to find out his mistake, for while he was stooping over the dead man, emptying his pockets, I crept across the road, got hold of the handkerchief, and slipped back to my hiding-place in the ditch again. I'm light of foot, you see, your honor, though an old woman."

"What next?"

"He opened the dead man's purse, emptied it, and put the contents in his own waistcoat pocket. Then he crammed watch and purse down into the ditch—the same ditch where I was hiding, but a little way off—took a stick which he had broken off the hedge, and thrust them down into the mud under the weeds, making sure, I suppose, that no one could ever find them there. When he had done this, he pulled himself together, as you may say, and hurried off as fast as he could go, panting like a hunted deer, across the swampy ground and toward the river, where they found his footsteps afterward. I think it would have been cleverer of him if he'd left his victim's pockets alone, and let those that found the body rob it, as they'd have been pretty sure to do. Yet it was artful of him to clean the pockets out, so as to make it seem a common case of highway robbery and violence."

"What did you do with the handkerchief?"

"Took it home with me, to that tent yonder—that's what we call home—and lighted an end of candle, and smoothed out the handkerchief to see if there was any mark upon it. Gentlemen are so particular about their things, you see, and don't like to get 'em changed at the wash. Yes, there the mark was, sure enough. The name in full—Christian and surname. It was as much as I could do to read 'em for the blood-stains."

"What was the name?"

"That's my secret. Every secret has its price, and I've put a price on mine. If I was sure of getting the reward, and not having the police turn against me, I might be more ready to tell what I know."

"You're a curious woman," said Churchill, after a longish pause. "But I suppose you've some plan of your own."

"Yes, your honor, I have my views."

"As to this story of yours, even supported by the evidence of this handkerchief which you pretend to have found, I doubt very much if it would have the smallest weight with a jury. I do not, therefore, press you to bring forward your information; though as my cousin's next of kin, it is, of course, my duty to do my best to bring his assassin to justice."

"That's just what I thought, your honor."

"Precisely. And you did quite right in bringing the subject before me. It will be necessary for me to know when and where I can find you in future, so that when the right time comes you may be at hand to make your statement."

"We are but wanderers on the face of the earth, kind gentleman," whined the gypsy. "It isn't very easy to find us when you want us."

"That's what I've been thinking," returned Churchill, musingly. "If you had some settled home, now? You're getting old, and must be tired of roving, I fancy—sleeping upon straw, under canvas, in a climate in which east winds are the rule rather than the exception. That sort of thing must be rather trying at your time of life, I should imagine."

"Trying! I'm racked with the rheumatics every winter, your honor. My bones are not so much bones as knawing wolves— they torment me so. Sometimes I feel as if I could chop off my limbs willingly, to be quit of the pain in 'em. A settled home, a warm bed, a fireside—that would be heaven to me."

" Well. I'll think about it, and see what can be done for you. In the meantime I'll give you a trifle to ward off the rheumatism."

He opened his purse, and gave the woman a bank-note—part of an advance made him by Mr. Pergament that morning. The gypsy uttered her usual torrent of blessings—the gratitude wherewith she was wont to salute her benefactors.

" Have you ever been in Cornwall?" asked Churchill.

" Lord love your honor. there isn't a nook or a corner in all England where I haven't been. '

"Good. If you happen to be in Cornwall any time during the next three months, you may look me up at Penwyn."

" Bless you, my generous gentleman; it won't be very long before you see me."

" Whenever you please," returned Churchill, with that air of well-bred indifference which he wore as a badge of his class. " Good-afternoon."

He turned to go back to the city, leaving the woman standing alone by the river-brink, looking after him, lost in thought, or lost in wonder.

CHAPTER XV.

" THEY SHALL PASS, AND THEIR PLACES SHALL BE TAKEN."

THE letter which told Miss Bellingham that her lover was master of Penwyn seemed to her almost like the end of a fairy tale. Lady Cheshunt had dropped in to afternoon tea only a quarter of an hour before the letter arrived, and Madge was busy with the old Battersea cups and saucers, and the quaint little Wedgwood teapot, when the accomplished serving man, who had never abated one iota of his professional solemnity because his wages were doubtful, presented Churchill's letter on an antique salver.

" Put it on the table, please," said Madge, busy with the tea-service, and painfully conscious that the dowager's eye was upon her. She had recognized Churchill's hand at a glance, and thought how daring, nay, even impudent, it was of him to write to her. It was mean of him to take such advantage of her weakness that Sunday morning. she thought. True that in one fatal moment she had let him discover the one secret she was most anxious to hide; but she had given him no right over her. She had made him no promise. Her love had been admitted hypothetically. " If we lived in a different world! If I had myself only to consider!" she said to him; which meant that she would have nothing to do with him under existing circumstances.

She glanced at Viola, that fragile Sevres china beauty, with her air of being unfitted for the vulgar uses of life.

" Poor child! For her sake I ought to marry Mr. Balecroft, that pompous Manchester merchant, or that vapid young fop, Sir Henry Flittergilt," she thought, with a sigh.

"Read your letter, my dear love," said Lady Cheshunt, leaning over the tray to put an extra lump of sugar into her cup,
and scrutinizing the address of that epistle which had brought
the warm crimson blood to Madge Bellingham's cheeks and
brow. The good-natured dowager permitted herself this breach
of good-breeding in the warmth of her affection for Madge. The
handwriting was masculine, evidently. That was all Lady
Cheshunt could discover.

Miss Bellingham broke the seal, trying to look composed and
indifferent, but after hurriedly reading Churchill's brief letter,
gave a little cry of horror.

"Good heavens! it is too dreadful!" she exclaimed.

"What is too dreadful, child?"

"You remember what we were talking about last Saturday
night, when you took so much trouble to warn me against allowing myself to—to entangle myself—I think that's what you
called it—with Mr. Penwyn?"

"With the poor Mr. Penwyn. I remember perfectly; and
that letter is from him—the man has had the audacity to propose to you? You may well say it is too dreadful."

"His cousin has been murdered, Lady Cheshunt—his cousin,
Mr. James Penwyn."

"And your man comes into the Penwyn estate," cried the en-
ergetic dowager. "My dearest Madge, I congratulate you!
Poor young Penwyn! A boy at school or a lad at the university,
I believe. Nobody seems to know much about him."

"He has been murdered. Shot from behind a hedge by some
midnight assassin. Isn't that dreadful?" said Madge, too much
shocked by the tidings in her lover's letter to consider the difference this event might make in her own fortunes. She could
not be glad all at once, though that the man whom her heart
had chosen for its master was raised from poverty to opulence.
For a little while, at least, she could only think of the victim.

"Very dreadful!" echoed Lady Cheshunt. "The police
ought to prevent such things. One pays highway rates and
sewer rates, and so forth, till one is positively ruined, and yet
one can be murdered on the very high-road one pays for with
impunity. There must be something wrong in the legislature.
I hope things will be better when our party comes in. Look at
that child Viola; she's as white as a sheet of paper—just as if
she were going to faint. You shouldn't blurt out your murders
in that abrupt way, Madge."

Viola gave a little hysterical sob, and promised not to faint
this time. She was but a fragile piece of human porcelain,
given to swooning at the slightest provocation. She went round
to Madge, and knelt down by her, and kissed her fondly, knowing enough of her sister's feelings to comprehend that this fatal
event was likely to benefit Madge.

"Odd that I did not see anything of this business in the papers," exclaimed Lady Cheshunt. "But then I only read the
Post, and that does not make a feature of murders."

"Papa is at Newmarket," said Viola, "and Madge and J never
look at the papers or hear any news while he is away."

Madge sat silent, looking at Churchill's letter till every word seemed to burn itself into her brain. The firm straight hand, the letters long and narrow and a little pointed—something like that wonderful writing of Joseph Addison's—how well she knew it!

"And yet he *must* have been agitated," thought Madge. "Even his quiet force of character could not stand against such a shock as this. After what he said to me, too, last Sunday, that wealth and position should have come to him so suddenly! There seems something awful in it."

Lady Cheshunt had quite recovered her habitual gayety by this time, and dismissed James Penwyn's death as a subject that was done with for the moment, merely expressing her intention of reading the details of the event in the newspapers at her leisure.

"And so, my dear Madge, Mr. Penwyn wrote to you immediately," she said. "Doesn't that look *rather* as if there were some kind of understanding between you?"

"There was no understanding between us, Lady Cheshunt, except that I could never be Mr. Penwyn's wife while he was a poor man. He understood that perfectly. I told him in the plainest, hardest words, like a woman of the world, as I am."

"You needn't say that so contemptuously, Madge. I'm a woman of the world, and I own it without a blush. What's the use of living in the world if you don't acquire worldly wisdom? It's like living ever so long in a foreign country without learning the language, and implies egregious stupidity. And so you told Churchill Penwyn that you couldn't marry him on account of his poverty; and you pledged yourself to wait ten or twenty years for him, I suppose, and refuse every decent offer for his sake?"

"No. Lady Cheshunt, I promised nothing."

"Well, my dear, Providence has been very good to you; for, no doubt, if Mr. Penwyn had remained poor, you'd have made a fool of yourself sooner or later for his sake. and gone to live in Bloomsbury, where even I couldn't have visited you on account of my servants. One might get over that sort of thing one's self, but coachmen are so particular where they wait."

Her ladyship rattled on for another quarter of an hour, promised Madge to come and stay at Penwyn Manor with her by and by, congratulated Viola on her sister's good fortune, hoped that her dear Madge would make a point of spending the season in London when she became Mrs. Penwyn, while Madge sat unresponsive, hardly listening to this flow of commonplace, but thinking how awful fortune was when it came thus suddenly, and had death for its herald. She felt relieved when Lady Cheshunt gathered up her silken train for the last time, and went rustling down-stairs to the elegant Victoria which appeared far too fairy-like a vehicle to contain that bulky matron.

"Thank Heaven, she's gone!" cried Madge. "How she does talk!"

35453

"Yes, dear, but she is always kind," pleaded Viola, "and so fond of you!"

Madge put her arms round the girl and kissed her passionately. That sisterly love of hers was almost the strongest feeling in her breast, and all Madge's affections were strong. She had no milk-and-water love.

"Dearest," she said, softly, "how happy we can be now! I hope it isn't wicked to be happy when fortune comes to us in such a dreadful manner."

"You do care a little for Mr. Penwyn, then, dear?" said Viola, without entering upon this somewhat obscure question.

"I love him with all my heart and soul."

"Oh, Madge, and you never told me!"

"Why tell you something that might make you unhappy? I should never have dreamed of marrying Churchill but for this turn in fortune's wheel. I wanted to make what is called a good marriage for your sake, darling, more than for my own. I wanted to win a happy home for you, so that when your time came to marry you might not be pressed or harassed by worldly people as I have been, and might follow the dictates of your own heart."

"Oh, Madge, you are quite too good!" cried Viola, with enthusiasm.

"And we may be very happy, mayn't we, my pet?" continued the elder, "living together at a picturesque old place in Cornwall, with the great waves of the Atlantic rolling up to the edge of our grounds—and in London sometimes, if Churchill likes—and knowing no more of debt and difficulty, or cutting and contriving so as to look like ladies upon the income of ladies'-maids. Life will begin afresh for us, Viola."

"Poor papa!" sighed Viola; "you'll be kind to him, won't you, Madge?"

"My dearest, you know that I love him. Papa will be very glad, depend upon it, and he will like to go back to his old bachelor ways, I dare say, now that he will not be burdened with two marriageable daughters."

"When will you be married, Madge?"

"Oh, not for ever so long, dear—not for a twelvemonth, I should think. Churchill will be in mourning for his cousin, and it wouldn't look well for him to marry soon after such a dreadful event."

"I suppose not. Are you to see him soon?"

"Very soon, love. Here is his postscript." Madge read the last lines of her lover's letter:

"I shall come back to town directly the inquest is over and all arrangements made, and my first visit shall be to you."

"Of course. And you really, really love him, Madge?" asked Viola, anxiously.

"Really, really. But why ask that question, Viola, after what I told you just now?"

"Only because you have taken me by surprise, dear, and—don't be angry with me, Madge—because Churchill Penwyn has never been a favorite of mine. But of course now I shall begin to like him immensely. You're so much better a judge of character than I am, you see, Madge, and if you think him good and true——"

"I have never thought of his goodness or his truth," said Madge, with rather a gloomy look. "I only know that I love him."

CHAPTER XVI.
"THERE IS A HISTORY IN ALL MEN'S LIVES."

UPON his return to London Churchill lost very little time before presenting himself in Cavendish Row. He did not go there on the day of his cousin's funeral. That gloomy ceremonial had unfitted him for social pleasures, above all, for commune with so bright a spirit as Madge Bellingham. He felt as if to go to her straight from that place of tombs would be to carry the atmosphere of the grave into her home. The funeral seemed to affect him more than such a solemnity might have been supposed to affect a man of his philosophical temper. But then these quiet, reserved men—men who hold themselves in check, as it were—are sometimes men of deepest feeling. So Mr. Pergament thought as he stood opposite the new master of Penwyn in the vault at Kensal Green, and watched his pallid face, the settled gloom of his brow.

Churchill drove straight back to the Temple, with Mr. Pergament for his companion, that gentleman being anxious to return to New Square for his afternoon letters before going down to his luxurious villa at Beckenham, where he lived sumptuously, or, as his enemies averred, battened, ghoul-like, on the rotten carcasses of the defunct chancery suits which he had lost. From Kensal Green to Fleet Street seemed an interminable pilgrimage in that gloomy vehicle. Mr. Pergament and his client had exhausted their conversational powers on the way to the cemetery, and now on the return home had but little to say for themselves. It was a blazing summer afternoon—an August day which had slipped unawares into June through an error in the calendar. The mourning-coach was like a locomotive oven; the shabby suburban thoroughfares seemed baking under the pitiless sky. Never had the Harrow Road looked dustier, never had the Edgeware Road looked untidier or more out at elbows than to-day.

"How I detest the ragged fringe of shabby suburbs that hangs round London!" said Mr. Penwyn. It was the first remark he had made after half an hour's thoughtful silence.

His only reply from the solicitor was a gentle snore—a snore which sounded full of placid enjoyment. Perhaps there is nothing more dreamily delightful than a stolen doze on a sultry afternoon, lulled by the movement of wheels.

"How the fellow sleeps!" muttered Mr. Penwyn, almost savagely. "I wish I had the knack of sleeping like that."

It is the curse of these hyperactive intellects to be strangers to rest.

The carriage drew up at one of the Temple gates at last, and
Mr. Pergament woke with a start, jerked into the waking world
again by the sudden pull-up.
"Bless my soul!" exclaimed the lawyer.   "I was asleep."
"Didn't you know it?" asked Churchill, rather pettishly.
"Not the least idea.   Weather very oppressive.   Here we are
at your place.   Dear me!   By the way, when do you think of
going down to Penwyn?"
"The day after to-morrow.   I should like you to go with me
and put me in formal possession.   And you may as well take the
title-deeds down with you.   I like to have those things in my
own possession.   The leases you can of course retain."
Mr. Pergament, hardly quite awake as yet, was somewhat
taken aback by this request.   The title-deeds of the Penwyn
estate had been in the offices of Pergament & Pergament for
half a century.   This new lord of the manor promised to be
sharper even than the old squire, Nicholas Penwyn, who among
some ribald tenants of the estate had been known as Old Nick.
"If you wish it, of course—yes—assuredly," said Mr. Pergament; and on this, with a curt good-day from Churchill, they
parted.
"How property changes a man!" thought the solicitor, as the
coach carried him to New Square.   "That young man looks as
if he had the cares of a nation on his shoulders already.   Odd
notion his wanting to keep the title-deeds in his own custody.
However, I suppose he won't take his business out of our hands
—and, if he should, we can do without it."

*   *   *   *   *   *   *

Churchill went up to his chambers, on a third floor.   They had
a somber and chilly look in their spotless propriety, even on this
warm summer afternoon.   The rooms were on the shady side
of the way, and saw not the sun after nine o'clock in the
morning.
Very neatly kept and furnished were those bachelor apartments, the sitting-room at once office and living-room, the
goods and chattels in it perhaps worth five-and-twenty pounds.
An ancient and faded Turkey carpet, carefully darned by the
deft fingers of a jobbing upholstress whom Churchill sometimes
employed to keep things in order; faded green cloth curtains,
an old oak knee-hole desk, solid, substantial, shabby, with all
the papers upon it neatly assorted; the ink-stand stainless, and
well supplied; a horse-hair covered arm-chair, high-backed,
square, brass-nailed, of a remote era, but comfortable withal;
armless chairs of the same period, with an unknown crest emblazoned on their mahogany backs; a battered old book-case,
filled with law-books, only one shelf reserved for that lighter
literature which soothes the weariness of the student; every object as bright as labor and furniture polish could make it; everything in its place—a room in which no ancient spinster, skilled
in the government of her own domestic, could have discovered
ground for a complaint.
Churchill looked round the room with a thoughtful smile—

not altogether joyous—as he seated himself in his arm-chair, and opened a neat cigar-box on the table at his side.

" How plain the stamp of poverty shows upon everything!" he said to himself; " the furniture the mere refuse of an auction-room, furbished and polished into decency; the faded curtains, where there is hardly any color visible, except the neutral tints of decay; the darned carpet—premeditated poverty, as Sheridan calls it; the mark of the beast shows itself on all. And yet I have known some not all unhappy hours in this room; patient nights of study, the fire of ambition, the sunlight of hope; hours in which I deemed that fame and fortune were waiting for me down the long vista of industrious years; hours when I felt myself strong in patience and resolve! I shall think of these rooms sometimes in my new life—dream of them perhaps—fancy myself back again."

He sat musing for a long time, so lost in thought that he forgot to light the cigar which he had taken from his case just now. He woke from that long reverie with a sigh, gave his shoulders an impatient shrug, as if he would have shaken off ideas that troubled him, and took a volume at random from a neat little book-case on his table, where about half a dozen favorite volumes stood ranged, all of the cynical school—Rabelais, Sterne, Goethe's "Faust," Voltaire—not books that make a man better, if one excepts Goethe, whose master-work is the gospel of a great teacher. Under that outer husk of bitterness, how much sweetness! With that cynicism, what depth of tenderness!

Churchill's hand lighted unawares upon "Faust." He opened the volume at that mightiest drama, and read on—read until the wearied student stood before him, tempting destiny with his discontent—read until the book dropped from his hand, and he sat, fixed as a statue, staring at the ground, in a gloomy reverie.

" After all, discontent is your true tempter—the fiend whose whisper forever assails man's ear. Who could be wiser than Faust, and yet how easy a dupe! Well, I have my Margaret, at least; and neither man nor any evil spirit that walks the earth in shape impalpable to man shall ever come between us two."

Churchill lighted his cigar, and left his quiet room, which seemed to him just now to be unpleasantly occupied by that uncanny poodle which the German doctor brought home with him. He went to the Temple Gardens, and walked up and down by the cool river, over which the mists of evening were gently creeping, like a veil of faintest gray. It was before the days of the embankment, and the Templars still possessed their peaceful walk on the brink of the river.

Here Churchill walked till late, thinking—always thinking: property has so many cares—and then, when other people were meditating supper, went out into Fleet Street to a restaurant that was just about closing, and ordered his tardy dinner. Even when it came, he seemed to have but a sorry appetite, and only took his pint of claret with relish. He was looking forward eagerly to the morrow, when he should see Madge Bellingham, and verily begin his new life. Hitherto he had known only the disagreeables of his position—the inquest, the funeral. To-morrow he was to taste the sweets of prosperity.

CHAPTER XVII.
"DEATH COULD NOT SEVER MY SOUL AND YOU."

CHURCHILL PENWYN lost little of the morrow to which he had looked forward so eagerly. He was in Cavendish Row at eleven o'clock, in the pretty drawing-room, among brightly bound books and music and flowers, surrounded by color, life, and sun-shine, and with Madge Bellingham in his arms.

For the first few moments neither of them could speak; they stood silent, the girl's dark head upon her lover's breast, her cheek pale with deepest feeling, his strong arms encircling her.

"My own dear love," he murmured, after a kiss that brought the warm blood back to that pale cheek. "My very own at last! Who would have thought when we parted that I should come back to you so soon with altered fortunes?"

"So strangely soon!" said Madge. "Oh, Churchill, there is something awful in it."

"Destiny is always awful, dearest. She is that goddess who ever was and ever will be, and whose veil no man's hand has ever lifted. We are blind worshipers in her temple, and must take the lots she deals from her inscrutable hand. We are among her favored children, dearest, for she has given us happiness."

"I refused to be your wife, Churchill, because you were poor. Can you quite forgive that? Must I not seem to you selfish and mercenary, almost contemptible, if I accept you now?"

"My beloved, you are truth itself. Be as nobly frank to-day as you were that day I promised to win fame and fortune for your sake. Fortune has come without labor of mine. It shall go hard with me if fame does not follow in the future. Only tell me once more that you love me, that you rejoice in my good fortune, and will share it and—bless it."

He made a little pause before the last two words, as if some passing thought had troubled him.

"You know that I love you, Churchill," she answered, shyly. "I could not keep that secret from you the other day, though I would have given so much to hide the truth."

"And you will be my wife, darling, the fair young mistress of Penwyn."

"By and by, Churchill. It seems almost wrong to talk of our marriage yet awhile. That poor young fellow, your cousin—he may have been asking some happy girl to share his fortune and his home—to be mistress of Penwyn—only a little while ago."

"Very sad," said Churchill, "but the natural law. You remember what the father of poets has said, 'The race of man is like the leaves on the trees.'"

"Yes, Churchill, but the leaves fall in their season. This poor young fellow has been snatched away in the blossom of his youth—and by a murderer's hand."

"I have heard a good deal of that sort of talk since his death," remarked Mr. Penwyn, with a cloudy look. "I thought you would have a warmer greeting for me than lamentations about my cousin. But for his death I should not have the right to hold you in my arms, to claim you for my wife. You rejected me on account of my poverty, yet you bewail the event that has made me rich."

Miss Bellingham withdrew herself from her lover's arms with an offended look.

"I would rather have waited for you ten years than that fortune should have come to you under such painful circumstances," she said.

"Yes, you think so, I dare say; but I know what a woman's waiting generally comes to—above all, when she is one of the most beautiful women in London. Madge, don't sting me with cold words or cold looks. You do not know how I have yearned for this hour."

She had seated herself by one of the little tables, and was idly turning the leaves of an ivory-bound volume. Churchill knelt down beside her, and took the white ringed hand away from the book, and covered it with kisses, and put his arm round her as she sat, leaning his head against her shoulder, as if he had found rest there after long weariness.

"Have some compassion upon me, darling," he pleaded. "Pity nerves that have been strained, a mind that has been overtaxed. Do not think that I have not felt this business. I have felt it, God knows how intensely. But I come here for happiness. Time enough for troublous thoughts when you and I are apart. Here I would remember nothing—know nothing but the joy of being with you, to touch your hand, to hear your voice, to look into those deep dark eyes."

There was nothing but love in the eyes that met his gaze now—love unquestioning and unmeasured.

"Dearest, I will never speak of your cousin again, if it pains you," Madge said, earnestly. "I ought to have been more considerate."

She pushed back a loose lock from the spacious forehead, where the hair grew sparsely, with a gentle, caressing hand—timidly, for it was the first time she had touched her lover's brow, and there was something of a wife's tenderness in the action.

"Churchill," she exclaimed, "your forehead burns as if you were in a fever. You are not ill, I hope."

"No, dear, not ill. But I have been over-anxious, over-excited, perhaps. I am calm now, happy now, Madge. When shall I speak to your father? I want to feel myself your acknowledged lover."

"You can speak to papa whenever you like, Churchill. He came home last night from Newmarket. I know he will be glad to see you either here or at his club."

"And our marriage, Madge, how soon shall that be?"

"Oh, Churchill, you cannot wish it to be soon after——"

"But I do wish it to be soon—as soon as it may be with decency. I am not going to pretend exaggerated grief for the death of a kinsman of whom I hardly knew anything. I am not going to sit in sackcloth and ashes because I have inherited an estate I never expected to own, in order that the world may look on approvingly, and say: 'What fine feelings! what tenderness of heart!' Society offers a premium for hypocrisy. No, Madge, I will wear crape on my hat for just three months, and wait just three months for the crowning happiness of my life, and then we will be married as quietly as you please, and slip away by some untrodden track to a Paradise of our own, some one fair scene among the many lovely spots of earth which has not yet come into fashion for honeymoons."

"You do not ask my terms, but dictate your own," said Madge, smiling.

"Dear love, are we not one in heart and hope from this hour, and must we not have the same wishes, the same thoughts?"

"You have no *trousseau* to think about, Churchill."

"No; a man hardly considers matrimony an occasion for laying in an unlimited stock of clothes, though I may indulge in a new suit or two in honor of my promotion. Seriously, dearest, do not trouble yourself to provide a mountain of millinery. Mrs. Penwyn shall have an open account with as many milliners and silk mercers as she pleases."

"You may be sure that I shall not have too expensive a *trousseau*, and that I shall not run into debt," said Madge, blushing.

And so it was settled between them that they were to be married before the end of September, in time to begin their new life in some romantic corner of Italy, and to establish them-selves at Penwyn before Christmas and the hunting season. Churchill had boasted friends innumerable as a penniless barrister; and this circle was hardly likely to become contracted by the change in his fortunes. Everybody would want to visit him during that first winter at Penwyn.

The lovers sat together for hours, talking of their future, opening their hearts to each other, as they had never dared to do before that day. They sat, hand clasped in hand, on that very sofa which Lady Cheshunt's portly form had occupied when she read Madge her lecture.

Viola was out riding with some good-natured friends who had a large stable, and gave the Misses Bellingham a mount as often as they chose to accept that favor; it was much too early for callers; Sir Nugent never came up-stairs in the morning; so Madge and her lover had the cool, shadowy rooms to themselves, and sat amidst the perfume of flowers, talking of their happy life to come. All the small-talk of days gone by—those many conversations at evening parties, flower-shows, picture-galleries —seemed as nothing compared with these hours of earnest talk; heart to heart, soul to soul, on one side, at least, without a thought of reserve.

Time flew on his swiftest wing for these two. Madge started up with a little cry of surprise when Viola dashed into the room, looking like a lovely piece of waxwork in a riding-habit and chimney-pot hat.

"Oh, Madge, we have had such a round; Ealing, Willesden,

Hendon, and home by Finchley. I beg your pardon, Mr. Penwyn, I didn't see you till this moment. This room is so dark after the blazing sunshine. Aren't you coming down to luncheon? The bell rang half an hour ago, and poor Rickson looks the picture of gloom. I dare say he wants to clear the table and compose himself for his afternoon siesta."

Madge blushed, conscious of having been too deep in bliss for life's common sounds to penetrate her Paradise—in a region where luncheon bells are not.

"You'll stay to luncheon, Churchill, won't you?" she said, and Viola knew it was all settled.

Miss Bellingham would not have called a gentleman by his Christian name unless she had been engaged to be married to him.

Viola got hold of her sister's hand as they went down-stairs, and squeezed it tremendously.

"I shall sit down to luncheon in my habit," she said, "if you don't mind, for I'm absolutely famishing."

That luncheon was the pleasantest meal Churchill Penwyn had eaten for a long time. Not an aldermanic banquet by any means, for Sir Nugent seldom lunched at home, and the young ladies fared but simply in his absence. There was a cold chicken left from yesterday's dinner, minus the liver wing, a tongue, also cut, a salad, a jar of apricot jam, some dainty little loaves from a German bakery, and a small glass dish of Roquefort cheese. The wines were vin ordinaire and sherry.

The three sat a long time over this simple feast, still talking of their future—the future which Viola was to share with the married people.

"Have you ever seen Penwyn Manor?" she asked, after having declared her acceptance of the destiny that had been arranged for her.

"Never," answered Churchill. "It was always a sore subject with my father. His father had not treated him well, you see; he married when he was little more than a boy, and was supposed to have married badly, though my mother was as good a woman as ever bore the name of Penwyn. My grandfather chose to take offense at the marriage, and my father resented the slight put upon his wife so deeply that he never crossed the threshold of Penwyn Manor-house again. Thus it happened that I was brought up with very little knowledge of my kindred, or the birth-place of my ancestors. I have often thought of going down to Cornwall to have a look at the old place, without letting anybody know who I was; but I have been too busy to put the idea into execution."

"How different you will feel going there as master!" said Viola.

"Yes, it will be a more agreeable sensation, no doubt."

It was between three and four o'clock when Churchill left that snug little dining-room to go down to Sir Nugent's club in St. James' Street, in the hope of seeing that gentleman and making all things straight without delay.

"Come back to afternoon tea, if you can," said Viola, who appeared particularly friendly to her future brother-in-law.

"If possible, my dear Viola. I may call you Viola, I suppose, now."

"Of course—are we not brother and sister henceforward?"

"Well, dear, have you been trying to like him?" asked Madge, when her lover had departed.

"Yes, and I found it quite easy, you darling Madge. He seemed to me much nicer to-day. Perhaps it was because I could see how he worships you. I never saw two people so intensely devoted. Prosperity suits him wonderfully; though that cloudy look which I have often noticed in him still comes over his face by fits and starts."

"He feels his cousin's awful death very deeply."

"Does he? That's very good of him, when he profits so largely by the calamity. Well, dearest, I mean to like him very much, to be as fond of him as if he really were my brother."

"And he will be all that a brother could be to you, dear."

"I don't quite know that I should care about that," returned Viola, doubtfully: "brothers are sometimes nuisances. A brother-in-law would be more likely to be on his good behavior for fear of offending his wife."

*   *   *   *   *   *   *

Churchill succeeded in lighting upon Sir Nugent at his club. He was yawning behind an evening paper in the reading-room when Mr. Penwyn found him. His greeting was just a shade more cordial than it had always been, but only a shade, for it was Sir Nugent's rule to be civil to everybody. "One never knew when a man might get a step," he said; and in a world largely composed of younger sons and heirs-presumptive this was a golden rule.

Sir Nugent expressed himself profoundly sympathetic upon the subject of James Penwyn's death. He was perfectly aware of Churchill's business with him that afternoon, but affected the most Arcadian innocence.

Happily Churchill came speedily to the point.

"Sir Nugent," he began, gravely, "while I was a struggling man I felt it would be at once presumption and folly to aspire to your daughter's hand, but to be her husband has been my secret hope ever since I first knew her. My cousin's death has made a total change in my fortune."

"Of course, my dear fellow. It has transformed you from a briefless barrister into a prosperous country gentleman. Pardon me if I remark that I might look higher for my eldest daughter than that. Madge is a woman in a thousand. If it had been her sister, now--a good little thing, and uncommonly pretty —but I have no lofty aspirations for her."

"Unhappily for your ambitious dreams, Sir Nugent, Madge is the lady of my choice, and we love each other. I do not think you ought to object to my present position; the Penwyn estate is worth six thousand a year."

"Not bad," said the baronet, blandly, "for a commoner. "But Madge could win a coronet if she chose, and I confess that I have looked forward to seeing her take her place in the peerage. However, if she really likes you, and has made up her mind about it, any objections of mine would be useless, no doubt; and as far as personal feeling goes, there is no one I should like better for a son-in-law than yourself."

The two gentlemen shook hands upon this, and Sir Nugent felt that he had not let his handsome daughter go too cheap, and had paved the way for a liberal settlement. He asked his future son-in-law to dinner, and Churchill, who would not have foregone that promised afternoon tea for worlds, chartered the swiftest hansom he could find, drove back to Cavendish Row, spent an hour with the two girls and a little bevy of feminine droppers-in, then drove to the Temple to dress, and 'reappeared at Sir Nugent's street door just as the neighboring clocks chimed the first stroke of eight.

" Bless the young man, how he do come backward and forward since he's come into his estates!" said the butler, who had read all about James Penwyn's death in the papers. " I always suspected that he had a sneaking kindness for our eldest young lady, and now it's clear they're going to keep company. If he's coming in and out like this every day, I hope he'll have consideration enough to make it worth my while to open the door for him."

    *   *   *   *   *   *   *

"I hope you are not angry with me, papa," said Madge, by and by, after her lover had bidden them good-night and departed, and when father and daughter were alone together.

" Angry with you! no, my love, but just a trifle disappointed. This seems to me quite a poor match for a girl with your advantages."

" Oh, papa, Churchill has six thousand a year: and think of our income."

" My love, that is not the question in point. What I have to think of is the match you might have made had it not been for this unlucky infatuation. There is Mr. Balecroft, with his palace in Belgravia, a picture-gallery worth a quarter of a million, and a superb place at Windermere——"

" A man who drops his h's, papa—complains of being 'ot!"

"Or Sir Henry Flittergilt, one of the oldest families in Yorkshire, with twelve thousand a year."

" And not an idea which he has not learned from his trainer or his jockey. Oh, papa, don't forget Tennyson's noble line:

" ' Cursed be the gold that gilds the straitened forehead of the fool.' "

" All very well for poets to write that sort of stuff, but a man in my position doesn't like to see his daughter throw away her chances. However. I suppose I mustn't complain. Penwyn Manor is a nice enough place, I dare say."

" You must come to stay with me, papa, every year."

" My love, that kind of place would be the death of me, except for a week in October. I suppose there are plenty of pheasants?"

" I dare say, papa. If not we'll order some."

" Well, it might have been worse," sighed Sir Nugent.

" You'll let Viola live with me when I am married, papa, won't you?" pleaded Madge, coaxingly, as if she were asking a tremendous favor.

" My dear child, with all my heart," replied her father, with amiable promptitude. " Where could she be so well off? In that case I shall give up housekeeping as soon as you are married. This house has always been a plague to me—taxes. repairs, no end of worry. I used to pay a hundred and fifty pounds a year for my rooms in Jermyn Street, and the business was settled. Bless you, my darling! You have always been a comfort to your poor old father."

And thus blandly, with an air of self-sacrifice, did Sir Nugent Bellingham wash his hands of his two daughters.

CHAPTER XVIII.
"THROUGH THE DESERT PAST MY FANCY MARCHES."

A YEAR had gone by since James Penwyn met his death by the lonely river at Eborsham, and again Humphrey Clissold spent his summer holiday in a walking tour. This time he was quite alone. Pleasant and social though he was, he did not make friendships lightly or quickly. In the year that was gone he had found no friend to replace James Penwyn. He had plenty of agreeable acquaintances, knew plenty of men who were glad to dine with him or to give him a dinner. He was famous already, in a small way, at the literary club where he spent many of his evenings when he was in London, and men liked to hear him talk, and prophesied fair things for his future as a man of letters, all the more surely because he was not called upon to write for bread, but could follow the impulse that moved him, and wait, were it ever so long, for the moment of inspiration; never forced to spur the jaded steed, or work the too-willing horse to death.

Not one of the comrades he liked well enough for a jovial evening or a cozy dinner had crept into his heart like the lad he had sworn to cherish in the ears of a dying woman five years ago. So when the roses were in bloom, and London began to look warm and dusty, the parks faded a little from their vernal green, Humphrey Clissold set forth alone upon a voyage of adventure, with a pocket Shakespeare, and a quire or so of paper in his battered old leathern knapsack, and just so much clothing and linen as might serve him for his travels.

Needless to say that he avoided that northern city of Eborsham, where such sudden grief had come upon him, and all that route which he had trodden only a year ago with the light-hearted, hopeful lad who now slept his sweetest sleep in one of the vaults at Kensal Green, beside the mother he had loved and mourned.

Instead of northward, to the land of lakes and mountains, Humphrey went due west. Many a time had he and James Penwyn talked of the days they were to spend together down at the old place in Cornwall; and behold, that visit to Penwyn Manor, deferred in order that James should see the lake country,

was destined never to be paid.   Never were those two to walk
together by the Atlantic, never to scale Tintagel's rugged height,
or ramble among the rocks of Bude.

Humphrey had a curious fancy for seeing the old home from
which death had ousted James Penwyn.   He might have gone
as a visitor to the Manor-house, had he pleased, for Churchill
had been extremely civil to him when they last met at the
funeral, and had promised him a hearty welcome to Penwyn
whenever he liked to come there.

Mr. Clissold infinitely preferred to go as an unknown pedestrian—knapsack on shoulder—having first taken the trouble to
ascertain that Churchill Penwyn and his beautiful young wife
were in London, where they had, for this season, a furnished
house in Upper Brook Street.   He saw their names in the list of
guests at a fashionable reception, and knew that the coast
would be clear, and that he could roam about the neighborhood of his dead friend's ancestral home without let or
hinderance.   He went straight to Plymouth by an express train,
crossed the Tamar, and pursued his journey on foot at a leisurely
pace, lingering at all the prettiest spots—now spending a day or
two at some rustic way-side inn—rambling about, sketching a
little, reading a little, writing a little, thinking and dreaming a
great deal.

It was an idle fancy that had brought him here, and he gave
a free rein to all other idle fancies that seized him by the way.
It was a morbid fancy, perhaps, for it must needs be but a melancholy pleasure at best to visit the domain which his friend had
never enjoyed, to remember so many boyish schemes unfulfilled, so many bright hopes snapped short off by the shears of
Atropos.

The long blue line of sea and the irregular green line of low
hills were steeped in the golden light of a midsummer afternoon
when Humphrey drew near Penwyn Manor.   The scene was far
more lonely than he had imagined it.   Measureless ocean stretched
before him, melting into the hazy summer sky—sea and heaven
so near of a color that it was hard to tell where the water ended
and the sky began—measureless hills around him, and except
the white sheep yonder, making fleecy dots upon the side of the
topmost hill, no sign of life.   He had left the village of Penwyn
behind him by a good two miles, but had not yet come in sight
of the Manor-house, though he had religiously followed the track
pointed out to him by the hostess of the little inn—a mere cottage—where he left his knapsack, and where he had been respectfully informed that he could not have a bed.

" At the worst I can sleep on one of these hills," he said to
himself.   " It can hardly be very cold, even at night, in this
western climate."

He walked a little further on, upon a narrow foot-path high
above the sea level.   On his right hand there were wide corn
fields, with here and there an open tract of turnip or mangel;
on his left only the wild-looking pastures. undulating like a sea
of verdure.   The ground had dipped a little while ago, and as it

rose again, with a gentle ascent, Humphrey Clissold saw the chimney-stacks of the Manor-house between him and the sea.

It was a substantial-looking house, built of a grayish stone—a long low building, with grounds that stretched to the edge of the cliff, sheltered by a belt of fir and evergreen oak. The blue sea showed in little patches of gleaming color through the dark foliage, and the spicy odor of the pines perfumed the warm still air. In its utter loneliness the house had a gloomy look, despite the grandeur of its situation on this bold height above the sea. The grounds were extensive, but to Humphrey Clissold they seemed somewhat barren: orderly, beyond doubt, and well-timbered, but lacking the smiling fertility, the richness of ornament which a student of Horace and Pliny desired in his ideal garden.

But Mr. Clissold did not make acquaintance with the inside of the shrubbery or gardens without some little difficulty. His foot-path led him ultimately into a villainous high-road, just in front of the gates of Penwyn, so the landlady of the village inn had not sent him astray. There was a lodge beside the gate, a square stone cottage, covered with myrtle, honeysuckle, and roses, from which emerged an elderly female, swarthy of aspect, her strongly marked countenance framed in a frilled cap, which gave an almost grotesque look to that tawny countenance.

" Can I see the house and grounds, ma'am?" asked Humphrey, approaching this somewhat grim-looking personage with infinite civility.

He had a vague idea that he must have seen that face before, or imagined it in a dream, so curiously did it remind him of some past occasion in his life—what, he knew not.

" The house is never shown to strangers," answered the woman.

" I know Mr. Penwyn, and will leave my card for him."

" You'd better apply to the housekeeper. As to the grounds, my little granddaughter will take you round, if you like. Elspeth!" called the woman; and a black-eyed girl of twelve appeared at the cottage-door, like a sprite at the sound of an incantation.

" Take this gentleman round the gardens," said the old woman, and vanished, before Humphrey could quite make up his mind as to whether he had seen a face like that in actual flesh and blood or only on a painter's canvas.

The girl, who had an impish look, he thought, with her loose black locks, scarlet petticoat, and scanty scarlet shawl pinned tightly across her bony shoulders, led the way through a wild-looking shrubbery, where huge blocks of granite lay among the ferns which grew with rank luxuriance between the straight pine stems. A sandy path wound in and out among trees and shrubs, till Humphrey and his guide emerged upon a wide lawn at the back of the house, whose many windows blinked at them, shining in the western sun.

There were no flower-beds on the lawn, but there was a small square garden, in the Dutch style, on one side of the house, and a bowling green on the other. A terraced walk stretched in front of the windows, raised three or four feet above the level of the lawn, and guarded by a stone balustrade, somewhat defaced by time. A fine old sun-dial marked the center of the Dutch garden, where the geometrical flower beds were neatly kept, and where Humphrey found a couple of gardeners, elderly men both, at work weeding and watering in a comfortable, leisurely manner.

"What a paradise for the aged!" thought Humphrey; "the woman at the lodge was old, the gardeners are old, everything about the place is old, except this impish girl, who looks the oldest of all, with her evil black eyes and vinegar voice."

Mr. Clissold had not come so far without entering into conversation with the damsel. He had asked her a good many questions about the place and the people to whom it belonged. But her answers were of the briefest, and she affected the profoundest ignorance about everything and everybody.

"You've not been here very long, I suppose, my girl," he said, at last, with some slight sense of irritation, "or you'd know a little more about the place."

"I haven't been here much above six months."

"Oh! But your grandmother has lived here all her life, I dare say."

"No, she hasn't. Grandmother came when I did."

"And where did you both come from?"

"Foreign parts," answered the girl.

"Indeed! you both speak very good English for people who come from abroad."

"I didn't say we were foreigners, did I?" asked the girl, pertly. "If you want to ask any more questions about the place or the people, you'd better ask 'em of the housekeeper, Mrs. Darvis; and if you want to see the house, you must ask leave of her; and this is the door you'd better ring at, if you want to see her."

They were at one end of the terrace, by a low, half-glass door which opened into a small and darksome lobby, where the effigies of a couple of ill-used ancestors frowned from the dusky walls, as if indignant at being placed in so obscure a corner. Humphrey rang the bell, and after repeating that operation more than once, and waiting with consummate patience for the result, he was rewarded by the appearance of an elderly female, homely, fresh-colored, comfortable-looking, affording altogether an agreeable contrast to the tawny visage of the lodge-keeper, whose countenance had given Humphrey an unpleasant feeling about Penwyn Manor. First impressions are so easily formed, and depend upon such trifles.

Mr. Clissold stated his business, and after spelling over his card and deliberating a little, Mrs. Darvis consented to admit him, and to show him the house.

"We used to show it to strangers pretty freely until the new squire came into possession," she said, "but he's rather particular. However, if you're a friend of his——"

"I know him very well; and poor James Penwyn was my most intimate friend."

"Poor Mr. James! I never saw him but once, when he came

down to see the place soon after the old squire's death. Such a frank, open-hearted young gentleman, and so free-spoken! It was a terrible blow to all of us down here when we read about the murder. Not but what the present Mr. Penwyn is a liberal master and a kind landlord and a good friend to the poor. There couldn't be a better gentleman for Penwyn."

"I am glad to hear you give him so good a character," said Humphrey.

The girl Elspeth had followed him into the house uninvited, and stood in the background, open-eyed, with her thin lips drawn tightly together, and a sharp, eager look in her face, listening intently.

"As for Mrs. Penwyn," said the housekeeper, "why, she's a lady in a thousand! She might be a queen, there's something so grand about her. Yet so affable that she couldn't pass one of the little children at the poor-school without saying a word; and so thoughtful for the poor that they've no need to tell her their wants; she provides for them beforehand."

"A model Lady Bountiful," exclaimed Humphrey.

"You may run home to your grandmother, Elspeth," said Mrs. Darvis.

"I was to show the gentleman the grounds," answered the damsel; "he hasn't half seen 'em yet."

In her devotion to the service she had undertaken, the girl followed at their heels through the old house, drinking in every word that was said by Mrs. Darvis or the stranger.

The house was old and somewhat gloomy, belonging to the Tudor school of architecture. when the heavy stonework of the window-frames, the lozenge-shaped mullions, the massive crossbars were eminently adapted to exclude light. Even what light they did admit was in many places tempered by stained glass emblazoned with the arms and mottoes of the Penwyn family in all its ramifications, showing how it had become entangled with other families, and bore the arms of heiresses on its shield, until the original badge which Sir Thomas Penwyn, the crusader, had first carried atop of his helmet was almost lost among the various devices in a barry of eight.

The rooms were spacious, but far from lofty, the chimney-pieces of carved oak and elaborate workmanship, the paneling between mantel-board and ceiling richly embellished, and over all the principal chimney-pieces appeared the Penwyn arms and motto, "*J'attends*."

There was much old tapestry, considerably the worse for wear, for the old house had been sorely neglected during that dreary interval between the revolution and the days of George the Third, when the Penwyn family had fallen into comparative poverty, and the fine old mansion had been little better than a farm-house. Indeed, brawny agricultural laborers had eaten and drunken in the banqueting-hall, now the state dining-room, and handsomely furnished with plain and massive oaken furniture by the old squire, Churchill's grandfather.

This room was one of the largest in the house, and looked toward the sea. Drawing-room, music-room, library, and boudoir were on the other side of the house, with windows opening on the terrace. The drawing-room and boudoir had been refurnished by Churchill since his marriage.

"The old squire kept very little company, and hardly ever went inside any of those rooms," said Mrs. Darvis. "In summer he used to sit in the yew-tree bower on the bowling-green after dinner, and in winter he used to smoke his pipe in the steward's room mostly, and talk to his bailiff. The dining-room was the only large room he ever used. So when Mr. Churchill Penwyn came he found the drawing-room very bare of furniture, and what there was was too shabby for his taste, so he had that and the boudoir furnished after the old style by a London upholsterer, and put a grand piano and harmonium in the music-room; and the drawing-room tapestry is all new, made by the Goblins, Mrs. Penwyn told me, which, I suppose, was only her fanciful way of putting it."

The dame opened the door as she spoke, and admitted Humphrey into this sacred apartment, where the chairs and sofas were shrouded with holland.

The tapestry was an exquisite specimen of that patient art. Its subject was the story of Arion; and the friendly dolphin and summer sea, the Greek sailors, Periander's white-walled palace, lived upon the work. Triangular cabinets of carved ebony adorned the corners of the room, and were richly furnished with the Bellingham *bric-a-brac*, the only dower Sir Nugent had been able to give his daughter. The chairs and sofas, from which Mrs. Darvis lifted a corner of the holland for the visitor's gratification, were of the same dark wood, upholstered with richest olive-green damask of mediæval diaper pattern. The window-curtains were of the same fabric, and their somber tint harmonized admirably with the brighter hues of the tapestry. The floor was darkest oak, only covered in the center of the room with a Persian carpet. The boudoir, which opened out of the drawing-rooms, was furnished in exactly the same style, only here the tapestried walls told the story of Hero and Leander.

"I believe it was all Mrs. Penwyn's taste," said the housekeeper, when Humphrey had admired everything. "Her rooms up-stairs are a picture—nothing out of character with the house, the head upholsterer said. 'There's so few ladies have got any notion of character,' he says. 'They'll furnish an old manor-house with flimsy white and gold of the Lewis Quince style, only fit for a drawing-room in the Shamps Eliza, and if you ask them why, they'll say because it's pretty, and they like it. Mrs. Penwyn is an artist,' says the upholsterer's foreman."

Humphrey did not hurry his inspection, finding the housekeeper communicative and the place full of interest. He heard a great deal about the old squire, Nicholas Penwyn, who had reigned for forty years, and for whom his dependents had evidently felt a curious mixture of fear, respect, and affection.

"He was a just man," said Mrs. Darvis, "but stern; and it was but rarely he forgave any one that once offended him. It took a good deal to offend him, you know, sir, but when he did take offense the wound rankled deep. I've heard our old doct

say the squire had bad flesh for healing. He never got on very
well with his eldest son, Mr. George, though he was the handsomest of the three brothers, and the best of them, too, to my
mind."

" What made them disagree ?" asked Humphrey. They had
made the round of the house by this time, and the traveler had
seated himself comfortably on a broad window-seat in the entrance hall—a window through which the setting sun shone
bright and warm. Mrs. Darvis sat on a carved oak bench by
the fireplace, resting after her unwonted exertions. Elspeth
stood at a respectful distance, her arms folded demurely in her
little red shawl, listening to the housekeeper's discourse.

" Well, you see, sir," returned Mrs. Darvis, in her slow, me-
thodical way, " the old squire would have liked Mr. George to
stop at home, and take an interest in the estate, for he was always adding something to the property, and his heart and mind
were wrapped up in it, as you may say. Folks might call him a
miser, but it was not money he cared for; it was land, and to
add to the importance of the family, and to bring the estate
back to what it had been when this house was built. Now Mr.
George didn't care about staying at home. It was a lazy, sleepy
kind of life, he said, and he had set his heart upon going into
the army. The squire gave way at last, and bought Mr. George
a commission, but it was in a foot regiment, and that went
rather against the grain with the young gentleman, for he
wanted to go into the cavalry. So they didn't part quite so cordial like as they might have done when Mr. George joined his
regiment and went out to India."

" You were here at the time. I suppose ?"

" Lord love you, sir, I was almost born here. My mother was
housekeeper before me. She was the widow of a tradesman in
Truro, very respectably connected. Mrs. Penwyn, the squire's
lady, took me for her own maid when I was only sixteen years
of age, and I nursed her all through her last illness twelve years
afterward, and when my poor mother died I succeeded her as
housekeeper, and I look forward to dying in the same room
where she died, and where I've slept for the last twenty years,
when my own time comes, please God."

" So the squire and his eldest son parted bad friends ?"

" Not exactly bad friends, sir, but there was a coolness between them, anybody could see that. Mr. George—or the captain, as we used generally to call him after he went into the
army—hadn't been gone a twelvemonth before there was a quarrel between the squire and his second son, Mr. Balfour, on account of the young gentleman marrying beneath him, according
to his father's ideas. The lady was a brewer's daughter, and
the squire said Mr. Balfour was the first Penwyn who had ever
degraded himself by marrying trade. Mr. Balfour was not
much above twenty at the time, but he took a high hand about
the matter, and never came to Penwyn Manor after his marriage."

" How was it that the eldest son never married ?" asked
Humphrey.

" Ah, sir, thereby hangs a tale, as the saying is. Mr. George came home from India after he'd been away about ten years, and had distinguished himself by his good conduct and his courage, people told me, who had read his name in the papers during the war. He looked handsomer than ever, I thought, when he came home, though he was browned by the sun. And he was just as kind and pleasant in his manner as he had been when he was a lad. Well, sir, the squire seemed delighted to have him back again, and made a great deal of him. They were always together about the place, and the squire would lean on his son's arm sometimes when he had walked a long way, and was a trifle tired. It was the first time any one had ever seen him accept anybody's support. They used to sit over their wine together of an evening, talking and laughing, and as happy as father and son could be together. All of us—we were all old servants—felt pleased to see it, for we were all fond of Mr. George, and looked to him as our master in days to come."

"And pray how long did this pleasant state of things endure?"

" Two or three months, sir; and then all at once we saw a cloud. Mr. George began to go out shooting early in the morning—it was the autumn season just then—and seldom came home till dark; and the squire seemed silent and grumpy of an evening. None of us could guess what it all meant, for we had heard no high words between the two gentlemen, till all at once, by some roundabout way which I can't call to mind now, the mystery came out. There was an elderly gentleman living at Morgrave Park, a fine old place on the other side of Penwyn village, with an only daughter, an heiress, and very much thought of. Mr. Morgrave and his daughter had been over to luncheon two or three times since Mr. George came home, and he and the squire had dined at Morgrave Park more than once; and I suppose Miss Morgrave and our Mr. George had met at other places, for they seemed quite friendly and intimate. She was a handsome young lady, but rather masculine in her ways —very fond of dogs and horses, and such like, and riding to hounds all the season through. But whatever she did was right, according to people's notions, on account of her being an heiress."

"And George Penwyn had fallen in love with this dashing young lady?"

"Not a bit of it, sir. It came to our knowledge somehow that the squire wanted Mr. George to marry her, and had some reason to believe that the young lady would say ' yes' if he asked her. But Mr. George didn't like her. She wasn't his style, he said, at which the squire was desperately angry. ' Join Penwyn and Morgrave, and you'll have the finest estate in the county,' he said—' an estate fit for a nobleman; a finer property than the Penwyns owned in the days of James the First.' Mr. George wouldn't listen. ' I see what it is,' the squire cried, in a rage; ' you want to disgrace me by some low marriage, to marry a shop-keeper's daughter, like your brother Balfour. But, by heavens! if you do, I'll alter my will and leave the estate away from my race. It didn't matter so much in Balfour's case; neither he nor his are ever likely to be masters here; but I won't stand disobedience in this matter from you. I won't have a pack of kennel-born mongrels rioting here when I'm moldering in my grave.'"

"What a sweet old gentleman!"

"Mr. George swore that he had no thought of making a low marriage; no thought of marrying at all yet awhile. He was happy enough. as he was, he said; but he wouldn't marry a woman he didn't like, even to please his father. So they went on pretty quietly together for a little while after this, the squire grumpy. but not saying much. And then Mr. George went up to London, and from there he went to join his regiment in Ireland, where they were stationed after they came from India, and he was about at different places for two or three years, during which time Miss Morgrave got married to a nobleman, much to the squire's vexation. But I'm afraid I'm tiring you, sir, with such a long story."

"Not at all. I like to hear it."

"Well, Mr. George came back one summer. He was home on leave for a little before he went on foreign service, and he and the squire were pretty friendly again. It was a very hot summer, and Mr. George used to spend most of his time out-of-doors, fishing or idling away the days somehow. The squire had a bad attack of gout that year, and was kept pretty close in his room. You couldn't expect a young man to sit in-doors all day, of course, but I've often wondered what Master George could find to amuse him among these solitary hills of ours, or down among the rocks by the sea. He staid all through the summer, however, and seemed happy enough, and in the autumn he went away to join his regiment, which was ordered off to Canada. I was thankful to remember afterward that he and the squire parted good friends."

"Why?" asked Humphrey.

"Because they were never to meet again. Mr. George was killed in a fight with the savages six months after he went away. I remember the letter coming that brought the news one fine spring evening. The squire was standing in this hall, just by that window, when Miles, the old butler, gave him the letter. He just read the beginning of it, and fell down as if he had been struck dead. It was his first stroke of apoplexy, and he was never quite the same afterward, though he was a wonderful old gentleman to the last."

CHAPTER XIX.
OVER THE HILLS.

THE old housekeeper's eyes were dim as she finished her story of the heir of Penwyn.

"He was the best of all," she said. "Mr. Balfour we saw very little of after he grew up, being the first to marry and leave home; Mr. James was a kind, easy-going young fellow enough; but Mr. George was everybody's favorite, and there

wasn't a dry eye among us when the squire called us together,
after his illness, and told us how his son had died. 'He died like
a gentleman, upholding the honor of his queen and his country—
and Penwyn,' said the master, without a tremble in his voice,
though it was feebler than before the stroke. 'And I am proud
to think of him lying in his far-off grave, and if I were not so
old I would go over the sea to kneel beside my poor boy's resting-place before I die. He displeased me once, but we are good
friends now, and there will be no cloud between us when we
meet in another world.' "

Here Mrs. Darvis was fairly overcome, much to the astonishment of the girl Elspeth, whose uncanny black eyes regarded
her with a scornful wonder. Humphrey noticed that look.

"Sweet child!" he said to himself. "What a charming helpmeet you will make for some honest peasant in days to come,
with your amiable disposition!"

He had taken his time looking at the old house and listening
to the housekeeper's story. The sun was low, and he had yet
to find a lodging for the night. He had walked far since morning, and was not disposed to retrace his steps to the nearest
town, a place called Seacomb, consisting of one long straggling
street, a market-place, parish church, lock-up, and five dissenting chapels of various denominations. This Seacomb was a
good nine miles from Penwyn Manor.

"Perhaps you'd like to see the young squire's portrait?" said
Mrs. Darvis, when she had dried her tears of tribute to the dead.

"The young squire?"

"Mr. George. We used to call him the young squire sometimes."

"Yes, I should like to have a look at the poor fellow, now
you've told me his history."

"It hangs in the old squire's study. It's a bit of a room, and
I forgot to show it to you just now."

Humphrey followed her across the hall to a small door in a
corner, deeply recessed and low, but solid enough to have
guarded the Tolbooth, one would suppose. It opened into a
narrow room, with one window looking toward the sea. The
wainscot was almost black with age, the furniture old walnut-
wood of the same time-darkened hue. There were a couple of
heavy old bureaus, brass-handled and brass-clamped, a ponderous writing-desk, and one capacious arm-chair, covered with
black leather. The high narrow chimney-piece was in an angle
of the room, and above this, inclining forward, hung the portrait of George Penwyn.

It was a kit-cat picture of a lad in undress uniform, the face
a long oval, fair of complexion, and somewhat feminine in
delicacy of feature, the eyes dark blue. The rest of the features,
though sufficiently regular, were commonplace enough; but the
eyes, beautiful alike in shape and color, impressed Humphrey
Clissold. They were eyes which might have haunted the fancy
of girlhood with the dream of an ideal lover—eyes in whose
somewhat melancholy sweetness a poet would have read some
strange life-history. The hair, a pale auburn, hung in a loosely

waving mass over the high narrow brow, and helped to give a picturesque cast to the patrician-looking head.

"A nice face!" said Humphrey, critically. "There is a little look of my poor friend James Penwyn, but not much. Poor Jim had a gayer, brighter expression, and had not those fine blue-gray eyes. I fancy Churchill Penwyn must be a plain likeness of his Uncle George—not so handsome, but more intellectual-looking."

"Yes, sir," assented Mrs. Darvis. "The present squire is something like his uncle, but there's a harder look in his face. All his features seem cut out sharper; and then his eyes are quite different. Mr. George had his mother's eyes. She was a Trevillian, and one of the handsomest women in Cornwall."

"I've seen a face somewhere which that picture reminds me of, but I haven't the faintest notion where," said Humphrey. "In another picture perhaps. Half one's memories of faces are derived from pictures, and they flash across the mind suddenly like a recollection from another world. However, I mustn't stand prosing here while the sun goes down yonder. I have to find a lodging before nightfall. What is the nearest place, village or farm house, where I can get a bed, do you think, Mrs. Darvis?"

"There's the Bell in Penwyn village."

"No good. I've tried there already. The landlady's married daughter is home on a visit, and they haven't a bed to give me for love or money."

Mrs. Darvis lapsed into meditation.

"The nearest farm-house is Trevanard's, at Borcel End. They might give you a bed there, for the place is large enough for a barracks, but they are not the most obliging people in the world, and they are too well off to care about the money you may pay them."

"How far is Borcel End?"

"Between two and three miles."

"Then I'll try my luck there, Mrs. Darvis," said Humphrey, cheerily. "It lies between that and sleeping under the open sky."

"I wish I could offer you a bed, sir; but in my position——"

"As custodian, such an offer would be a breach of good faith to your employers. I quite understand that, Mrs. Darvis. I come here as a stranger to you, and I thank you kindly for having been so obliging as to show me the house."

He dropped a couple of half-crowns into her hand as he spoke, but these Mrs. Darvis rejected most decidedly.

"Ours has never been what you can call a show-place, sir, and I've never looked for that kind of a perquisite."

"Come, young one," said Humphrey, after taking leave of the friendly old housekeeper, "you can put me into the right road to Trevanard's, and you shall have one of these for your reward."

Elspeth's black eyes watched the rejection of the half-crowns with unmistakable greed. Her sharp face brightened at Humphrey's promise.

"I'll show you the way, sir," she said; "I know every step of it."

"Yes, the lass is always roaming about like a wild creature over the hills and down by the sea," said Mrs. Darvis, with a disapproving air. "I don't think she knows how to read or write, or has as much Christian knowledge as the old jackdaw in the servants' hall."

"I know things that are better than reading and writing," said Elspeth, with a grin.

"What kind of things may those be?" asked Humphrey.

"Things that other people don't know."

"Well, my lass, I won't trouble you by sounding the obscure depths of your wisdom. I only want the straightest road to Trevanard's farm. He is a tenant of this estate, I suppose, Mrs. Darvis."

"Yes, sir. Michael Trevanard's father was a tenant of the old squire's before my time. Old Mrs. Trevanard is still living, though stone-blind, and hardly right in her head, I believe."

They had reached the lobby door by this time, the chief hall-door being kept religiously bolted and barred during the absence of the family.

"I shall come and see you again, Mrs. Darvis, most likely, before I leave this part of the country," said Humphrey, as he crossed the threshold. "Good-evening."

"You'll be welcome at any time, sir. Good-evening."

Elspeth led the way across the lawn with a step so light and swift that it was as much as Humphrey could do to keep pace with her, tired as he was after a long day afoot. He followed her into the pine wood. The trees were not thickly planted, but they were old and fine, and their dense foliage looked inky black against the primrose-colored sky. A narrow foot-path wound among the tall black trunks only a few yards from the edge of the cliff, which was poorly guarded by a roughly fashioned timber railing, the stakes wide apart. The vast Atlantic lay below them, a translucent green in the clear evening light, melting into purple far away on the horizon.

Humphrey paused to look back at Penwyn Manor-house, the grave, substantial old dwelling-house which had seen so little change since the days of the Tudors. High gable ends; latticed windows gleaming in the last rays of the setting sun; stone walls moss-darkened and ivy-shrouded; massive porch with deep recesses, and room enough for a small congregation; mighty chimney stacks, and quaint old iron weather-cock, with a marvelous specimen of the ornithological race pointing its beak due west.

"Poor old James, what good days we might have had here!" sighed Humphrey, as he looked back at the fair domain. It seemed a place saved out of the good old world, and was very pleasant to contemplate after the gimcrack palaces of the age we live in, in which all that architecture can conjure from the splendors of the past is more or less disfigured by the tinsel of the present.

"Dear old James! to think that he wanted to marry that poor

little actress girl, and bring her to reign down here in the glow
and glory of those stained glass windows, gorgeous with the
armorial devices of a line of county families—innocent, simple-
hearted lad, wandering about like a prince in a fairy tale, ready
to fall in love with the first pretty girl he saw by the roadside,
and to take her back to his kingdom!"

"If you want to see Trevanard's farm before dark, you must
come on, sir," said Elspeth.

Humphrey took the hint, and followed at his briskest pace.
They were soon out of the pine grove, which they left by a little wooden gate, and on the wide wild hills where the distant
sheep-bell had an eerie sound in the still evening air.

Even the gables of the Manor-house disappeared presently,
as they went down a dip in the hills. Far off in the green hollow Humphrey saw some white buildings—scattered untidily
near a patch of water, which reflected that saffron-hued evening
sky.

"That's Trevanard's," said Elspeth, pointing to this spot.

"I thought as much," said Humphrey. "Then you need go
no further. You've fairly earned your fee."

He gave her the half crown. The girl turned the coin over
with a delighted look before she put it in her pocket.

"I'll go to Borcel End with you," she said. "I'd as lief be on
the hills as at home—sooner—for grandmother is not overpleas-
ant company."

"But you'd better go back now, my girl, or it'll be dark long
before you reach home."

Elspeth laughed, a queer impish cachinnation, which made Mr.
Clissold feel rather uncomfortable.

"You don't suppose I'm afraid of the dark?" she said, in her
shrill young voice, so young and yet so old in tone. "I know
every star in the sky. Besides, it's never dark at this time of
year. I'll go on to Borcel End with you. Maybe you mayn't
get accommodated there, and then I can show you a near way
across the hills to Penwyn village. You might get shelter at
one of the cottages anyhow."

"Upon my word you are very obliging," said Humphrey,
surprised by this show of benevolence upon the damsel's part.

"Do you know anything about this Borcel End?" he asked,
presently, when they were going down into the valley.

"I've never been inside it," answered Elspeth, glibly, more
communicative now than she had been an hour or two ago when
Clissold questioned her about the house of Penwyn. "Mrs.
Trevanard isn't one to encourage a poor girl like me about her
place. She's a rare hard one, they say, and would pinch and
scrape for a sixpence, yet dresses fine on Sundays, and lives well.
There's always good eating and drinking at Borcel End, folks
say. I've heard tell as it was a gentleman's house once, before
old Squire Penwyn bought it, and that there was a fine park
round the house. There's plenty of trees now, and a garden that
has all gone to ruin. The gentleman that owned Borcel spent
all his money, people say, and old Squire Penwyn bought the
place cheap, and turned it into a farm, and it's been in the hands

of the Trevanards ever since, and they're rich enough to buy the place three times over, people say, if Squire Penwyn would sell it."

"I don't suppose I shall get a very warm welcome if this Mrs. Trevanard is such a disagreeable person," said Humphrey, beginning to feel doubtful as to the wisdom of asking hospitality at Borcel End.

"Oh! I don't know about that. She's civil enough to gentle-folks, I've heard say. It's only her servants and such·like she's so stiff with. You can but try."

They were at the farm by this time. The old house stood before them—a broad stretch of greensward in front of it, with a pool of brackish·looking water in the middle, on which several broods of juvenile ducks were swimming gayly.

The house was large, the walls rough-cast, with massive timber frame-work. There was a roomy central porch, also of plaster and timber, and this and a projecting wing at each end of the house gave a certain importance to the building. Some relics of its ancient gentility still remained to show that Borcel End had not always been the house of a tenant-farmer. A coat of arms roughly cut on a stone tablet over the front-door testified to its former owner's pride of birth, and the quadrangular range of stables, stone-built, and more important than the house, indicated those sporting tastes which might have helped to dissipate the fortunes of a banished and half-forgotten race. But Borcel End, in its brightest day, had never been such a mansion as the old Tudor Manor-house of Penwyn. There was a homeliness in the architecture which aspired to neither dignity nor beauty—low ceilings, square latticed windows, dormers in the roof, and heavy chimney-stacks. The only beauty which the place could have possessed at its best was the charm of rusticity—an honest, simple, English home. To-day, however, Borcel End was no longer at its best. The stone quadrangle, where the finest hunting stud in Cornwall had once been lodged, was now a straw-yard for cattle; one side of the house was overshadowed by a huge barn, built of the *debris* of the park wall; a colony of jovial pigs disported themselves in a small inclosure which had once been a maze. A remnant of hedge-row, densest yew, still marked the boundary of this ancient pleasance, but all the rest had vanished beneath the cloven hoof of the unclean animal.

Though the farmyard showed on every side the tokens of agricultural prosperity, the house itself had a neglected air. The plaster walls, green and weather-stained, presented the curious blended hues of a Stilton cheese in prime condition; the timber seemed perishing for want of a good coat of paint. Poultry were pecking about close under the latticed windows, and even in the porch, and a vagabond pigling was thrusting his black nose in among the roots of one solitary rose-bush which still lingered on the barren turf. Borcel End, seen in this fading light, was hardly a homestead to attract the traveler.

"I don't think much of your Borcel End," said Humphrey, with a disparaging air. "However, here goes for a fair trial of Western hospitality."

CHAPTER XX.
BORCEL END.

MR. CLISSOLD entered the porch, scattering the affrighted fowls right and left. As they sped cackling away, the house-door, which had stood ajar, was opened wider by a middle-aged woman, who looked at the intruder frowningly. "We never buy anything of peddlers," she said, sharply. "It's no use coming here."

"I'm not a peddler, and I haven't anything to sell. I am going through Cornwall on a walking tour, and want to find a place where I could stop for a week or so and look about the country. I am prepared to pay a fair price for a clean homely lodging. The housekeeper at Penwyn Manor told me to try here."

"Then she sent you on a fool's errand," replied the woman; "we don't take lodgers."

"Not as a rule, perhaps; but you might strain a point in my favor, I dare say."

Humphrey Clissold had a pleasant voice and a pleasant smile. Mrs. Trevanard looked at him doubtfully, softened in spite of herself by his manner. And then no Trevanard was ever above earning an honest penny. They had not grown rich by refusing chances of small profits.

"Come, mother," cried a cheery voice from within, while she was hesitating, "you can ask the gentleman to come in and sit down a bit, anyhow. That won't make nor break us."

"You can walk in and sit down, sir, if you like," said Mrs. Trevanard, with a somewhat unwilling air.

Humphrey crossed the threshold and found himself in a large, stone-paved room which had once been the hall, and was now half kitchen, half living-room. The staircase, with its clumsy, black painted balustrades, shaped like gouty legs, occupied one side of the room; on the other yawned the mighty chimney, with a settle on each side of the wide hearth, a cozy retreat on winter's nights. The glow of the fire had a comfortable look even on this midsummer evening.

A young man—tall, stalwart, good-looking, clad in a suit of velveteen which gave him something the air of a gamekeeper—stood near the hearth, cleaning a gun. He it was who had spoken just now—Martin Trevanard, the only son of the house, and about the only living creature who had any influence with his mother. Pride ruled her, religion or bigotry had power over her, gold was the strongest influence of all; but of all the mass of humanity there was but one unit she cared for after herself, and that one was Martin.

"Sit down and make yourself at home, sir," said the young man heartily. "You've walked far, I dare say."

"I have," answered Humphrey, "but I don't want to rest anywhere until I am sure that I can get a night's shelter. There was no room for me at the Bell at Penwyn, but I left my knapsack there, thinking I should be forced to go back to

the village anyhow. It was an after-thought coming on
here. Oh, by the way, there's a girl outside, the lodge-keeper's
daughter, who has been my guide so far, and wants to know
my fate before she goes home. What can you do with me,
Mrs. Trevanard? I'm not particular. Give me a truss of clean
hay in one of your barns if you're afraid to have me in the
house."

"Don't be ill-natured, old lady," said the young man; "the
gentleman is a gentleman. One can see that with half an
eye."

"That's all very well, Martin; but what will your father
say to our taking in a stranger without so much as knowing his
name?"

"My name is Humphrey Clissold," said the applicant, taking
a card out of his pocket-book and throwing it on the polished
beech-wood table, the only handsome piece of furniture in the
room—a massive, oblong table big enough for twelve or fourteen people to sit at. "There are my name and address. And
so far as payment in advance goes"—he put a sovereign down
beside the card—"there's for my night's accommodation and
refreshment."

"Put your money in your pocket, sir. You're a friend of
Mr. Penwyn's, I suppose?" asked Mrs. Trevanard, still doubtful.

"I know the present Mr. Penwyn, but I cannot call myself
his friend. The poor young fellow who was murdered, James
Penwyn, was my nearest and dearest friend, my adopted
brother."

"Let the gentleman stop, mother. We've rooms enough and
to spare in this gloomy old barrack. A fresh face always
brightens us up a little, and it's nice to hear how the world goes
on. Father's always satisfied when you are. You can put the
gentleman in that old room at the end of the corridor. You
needn't be frightened, sir; there are no ghosts at Borcel End,"
added Martin Trevanard, laughing.   •

His mother still hesitated, but after a pause she said. "Very
well, sir. You can stop to-night, and as long as you please afterward at a fair price—say a guinea a week for eating, drinking, and sleeping, and a trifle for the servant when you go
away."

Even in consenting the woman seemed to have a lingering
reluctance, as if she were giving assent to something which she
felt should have been refused.

"Your terms are moderation itself, madam, and I thank you.
I'll send away my small guide."

He went out to the porch, where Elspeth sat waiting—no
doubt a listener to the conversation. Humphrey rewarded her
devotion with an extra sixpence, and dismissed her. Away she
sped through the gathering gloom, light of foot as a young
fawn. Humphrey felt considerably relieved by the comfortable
adjustment of the lodging question. He seated himself in an
arm-chair by the hearth, and stretched out his legs in the ruddy
glow with a blissful sense of repose.

"Is there such a thing as a lad about the place who would go to the Bell at Penwyn to fetch my knapsack, for a consideration?" he asked.

There was a cow-boy who would perform that service, it seemed. Martin went out himself to look for the rustic Mercury.

"He's a good-natured lad, my son," said Mrs. Trevanard, "but full of fancies. That comes of idleness, and too much education, his father says. His grandmother yonder never learned to read or write, and 'twas she and her husband made Borcel End what it is."

Following the turn of Mrs. Trevanard's head, Humphrey perceived that an object which in the obscurity of the room he had taken for a piece of furniture was in reality a piece of humanity —a very old woman, dressed in dark garments, with only a narrow white border peeping from under a cowl-shaped black silk cap, a dingy red handkerchief pinned across her shoulders, and two bony hands, whose shriveled fingers moved with a mechanical regularity in the process of stocking-knitting.

- "Ay," said a quivering voice, "I can't read or write—that's to say, I couldn't even when I had my sight—but between us Michael and I made Borcel what it is. Young people don't understand the old ways—they have servants to wait upon 'em, and play the harpsicord; but little good comes of it."

"Is she blind?" asked Humphrey of the younger Mrs. Trevanard, in a whisper.

The old woman's quick ear caught the question.

"Stone-blind, sir, for the last eighteen years. But the Lord has been kind to me. I've a comfortable home and kind children, and they don't turn me out of doors, though I'm such a useless creature."

"Why, mother, you know the place is your own for life," said Bridget Trevanard, sharply. "Michael's father left it so in his will."

"You might turn me out for all that. Who'd see an old blind woman righted?"

"A gloomy figure in that dark corner beyond the glow of the fire! Humphrey felt that the room was less comfortable somehow since he had discovered the presence of this old woman, with her sightless orbs and never-resting fingers, long and lean, weaving her endless web gloomy as Clotho herself.

A plump, ruddy-cheeked maid-servant came bustling in with preparations for supper, making an agreeable diversion after this sad little episode. She lighted a pair of tall tailow candles in tall brass candlesticks, which feebly illumined the large low room. The wainscoted walls were blackened by smoke and time, and from the cross-beams that sustained the low ceiling hung a grove of hams, while flitches of bacon adorned the corners, where there was less need of headway. Every object in the room belonged to the useful rather than the beautiful. Yet there was something pleasant to Humphrey's unaccustomed eye in the homely old-world comfort of the place.

He took advantage of the light to steal a glance at the face of

his hostess. as she helped the servant to lay the cloth and place
the viands on the table. Bridget Trevanard was about fifty
years of age, but there were few wrinkles on the square brow or
about the eyes and mouth. She was tall, buxom, and broad-
shouldered; a woman who looked as if she had few feminine
weaknesses, either moral or physical. The muscular arm and
broad, open chest betokened an almost virile strength. Her skin
was bright and clear, her nose broad and thick, but fairly mod-
eled of its kind, her under lip full and firm, as if wrought
in iron, the upper lip long, straight, and thin. Her eyes
were dark brown, bright and hard, with that sharp, penetrating
look which is popularly supposed to see through deal boards and
even stone walls on occasion. So, at least, thought the servants at Borcel End.

A model farmer's wife this Mrs. Trevanard, a severe mistress,
yet not unjust or unkind, a proud woman, and in her own particular creed something of a zealot: a woman who loved money,
not so much for its own sake, as because it served the only ambition she had ever cherished, namely, to be more respectable
than her neighbors. Wealth went a long way toward this superior respectability, therefore did Mrs. Trevanard toil and spin,
and never cease from labor in the pursuit of gain. She was the
motive power of Borcel End. Her superlative energy kept
Michael Trevanard, a somewhat lazy man by nature, a patient
slave at the mill. Martin was the only creature at Borcel who
escaped her influence. For him life meant the indulgence of
his own fancies, with just so much work as gave him an appetite for his meals. He would drive the wagon to the mill. or
superintend the men at hay-making and harvest. He rather
liked attending market, and was a good hand to a bargain; but
to the patient drudgery of every-day cares young Trevanard
had a rooted objection. He was g   -looking. good-natured,
walked well, sang well, whistled bett.. than any other man in
the district, and was a general favorite. People said that the
good blood of the old Trevanards showed in young Martin.

CHAPTER XXI.
"'HE COMETH NOT,' SHE SAID."

· WHEN the supper-table was ready, the servant-girl ran to the
porch and rang a large bell, which was kept under one of the
benches—a bell that pealed out shrilly over the silent fields.
This summons brought home Michael Trevanard, who appeared
about five minutes after the peal, pulling down his shirt sleeves.
and carrying his coat over his arm. while some stray wisps of
hay which hung about his hair and clothes indicated that he
had but that moment left the yard where they were building a
huge stack, which Humphrey had seen looming large through
the dusk as he approached Borcel.

"We've stacked the fourteen-acre piece, mother," said the
farmer, as he pulled on his coat, "and a fine stack it is, too, as
sweet as a hazel-nut. No fear of mildew. this year. And now
I'll give myself a wash——"

He stopped, surprised at beholding a stranger standing by his hearth. Humphrey had risen to receive the master of the house.

Martin explained the traveler's presence.

" We've taken to lodging-letting since you've been out, father," he said, in his easy way. " This gentleman wants to stay here and to look about the country round for a few days, and as mother thought he'd be company for me, and knew you wouldn't have any objection, she said yes. Mr. Clissold, that's the gentleman's name, is a friend of the family up yonder." An upward jerk of Martin's head indicated the Manor-house.

" Any friend of the squire's, or any one your mother thinks proper to accommodate, my lad; she's missus here," answered Mr. Trevanard. " You're kindly welcome, sir."

The farmer went out to some back region, whence was immediately heard an energetic pumping and plashing, and a noise as of a horse being rubbed down, after which Mr. Trevanard reappeared, lobster-like of complexion, and breathing hard after his rapid exertions.

He was a fine-looking man, with a face which might fairly be supposed to show the blood of the Trevanards, for the features were of a patrician type, and the broad open brow inspired at once respect and confidence. That candid countenance belonged to a man too incapable of deceit to be capable of suspicion—a man whom an artful child might cheat with impunity—a man who could never have grown rich unaided.

Mr. and Mrs. Trevanard, their son, and their guest sat down to supper without delay; but the old blind mother still kept her seat in the shadowy corner, and ate her supper apart. It consisted only of a basin of broth, sprinkled with chopped parsley, in which the old woman sipped slowly, while the rest were eating their substantial meal.

Humphrey had eaten nothing since noon, and did no scant justice to the lordly round of corned beef and home-cured chine, nor to the freshly gathered lettuces, or even the gooseberry pie and clotted cream. He and Martin talked all supper-time, while the house-mother carved, and the farmer abandoned himself to the pleasures of the table, and drank strong cider with easy enjoyment after the toilsome day.

" There's no place like a hay field for making a man thirsty," he said, by way of apology, after one of his deep draughts; " and I can't drink the cat-lap mother sends to the men."

Martin talked of field-sports and boating. He had a little craft of his own, four or five tons burden, and was passionately fond of the water. By and by the conversation drifted round to the Squire of Penwyn.

" He rides well," said Martin; " but I don't believe he's over-fond of hunting, though he subscribes handsomely to the hounds. I never knew such a fellow for doing everything liberally. He's bound to be popular, for he's the best master they ever had at the Manor."

" And is he popular?" asked Humphrey.

"Well, I hardly know what to say about that. I only know
that he ought to be. People are so hard to please. There are
some say they liked the old squire best, though he wasn't half so
generous, and didn't keep any company worth speaking of. He
had a knack of talking to people and making himself one of
them that went a long way. And then some people remember
Mr. George, and seem to have a notion that this man is an in-
terloper. He oughtn't to have come into the property, they say.
Providence never could have meant the son of the youngest son
to have Penwyn. They're as full of fancies as an egg is full of
meat in our parts."

"So it seems. Mrs. Penwyn is liked, I suppose?"

"Yes; she made friends with the poor people in no time. And
then she's a great beauty; people go miles to see her when she
rides to cover with her husband. There's a sister, too, still
prettier, to my mind."

Martin promised to show his new friend all that was worth
seeing for twenty miles round Borcel. He would have the dog-
cart ready early next morning, directly after breakfast, in fact,
and six o'clock was breakfast-time at the farm. Humphrey was
delighted with the friendly young fellow, and thought that he
had stumbled upon a very agreeable household.

Mrs. Trevanard was somewhat stern and repellent in manner,
no doubt, but she was not absolutely uncivil, and Mr. Clissold
felt that he should be able to get on with her pretty well.

She had said grace before meat, and she stopped the two young
men in their talk presently, and offered a thanksgiving after the
meal. It was a long grace, Methodistical in tone, with an allusion to Esau's mess of pottage, which was brought in as a dreadful example of gluttony.

After this ceremonial Mrs. Trevanard went up-stairs to superintend the preparation of the stranger's apartment. The grandmother vanished at the same time, spirited away by the serving-
wench, who led her out by a little door that opened near her
corner, and the three men drew round the hearth, lighted their
pipes, and smoked and talked in a very friendly fashion for the
next half hour or so. They were talking merrily enough when
Mrs. Trevanard came down-stairs again, candle in hand. She
had taken out one of the old silver candlesticks, which had been
part of her dower, in order to impress the visitor with the proper
notion of her respectability.

"Your room's ready, Mr. Clissold," she said, "and here's your
bedroom candle."

Humphrey took the hint, and bade his new friends good-
night. He followed Mrs. Trevanard up the broad, bulky old
staircase, and to the end of the corridor. The room into which
she led him was large, and had once been handsome, but some
barbarian had painted the oak paneling pink, and the wood-
carving over the fire-place had been defaced by the industrious
knives of several generations of school-boys: there was a good
deal of broken glass in the lattices, and a general air of dilapitude.
A fire burned briskly in the wide basket-shaped grate, and,

though it brightened the room, made these traces of decay all the more visible.

"It's a room we never use," said Mrs. Trevanard, "so we haven't cared to spend money upon it. There's always enough money wanted for repairs, and we haven't need to waste any upon fanciful improvements. The place is dry enough, for I take care to open the windows on sunny days, and there's nothing better than air and sun to keep a room dry. I had a fire lighted to-night for cheerfulness' sake."

"You are very kind," replied Humphrey, pleased to see his knapsack on a chair by the bed, "and the room will do admirably. It looks the pink of cleanliness."

"I don't harbor dirt, even in unused rooms," answered Mrs. Trevanard. "It needs a mistress' eye to keep away cobwebs and vermin, but I've never spared myself trouble that way. Good-night, sir."

"Good-night, Mrs. Trevanard. By the way, you've no ghosts here, I think your son said."

"I hope both you and he know better than to believe any such rubbish, sir."

"Of course, only this room looks the very picture of a haunted chamber, and if I were capable of believing in ghosts I should certainly lie awake on the look-out for one to-night."

"Those whose faith is surely grounded have no such fancies, sir," replied Mrs. Trevanard, severely, and closed the door without another word.

"The room looks haunted, for all that," muttered Humphrey, and then involuntarily repeated those famous lines of Hood's:

> "O'er all there hung a shadow and a fear;
> A sense of mystery the spirit daunted,
> And said as plain as whisper in the ear,
> The place is haunted."

The bedstead was a four-poster, with tall, spirally twisted posts, and some dark drapery, which looked shrunken with age, and too small for the wooden framework. There was an old-fashioned press or wardrobe of black wood, whose polished surface reflected the fire-light. A corner wash-hand stand of more modern make, and a clumsy-looking chest of drawers between the windows, surmounted by a cracked looking-glass, completed the furniture of the room. The boards were uncarpeted, and showed knots and dark patches in the worm-eaten wood, which a morbid fancy might have taken for blood stains.

"Not a cheerful-looking room by any means, even with the aid of that blazing fire," thought Humphrey.

He opened one of the casements and looked out. The night air was soft and balmy, perfumed with odors of clover and the newly stacked hay. The Atlantic lay before him, shining under the great red moon, which had but just risen; a pleasanter prospect this than the bare walls of faded dirty pink, the black clothes-press, and funereal four-poster.

Humphrey lingered at the window, his arms folded on the broad ledge, his thoughts wandering idly—wandering back to last year and the moonlight that had shone upon the cathedral towers of Eborsham, the garden of the Waterfowl Inn, and the winding river.

"Poor James!" he mused; "how happy that light-hearted fellow might have been at Penwyn Manor—how happy, and how popular! He would have had the knack of pleasing people with that frank, easy kindness of his, and would have made friends of half the county. And if he had married that actress girl? A folly, no doubt, but who knows if all might not have ended happily? There was nothing vulgar or low about that girl—indeed, she had the air of one of nature's gentlewomen. It would have been a little difficult for her to learn all the duties of a chatelaine, perhaps—how to order a dinner and whom to invite, the laws of precedence, the science of morning calls. But if James loved her, and chose her from all other women for his wife, why should he not have been happy with her? I was a fool to oppose his fancy—a worse fool for leaving him. He might be alive now, perhaps, but for that wild-goose journey of mine."

Here his thoughts took another turn. They went back to that train of circumstances which had brought about his absence from Eborsham on the night of James Penwyn's murder.

It was past midnight when Humphrey Clissold roused himself from that long reverie, and prepared for peaceful slumber in the funereal bed. His fire had burned low by this time, and the red glow of the expiring embers was drowned in the full splendor of the risen moon, whose light silvered the bare boards, and brought into strong relief those stains and blotches upon the wood which looked so like the traces of ancient murder. The bed was luxurious, for there was no stint of feathers at Borcel End; yet Humphrey wooed the god of sleep in vain. He began to think that there must be some plumage of game birds mingled with the stuffing of his couch, and that, soft and deep as it was, this was one of those beds upon which a man could neither sleep nor die comfortably.

"I ought to be tired enough to sleep on a harder bed than this, considering the miles I've walked to-day," thought Humphrey.

It may have been that he was overtired, or it may have been that flood of silver light streaming through the diamond panes of yonder lattic; whatever might be the reason of his restlessness, sleep came not to straighten his unquiet limbs, to steep his wandering thoughts in her cool waters of forgetfulness.

He heard a distant clock—in the hall where he had supped, most likely—strike two, and just at this time a gentle drowsiness began to steal over him. He was just falling deep down into some sleepy hollow, soft as a bed of poppies, when his door was opened by a cautious hand, and a light footstep sounded on the floor. He was wide awake in a minute, and without moving from his recumbent position, drew the dark curtain back a little way and looked toward the door. The shadow of the curtain fell upon him as he lay, and the bedstead looked unoccupied.

"The ghost!" he said to himself, with rather an awful feeling. "I knew there must be one in such a room—or perhaps the house is on fire, and some one has come to warn me."

No; that wanderer through the deep of night had evidently no business with Mr. Clissold—nay, was unconscious of, or indifferent to. the fact of his existence. The figure slowly crossed the floor, with a light step, but a little sliding noise as of a foot ill shod, a slipper down at the heel.

It came full in the moonlight presently, between the bedstead and the two windows.

"Ay, verily a ghost," thought Humphrey, with a feeling like ice-cold water circulating slowly through every artery in his body.

Never had he seen, or conceived within his mind, a figure more spectral, yet with a certain wild beauty in its ghastliness. He raised himself in his bed, still keeping well within the shadow of the curtains, and watched the specter with eyes which seemed endowed with a double power of vision in the thrilling intensity of•that moment.

The specter was a woman's form; tall, slender—nay, so wasted that it seemed almost unnaturally tall. The face was death-pale in that solemn light, the eyes large and dark, the hair ebon black, and falling in long loose masses over the white garment, whose folds were straight as those of a winding-sheet. So might the dead risen from a new-made grave have looked.

The figure went straight to one of the casements—that furthest from the bed, and at right angles with it—unfastened the hasp and flung the window wide open. She drew a chair close to the open window, and kneeled upon it, resting her arms on the sill, and leaning out of the window, as if watching for some one to come, thought Humphrey, that frozen blood of his beginning to thaw a little.

"Those actions seem too deliberate and real for a ghost," he told himself. "Phantoms must surely be soundless. Now I heard the slipshod feet upon the floor. I heard the scrooping of the chair. I can see a gentle heaving of the breast under that white shroud. *Ergo* my visitor is not a ghost. Who can she be? Not Mrs. Trevanard assuredly, nor the old blind grandmother, nor the buxom lass who waited on us at supper. I thought those were all the womenkind in the house."

A heavy sigh from that unearthly looking intruder startled him—a sigh so long, so full of anguish, so like the utterance of some lost soul in pain! Difficult not to yield to superstitious fear as he gazed at that kneeling figure. with its long dark hair and delicate profile sharply outlined against the black shadow of the deep-sunk casement.

Again came the sigh, despairing, desolate.

"Oh, my love, my love, why don't you come back to me?" The words broke like a cry of despair from those pale lips. Not loud was the sorrowful appeal, but so full of pain that it touched the listener's heart more deeply than the most passionate burst of louder grief could have done.

"Dear love. you promised, you promised me. How could I have lived if I hadn't thought you would come back?"

Then the tone changed. She was no longer appealing to another, but talking to herself, hurriedly, breathlessly, with ever-increasing agitation.

" Why not to-night? Why shouldn't he come back to-night? He. was always fond of moonlight nights. He promised to be true to me, and stand by me, come what might. No harm should ever come to me. He swore that. swore it with his arms round me, his eyes looking into mine. No man could be false, and yet look as he looked, and speak as he spoke."

Silence for a brief space, and then a sudden cry—a sharp, anguish-stricken cry, as of a broken heart.

" Who said he was dead and gone—dead and gone years ago? The world wouldn't look as bright as it does if he were dead. He loved the moonlight. Could you shine, false moon, if he were dead?" Again a pause; and then, in a slower, more thoughtful tone, as if doubts disturbed that demented brain, " Was it last year he used to come—last year, when we were so happy together—last year, when——"

A sudden burst of tears interrupted the sentence. The woman's face fell forward on her folded arms, and the frail body was shaken by her sobs.

Humphrey Clissold no longer doubted his visitant's humanity. This was real grief. perchance real madness. For a little while he had fancied it a case of somnambulism; but the eyes which he had seen lifted despairingly to that moonlit sky had too much expression for the eyes of a somnambulist.

For a long time—or time that seemed long to Clissold's mind —the woman knelt by the window, now silent, motionless as an inanimate figure, now talking rapidly to herself, anon invoking that absent one whose broken promises were perhaps the cause of her wandering wits. Never had the young man beheld a more piteous spectacle. It was as if one of Wordsworth's most pathetic pastorals were here realized. His heart ached at the sound of those heart-broken sighs. This flesh-and-blood sorrow moved him more deeply than any spectral woe. This was no ghostly revisitant of earth, who acted over agonies dead and gone, but a living, loving woman, who mourned a lost or a faithless lover.

At last, with one farewell look seaward, as if it were along yon moon-lit track across the waves she watched for the return of her lover, this new Hero turned from the casement, closed it carefully and quietly, and then slowly left the room. Humphrey heard that slipshod foot going slowly along the passage until the sound dwindled and died in the distance.

He fancied sleep would have been impossible after such a scene as this; but perhaps that overstrained attention of the last hour had exhausted his wakefulness, for he fell off presently into a sound slumber, from which he was only awakened by a friendly voice outside his door saying, " Six o'clock, Mr. Clissold! If you want the long round I promised you last night, we ought to start at seven."

" All right," answered Humphrey, as gayly as if no uncanny visitor had shortened his slumbers; " I'll be with you in half an hour."

He kept his word, and was down in the hall, or family sitting-room, just in time to hear the noisy old eight-day clock strike the half hour, with a slow and laborious groaning of its inward anatomy, as if fast subsiding into dumbness and decrepitude. Mr. Trevanard had breakfasted an hour ago, and gone forth to his hay-makers. Mrs. Trevanard was busy about the house, but the old blind grandmother sat in her corner plying those never-resting needles, just as she had sat, just as she had knitted, last night, with no more apparent share or interest in the active life around her than the old clock had.

There was a liberal meal ready for the stranger. Last night's round of beef, and a Cornish ham, archetype of hams, adorned the board, but were only intended as a reservè force in case of need, while the breakfast proper consisted of a dish of broiled ham and eggs, and another of trout, caught a hundred yards or so from the house that morning. Home-baked bread, white and brown, a wedge of golden honey-comb, and a plate of straw-berries, counted for nothing.

Both young men did justice to the breakfast, which they ate together, making the best use of the half hour allotted for the meal, and not talking so much as they had done last night at the more leisurely evening repast.

" I hope you slept pretty well," said Martin, when he had taken the edge off a healthy appetite, and was trifling with a slice of cold ham.

" Not quite so well as I ought to have done in so comfortable a bed. My brain was a little overactive, I believe."

" Ah, that's a complaint I don't suffer from. Father says I haven't any brains. I tell him brains don't grow at Borcel End. One year is so like another that we get to be a kind of clock-work, like poor old granny yonder. We get up every morning at the same hour, look out of our windows to see what sort of weather it is, eat and drink, and walk about the farm, and go to bed again, without using our minds at all from the beginning to the end of the business. Father and I brighten up a little on market days, but for the rest of our lives we might just as well be a couple of slow-going machines."

" There is nothing drowsy or mechanical about your mother's nature, I should think, in spite of the quiet life you all lead here."

" No; mother's mind is a candle that would burn to waste in a dark cellar. Her blood isn't poppy-juice, like the Trevanards'. Do you know that my father has never been as far as Plymouth one way, or as far as Penzance the other way, in his life. He has no call to go, he says, so he doesn't go. He squats here upon his land like a toad, and would if his life was to be threescore and ten centuries instead of as many years."

" You would like a different kind of life, I dare say," suggested Humphrey.

The young man's bright eye reminded him of a caged squirrel's —a wild, free-born creature, longing for the liberty of forests and untrodden groves.

" Yes, if I could have chosen my own life, I would have been a soldier, like George Penwyn."

" To die by the hands of savages."

" Yes, they say he had a hard death; that those copper-colored devils scalped him, tied him to a tree, tortured him. His soldiers went mad with revenge, and roasted some of the miscreants alive afterward, I believe, but that wouldn't bring the captain to life again."

" Do you remember him ?"

" Well. He used to come fishing in our water—the very stream that trout came out of this morning. I was a little chap of eight or nine years old when the captain was last home, and used to catch flies for him, and carry his basket many a time, and loaf about with him half the day through; and many a half-crown has he given me, for he was an open-handed fellow always, and one of the handsomest, pleasantest young men I ever remember seeing; when I say young 1 suppose he must have been past thirty at this time, for he was the oldest of the three brothers, and Balfour, the youngest, had been married ever so many years. But here's the trap, and we'd better be off. Goodbye, granny."

The old woman gave a hoarse chuckle of response, marvelously like the internal rumbling of the ancient clock.

" Good-morning, ma'am," said Humphrey, anxious to be civil, but of his salutation the dame took no notice.

The horse, though clumsily built, and not unacquainted with the plow, was a good goer. The two young men had soon left Borcel End behind them, down in its sleepy hollow, and were driving over the fair green hills.

" Now to fathom the mystery of last night's adventure," thought Humphrey, when they were out of sight of Borcel. " I think I can venture to speak pretty freely to this good-natured young man."

He meditated a few minutes, and then began the attack.

" When you asked me at breakfast how I rested last night I didn't give you quite a straightforward answer," he said. " There was a reason for my not getting a full allowance of sleep which I didn't care to speak of till you and I were alone."

" Indeed!" said Martin Trevanard, looking round at him sharply. " What was that ?"

There was a lurking anxiety in that keen glance of scrutiny, Humphrey Clissold thought.

" Some one came to my room in the dead of the night—a woman," said Humphrey Clissold, in answer to that question of Martin Trevanard's. " At first I almost thought she was a ghost. I was never so near yielding to superstitious terror in my life. But I soon discovered my mistake, and that the poor soul was only a living, suffering fellow-creature."

" I am very sorry such a thing should have happened," said Martin, gravely. " She ought to be better taken care of. The person you saw must have been my unfortunate sister."

" Your sister ?" ·

" Yes. She is ten years older than I, and not quite right in
her mind. But she is perfectly harmless—has never in her
life attempted to injure any one—not even herself, poor soul,
though her own existence is dreary enough; and neither my
father nor my mother will consent to send her away to be taken
care of. Our old doctor sees her now and then, and doesn't
call her mad. She is only considered a little weak in her intellect."

" Has she been so from childhood?" asked Humphrey.

" Oh, dear, no. She went to school at Helstone, and was quite
an accomplished young woman, I believe—played the piano, and
painted flowers, and was brought up quite like a young lady;
never put her hand to dairy work, or anything of the kind. She
was a very handsome girl in those days, and father and mother
were uncommonly proud of her. I can just remember her when
she first came from school. I was always hanging about her,
and I used to think she was like a beautiful princess in a fairy
tale. She was very good to me, told me fairy stories, and sung
to me in the twilight. Many a time I've fallen asleep in her lap,
lulled by her sweet voice, when I was a little chap of seven or
eight. There were only us two, and she was very fond of me.
Poor Muriel!"

" What was it brought about such a change in her ?"

" Well, that's a story I never quite got to the bottom of. It's
a sore subject even with father, who's easy enough to deal with
about most things. And as to mother, you have but to mention
Muriel's name to make her look like thunder. Yet she's never
unkind to the poor soul. I know that."

" Does your sister live among you when you are alone?"

" No; she has a little room over granny's, with a little old-
fashioned staircase leading up to it—a room quite cut off from
the rest of the house. You can't reach it except by coming
through granny's bedroom, which is on the ground-floor, you
must understand, on account of the old lady's weak legs. Now
one of poor Muriel's fancies is to roam about the house in the
middle of the night, especially moonlight nights, for the moonlight makes her wakeful. So, as a rule, granny locks her door
of a night. However, I suppose, last night the old lady forgot,
in consequence of the excitement caused by your arrival, and
that's how you happened to have such an uncomfortable night."

" You haven't told me even the little you do know as to the
cause of your sister's state."

" Haven't I? All I know is what my father told me once.
She was crossed in love, it seems—loved some one rather above
her station—and never got over it. That comes of being constant to one's first fancy."

" You say she lives in a room by herself. Does she never have
air or exercise ?"

" Do you imagine us barbarians? Yes, she roams about the
old, neglected gardens just as she pleases, but never goes beyond.
She has a pretty clear notion that it is her beat, poor girl, and
I've never known her to break bounds. Mother fetches her in-
doors at sunset, and gives her her supper, and sees that she's com-

fortable for the night, and tries to keep her clothes decent and tidy, but the poor soul tears them sometimes, when her melancholy fit is upon her."

CHAPTER XXII.
"AND I SHALL BE ALONE UNTIL I DIE."

THE image of that white-robed figure, pallid face, and ebon hair haunted Humphrey Clissold throughout the day, though his day was very pleasant, and Martin Trevanard the most cheerful of companions. They halted at various villages, explored old parish churches, where tarnished and blackened brasses told of mitered abbots and lords of the soil, otherwise unrecorded and forgotten. Clissold was learned in church architecture, and not a gargoyle escaped his keen eye. Martin was pleased to exhibit the interesting features of his native land, and listened deferentially to Humphrey's disquisitions on brasses, fonts, and piscinæ.

They stopped at a way-side inn, lunched heartily on bread and cheese and cider, and were altogether as companionable as young men can well be. Martin had read about half a dozen books since he left Helstone grammar school, but those were of the highest character, and he had them in his heart of hearts. Shakespeare, Pope, and Byron were his poets, and Fielding, Goldsmith, and Scott his only romancers.

From Shakespeare and Scott he had learned history, from Fielding and Goldsmith he had caught the flavor of wit and humor that are dead as the Latin classics. Thus Clissold found, not without a touch of surprise, that the farmer's son was no unworthy companion for a man who had made literature his profession.

On their homeward round they pulled up at Penwyn Church, which stood high and dry on the green hillside, midway between the village and the manor, and looked like a church that had fallen from the sky, so completely was it out of everybody's way. Tradition insisted that in the Middle Ages there had been a village close to the church, but no trace of that vanished settlement remained. There stood the temple, square-towered, with crocketed finials at the four angles of the tower. There lay its ancient slumberous graveyard on the slope of the hill, the dead forever basking in the southern sun, which in this midsummer weather seemed to have power enough to warm them back to life again.

Here Humphrey saw the resting-place of the Penwyns, almost as old as the church itself—a vault so large that these lords of the soil seemed to have a whole crypt to themselves. Very moldy and cold and dark was this last abode of the squires and their race. Here he saw also the parish registers. which contained a concise synopsis of the history of the Penwyns since the Middle Ages—how they had been christened, married, and buried.

"James ought to have been brought down here," said Humphrey, when they were in the churchyard, where the deep soft grass was full of field flowers, and the air of sweet, homely odors: "not in that moldy old crypt with his ancestral dust, but here among this thymey grass, face to face with the sun and the sea, and with the skylark singing above his grave. It would have been ever so much better than Kensal Green."

It was eight o'clock when they drove down into the valley where the old white house and its numerous barns and out-buildings looked like a village nestling in that grassy hollow. The scene looked just the same as last night, when Humphrey Clissold approached it for the first time—the same stillness upon all things, the same low yellow light in the western sky, the same red glow from the hall fire, the same changeless figure of the old grandmother in her high-backed leather-covered arm-chair, half hidden in the shadow of the corner where she sat.

It wanted an hour to supper, and Mr. Trevanard was strug-gling with some accounts at a table by one of the windows, where he had the last of the dying daylight.

"Hope you've had a pleasant day. sir," he said, without looking up from his papers, or relaxing the frown with which he contemplated a long column of figures. "Take a pull of that cider after your drive; it's only just drawn. You might give me a hand with these accounts, Martin; I never was a dab at figures."

"All right, father, we'll soon tot 'em up."

Martin sat down by his father, and took the pen out of his hand. Humphrey refreshed himself with a draught of cider, and then went to the porch.

"I should like to take a look round the place between this and supper-time, if you don't mind, Mr. Trevanard," he said.

"Look where you please, sir; you're free and welcome. You'll hear the supper-bell at nine o'clock."

Humphrey lighted a cigar as he left the porch, and prepared for a contemplative, dreamy stroll, one calm hour of solitude before the day was done.

He avoided the stack-yard, and did not honor the various families of black and white piglings, in divers stages of infancy and adolescence, with his attention. He made a circuit of the pond, and went round to the back of the homestead, where lay that neglected garden which he had seen from the distance. At this midsummer time it was a wilderness of verdure and flowers run wild. Great gray lavender bushes, forests of unpruned roses, tall white lilies, seringa, carnations, weeds, and blossoms growing as they would; moss-grown paths, a broken sun-dial fallen across a bed of heart's ease and mignonette. Beyond the flower garden there was a still deeper wilderness of hazel, quinces, and alders, which drew their chief sustenance from a shallow pool, whose dark shining surface was almost hidden by the spreading branches, the gray old trunks, the thick screen of leaves, through which the light came dimly even at noon.

A delightful spot for a meditative poet. Humphrey was charmed with garden and wilderness, and lighted a second cigar on the strength of his discovery of the alder and quince grove.

It was not easy walking here by reason of the undergrowth of

St. John's wort, fern, and brier, which made a dense jungle, but after a little exploration Mr. Clissold came upon a narrow footpath, evidently well trodden, which wound in and out among the old gray trunks and under the hazel boughs, till it brought him to the brink of the water.

The pool was wider than he had thought, but so covered with water-lilies that the dark water only showed in patches upon that thick carpet of shining leaves. Just such a pool as a stranger might easily walk into unawares. Humphrey pulled up in time, and seated himself on the gnarled trunk of a peculiarly ancient alder, whose roots straggled deep down into the water, among sedges, and innocent, harmless cresses. Here he slowly pulled at his cigar, abandoning himself to such thought as a poet has in such a scene and such an hour.

The last yellow gleam of the sun shone faintly behind the low thick trees, and through the one break in the wood the distant sea line showed darkly gray, just where the ocean merged into sky.

"I should write better verses if I lived here for a year," thought Humphrey, musing upon a certain volume which he meant to give the world by and by. He hardly knew whether there would be much in it worthy the world's acceptance. It was only the outpouring of a strong, fresh soul, a soul that had known its share of human sorrow, and done a brave man's battle with care.

He was deep in a reverie that had led him very far away from Borcel End, when he heard a rustling of the branches near him, and turned quickly round, expecting to see Martin Trevanard.

The face that looked at him from between the parted hazel boughs startled him almost as much as that white-robed figure last night. It was the face he had seen in the moonlight, and which he saw now with peculiar distinctness in the clear gray light—a wan, white face, with large, dark eyes—a face which once must have been most beautiful. The dark eyes, the delicate features, were still beautiful, but the complexion was almost ghastly in its pallor, and the eyes were unnaturally bright. This was Muriel Trevanard.

Humphrey thought she would have been frightened at sight of him, and would have hurried away. But to his surprise, she came a little nearer him, cautiously, stealthily even, those restless eyes glancing right and left as she approached. There was a curious intensity in her gaze when her eyes fixed themselves at last upon his face, peering at him, scrutinizing him with something of her mother's keen look. One hand was lifted to her head to push back the wild mass of tangled hair, and the loose sleeve of her dark cotton gown fell back from the white, wasted arm. Face and body seemed alike wasted by the mind's consuming fire.

" You can tell me, perhaps," she said, in a quick, eager voice. " Others won't; they're too unkind, for they must know. You can tell me, I'm sure. When will he come back ?"

" My poor soul, I would gladly tell you if I knew. But I don't even know whom you are talking of."

"Oh, yes, you do, Mother knows. She's told you, I dare say. I m not going to tell bis name. I promised to keep that secret, whatever it cost me to be silent, and I'm not going to break my promise. When is he coming back ?"

She paused, looking at Humphrey with beseeching, expectant eyes, as if she waited breathless for his answer.

"Is he ever coming back ?"

She waited again.

"Indeed, Miss Trevanard, I know nothing about it."

"How dare you call me Miss Trevanard? That's not my name."

"Muriel, then."

"That's better. He sometimes called me Muriel."

Her chin dropped on her breast, and she stood for a few mo- ments looking down at the water, all her face softened by some sweet sad thought.

"He called me Muriel," she repeated. "Muriel, Muriel. I can hear his voice now—hear it! ay, as plainly as I can see him when I close my eyes."

Again a pause, and then an eager question.

"How can he be dead, when he is so near me? How can he be dead, when I hear him and see him, and can even feel the touch of his hand upon my head, his lips upon my lips? He awakes me from my sleep sometimes with a kiss, but when I open my eyes he is gone. Was he always a spirit ?"

She seemed unconscious of Humphrey's presence as she moved a few paces further along the water's edge, always looking down- ward, in self-communion.

"My love, how can they say that you are dead, when I am waiting for you so patiently, and will wait for you to the end— wait till you come to take me away with you? It was to be ltle more than a year, you told me. O God! what a long year!"

The anguish in that last ejaculation pierced Humphrey's heart as it had been pierced by her wild cry of sorrow last night. He followed her along the brink of the pool, put his arm round her shrunken form protectingly, and tried to comfort her as best he might, knowing so little of her grief.

"Muriel," he said, gently—and her name so spoken seemed to have a softening influence upon her—"I am almost a stranger to this place and to you, but I would gladly be your friend if I could. Tell me if there is anything I can do to comfort you. Are you happy in your home, with your poor old grandmother, or would you rather be somewhere else ?"

He wanted to find out if she was suffering from any sense of ill-usage—if she felt herself a prisoner and an alien in her father's house.

"No," she said, resolutely, "I must stay here. He will come and fetch me."

"But you speak sometimes as if you knew him to be dead. Is it not foolish, vain, to hope for that which cannot happen ?"

"He is not dead. People have told me so on purpose to

break my heart, I think. Haven't I told you that I see him often?"

" Then why are you so unhappy?"

" Because he will not stay with me, because he does not come to fetch me away as he promised, in a little more than a year. Because he comes and goes like a spirit. Perhaps they are right, and he is really dead."

" Would it not be better to make up your mind to that, and to leave off watching for him, and roaming about the house at night?"

" Who told you that?" she asked, quickly.

" Never mind who told me. You see I know how foolish you are. Wouldn't it be wiser to try and go back to the common business of life, to bind up all that loose hair neatly, like a lady, and to try to be a comfort to your father and mother?"

At that last word an angry cry broke from the pale lips.

" Mother!" echoed Muriel; " I have no mother. That woman yonder," pointing toward the house, " is my worst enemy. Mother! my mother!" with a bitter laugh. " Ask her what she has done with my child!"

That question came upon Humphrey Clissold like a revelation. Here was a sadder story than he had dreamed of—a story which no words of Martin's had hinted at—a story of shame as well as of sorrow, perchance. He remained silent, troubled and perplexed by this new turn of affairs. His office of consoler, his attempt to smooth the tangled threads of a disordered brain, came to an end all at once.

The woman turned from him impatiently, muttering to herself as she went away. He followed her along the sinuous footpath and across the garden, and watched her as she entered by a low half-glass door at the back of the house. He passed this door afterward, and stole a glance through the glass into a large low room where there was a fire burning, a room which he divined to be the grandmother's chamber.

An old-fashioned tent bedstead, with red and white chintz curtains, occupied one side of the room; a ponderous old armchair stood near the fireplace; a huge wooden chest made at once a seat and a receptacle for all kinds of household stores; a corner cupboard filled with crockery-ware and a small round table near the hearth completed the catalogue of furniture.

Here on the ground by the fender sat Muriel, her wild hair falling about her face, her hands clasped upon her knees, her eyes bent gloomily upon the burning log.

The bell rang from the porch on the other side of the homestead while Humphrey Clissold was watching that melancholy figure by the hearth.

" She has taken away my appetite for supper," he said to himself, " and has almost set me against Borcel End."

That last speech of Muriel Trevanard's troubled him. " Ask her what she has done with my child."

It set him thinking of dark stories of family pride and hidden crime. It took the flavor of enjoyment out of this rustic home, and imparted a taint of mystery and suspicion which poisoned the atmosphere.

CHAPTER XXIII.

"SURELY MOST BITTER OF ALL SWEET THINGS THOU ART."

HUMPHREY CLISSOLD keenly scrutinized Bridget Trevanard's face as they sat at supper that evening. Muriel's look of horror at the mention of her mother's name had inspired unpleasant doubts upon the subject of his hostess' character. He remembered how Elspeth had told him that Mrs. Trevanard was known as a hard woman; and he told himself that cruelty or even crime might be consistent with that hard nature which had won for the farmer's wife the reputation of a stern and exacting mistress. His closer examination of that face showed him no indication of lurking evil. That square unwrinkled brow, those dark brown eyes with their keen straight-out look, denoted at least an honest nature. The firm lips, the square jaw, gave severity to the countenance—a resolute woman—a woman not to be turned from her purpose, thought Humphrey, but a woman whom he could hardly imagine capable of crime.

And then why give credence to the rambling assertions of lunacy? It is the nature of madness to accuse the sane. Humphrey tried to put the thought of Muriel's wild talk out of his mind; yet that awful question, "What has she done with my child?" haunted him.

He felt less desire to prolong his stay at Borcel. The restful tranquillity of the place seemed to have departed. Muriel's fevered mind had its influence upon the atmosphere. He could not forget that she was near—wakeful, unhappy—waiting for the lover who was never to return to her.

He took good care to lock his door that night, and his slumbers were undisturbed. The next morning was devoted to a long ramble with Martin. They walked to a distant hillside, where there were some Druidic remains well worthy inspection, came back to the farm in time for the substantial early dinner, had a look at the hay-makers dining plenteously in a great stone kitchen, and then retired to a field where the hay was cocked, to lie basking in the sun, with their faces seaward, dreaming away the summer afternoon.

Here Humphrey told Martin the story of James Penwyn's death, and that brief love-story which had come to so pitiful an ending.

"Poor child!" he said musingly, recalling his last interview with Justina, "I verily believe she loved him truly and honestly, and would have made him a good wife. I never saw a nobler countenance than that player-girl's. I'm sorry I thrust myself between them with so much as one hard word."

"Was no one ever suspected of the murder?" asked Martin.

"Yes," replied Humphrey, without taking his cigar from his lips, "I was, for a little while."

This was rather startling. Martin Trevanard stared at his

new acquaintance with a curious look for a moment or so, before he recovered himself.

" You were ?"

" Yes. Didn't you know ? My name was in the papers, but I believe they did me the favor to spell it wrong. Perhaps I ought to have mentioned the fact when I was asking Mrs. Trevanard to take me in. Yes, I, his bosom friend, was the only person they could pitch upon when they wanted to find the murderer. Yes, I have been in Eborsham jail under suspicion of homicide. The charge broke down at the inquest, and I came off with flying colors, I believe. Still, there the fact remains. The Spinnersbury detectives put the crime down to me."

" It would need pretty strong proof to make *me* suspect you," said Martin heartily.

" I was a good many miles away from the spot when that cursed deed was done, but it did not suit me to advertise my exact whereabouts to the world."

" Why not ?"

" Because to have told the truth would have been to have compromised a woman, the only one I ever loved, as a man loves one chosen woman out of all the world."

Martin threw away his unfinished cigar, turned himself about on the hay-cock which he had chosen for his couch, and settled himself to hear something interesting, with a bright, eager look in his dark eyes.

" Tell me all about it," he said.

" Bah! weak sentimentality," muttered Humphrey. " I should only bore you."

" No. you wouldn't. I should like to hear it."

" Well. naming no names, and summing up the matter briefly, there will be no harm done. It's the story of a dead and buried folly, that's all—a hackneyed, commonplace story enough."

He sighed, as if the recollection hurt him a little, dead as this old foolishness might be—sighed, and looked seaward dreamily, as if he were looking back into the past.

" You must know that when I was a year or two younger, and life was fresher to me, I went a good deal into what people call society—didn't set my face against new acquaintances, dinner-parties, dances, and so forth, as I do now. I've a fair income for a bachelor, belong to a good family, and can hold my own position well in a crowd. Now, among the houses I visited in those days there were only two or three where I went from sheer honest regard for the people I visited. Among these was the house of a certain fashionable physician, not a hundred miles from Cavendish Square. He was a widower, with three daughters, the two elder thorough women of the world, and most delightful girls to know. We were chums from the outset. They drove me about in their barouche, made me useful as an escort at flower-shows, a perambulatory catalogue at picture-galleries, and we all three comprehended perfectly that I was not to dream of marrying either of them."

" Dangerous, I should think," suggested Martin.

" Safe as the Tarpeian rock. My feelings for the dear girls

were of a purely fraternal character from the first. I would as
soon have bought the winner of the last Derby for a Park hack
as had one of these two for my wife. I went shopping with
them occasionally, twiddled my thumbs at Peter Robinson's
while they turned over silks, and I knew the amount of mil·
linery required for their sustenance. No, Martin, there was no
peril here. Unluckily there was the third daughter, a tender
slip of a girl, hardly out of the school-room—a child who had her
gowns meted out to her by her sisters, and wore perpetual white
muslin for dress and brown holland for morning. Good
heavens! I can see her this moment standing by the piano in her
holland frock, with a blue ribbon twisted through her loose
brown hair, and those divine hazel eyes looking at me plead-
ingly, as who should say, ' Be gentle to me; you see what a
child I am.' No worldliness here, no ambition here, no avid desire of millinery, no set purpose of making a great marriage, I
said to myself. Only innocence and trustfulness and child-like
meekness. So I fell over head and ears in love with my friend's
third daughter."

" Very natural," said Martin. " I don't see why it shouldn't
have ended pleasantly."

" I didn't act like a sneak—make love to the girl behind her
sisters' backs, and bide my time for winning her. I went to the
doctor at once, told him what had happened, ventured to add
that I thought my darling liked me, and asked his permission to
offer her my hand. He hummed and hawed; said there was no
one he would like better for a son-in-law; but his youngest child
was really not out of the nursery; any question of an engagement was absurd; it seemed only yesterday that he had bought
her a Shetland pony. However, he gave me to understand, in a
general way, that I was free to come and go; so our intimacy
knew no abatement. I still did the walking-stick business at
flower-shows and the catalogue business at exhibitions, and
made myself generally useful, seeing a good deal of my fair
blossom-like maiden in the meanwhile. We met very often, sat
together of an evening unnoticed when the room was full, and
before long we knew that we loved each other, and we had
sworn that for us two there should be no love but this. Papa
might say what he liked about youth and foolishness and Shetland ponies. We were not impatient, we would wait for ever so
many years if necessary, but in good time we two should be one.
Sweet and tender promises breathed in the twilight from lips too
lovely to betray, dove-like eyes lifted shyly to mine, soft little
hand resting so fondly within my arm! I laugh when I think
of you and how it all ended."

He did laugh bitterly, savagely almost, as he flung the stump
of his cigar across the hay-cocks toward the sea. Martin waited
in respectful silence, awed by this little gust of passion.

" Well, we were pledged to each other, and happy. This
went on for a year. Nobody took any notice of us any more
than if we had been children playing at lovers. We lived in a
foolish paradise of our own—at least I did; Heaven only knows
what her thoughts may have been. One day, when I had been

away from town for a week or so, I called in Cavendish Square, saw the two elder girls, and heard that my betrothed had gone for a long visit to some friends in Yorkshire, at a place called Tilney Longford, a fine old country seat. Papa had thought her looking pale and thin, and had sent her off at a day's notice. She might be away two or three months. Lady Longford was the kindest of women, and was always asking them to stay at her place. 'We can't go, of course,' they said, 'with our large circle; but that child has no ties, and can stay as long as they like to keep her.'

"This was hard upon me. The privilege of correspondence was denied us, for I could not write my darling a clandestine letter. I went to the doctor a second time, and told him that I had waited a year, that I was so much deeper in love by every day of that blessed year, and urged him to receive me as his daughter's suitor. He treated the question rather more seriously than before, repeated his assurance that I was the very man he would have liked for a son-in-law, but added that he did not consider my income sufficiently large or my profession sufficiently lucrative to allow of his intrusting his daughter's happiness to my care. 'My girls have been expensively brought up,' he said. 'You have no notion what they cost me. I have been too busy to teach them prudence. It has been easier for me to earn money for them to waste than to check their extravagance. We live in too fast an age for the vulgar virtues.' I argued the point, but vainly, and told him that whatever decision he might arrive at, his youngest daughter and I had made up our minds to be true to each other against all opposition. 'I am sorry to hear that,' he replied, 'for it will oblige me to ask you to discontinue your visits here when my little girl comes back, a discourtesy which goes very much against the grain.' I left him in a white heat, went straight off to James Penwyn, and arranged a tour which we had been talking about ever so long. We were to walk through the north of England, and I was to coach poor Jim for his last struggle at Oxford. London was hateful to me now that my darling had left it, and James Penwyn's company the only society I cared for."

He paused, abandoned himself to moody thought of that vanished past for a little, and then went on more hurriedly.

"It was at Eborsham, the morning before James Penwyn's murder, that I received the first and last letter I was ever to get from my love. She had addressed it to me at my London lodgings, and it had been traveling about after me for the last three weeks. Her first letter! I opened it with such a thrill of joy, thinking how divine it was of her to be so daring as to write to me. Such a broken-hearted letter! telling me how a certain rich land-owner near Lady Longford's had proposed to her—she broke into a parenthesis a page long to assure me she had never given him the faintest encouragement—and how everybody persuaded her to accept him, and how her father himself had come down to Tilney to lecture her into subjection. 'But it is all useless,' she said; 'I will marry no one but my own dear love,

and oh, please write, and tell me what I am to do.' Think what
I must have felt, Trevanard, when I considered that the letter
was three weeks old, and what persecution the poor little soul
might have had to suffer in the interval!"

"What did you do?"

"Can you ask me? Started off without a quarter of an hour's
delay, and got to Tilney as soon as the trains would carry me.
It was an abominable cross-country journey, and there I was,
eating my heart out at dismal junctions for half the day. It
was past three o'clock when I ended my journey of something
less than a hundred miles, and found myself at a detestable little
station called Tilney Road, eight miles from Tilney Longford,
and no conveyance of any kind to be had. I did the distance in
something under two hours, and entered the park gates just as
the church clock hard by was striking five."

"You went straight to the house?"

"No, I didn't want to bring trouble upon that poor child, so
I prowled about the place like a poacher, skirting the carriage
roads. Luckily for me, there was a right of way through the
park, so I was able to get pretty close to the house without at-
tracting any one's particular attention. I reflected that unless
the doctor was still there—not a likely thing for a man whose
moments were gold—there was no one to recognize me except
my poor pet. As I approached the gardens I heard laughter and
fresh young voices and a general hubbub on the other side of
the haw-haw which divided the park from a croquet lawn.
There was a gayly striped marquee on one side of the lawn, a
group of people taking tea under a gigantic cedar, and a double
set of croquet players disporting on a level sward. My eyes
were keen as a hawk's to distinguish my dearest in a mauve
muslin and an innocent little chip hat trimmed with daisies—I
observed even details, you see—busily engaged with her attendant cavalier, and with no appearance of being bored by his society. Her fresh young laugh rang out silver-clear, that girlish
laugh which had been one of her many charms to my mind.
'That hardly sounds like a broken heart,' I said to myself."

He sighed, and waited for a minute or so, and then resumed
in a harder voice:

"Well, I was determined to follow no judgment from appearances: and I could not stand on the other side of the haw-haw
taking observations from the covert of an old hawthorn forever;
so I went round to the back of the house, waylaid a neat little
abigail, and asked her if she could find Miss Blank's maid for
me. I accompanied my question with a fee which insured
compliance, and my pretty one's hand-maiden appeared presently at the gate where I was waiting. She remembered me
among the intimates in Cavendish Square, and consented to give
her mistress the note I scribbled on a leaf of my pocket-book.
'I hope I am not doing wrong, sir,' she said, 'but a young lady
in my mistress' position cannot be too careful how she acts——'
'In what position?' I asked. 'Didn't you know, sir? My young
lady is to be married the day after to-morrow.'"

"That was a facer!" exclaimed Martin.

"It wasn't a pleasant thing to hear, was it?—with that letter in my pocket vowing eternal fidelity. The remembrance of that gay young laughter was hardly pleasant either. The man I had seen on the croquet lawn was a good-looking fellow enough; and then one man is so like another nowadays. A woman may be constant to the type while she jilts the individual. I had written to my betrothed asking her to meet me in the park at nine o'clock by a certain obelisk which I had observed on my way. By nine she would be free, I fancied, in that half hour of liberty which the women get after dinner, while the men are talking politics and pretending to be very wise about claret."

" Did she come?"

" Yes, poor, pretty, shallow-hearted thing, looking very sweet in the moonlight, but tearful and trembling as if she thought I should beat her. She sobbed out her wretched little story. Papa had been so kind, her elder sisters had badgered her. Poor Reginald, the lover, had been so good, so generous, so self-sacrificing; and it had ended as such things generally do end, I dare say. She was to be married to him the day after to-morrow. 'And oh, Humphrey, pray give me back my letter!' she said, ' for I don't know what would become of me if it ever fell into Reginald's hands.'"

" How did you answer her?"

." With never a word. I tore the lying letter into atoms, and threw them away into the summer wind. I made my love a respectful bow, and left her, never, I trust in God to see her fair false face again."

CHAPTER XXIV.
" WE ARE PAST THE SEASON OF DIVIDED ILLS."

IF any one had asked Humphrey Clissold why he had bared old wounds in the dreamy restfulness of that June afternoon in the hay field, and why he had chosen Martin Trevanard for his father confessor, he would have been sorely puzzled to answer so natural a question. That inexpressible longing to talk of himself and his own sorrows which seizes upon men now and then had laid hold of him, and there had been a kind of bitter pleasure, a half-cynical enjoyment, in going over that story of the dead past. There was something sympathetic about Martin, too. a man who might have been crossed in love himself, Humphrey thought, or who at least had a latent capacity for sincerest passion. Friendship had proved a plant of rapid growth in the utter solitude of Borcel End. Humphrey felt that he could talk to this young Trevanard very much as he had talked to James Penwyn, knowing very well that he might not be always understood when his flights of fancy went widest, but very sure of sympathy at all times.

That afternoon was Saturday, and on the following morning perfect rest reigned at Borcel End. Even the ducks seemed less noisy than usual. as if their own voices startled them unpleasantly in the universal silence. Mr. and Mrs. Trevanard cam/

down to the eight o'clock breakfast—luxurious Sabbath hour!—
in their best clothes, the farmer seeming somewhat embarrassed
by the burden of respectability involved in sleek new broadcloth, and a buff waistcoat starched to desperation, Mrs. Trevanard stern and even dignified of aspect in her dark gray silk
gown and smart Sunday cap.

"Would you like to go to church?" Martin asked, with some
faint hesitation, lest his new friend, being something of a poet,
should also be something of an infidel.

"By all means. You drive, I suppose, as it's so far?"

Penwyn Church, that lonely church among the hills, was the
nearest to Borcel—a good seven miles off, at least.

"Yes, we drive to church and back. Mother says it goes
against her to have the horse out on Sabbath, but the distance
is more than she could manage."

The morning service began at half-past ten, so, soon after nine,
the dog-cart was at the door, for there was a good deal of walking up and down hill to be allowed for, driving in this part of
the country being not altogether a lazy business. The two
young men, who occupied the back seat, were continually getting up and down, and had walked about half the distance by
the time they came to the quiet old church, whose single bell
clanged over the green hillside.

"I'm blest if the squire and Mrs. Penwyn haven't come back!"
cried Martin, descrying a handsome landau and pair in front of
them as they drew near the church.

"Are you sure that's the Penwyn carriage? They were not
expected three days ago," said Humphrey.

"Quite sure. We've no other gentry hereabouts, except the
Morgrave Park people, and they hardly ever are at home. There
is no doubt about it; that is Mr. Penwyn's carriage."

"Then I'll renew my acquaintance with him after church,"
said Humphrey.

The old gray church, which he had explored two days ago, had
quite a gay look in its Sunday guise. The farmers' wives and
daughters in their fine bonnets, the villagers with their sun-
burned faces and Sabbath cleanliness; the servants from the
Manor, occupying two pews under the low gallery, within
which dusky recess the livery of Churchill Penwyn's serving-
men gleamed gayly, while the bonnets of the maids, all more
or less in the past Parisian fashion, made the shadowy corner a
perfect flowerbed. And, most important of all, in a large
square pew in the chancel appeared the Manor-house family—
Churchill, gentleman-like and inscrutable, with his pale thoughtful face and grave gray eyes; Madge, looking verily the young
queen of that far western land; and Viola, fair and flower-like,
a beauty to be worshiped so much the more for that frail loveli-
ness which had a fatal air of evanescence.

"I'm afraid she won't live long," whispered Martin to his
companion, in one of the pauses of the service, while the pur-
blind old clerk was hunting for the antiquated psalm, Tate
and Brady, which it was his duty to give out.

"Not Mrs. Penwyn? Why, she looks the picture of health," replied Humphrey, in a similar under-tone.

Martin colored like a school-boy justly suspected of felonious views in relation to apples.

"I meant the fair one," he gasped; "her sister.".

"She? Ah! looks rather consumptive," replied Humphrey, heartlessly.

The Borcel End and Manor-house families met in the church-yard after the service—Borcel End respectful and not intrusive; the Manor-house kindly, cordial even, with no taint of patron-age. In sooth, Michael Trevanard was the best tenant a land-owner could have; a man who was always improving his hold-ing, and paid his rent to the hour; a man to take a chair at audit dinners, and stumble through a limping proposal of his landlord's health.

"You didn't expect to see us so soon, did you, Mrs. Treva-nard?" said Madge, with her bright smile; "but we all got tired of town in the middle of the season."

There was another reason for Mrs. Penwyn's return to Corn-wall, but it was one she did not care to talk about.

"We're always glad to see you back," said Michael, screw-ing up his courage and jerking out the words as if they were likely to choke him. "The place doesn't seem home-like when there's no family at the Manor-house. You see, we were accus-tomed to see the old squire pottering about the place from year's end to year's end, and entering into every little bit of improve-ment we made; and as familiar, you know, as if he was one of ourselves. That spoiled us a bit, I make no doubt."

"It shall not be my fault if you do not come to consider me one of yourselves in good time, Mr. Trevanard," said Churchill, kindly—kindly, but without that real heartiness which makes a country gentleman popular among his vassals.

Humphrey was standing in the background, and it was only at this moment that Mr. Penwyn recognized him. Something like a spasm of pain changed his face for a moment, as if some unwelcome memory were suddenly brought back to him.

"Natural enough," thought Humphrey. "The last time we met was at his cousin's funeral, and it is hardly a pleasant idea for any man that he stands in the shoes of the untimely dead."

That momentary flush of pain past, Mr. Penwyn welcomed the stranger in the land with exceeding cordiality.

"How long have you been in Cornwall, Mr. Clissold?" he asked. "You ought not to come to Penwyn without putting up at the Manor-house."

"You are very good. I have been to the Manor-house, and ventured to put forward my acquaintance with you as a reason why your faithful old housekeeper should let me see your house. I dare say she has forgotten to mention the fact."

"There has been scarcely time. We only arrived last night. Let me present you to my wife. Madge, this is the Mr. Clissold of whom you have heard me speak; Mr. Clissold, Mrs. Penwyn; her sister, Miss Bellingham."

Madge acknowledged the introduction with something less

than her accustomed sweetness. Although Churchill was so thoroughly convinced of the man's innocence, Madge had not quite made up her mind that he was guiltless of his friend's blood. He had been suspected, and the taint clung to him yet.

Still when she looked at the dark earnest eyes, the open brow, the firm mouth, with its expression of subdued power, the countenance on which thought had exercised its refining influence, she began to think that Churchill must be right in this opinion as in all other things, and that this man was incapable of crime.

So when, after questioning Mr. Clissold as to his whereabouts, Churchill asked him to go back to the Manor-house with them for luncheon, and to bring his friend Martin Trevanard, Madge seconded the invitation. "If Mrs. Trevanard can spare her son for a few hours," she added graciously.

Mrs. Trevanard courtesied, and thanked Mrs. Penwyn for her condescension. but added that she did not hold with young people keeping company with their superiors, and thought that Martin would be better at home in his own sphere.

"If I had ever seen good come of it, I might think differently," said the farmer's wife, with a gloomy look; "but I never have."

Martin looked angry, and his father embarrassed.

"I hope you'll excuse my wife for being so free spoken," Mr. Trevanard said, in a rather clumsy apology. "She doesn't mean to be uncivil, but there are points"—here he stuck hopelessly, and could only repeat, in a feebler tone—"there are points."

"Thanks for your kind invitation, Mr. Penwyn," said Martin, still flushed with shame and anger; "but you see I'm not supposed to have a will of my own yet awhile, and must do as my mother tells me."

"Come along, old lady," said Michael; and after making their salaams to the quality, the Borcel End party retired to the dog-cart. The horse had been tethered on the sward near at hand, browsing calmly throughout the hour-and-a-half service.

Humphrey drove off with the Penwyns in the landau.

"What a very disagreeable person that Mrs. Trevanard seems!" said Madge. "I should think it could be hardly pleasant staying in her house, Mr. Clissold."

"She is eccentric rather than disagreeable, I think," replied Humphrey—"a woman with a fixed idea which governs all her conduct. I had hard work to persuade her to let me stop at the farm, but she has been an excellent hostess. And her son Martin is a capital fellow—one of nature's gentlemen."

"Yes, I liked his manner, except when he got so angry with his mother. But she was really too provoking, with her preachment about equality, more especially as these Trevanards belong to a good old Cornish family. Do they not, Churchill?"

"Yes, love. By Tre, Pol, and Pen, you may know the Cornish men. I believe these are some of the original Tres. Admirable tenants, too. One can hardly make too much of them."

"Do you know anything about their daughter?" asked Humphrey of Mr. Penwyn.

"Yes, I have heard of her, but never seen her. A poor half-witted creature, I believe."

"Not half-witted, but deranged. Her brain has evidently been turned by some great sorrow. From what I can gather she must have loved some one superior to her in rank, and been ill-treated by him. I fancy this is why Mrs. Trevanard says bitter things about inequality of station."

"An all-sufficient reason. I shall never feel angry with Mrs. Trevanard again," said Madge.

The Manor-house looked so much gayer and brighter to-day with servants passing to and fro, great bowls of roses on all the tables; banks of flowers in the windows, new books scattered on the tables, holland covers banished to the limbo of household stores, and two pretty women lending the charm of their presence to the scene.

Never had Humphrey Clissold seen husband and wife so completely happy, or more entirely suited for each other, than these two seemed. Domestic life at Penwyn Manor-house was like an idyl; simple, unaffected happiness showed itself in every look, in every word and tone. There was just that amount of plenteousness and luxury in all things which makes life smooth, without the faintest ostentation. A certain subdued comfort reigned everywhere, and Churchill in no wise fell into the common errors of men who have suffered a sudden elevation to wealth. He neither "talked rich" nor told his friends, with a deprecating shrug of his shoulders, that he had just enough for bread and cheese. In a word, be took things easily.

As a husband he was, in Viola's words, "simply perfect." It was impossible to imagine devotedness more thorough, yet less obtrusive. His face never turned toward his wife without brightening like a landscape in a sudden gleam of sunlight. There was nothing that could be condemned as "spooning" between these married lovers, yet no one would fail to understand that they were all the world to each other.

Viola had long since altered her mind about Mr. Penwyn. From thinking him not "quite nice," she had grown to consider him adorable. To her he had been all generosity and kindness, treating her in every way as if she had been his own sister, and a sister well beloved. She had the prettiest possible suit of rooms at Penwyn, a horse of Churchill's own choosing, her own piano, her own maid, and more pocket money than she had ever had in all her life before.

"It comes rather hard upon Churchill to have two people to provide for instead of one," Viola remarked to her sister; "but he is so divinely good about it"—she was a young lady who delighted in strong adverbs—"that I hardly realize what a sponge I am."

And then came sisterly embracings and protestations. Thus the Penwyn Manor people were altogether the happiest of families.

Humphrey Clissold thoroughly enjoyed his day at Penwyn. After luncheon they all rambled about the grounds, Churchill and his wife always side by side, so that Humphrey had the pretty Miss Bellingham for his companion.

"It might be dangerous for another man," he said to himself, "but I've had my lesson. No more fair soft beauties for me. If ever I suffer myself to fall in love again, it shall be with a girl who looks as if she could knock me down if I offended her—a girl with as much character in her face as that actress poor James was so fond of. Of the two, I think I would rather have Clytemnestra than Helen. I dare say Menelaus believed his wife a pattern of innocence and purity till he woke one morning and found she had levanted with Paris."

Thus secure from the influence of her attractions, Mr. Clissold made himself very much at home with Miss Bellingham. She showed him all the beauties of Penwyn, spots where a glimpse of the sea looked brightest through a break in the pine grove, hollows where the ferns grew deepest and greenest, and proved a very different guide from Elspeth.

"I have been through the grounds before," said Humphrey, "but my companion was not calculated to enhance the beauties of nature by the charm of her society."

"Who was that?"

"The granddaughter of the woman at the lodge. Rather curious people, are they not?"

"Yes, I have often wondered how my brother-in-law came to pick them up, for they are not natives of the soil, as almost every one else is at Penwyn. But Churchill says the old woman is a very estimable person, well worthy of her post, so one can say no more about it."

When Humphrey wanted to take leave, his new friends insisted that he should stay to dinner. Mr. Penwyn offering to send him home in a dog cart. This favor, however, the sturdy pedestrian steadfastly declined.

"I'm not afraid of a night walk across the hills," he said, "and am getting as familiar with the country about here as if I were to the manner born."

So he staid to dinner, and assisted at Mrs. Penwyn's kettledrum, which was held in the old squire's yew-tree bower on the bowling-green—an arbor made of dense walls of evergreen, cool in summer, and comfortably sheltered in winter.

Here they drank tea, lazily enjoying the freshening breeze from the great wide sea—the sea which counts so many argosies for her spoil, the mighty Atlantic! Here they talked of literature and the world, and rapidly progressed in friendliness. But not one word was said of James Penwyn, who save for that shot fired from behind a hedge would have been master of grounds and bower, manor and all thereto belonging. That was a thought which flashed more than once across Humphrey's mind.

"How happy these people seem in the possession of a dead man's goods!" he thought; "how placidly they enjoy his belongings! how coolly they accept fate's awful decree! Only human nature, I suppose. 'Les morts durent bien peu, laissons les sous la pierre.'"

Humphrey staid till ten o'clock, and left, charmed with host and hostess.

Churchill Penwyn had been at his best all day—a man whose talk was worth hearing, and whose opinions were not feeble echoes of Saturday's literary journals. After dinner they had music, as well as conversation, and Madge played some of Mozart's finest sacred music, choice bits culled from the Masses.

"How long do you stay in Cornwall?" was the question at parting.

"About a week longer at Borcel End, I suppose. But I am my own master as to time. I have no legitimate profession—for I believe literature hardly counts under that head—and am therefore something of a Bohemian; not in a bad sense, Miss Bellingham, so please don't look alarmed."

"Why not come to us instead of staying at Borcel End?" asked Churchill.

"You are too good. But I could hardly do that. When I offered myself to Mrs. Trevanard as a lodger I said I should stay for a week or two, and she is just the kind of a woman to feel wounded if I left her abruptly. And then Martin and I are great friends. He is really one of the best fellows I ever met, except—except the friend I lost," quickly and huskily, feeling that any allusion of that kind was ill-judged here.

"Well, you must do just as you please about it, but give us as much of your company as you can. We shall have a dinner next week, I believe."

"Saturday," said Madge.

"You will come to us then, of course. And as often in the meanwhile as you can."

"Thanks. The dinner-party is out of the question. I travel with a knapsack, and am three hundred miles from my dress suit. But if you will allow me to drop in now and then between this and Saturday I shall be delighted."

CHAPTER XXV.
"THE DROWSY NIGHT GROWS ON THE WORLD."

THE advent of the Manor-house family made life all the more pleasant to Mr. Clissold at Borcel End. It imparted variety to his existence, and the homely comfort of the farm-house was agreeably contrasted by the refinement of Mr. Penwyn's surroundings. He dined at Penwyn during the week, and as he became more familiar with the interior of Churchill's home, only saw fresh proofs of its perfect happiness. Here were a man and a woman who made the most and the best of wealth and position, and shed an atmosphere of contentment around them.

With Martin for his companion, Humphrey saw all that was worth seeing within reach of Borcel End. They drove to Seacomb, the nearest market-town, and explored the church there, which was old and full of interest. Here, in looking over the register for some name of world-wide renown, Humphrey stumbled upon an entry that aroused his curiosity.

It was the register of baptisms:

"Emily Jane, daughter of Mathew Elgood, comedian, and Jane Elgood, his wife." The date was just eighteen years ago.

"Mathew Elgood! That girl's father was Mathew," thought Humphrey. "Can it be the same man, I wonder? Yes, Mathew Elgood, comedian; there would hardly be two men of the same name and calling. His daughter must be the age of the child baptized here, for I remember James telling me that she was just seventeen."

The infant was certainly recorded in the register as Emily Jane, and the young actress' name was Justina. But Mr. Clissold concluded that this was merely a fictitious appellation, chosen for euphony. He made up his mind that the child entered in these old yellow pages and the girl he had seen weeping for his friend's untimely death were one and the same. Strange that the sweetheart of James Penwyn's choice had been born so near the cradle of his own race! It was as if there had been some subtle sympathy between these children of the same soil, and their hearts held forth to each other spontaneously.

"Is there a theater at Seacomb?" asked Humphrey, wondering how that quiet old town could have afforded a field for Mr. Elgood's talents.

"Not now," replied Martin; "there used to be some years ago. The building exists still, but it has been converted into a Wesleyan chapel. It answers better than the theater did, I believe."

The week came to an end. Humphrey Clissold attended a second service at Penwyn church and paid a farewell visit to the Manor-house on Sunday afternoon. This time he refused Mr. Penwyn's hearty invitation to dinner, and wished his new friends good-bye shortly after luncheon, with cordial expressions of friendship on both sides.

He walked across the hills ruminating upon all that had happened since he first followed that track, with Elspeth for his guide. He had made acquaintance with the interior of two families since then, in both of which he felt considerable interest.

"Churchill Penwyn must be a thoroughly good fellow," he said to himself, "or he would never have behaved so well as he has to me. It would have been so natural for him to be prejudiced against me by that business at Eborsham. But he has not only done me the justice to disbelieve the accusation from the very first—he has taken pains to let me see I am in no way damaged in his opinion by the suspicion that has attached to me."

Humphrey had made up his mind to leave Borcel End next day. He had thoroughly explored the neighborhood, and thoroughly enjoyed the tranquil pastoral life at the farm-house, and he saw no reason for delaying his departure to fresher scenes. Mrs. Trevanard had heard of his resolution with indifference, her husband with civil regret, Martin with actual sorrow.

"I don't know how I shall get on when you are gone," he said;

" it has been so nice to have some one to talk to whose ideas rise
above threshing-machines and surface-drainage.   Father's a good
old soul, but he and I have precious little to say to each other.
Now, with you, the longest day seems short.   I think you've
taught me more since we've been together than all I learned at
Helstone."

" No, Martin, I haven't taught you anything; I've only stirred
up the old knowledge that was in you, hidden like stagnant
water under a mass of duck-weed," answered Humphrey.   " But
we are not going to bid each other good-bye forever.   I shall
come down to Borcel End again, you may be very sure, if your
people will let me, and whenever you come to London you must
come and take up your quarters with me, and I'll show you some
of the pleasantest part of London life."

Humphrey Clissold really regretted parting from the young
man who had been the brightest and most light-hearted of companions, and he regretted leaving Borcel End without knowing
a little more of Muriel Trevanard's history.

He had thought a good deal upon this family secret during
the past week, though in all his wanderings about the old
neglected garden or down in the wilderness of hazel by the pond
—and he had smoked many a cigar there in the interval—he
had never again encountered Muriel.   He had no reason to suppose there was any undue restraint placed upon her movements,
or that she was unkindly treated by any one.   Yet the thought
that she was there, a part of the family, yet divided from it,
banished from the home circle, yet so near, cut off from all the
simple pleasures of her father's hearth, haunted him at all times.
He was thinking of her this afternoon during his lonely walk
across the hills.   She was more in his thoughts than the people
he had left.

It was past six o'clock when he entered the old hall at Borcel End, and he was struck at once by· the quietude of the
place.   The corner where old Mrs. Trevanard was wont to sit
was empty this evening.   The hearth was newly swept, as it
always seemed to be, and the fire, not unacceptable on this dull
gray afternoon, _burned bright and red.   The table was laid
with a composite kind of meal: on one side a small tea-tray,
on the other the ponderous Sunday sirloin and a tempting
salad, a meal prepared for himself, Humphrey felt sure.   The
maid-servant entered from the adjoining kitchen at the sound of
his footsteps.

" Oh, if you please, sir, they're all gone to tea at Limestone
Farm.   Mr. Spurcombe, at Limestone, is an old friend of master's.   And missus said if you should happen to come home
before they did, would you please to make yourself comfortable,
and I was to lay tea for you."

" Your mistress hardly expected me, I suppose ?"

" I don't think she did, sir.   She said she thought you would
dine up at Penwyn, most likely."

Humphrey was not long about his evening meal.   Perhaps he
made shorter work of it than he might have done otherwise,
perceiving that the maid was longing for the moment when she

might clear the table, and slip away by the back-door to her Sunday evening tryst. Maid-servants at Borcel were kept very close, and were almost always under the eye of their mistress, yet, as a rule, the Borcel End domestic always had her "young man." Humphrey heard the back-door shut stealthily, and felt very sure that the kitchen was deserted. He drew his chair nearer to the hearth, and lighted a cigar and abandoned himself to idle thought.

CHAPTER XXVI.
"GOOD-NIGHT, GOOD REST. AH! NEITHER BE MY SHARE."

HUMPHREY CLISSOLD sat for some time smoking and musing by the wide old hearth—sat till the light faded outside the diamond-paned windows, and the shadows deepened within the room. He might have sat on longer had he not been surprised by the opening of a door in that angle of the hall which was sacred to age and infirmity in the person of old Mrs. Trevanard.

It was the door of her room which had opened. "Have they come back yet?" asked her feeble old voice.

"No, ma'am," answered Humphrey, "not yet. Can I do anything for you?"

" No, sir. It's the strange gentleman, Mr.—Mr.——"

" Clissold. Yes, ma'am. Won't you come to your old place by the fire?"

" No; I've my fire in here, thank you kindly. But the place seems lonesome when they're away. I'm not much of a one to talk myself, but I like to hear voices. The hours seem so long without them. You can come in, if you please, sir. My room is kept quite tidy, I believe; I should fret if I thought it wasn't."

The old woman was standing on the threshold of the door opening between the two rooms. Humphrey had risen to offer her assistance.

" Come in and sit down a bit," she said, pleased at having found some one to talk to, for it was a notorious fact at Borcel End that old Mrs. Trevanard always had a great deal more to say for herself when her daughter-in-law was out of the way than she had in the somewhat freezing presence of that admirable housewife.

Humphrey complied, and entered that room which he had observed through the half-glass door, a comfortable, homely room enough in the light of an excellent fire. Old Mrs. Trevanard required a great deal of warmth.

She went back to her arm-chair, and motioned her visitor to a seat on the other side of the hearth.

" It's very kind of you to be troubled with an old woman like me," she mumbled.

" I dare say you could tell me plenty of interesting stories about Borcel End if you were inclined, Mrs. Trevanard," said Humphrey.

" Ah, there's few houses without a history, few women of my age that haven't seen a good deal of family troubles and family secrets. The best thing an old woman of my age can do is to hold her tongue. That's what my daughter-in-law's always telling me. ' Least said soonest mended.' "

" Ah," thought Humphrey, " the dowager has been warned against being over communicative."

Contemplating the room more at his leisure now than he had done from outside, he perceived a picture hanging over the chimney-piece which he had not noticed before. It was a common-place portrait enough, by some provincial limner's hand, the portrait of a young woman in a gypsy hat and flowered damask gown—a picture that was perhaps a century old.

" Is that picture over the chimney a portrait of one of your son's family, ma'am ?" asked Humphrey.

"Yes. That's my husband's mother, Justina Trevanard."

Justina! The name startled him—so uncommon a name—and to find it here in the Trevanard family!

" That's a curious name," he said, " and one which recalls a person I met under peculiar circumstances. Have you had many Justinas in the Trevanard family since that day ?"

" Only one."

" Is she living ?"

" I don't know. I know nothing about her."

" A distant relation, I suppose ?" hazarded Humphrey.

" Yes."

" I met your granddaughter in the garden the other night, Mrs. Trevanard," he said, determined to find out whether this blind woman was a friend of Muriel, " and I was grieved to see her in so sad a condition."

" Muriel ? Yes, poor girl. it's very sad—sad for all of us," answered the old woman, with a sigh; " saddest of all for her father. He was so proud of that girl—spared no money to make her a lady, and now he can't bear to see her. It wounds him too deep to see such a wreck. Yet he won't have her away from the house. He likes to know that she's near him, and as well cared for as she can be—in her state."

" It must have been a great sorrow that so changed her ?"

" It was more sorrow than she could bear, poor child; though others have borne harder things."

" She was crossed in love, her brother told me."

" Yes, yes—crossed in love, that was it. The young man that she loved died young, and she was told of it suddenly. The shock turned her brain. She had a fever, and every one thought she was going to die. She got the better of the illness. but her senses never came back to her. She's quite harmless, as you've seen, I dare say: but she has her fancies, and one is to think that the young man she was fond of is still alive, and that he'll keep his promise, and come back to her."

Humphrey told Mrs. Trevanard of his first night at Borcel End, and the intrusion that had shortened his slumbers.

" Ah! to think that she should have happened to find her way there that night, close as we keep her! My door is always locked, and she can't get out into the house without coming through this room; but I suppose that night I must have forgotten to take the key out of the door and put it under my pillow, as I do mostly. And the poor child went roaming about the house by moonlight. That's an old trick of hers. The room where you sleep was her room once upon a time, and she always goes there if she gets the chance. It was unlucky that it should have happened the first night of your being here!"

"She is very fond of you, I suppose?" said Humphrey, anxious to hear more of one in whom he felt a strong interest.

"Yes, I think she likes me better than any one else now."

"Better even than her own mother?"

"Why, yes; she does not get on very well with her mother; she has odd fancies about her."

"I thought as much. I have heard her speak of a child. That was a mere delusion, I conclude."

"Yes, that was one of her fancies."

"Has Mrs. Trevanard never consulted any medical man upon the state of her daughter's mind?"

"Medical man?" repeated the old woman, dubiously. "You mean a doctor, I suppose? Yes, Dr. Mitchell, from Seacomb, has seen the poor child many a time, and given her physic for this, that, and the other, but he says her mind will never be any different. There's no use worrying about that. He gives her stuff for her appetite sometimes, for she has but a poor appetite at the best. She's sorely wasted away from the figure she was once upon a time."

"She was a very beautiful girl. I have heard from Martin."

"Yes, I never saw a handsomer girl than Muriel when she came from school. It was all along of sending her to boarding-school things went wrong."

"How do you mean?"

"Oh, dear me, sir, you mustn't listen to my rambling talk. I'm a weak old woman, and I dare say my mind goes astray sometimes, just like Muriel's."

A light step sounded on the narrow stairs, a door in the paneling opened, and the figure Humphrey had first seen in the spectral light of the moon came toward the hearth, and crouched down at the grandmother's knees. A slender figure, dressed in a light-colored gown, which looked white in the uncertain flare of the fire, a pale, wan face, a mass of tangled hair.

Muriel took the old woman's withered hand, laid her hollow cheek against it, and kissed it fondly.

"Granny," she murmured, "patient, loving granny. Muriel's only friend."

Mrs. Trevanard smoothed the dark hair with her tremulous hand.

"How tangled it is, Muriel! Why won't you let me brush it, and keep it nice for you? My poor old hands can do that without the help of eyes."

"Why should it be made smooth or nice? He isn't coming back yet. See here, granny, you shall dress me the day he comes home—all in white—with myrtle in my hair, like a bride. I would have orange-blossoms if I knew where to get any.

There are some orange trees up at the Manor-house. I'll ask him to bring me some. I was never dressed like a bride."

"Oh, Muriel, Muriel! so full of fancies!"

"Ah, but there are some of them real—too real. Where is the old cradle that my little brother used to sleep in ?"

"I don't know, darling. In the lumber-room, perhaps."

"They should have burned it. I peeped into the lumber-room one day, and saw it in a corner—the old cradle. It set me thinking—such strange thoughts!"

She remained silent for a few minutes, still crouching at her grandmother's knees, and with her hollow eyes fixed on the low fire.

"Didn't you hear a child's cry ?" she asked, suddenly, looking up with a listening face, first at the old woman, then at Humphrey. "Didn't you, granny ?"

"No, love. I heard nothing."

"Didn't you, then ?" to Humphrey.

"No, indeed."

"Ah, you are all of you deaf. I hear that crying so often—a poor little feeble voice. It comes and goes like the wind in the long winter nights, but it sounds so distant. Why doesn't it come nearer? Why doesn't it come close to us that we may take the child in, and comfort it ?"

"Ah, Muriel, Muriel! so full of fancies!" repeated the old woman, like the refrain of an ancient ballad.

The sound of doors opening and loud voices announced the return of the family.

"You'd better go back to the hall, sir. Bridget won't like to find you here, with *her*," said Mrs. Trevanard, in a hurried whisper, pointing to the figure leaning against her knees.

Humphrey obeyed without a word. His last look at Muriel showed him the great haggard eyes gazing at the fire, the wasted hands clasped upon the grandmother's knee.

He left Borcel early next morning. Martin insisting upon bearing him company for the first few miles of his journey. He had paid liberally for his entertainment, rewarded the servant, and parted upon excellent terms with Mr. and Mrs. Trevanard and the blind grandmother. But he saw no more of Muriel, and it was with her image that Borcel End was most associated in his mind. When he was parting with Martin he ventured to speak of her for the first time since that conversation in the dog-cart.

"Martin, I am going to say something which will perhaps offend you, but it is something I can't help saying."

"I don't think there's much fear of offense between you and me—at least not on my side."

"I am not so sure of that; some subjects are hazardous even between friends. You remember our talk about your sister ? Well, I have seen her twice since then—never mind how or where; and I am more interested in her sad story than I can well express to you. It seems to me that there is something in that story which you, her only brother, ought to know, or, in a word, that she has need of your love and protection. Do not suppose for a moment that I would insinuate anything against your father and mother. They have doubtless done their duty to her according to their lights, but it is just possible that she has need of more active friendship, more sympathetic affection, than they can give. She clings to her old grandmother—a fading succor. When old Mrs. Trevanard dies, your sister will lose a natural nurse and protector. It will be your duty to lighten that loss for her, to interpose your love between her and the sense of desolation that may then arise. You are not angry with me for saying so much?"

"Angry with you! no, indeed. You set me thinking, that's all. Poor Muriel! I used to be so fond of her when I was a little chap, and perhaps I have thought too little about her of late years. My mother doesn't like any interference upon that point—doesn't even like me to talk of my poor sister, and so I've got into the way of taking things for granted, and holding my tongue. Honestly, if I had thought there was anything to be done for Muriel, that she could be better off than she is or happier than she is, I should have been the first to make the attempt to bring about that improvement. But my mother has always told me there was nothing to be done except submit to the will of Providence."

"Your mother may be right, Martin; it is not for me, a stranger in your home, to gainsay her. But your sister's case seems to me most pitiful, and it will be long before I shall get her image out of my mind. If ever there should come a time when you may need the advice or the assistance of a man of the world upon that subject, be very sure my services will be at your disposal. And whenever you come to London on business or pleasure, remember that you are to make my home yours."

"I shall take you at your word. But you are more likely to come back to Borcel than I to come to London, for, mind, I count upon your coming next summer. And now you are so thick with the Manor-house people, you've some inducement for coming," added Martin, with the faintest touch of bitterness.

"There is temptation enough for me at Borcel End, Martin, without any question of the Manor-house."

Martin shook his head incredulously.

"Miss Bellingham is too pretty to be left out of the question," he said.

"Miss Bellingham! A mere Dresden China beauty, a very fine specimen of human wax-work. I have told you my adventure in that line, Martin. I'm not likely to make a second venture."

They parted with the friendliest farewell, and Humphrey felt that he was leaving something more than a chance acquaintance behind him at Borcel End.

CHAPTER XXVII.
"SUCH A LORD IS LOVE."

NOTHING could be more perfect than that serenity which ruled the domestic life of Penwyn Manor. The judgment which Humphrey Clissold had formed of that life, as seen from the outside, was fully confirmed by its inner every day aspect. Mr. and Mrs. Penwyn had no company manners. They did not pose themselves before a stranger as model husband and wife, and settle their small differences at their leisure in the sanctuary of the lady's dressing-room or the gentleman's study. They had no differences, but lived in each other and for each other.

Yet, so impossible is perfect happiness to erring mortality, even here there was a hitch. Affection the most devoted. peace that knew not so much as a summer cloud across its fair horizon —these there were truly—but not quite happiness. Madge Penwyn had discovered somehow, by some subtle power of intuition given to anxious wives, that the husband she loved so fondly was not altogether happy. that he had his hours of lassitude and depression, when the world seemed to him, like Hamlet's world, "out of joint"—his dark moments, when even she had no spell that could exorcise his demon.

Vainly she sought a cause for these changeful moods. Was he tired of her? Had he mistaken his own feelings when he chose her for his wife? No, even when most perplexed by his fitful spirits. she could not doubt his love. That revealed itself with truth's simple force. She knew him well enough to know that his love for her was the diviner half of his nature.

Once, on the eve of an event which was to complete the sacred circle of their home life, when her nature was most sensitive and she clung to him with a pathetic dependence, Madge ventured to speak of her husband's intervals of gloom.

"I'm afraid there is something wanting even in your life, Churchill," she said, gently, fearful lest she should touch some old wound, "that you are not quite happy at Penwyn."

"Not happy! My dear love, if I am not happy here, and with you, there is no such thing as happiness for me. Why should I not be happy? I have no wish unfulfilled, except, perhaps, some dim, half-formed aspiration to make my name famous— an idea with which most young men begin life, and which I can well afford to let stand over for future consideration while I make the most of the present here with you."

"But, Churchill, you know that I would not for the world stand between you and ambition. You must know how more than proud any success of yours would make me."

"Yes, dearest, and by and by I will put up for Seacomb, and try to make a little character in the House, for your sake," replied Mr. Penwyn, with a yawn. "It's a wonderful thing how ambitious a man feels while he has his living to win, and only his own wits to help him. Then, indeed, the distant blast of Fame's trumpet is a sound that wakes him early in the morning, and keeps him at his post in the night-watches, But then

Fame means income, position, the world's esteem, all the good things of life. The penniless struggler knows he must be Cæsar or nothing. Give the same man a comfortable estate like Pen· wyn, and Fame becomes a mere addendum to his life—an orna· ment which vanity may desire, but which hardly weighs against the delight of idle days and nights that know no care. In short, darling, since I won fortune and you, I have grown somewhat forgetful of the dreams I cherished when I was a struggling bachelor."

" Is it regret for those old dreams that makes you so gloomy sometimes, Churchill ?"

" I do not regret them. I regret nothing. I am not gloomy," said Churchill, eagerly. " Never question my happiness, Madge. Joy is a spirit too subtle to endure a doubter's analysis. God forbid that you and I should be otherwise than utterly happy! Oh, my dear love, never doubt me! Let us live for each other, and let me at least be sure that I have made your life all sun· shine!"

" It has never known a cloud since our betrothal, Churchill, except when I have thought you depressed and despondent."

" Neither depressed nor despondent, Madge, only thoughtful. A man whose early days have been for the most part given up to thinking must have his hours of thoughtfulness now and then. And perhaps my life here has smacked a little too much of the Lotus Land. I must begin to look about me, and take more interest in the estate; in short, follow in the footsteps of my worthy grandfather, the old squire, as soon as I can add the respectable name of father to my qualifications for the post."

That time came before the sickle had been put to the last patch of corn upon the uplands above Penwyn Manor. The halting bell of Penwyn Church rang out its shrill peal one Au· gust morning, and the little world within ear·shot of the Manor knew that the squire rejoiced in the coming of his first-born. There were almost as many bonfires in the district that summer night, outflaring the mellow harvest moon, as at Penzance on the eve of St. John the Evangelist. The first·born was a son, whose advent the newspapers, local and metropolitan, duly re· corded: " At Penwyn Manor, August 25, the wife of Churchill Penwyn, Esq., of a son (Nugent Churchill)." The new-comer's names had been settled beforehand.

" The sweet thing!" exclaimed Lady Cheshunt, when she read the announcement in the reading-room of a German Kursaal. " I feel as if she had made me a grandmother."

And Lady Cheshunt wrote straight off to her silversmith and ordered him to make the handsomest thing in christening cups, and sent a six-page letter to Mrs. Penwyn by the same post, re· questing, in a manner that amounted to a command, that she might be represented by proxy as sponsor to the infant.

The child's coming gave new brightness to the domestic hori· zon. Viola was in raptures. This young nephew was the first baby that had ever entered into the sum of her daily life. She seemed to regard him as a phenomenon; very much as **grave**

fellows of the Zoological Society regarded the first hippopotamus
born in Regent's Park.

Madge saw no more clouds on her husband's brow after that
gentle remonstrance of hers. Indeed, he took pains to demonstrate his perfect contentment. His naturally energetic character reasserted itself. He threw himself heart and soul into that
one ambition of the old squire—the improvement and aggrandizement of the Penwyn estate. He made a fine road across
those lonely hills. and planted the land on both sides of it with
Scotch and Norwegian firs, wherever there was ground available for plantation. The young groves arose, giving a new
charm to the face of the landscape, and a new source of rev-
enue to the lord of the soil. Mr. Penwyn also interested himself
in the mining property, and finding his agent an easy-going,
incapable sort of person, took the collection of the royalty into
his own hands, much to the improvement of his income. People shrugged their shoulders and said that the new squire was
just such another as "Old Nick," meaning the late Nicholas
Penwyn. But careful as he was of his own interests, Churchill
did not prove himself an illiberal landlord or a bad paymaster.

Those plantations and new roads of his gave employment
enough to use up all the available labor of the district, and im-
part new prosperity to the neighborhood. When he suggested
an improvement to a tenant, he was always ready to assist in
carrying it out. He renewed leases to good tenants upon the
easiest terms, but was merciless in the expulsion of bad tenants.
He was just one of those landlords who do most to improve the
condition of an estate and the people on it, and in Ireland would
inevitably have met with a violent death. The Celts of Western
England took matters more quietly, abused him a good deal,
owned that he was the right sort, of man for the improvement
of the soil, and submitted to fate, which had given them King
Stork rather than King Log for a ruler.

When the election came on Mr. Penwyn put himself into
nomination for Seacomb, and came in with flying colors. All
the trading classes voted for him out of self-interest. He had
spent more money in the town than any one of his name had
ever expended there. Madge's popularity secured the lower
.classes. Her schools were the admiration of the district, and
she was raising up a model village between Old Penwyn and the
Manor-house. "Madge's folly," Mr. Penwyn called the pretty
cluster of cottages on the slope of the hill; but he allowed his
wife to draw upon his balance to any extent she pleased, and
never grumbled at the builder's bills, or troubled her by suggesting that the money she was laying out was likely to produce
something less than two per cent.

So Churchill Penwyn wrote himself down M. P. and might
be fairly supposed to have conquered all good things which fortune could bestow upon a deserving scion of Burke's "Landed
Gentry." He had a fair young wife, who won love and honor
from all who knew her. His infant heir was esteemed a model
of all that is most excellent in babyhood. His sister-in-law believed in him as the most wonderful and admirable of husbands

and men. His estate prospered, his plantations grew and flourished. The vast Atlantic itself was as a lake beneath his windows, and seemed to call him lord. No cloud, were it but the bigness of a man's hand, obscured the brightness of his sky.

Mr. and Mrs. Penwyn spent their second season in town with greater distinction than their first. More people were anxious to know them, more exalted invitation cards showered in upon them; and Churchill, who had been a successful man even in the days of his poverty, felt that he had then only tasted the skimmed milk of success, and that this which was offered to his lips to-day was the cream. There was a subtle difference in the manner of his reception by the same world nowadays. If he had been only a country gentleman, with the ability to take a furnished house in Belgravia, the difference might have been slight enough; or, indeed, the advantage might have been on the side of the portionless barrister, with his way to make in life, and his chances of success before him. But Churchill's maiden speech had been a success. He had developed a special capacity for committees, had shown slow-going county members how to get through their work in about one-fifth of the time they had been in the habit of giving to it, had proved himself a master of railway and mining economics—in a word, without noise, or bluster, or assumption, had infused something of transatlantic goaheadishness into all the business to which he put his hand. Men in high places marked him as a young man worth cultivating, and thus, before the session was over, Churchill Penwyn had tasted the first fruits of Parliamentary success.

Perhaps if ever a man went in danger of being spoiled by a wife, Churchill Penwyn was that man. Madge simply worshiped him. To hear him praised, to see him honored, was to her of all praise and honor the highest. She shaped all the circumstances of her life to suit his interest and his convenience; chose her acquaintance at his bidding, would have given up the greatest party of the season to sit by his side in the dingy Eton Square study, copying paragraphs out of a blue-book for his use and advantage. Churchill, on his side, was careful not to impose upon devotion so unselfish, and was never prouder than in assisting at his wife's small social triumphs. He chose the colors of her dresses, and took as much interest in her toilet as in the state of the mining market. He never seemed so happy as in those rare evenings which he contrived to spend alone with Madge, or hearing some favorite opera with her, and going quietly home afterward to a snug little *tete-a-tete* supper, while Viola was dancing to her heart's content under the wing of some good-natured chaperon, like Lady Cheshunt.

That friendly dowager was enraptured with her *protegee's* domestic life.

" My sweet love, you renew one's belief in Arcadia!" she exclaimed, to Madge, after her enthusiastic fashion. " I positively must buy you a crook, and a lamb or two to lead about with blue ribbons. You are the simplest of darlings. To see how you worship that husband of yours puts me in mind of Baucis

and what's his name, and all that kind of thing. And to think
that I should have taken such trouble to warn you against this
very man! But then who could imagine that young Penwyn
would have been so good-natured as to die?"

"When are you coming to see me at the Manor, Lady Cheshunt?" asked Madge, laughing at her friend's raptures. "You
can form no fair idea of my domestic happiness in London.
You must see me at home in my Arcadia, with my crook and
flock."

"You dear child, I shall ce:tainly come in August."

"I'm so glad. You must be sure to come before ·the twenty-
fifth. That's Nugent's birthday, you know, and I mean to give
a pastoral *fete* in honor of the occasion, and you will see all my
cottagers and their children, and the rough miners, and discover what a curious kingdom we reign over in the West."

"My dearest love, I detest poor people and tenants and cottagers—but I shall come to see *you*."

CHAPTER XXVIII.
"THEN STREAMED LIFE'S FUTURE ON THE FADING PAST."

MORE than a year had gone by since Humphrey Clissold had
said farewell to Borcel End, and he had not yet found leisure to
revisit that peaceful homestead. He had corresponded with
Martin Trevanard regularly during the interval, and had heard
all that was to be told of Borcel and its neighborhood; how Mrs.
Penwyn was daily becoming more and more popular, how her
schools flourished, her cottagers thrived, her cottage gardens
blossomed as the rose; and how Mr. Penwyn, though respected
for his liberality and justice, and looked up to very much in his
Parliamentary capacity. had not yet found the knack of making himself popular. From time to time, in reply to Humphrey's inquiries, Martin had written a few words about Muriel.
She was always the same—there was no change. She was neither better nor worse, and the good old grandmother was very
careful of her, and kept her from wandering about the house at
night. Nothing had happened to disturb the even current of
life at Borcel End.

This year that had gone had brought success, and in some
measure fame. to Humphrey Clissold. He had published the
long-contemplated volume of verse, the composition whereof
had been his labor and delight since he left the university. His
were not verses "thrown off" in the leisure half hours of a
man whose occupations were more serious—verses to be apolo-
gized for with a touch of proud humility in a preface. They contained the full expression of his life. They were strong with all
the strength of his manhood. Passion, fervor, force, intensity,
were there; and the world, rarely slow to appreciate youthful
fire, was quick to recognize their real power. Humphrey Clissold slowly awoke to the fact that under his *nom de plume* he
was famous. He had taken care not to affix his real name to
that confession of faith—not to let all the world know that his
was the inner life which a poet reveals half unconsciously,

even when he writes about the shadows his fancy has created. In the story-poem which made the chief portion of his volume, Humphrey, had, in some wise, told the story of his own passion and his own disappointment. Pain and disillusion had given their bitter flavor to his verse; but, happily for the poet's reputation, it was just that bitter-sweet, that sub-acid, which the lovers of sentimental poetry like. That common type of womanhood, fair and lovable, and only false under the pressure of circumstances, was here represented with undeniable vigor. The modern Helen, the woman whose passive beauty and sweetness are the source of tears and death, and whom the world forgives because she is mild and fair, here found a powerful limner. He had spared not a detail of that cruel portrait. It was something better than a miniature of that one girl who had jilted him; it was the universal image of weakly selfish womanhood, yielding, unstable, caressing, dependent, and innately false.

Side by side with this picture from life he had set the ideal woman, pure and perfect and true, lovely in face and form, but more lovely in mind and soul. Between these two he had placed his hero, wayward, mistaken, choosing the poison-flower instead of the sweet thornless rose, led through evil ways to a tragical end, comforted by the angel-woman only as chill death sealed his lips. Bitterness and sorrow were the dominant notes of the verse, but it was a pleasing bitterness, and a melodious sadness.

There was a run on Mudie's for a "Life Picture, and other Poems," by Clifford Hawthorn. The book was widely reviewed, but while some critics hailed the bard as that real poet for whom the age had been waiting, others dissected the pages with a merciless scalpel, and denounced the writer as a profligate and an infidel. The fugitive pieces—brief lyrics some of them—with the delicate finish of a cabinet picture, won almost universal favor. In a word, Humphrey Clissold's first venture was a success.

He was not unduly elated. He did not believe in himself as the poet for whom the expectant age had been on the lookout. He had measured himself against giants, and was pretty clear in the estimate of his own powers. This pleasant taste of the strong wine of success made him only more intent upon doing better. It stimulated ambition, rather than satisfied it. Perhaps the adverse criticism did him most good, for it created just that spirit of opposition which is the best incentive to effort.

Very happy was the bachelor-poet's life in those days. He had lived just long enough to survive the pain of his first disappointment. It was a bitter memory still, but a memory which but rarely recurred to mar his peace. He had friends who understood him—two or three real friends, who, with his publisher, alone knew the secret of his authorship. He had an occupation he loved, just enough ambition to give stimulus to life, and he had not a care.

He had visited the Penwyns in Eton Square several times

during the course of the season, but he had been careful not to go to that very pleasant house too often. Afternoon tea in Mrs. Penwyn's drawing-room—the smaller drawing-room with its wealth of flowers—was a most delightful manner of wasting an hour or so. But Humphrey felt somehow that it was an indulgence he must not give himself too often. He had a lurking fear of Viola. She was very fair and sweet and gentle, like the girl he had loved, and though he had as yet regarded her with only the most fraternal feeling—nay, a sentiment approaching indifference—he had an idea that there might be peril in too much friendliness.

Dropping in one afternoon at the usual hour, he was pleased to see his own book on one of the gypsy tables.

"Have you read this ' Life Picture' which the critics have been abusing so vigorously?" he asked.

"Yes, I saw it dreadfully cut up in the *Saturday Review;* so I thought it must be nice, and sent to the publishers for a copy," answered Madge. "I've had it down on my Mudie's list ever so long, without effect. It's a wonderful book. Viola and I were up till three o'clock this morning reading it together. Neither of us could wait. From the moment we began with that picture of a London twilight, and the two girls and the young lawyer sitting in a balcony talking, we were riveted. It is all so easy, so lifelike, so full of vigor and freshness and color!"

"The author would be very much flattered if he could hear you," said Humphrey.

"The author—oh, I'm afraid he must be rather a disagreeable person. He seems to have such a bad opinion of women."

"Oh, Madge, his heroine is a noble creature!" cried Viola.

"Yes, but the woman his hero loves best is worthless."

"Well, I should like to know the author," said Viola.

"I don't think Churchill would get on very well with him," said Madge. And that, to her mind, made an end of the question.

The only people she sought were people after Churchill's own heart. This poet had a wildness in his ideas which the squire of Penwyn would hardly approve.

* * * * * * *

Among Humphrey's literary acquaintance was a clever young dramatic author, whose work was just beginning to be popular. One afternoon at the club (a rather Bohemian institution for men of letters, in one of the streets of the Strand) this gentleman—Mr. Flittergilt—invited Humphrey to assist at the first performance of his last comedietta at a small and popular theater near at hand.

They dined together, and dropped in at the theater just as the curtain was falling on a half-hour farce played while the house was filling. The piece of the evening came next. "No Cards," an original comedy in three acts; which announcement was quite enough to convince Humphrey that the motive was adapted from Scribe, and the comic underplot conveyed from a Palais Royal force.

"There's a new girl in my piece," said Mr. Flittergilt, on the tiptoe of expectation; "such a pretty girl and by no means a bad actress."

"Where does she come from?"

"Goodness knows. It's her first appearance in London."

"Humph, comes to the theater in her brougham, I suppose, and has her dresses made by Madame Devy."

"Not the least in the world. She wore a shabby gray thing, which I believe you call alpaca, at rehearsal this morning, and she ran into the theater, dripping like a naiad, in a waterproof —if you can imagine a naiad in a waterproof—having failed to get a seat in a twopenny omnibus."

"That is the prologue," said Humphrey, with a slight shoulder shrug. Perhaps Madge was right, and that he really had a bad opinion of women.

He turned to the programme listlessly presently, and read the old names he knew so well, for this house was a favorite lounge of his.

"Is the piece really original, Jack?" he inquired of his friend.

"Well," said Mr. Flittergilt, pulling on a new glove, and making a wry face, perhaps at the tightness of the glove, perhaps at the awkwardness of the question, "I admit there was a germ in that last piece at the Vaudeville, which I have ripened and expanded, you know. There always is a germ, you see, Humphrey. It's only from the brains of a Jove that you get a full-grown Minerva at a rush."

"I understand. The piece is a clever adaptation. Why, what's this?"

It was a name in the programme which evoked that sudden question.

"Celia Flower, Miss Justina Elgood."

"Flittergilt," said Humphrey, solemnly, "I know that young woman, and I regret to inform you that, though a really superior girl in private life, she is a very poor actress. If the fortunes of your piece are intrusted to her, I am sorry for you."

"If she acts as well to-night as she did this morning at rehearsal, I shall be satisfied," replied Mr. Flittergilt. "But how did you come to know her?"

Humphrey told his story of those two days at Eborsham. "Poor child, when last I saw her she was bowed down with grief for my murdered friend. I dare say she has forgotten all about him by this time."

"She doesn't look like a girl who could easily forget," said the dramatist.

The curtain rose on one of those daintily furnished interiors which the modern stage realizes to such perfection. Flowers, birds, statues, pictures, a glimpse of sun-lit garden on one side, and an open piano on the other. A girl was seated on the central ottoman, looking over a photograph album. A young man was in a half-recumbent position at her feet, watching her with upward-looking, earnest eyes. The girl was Justina Elgood—the old Justina, and yet a new Justina, so wondrously had the overgrown girl of seventeen improved in womanly beauty and grace. The dark blue eyes, with their depth of thought and tenderness of expression, were alone unchanged. Humphrey could have recognized the girl anywhere by those eyes.

The management had provided the costumes for the piece, and Justina, in her white silk dress, with its voluminous frills and flouncings, looked as elegant a young woman as one could desire to see offered up, Iphigenia-like, on the altar of royalty at St. James' Palace, to be almost torn to pieces on a drawing-room day. Celia Flower is the heroine of the comedy, and this is her wedding morning, and this young man at her feet is a cousin and rejected lover. She is looking over the portraits of her friends, in order to determine which she shall preserve and which drop after marriage.

Mr. Flittergilt's comedy goes on to show that Celia's intended union is altogether a mistake, that she really loves the rejected cousin, that he honestly loves her, that nothing but misery can result from the marriage of interest which has been planned by Celia's relatives.

Celia is at first indifferent and frivolous, thinking more of her bridal toilet than of the bond which it symbolizes. Little by little she awakens to deeper thought and deeper feeling, and here, slender as Mr. Flittergilt's work is, there is scope for the highest art.

Curiously different is the actress of to-day from the girl whose inaptitude the strolling company at Eborsham had despised. There is a brightness and spontaneity about her comedy, a simple artless tenderness in her touches of sentiment, which show the untaught actress, the actress whose art has grown out of her own depth of feeling, whose acting is the outcome of a rich and thoughtful mind rather than the hard and dry result of tuition and study, or the mechanical art of imitation. Impulse and fancy give their bright brief flashes of light and color to the interpretation, and the dramatist's creation lives and moves before the audience—not a mere mouth-piece for smart sayings or graceful bits of sentiment—but a being with a soul, an original absolute creation of an original mind.

The audience is enchanted, Mr. Flittergilt is in fits of admiration of himself and the actress. "By Jove, that girl is as good as Nesbitt, and my dialogue is equal to Sheridan's!" he ejaculates, when the first act is over, and the rashly enthusiastic without waiting for the end, begin to clamor for the author. And Humphrey—well, Humphrey sits in a brown study, far back in the shadow of the cavernous private box, astride upon his chair, his arms folded upon the back of it, his chin upon his folded arms, the image of intense contemplation.

"By Heaven, the girl is a genius!" he says, to himself. "I thought there was something noble about her, but I did not think two short years would work such a change as this."

At the end of the piece Justina was received with what it is the fashion to call an ovation. There were no bouquets thrown to her, for these floral offerings are generally pre-arranged by the friends and admirers of an actress, and Justina had neither friends nor admirers in all the great city to plan her triumph. She had conquered by the simple force of an art which was spontaneous and unstudied as the singing of a nightingale. Time and practice had made her mistress of the mechanism of her art, had familiarized her with the glare of the lights and strange faces of the crowd, had made her as much at ease on the stage as in her own room. The rest had come unawares; it had come with the ripening of her mind, come with the thoughtfulness and depth of feeling that had been the growth of that early disappointment, that first brief dream of love, with its sad sudden ending.

When the piece was over, and Justina and Mr. Flittergilt had enjoyed their triumph, and all the actors had been called for and applauded by a delighted audience, Humphrey suddenly left the box. He had done nothing to help the applause, but had stood in his dark corner like a rock while the little theater shook with the plaudits of pit and gallery.

" Come, I say, that's rather cool," the dramatist muttered to himself. " He might have said something civil anyhow. I was just going to ask him if he'd like to go behind the scenes, too." The accomplished Flittergilt had contented himself with bowing from his box, and he was now in haste to betake himself to the green-room, there to receive the congratulations of the company, and to render the usual meed of praise and thanks for the interpretation of his play.

The green-room at the Royal Albert Theater was a very superior apartment to the green-room at Eborsham. It was small, but bright and comfortable-looking, with carpeted floor, looking-glasses over chimney-piece and console table, photographs and engraved portraits of popular actors and actresses upon the gayly papered walls, a cushioned divan all around the room, and nothing but the table and its appurtenances wanted to make the apartment resemble a billiard-room in a pleasant, unpretentious country-house.

Here, standing by the console table, and evidently quite at his ease, Mr. Flittergilt found his friend talking to the new actress. Mr. Clissold penetrated to the sacred chamber somehow, without the dramatist's safe-conduct.

" How did you get here?" asked Flittergilt, annoyed.

" Oh, I hardly know. The old man at the stage-door didn't want to admit me. I'm afraid I said I was Miss Elgood's brother, or something of that kind, I was so desperately anxious to get in."

He had been congratulating Justina on her developed talents. The girl's success had surprised herself more than any one else. She had been applauded and praised by provincial critics of late, but she had not thought that a London audience was so easily conquered. The dark violet eyes shone with a new light, for success was very sweet. In the background stood a figure that Humphrey had not observed till just now, when he made way for Mr. Flittergilt.

This was Mathew Elgood, clad in the same greasy-looking frock-coat, or just such a coat as that which he had worn two years ago at Eborsham, but smartened by an expanse of spotless shirt front which a side view revealed to be only frontage, and not an integral part of his shirt, and a purple-satin cravat.

"How do you do, Mr. Elgood? Are you engaged here, too?" asked Humphrey.

"No, sir. There was no opening for a man of my standing. The pieces which are popular nowadays are too flimsy to afford an opening for an actor of weight, or else they are one-part pieces written for some mannerist of the hour. The genuine old legitimate school of acting—the school which was fostered in the good old provincial theaters—is nowhere nowadays. I bow to the inevitable stroke of Time. I was born some twenty years too late. I ought to have been the compeer of Macready."

"Your daughter has been fortunate in making such a hit."

"Ay, sir. The modern stage is a fine field for a young woman with beauty and figure; and when that young woman's talents have been trained and fostered by a man who knows his art, she enters the arena with the assurance of success. There was a time when the malignant called my daughter a stick. There was a time when my daughter hated the profession. But my fostering care has wrought the change which surprises you to-night. A dormant genius has been awakened—I will not say by a kindred genius, lest the remark should savor of egotism."

"You are without occupation, then, in London, Mr. Elgood?"

"Yes, Mr. Clissold; but I have my vocation. I am here as guardian and protector of my innocent child."

"I told Miss Elgood two years ago that if ever she came to London, and needed a friend, my best services should be at her disposal. But her success of to-night has made her independent of friendship."

"I don't know about that, Mr. Clissold. You are a literary man, I understand, a friend of Mr. Flittergilt's, and you have doubtless some influence with dramatic critics. One can never have too much help of that kind. There is a malevolent spirit in the press which requires to be soothed and overcome by friendly influences. Beautiful, gifted, as my daughter is, I feel by no means sure of the newspapers. Our unpretending domicile is at No. 27 Hudspeth Street, Bloomsbury, a lowly but a central locality. If you will favor us with a call, I shall be delighted. Our Sunday evenings are our own."

"I shall lose no time in availing myself of your kind permission," said Humphrey; and then he added, in a lower tone, for Mr. Elgood's ear only, "I hope your daughter has got over the grief which that dreadful event at Eborsham occasioned her."

"She has recovered from the blow, sir, but she has not forgotten it. A curiously sensitive child, Mr. Clissold. Who could have supposed that so brief an acquaintance with your murdered friend could have produced so deep an impression upon that young mind? She was never the same girl afterward. From that time she seemed to me to dwell apart from us all, in a world of her own. She became, after a while, more attentive to her professional duties, more anxious to excel, more interested in the characters she represented, and she began to surprise us all by touches of pathos which we had not expected from her. She engaged with Mr. Tilberry, of the Theater Royal, Westborough, for the juvenile lead about six months after your young friend's death, and has maintained a leading position in the provinces ever since. 'Sweet are the uses of adversity.' Her genius seemed to have been called into being by sorrow. Good-night, Mr. Clissold. I dare say Justina will be ready to go home by this time. If you *can* square any of the critics for us, you will discover that Mathew Elgood knows the meaning of the word gratitude."

Humphrey promised to do his best, and that evening at his club near the Strand used all the influence he had in Justina's favor. He found his task easy. The critics who had seen Mr. Flittergilt's new comedy were delighted with the new actress. Those who had been elsewhere, assisting at the production of somebody else's new piece, heard their brothers of the pen enthusiastic in their encomiums, and promised to look in at the Royal Albert Theater on Monday.

To-night was Saturday. Humphrey promised himself that he would call in Hudspeth Street to-morrow evening. He had another engagement, but it was one that could be broken without much offense. And he was curious to see the successful actress at home. Was she much changed from the girl he had surprised on her knees by the clumsy old arm-chair, shedding passionate tears for James Penwyn's death? He had thought her half a child in those days, and the possibilities of fame whereof he had spoken consolingly very far away. And behold, she was famous already—in a small way, perhaps, but still famous. On Monday the newspapers would be full of her praises. She would be more immediately known to the world than he, the poet, had made himself yet. And she had already tasted the sweetness of applause coming straight from the hearts and hands of her audience, not filtered through the pens of critics, and losing considerable sweetness in the process.

   *   *   *   *   *   *   *

The illimitable regions of Bloomsbury have room enough for almost every diversity of domicile, from the stately mansions of Russell Square to the lowly abode of the mechanic and charwoman. Hudspeth Street is an old-fashioned, narrow street of respectable and substantial-looking houses, which must once have been occupied by the professional classes, or have served as the private dwellings of wealthy traders, but which now are for the most part let off in floors to the shabby genteel and struggling section of humanity, or to more prosperous mechanics who ply their trades in the somber old-paneled rooms, with their tall mantel-boards and deep-set windows.

The street lies between the oldest square of this wide district and a busy thoroughfare, where the costermongers have it all their own way after dark; but Hudspeth Street wears at all times a tranquil gloom, as if it had been forgotten somehow by the majority, and left behind in the general march of progress. Other streets have burst out into stucco, and masked their aged walls with fronts of plaster, as ancient dowagers hide their wrinkles under Bloom de Ninon or Blanc de Rosati. But here the dingy old brick facades remain undisturbed, the old carved garlands still decorate the doorways, the old extinguishers still stand ready to quench torches that have gone to light the dark way of Hades.

To Humphrey Clissold on this summer evening—Sunday evening, with the sound of many church bells filling the air—Hudspeth Street seemed a social study, a place worth half an hour's thought from a philosophical lounger, a place which must have its memories.

Number 27 is cleaner and brighter of aspect than its immediate neighbors. A brass plate upon the door announces that Louis Charlevin, artist in buhl and marquetry, occupies the ground floor. Another plate upon the door-post bears the name of Miss Girdleston, teacher of music; and a third is inscribed with the legend, "Mrs. Mapes, Furnished Lodgings," and has furthermore a little hand pointing to a bell, which Humphrey rings.

The door is opened by a young person, who is evidently Mrs. Mapes' daughter. Her hair is too elaborate, her dress too smart, her manner too easy for a servant under Mrs. Mapes' dominion. She believes that Mr. Elgood is at home, and begs the visitor to step up to the first floor front, not troubling herself to precede and announce him.

Humphrey obeys, and speeds with light footsteps up the dingy old staircase. The house is clean and neat enough, but has not been painted for the last thirty years, he opines. He taps lightly at the door, and some one bids him enter. Mr. Elgood is lying on a sofa, smoking luxuriously, with a glass of cold punch on the little table at his elbow. The Sunday papers lie around him. He has been reading the records of Justina's success, and is reveling in the first-fruits of prosperity.

Justina is sitting by an open window, dressed in some pale lavender-hued gown, which sets off the tall and graceful figure. Her head leans a little back against the chintz cushion of the high-backed chair; an open book lies on her lap. It falls as she rises to receive the visitor, and Humphrey stoops to pick it up.

His own poem.

It gives him more pleasure, somehow, to find it in her hand than he derived from the praises of those two fashionable and accomplished women, Mrs. Penwyn and her sister. It touches him more deeply still to see that Justina's cheeks are wet with tears.

"She has been crying over some foolish poetry, instead of thanking Providence for such criticism as this," said Mr. Elgood, slapping his hand upon the *Sunday Times.*

CHAPTER XXIX.
"A MERRIER HOUR WAS NEVER WASTED THERE."

AUGUST came—a real August—with cloudless blue skies and scorching noontides and a brief storm now and then to clear the atmosphere. The yellow corn-fields basked in the sun's hot rays, scarce stirred to a ripple by the light summer air. The broad Atlantic lay still as that great jasper sea men picture in their dreams of Heaven. The pine-trees stood up straight and dark and tall and solemn against a background of azure sky. Ocean's wide waste of waters brought no sense of coolness to the parched wayfarer, for all that vast expanse glowed like burnished gold beneath the splendor of the sun-god. The road across the purple moor glared whitely between its fringe of plantations, and the flower gardens at Penwyn Manor blazed like one broad mass of color, not a petal ruffled by the still clear air. The birthday of the heir had come and gone with many bonfires, skyrockets, much rejoicing of tenants and peasantry, eating and drinking, bounties to the poor, speechifying and general exultation. At twelve months old Churchill Penwyn's heir, if not quite the paragon his parents and his aunt believed him, was fairly worth some amount of rejoicing. He was a sturdy, broad-shouldered little fellow, with chestnut locks cut straight across his wide fair forehead, and large blue eyes, dark and sweet and truthful—a loving, generous-hearted little soul, winning the love of all creatures, from the grave, thoughtful father who secretly worshiped him, to the kitten that rolled itself into a ball of soft white fur in his baby lap.

The general rejoicings for tenants and cottagers, the public celebration, as it were, of the infant's first anniversary, being happily over, with satisfaction to all—even to the Irish reapers, who were regaled with supper and unlimited whisky-punch, in one of the big barns, Mrs. Penwyn turned her attention to more refined assemblies. Lady Cheshunt was at Penwyn, and had avowed herself actually charmed with the gathering of the vulgar herd.

"My dear, they are positively refreshing in their absolute *naivete*," she exclaimed. when she talked over the day's proceedings with Madge and Viola in Mrs. Penwyn's spacious dressing-room. "To see the colors they wear, and the unsophisticated width of their boots, and skimpiness of their petticoats, and the way they perspire, and get ever so red in the face without seeming to mind it, and the primitive way they have of looking really happy—it is positively like turning over a new leaf in the book of life. And when one can see it all without any personal exertion, sitting under a dear old tree and drinking iced claret-cup—how admirably your people make claret-cup!—it is intensely refreshing."

"I hope you will often turn over new leaves, then, dear Lady Cheshunt," Madge answered, smiling.

"And on Thursday you are going to give a dinner-party, and show me the genteel aborigines, the county people: poor creatures who have no end of quarterings on their family shields, and never wear a decently-cut gown, and drive horses that look as if they had been just taken from the plow."

"I don't know that our Cornish friends are quite so benighted as you suppose them," said Madge, laughing. "Brunel has brought them within a day's journey of civilization, you know,

They may have their gowns made in Bond Street without much trouble."

"Ah, my love, these are people who go to London once in three years, I dare say. Why, to miss a single season in town is to fall behind one's age; one's ideas get moldy and moss-grown; one's sleeves look as if they had been made in the time of George the Third. To keep abreast with the march of time one must be at one's post always. One might as well be the sleeping beauty at once, and lose a hundred years, as skip the London season. I remember one year that I was out of health, and those tiresome doctors· sent me to spend my spring and summer in Germany. When I came to London in the following March I felt like Rip Van Winkle. I hardly remembered the names of the ministry, or the right use of asparagus tongs. However, sweet child, I shall be amused to see your county people."

The county families assembled a day or two afterward, and proved not unintelligent, as Lady Cheshunt confessed afterward, though their talk was for the most part local, or of field sports. The ladies talked chiefly of their neighbors. Not scandal by any means; that would have been most dangerous; for they could hardly have spoken of any one who was not related by cousinship or marriage with somebody present. But they talked of births and marriages and deaths, past or to come; of matrimonial engagements. of children, of all simple, social, domestic subjects, all which Lady Cheshunt listened to wonderingly. The flavor of it was to the last degree insipid to the metropolitan worldling. It was like eating white-bait without Cayenne or lemon—white-bait that tasted only of frying-pan and batter. The young ladies talked about curates, point lace, the penny readings of last winter, amateur concerts, new music —ever so old in London—and the school children; or, grouped round Viola, listened with awful interest to her descriptions of the season's dissipations—the balls and flower shows and races and regattas she had assisted at, the royal personages she had beheld, the various *on dits* current in London society about those royal personages, so fresh and sparkling, and, if not true, at least possessing a richness of detail that seemed like truth.

Viola was eminently popular among the younger branches of the county families. The sons played croquet and billiards with her, the daughters copied the style of her dresses, and chose their new books and music at her recommendation. Mrs. Penwyn was popular with all—matrons and maidens, elderly squires and under-graduates, rich and poor. She appealed to the noblest and widest feelings of human nature, and not to love her would have been to be indifferent to virtue and sweetness.

This first dinner after the return to Penwyn Manor was more or less of a state banquet. The Manor-house put forth all its forces. The great silver-gilt cups and salvers, and ponderous old wine-coolers, and mighty venison dishes, a heavy load for a strong man, came forth from their retirement in shady groves of green baize. The buffet was set forth as at a royal feast; the

long dinner-table resembled a dwarf forest of stephanotus and
tremulous dewy-looking fern. The closed Venetians excluded
the lurid light of a crimson sunset, yet admitted evening's refreshing breeze. The many tapers twinkled with a tender,
subdued radiance. The moonlike silver lamps on the sideboard
and mantelpiece gave a tone of coolness to the room. The
women in their gauzy dresses, with family jewels glittering star-
like upon the white throats and fair round arms, or flashing
from coils of darkest hair, completed the pleasant picture.
Churchill Penwyn looked down at the table with his quiet
smile.

"After all, conventional, commonplace, as this sort of thing
may be, it gives one an idea of power," he thought, in his half-
cynical way, "and is pleasant enough for the moment. Sar-
danapalus, with a nation of slaves under his heel, could only
have enjoyed the same kind of sensation on a larger scale."

CHAPTER XXX.
"IT WAS THE HOUR WHEN WOODS ARE COLD."

WHILE the Squire of Penwyn surveyed his flower and fern
bedecked board, and congratulated himself that he was a power
in the land, his lodge-keeper, the woman with tawny skin, sun-
browned almost to mahogany color, dark brows, and night-black
eyes, sat at her doorstep watching the swiftly changing splendors
of the west, where the sky was still glorious with the last radiance of the sunken sun. The crimson light glows on the brown
skin and gleams in the dusky eyes as the woman sits with her
face fronting westward.

She has a curious fancy for out-of-door life, and is not often
to be found inside the comfortable lodge. She prefers the door-
step to an arm-chair by the hearth, even in winter; nay, she has
been seen to sit at her threshold, with a shawl over her head,
during a pitiless storm, watching the lightning with those
bright, bold eyes of hers. Her grandchild Elspeth has the same
objection to imprisonment within four walls. She has no gates
to open, and can roam where she lists. She avails herself of
that privilege without stint, and wanders from dawn till sunset,
and sometimes late into the starry night. She has resisted all
Mrs. Penwyn's kind attempts to beguile her along the road to
knowledge by the easy steps of the parish school. She will not
sit among the rosy-cheeked Cornish children, or walk to church
with the neatly clad procession from the Sunday-school. She is
more ignorant than the small toddlers of three or four, can
neither read nor write, hardly knows the use of the needle, and
in the matter of Scriptural and theological knowledge is a very
heathen.

If these people had not been the squire's *protegees* they would
have been dismissed from orderly Penwyn long ere now. They
were out of harmony with their surroundings; they made a discordant note in the calm music of life at the Manor. While all
else was neatness, exquisite cleanliness, the north lodge had a
look of neglect, a slovenliness which struck the observer's eye

disagreeably—a curtain hanging awry at one of the lattices, a tattered garment flying like a pennant from an open casement, a trailing branch of jasmine, a handless jug standing on a window-sill, a muddy door-step. Trifles like these annoyed Mrs. Penwyn, and she had more than once reproved the lodge-keeper for her untidiness. The woman had heard her quietly enough, had uttered no insolent word, and had courtesied low as the lady of the mansion passed on. But the dark face had been shadowed by a sullen frown, and no amendment had ever followed Mrs. Penwyn's remonstrances.

"I really wish you would get rid of those people at the north lodge," Madge said to Churchill one day, after having her patience peculiarly tried by the spectacle of a ragged blanket hanging to dry in the lodge-garden. "They make our grounds look like some Irish squireen's place, where the lodge-keeper is allowed a patch of potatoes and a drying-ground for the family linen at the park gates. If they are really objects of charity, it would be better to allow them a pension, and let them live where they like."

"We will think about it, my love, when I have a little more time on my hands," answered Mr. Penwyn.

He never said an absolute "No" to his wife; but a request which had to be thought about by him was rarely granted.

Madge sighed and tapped the ground with the toe of her little morocco boot. These people at the lodge exercised her patience severely.

"Waiting till you have leisure seems absurd, Churchill," she said. "With your Parliamentary work, and all that you have to see to here, there can be no such thing as spare time. Why not send these people away at once? They make the place look so horrid."

"I'll remonstrate with them," replied Churchill.

"And then they are such queer people!" continued Madge. "That girl, Elspeth, is as ignorant as a South Sea Islander, and I dare say the grandmother is just as bad. They never go to church, setting such a shocking example to the villagers."

"My love, there are many respectable people who never go to church. I rarely went myself in my bachelor days. I used to reserve Sunday morning for my arrears of correspondence."

"Oh, Churchill!" cried Madge, with a shocked look.

"My dearest love, you know I do not set up for exalted virtue."

"Churchill!" she exclaimed, tenderly, but still with that shocked look. She loved him so much better than herself that she would have liked heaven to be a certainty for him, even at the cost of a cycle in purgatory for her.

"Come, dear, you know I have never pretended to be a good man. I do the best I can with my opportunities, and try to be as much use as I can in my generation."

"But you call yourself a Christian, Churchill?" she asked, solemnly. Their life had been so glad, so bright, so busy, so full of action and occupation, that they had seldom spoken of serious things. Never till this moment had Madge asked her husband that simple, solemn question.

He turned from her with a clouded face—turned from her impatiently even—and walked to the other end of the room.

"If there is one thing I hate more than another, Madge, it is theological argumentation," he said, shortly.

"There is no argument here, Churchill. A man is or is not a follower of Christ."

"Then I am not," he said.

She shrunk away from him as if he had struck her, looked at him for a few moments with a pale, agonized face, and left him without a word. She could not trust herself to speak—the blow had been too sudden, too heavy. She went away to her own room and shut herself in, and wept for him and prayed for him. But she loved him not the less because by his own lips he stood confessed an infidel; that was how she interpreted his words of self-condemnation. She forgot that a man may believe in Christ, yet not follow him—believe, like the devils, and, like the devils, tremble.

*　　*　　*　　*　　·　　*　　*　　*

Mrs. Penwyn never spoke to her husband of the people of the north lodge after this. They were associated with a too painful memory. Churchill, however, did not forget to reprove the lodge-keeper's slovenliness, and his brief and stern remonstrance had some effect. The lodge was kept in better order—at least so far as its external appearance went. Within it was still a disorderly den.

The lodge-keeper's name was Rebecca. By this name at least she was known at Penwyn. Whether she possessed the distinction of a surname was a moot-point. She had not condescended to communicate it to any one at the Manor. She had been at Penwyn nearly two years, and had not made a friend, nay, not so much as an acquaintance who cared to "pass the time of day" as he went by her door. The peasantry secretly thought her a witch—a dim belief in witchcraft and wise women still lingering in nooks and corners of this remote romantic West, despite the printing-press and the School Board. The women-servants were half disposed to share that superstition. Everybody avoided her. Unpopularity so obvious seemed a matter of supreme indifference to the woman who called herself Rebecca. Certain creature comforts were needful to her well-being, and these she had in abundance.

The sun and the air were indispensable to her content. These she could enjoy unhindered. Her ruling vice was slothfulness, her master-passion love of ease. These she could indulge. She therefore enjoyed as near an approach to positive happiness as mere animal mankind can feel. Love of man or of God, the one divine spark which lights our clay, shone not here. She had a vague sense of kindred which made some kind of tie between her and her own flesh and blood: but she had never known what it was to love anything. She kept her grandchild Elspeth, gave her food and raiment and shelter, first, because what she gave cost her nothing, and secondly, because Elspeth

ran errands for her, did whatever work there was to be done in
the lodge, and saved her trouble generally. The delicious lazi-
ness of her days would have been less perfect without Elspeth's
small services. Otherwise it would have given this woman little
pain to know that Elspeth was shelterless and starving.

She sat and watched the light fade yonder over the lake-like
sea, and heavy mists stealing up the moorlands as the day died.
Presently, sure that no one would come to the gates at this hour,
she drew a short blackened clay pipe from her pocket, filled and
lighted it, and began to smoke—slowly, luxuriously, dreamily,
if so mindless a being could dream.

She emptied her pipe, and filled again, and smoked on, happy,
while the moon showed silver-pale in the opal sky. The opal
faded to gray; the gray deepened to purple. The silver shield
grew brighter while she sat there, and the low murmur of summer waves made a soothing music, soft, slow, dreamily monotonous. The brightening moon shone full upon that moorland
track by which Humphrey Clissold first came to Penwyn Manor.
In making his road across the uplands the squire had not followed this narrow track. The foot-path still remained at some
distance from the road.

Turning her eyes lazily toward this path, Rebecca was startled
by the sight of a figure approaching slowly in the moonlight—a
man, broad-shouldered, stalwart, walking with that careless
freedom of gait which betokens the habitual pedestrian, the
wanderer who has tramped over many a hillside and traversed
many a stony road, a nomad by instinct and habit.

He came straight on, without pause or uncertainty—came
straight to the gate, and looked in at the woman sitting on the
door-step.

" Ah!" he said. " It was the straight tip Josh Collins gave me.
Good-evening, mother."

The woman emptied the ashes of her pipe upon the door-step
before she answered this filial greeting. Then she looked up at
the wanderer frowningly.

" What brings you here ?"

" There's a heartless question!" cried the man. " What brings
a son to look after his blessed old mother? Do you allow nothing for family feeling?"

" Not in you, Paul, or any of your breed. What brought you
here ?"

" You'd better let me in first, and give me something to eat
and drink. I don't care about looking through iron bars like a
wild beast in Wombwell's show."

Rebecca hesitated, looked at her son doubtfully for a minute
or so before she made up her mind to admit him, weighed the
possibilities of the case, and then took her key and unlocked the
gate. If it had been practicable to keep this returned prodigal
outside without peril to herself, she would have done it. But
she knew her son's disposition too well to trifle with feelings
which were apt to be violent.

" Come in," she said, sulkily, " and eat your fill, and go you way when you've eaten. It was an ill wind for me that blew you this way."

"That's not overkind from a mother," responded the nomad, carelessly. "I've had work enough to find you since you gave us the slip at Westerham Fair."

"You might have been content to lose me, considering the little store you ever set by me," retorted Rebecca, bitterly.

"Well, perhaps I might have brought myself to look at it in that light, if I hadn't heard of you two or three months ago from a mate of mine in the broom trade, who happened to pass this way last summer, and saw you here, squatting in the sun like a toad. He made a few inquiries about you—out of friendliness to me—in the village yonder, and heard that you were living on the fat of the land, and had enough to spare. Living in service —you that were brought up to something better than taking any man's wages—and eating the bread of dependence. So 1 put two and two together, and thought perhaps you'd contrived to save a little bit of money by this time, and would help me with a pound or two if I looked you up. It would be hard lines if a mother refused to help her son."

"You treated me so well when we were together that I ought to be very fond of you, no doubt," said Rebecca. "Come in and eat. I'll give you a meal and a night's lodging if you like, but I'll give you no more, and you'd better make yourself scarce soon after daybreak. My master is a magistrate, and has no mercy on tramps."

"Then how did he come to admit you into his service? You hadn't much of a character from your last place, I take it."

"He had his reasons."

"Ay, there's a reason for everything. I should like to know the reason of your getting such a berth as this, I must say."

He followed his mother into the lodge. The room was furnished comfortably enough, but dirt and disorder ruled the scene. Of this, however, the wanderer's eye took little note as he briefly surveyed the chamber, dimly lighted by a single tallow-candle burning in a brass candle-stick on the mantelpiece. He flung himself into the high-back Windsor chair, drew it to the table, and sat there waiting for refreshments, his darkly bright eyes following Rebecca's movements as she took some dishes from a cupboard and set them on the board, without any previous ceremony in the way of spreading a cloth or clearing the litter of faded cabbage leaves and stale crusts which encumbered one side of the table.

The tramp devoured his meal ravenously, and said not a word till the cravings of hunger were satisfied. At the rate he ate, this result was quickly attained, and he pushed away the empty dish with a satisfied sigh.

"That's the first hearty feed I've had for a week," he said. "A snack of bread and cheese and a mug of beer at a roadside public has had to serve me for breakfast and dinner and supper, and a man of my stamina can't live on bread and cheese. And now tell me all about yourself, mother, and how you came into this comfortable berth—plenty to eat and drink, and nothing to do."

" That's my business, Paul," answered the woman, with a dogged air which meant resistance.

" Come, you needn't make a secret of it. Do you suppose I haven't brains enough to find out for myself if you refuse to tell me? It isn't every day in the year that a fine gentleman and lady take a gypsy fortune-teller into their service. Such things are not done without good reason. What sort of a chap is this Squire Penwyn ?"

" I've nothing to tell you about him," answered the woman, with the same steady look.

" Oh, you're as obstinate as ever, I see! All the winds that blow across the Atlantic haven't blown your sullen temper out of you. Very well, since you're so uncommunicative, suppose I tell you something about this precious master of yours. There are other people who know him—people who are not afraid to answer a civil question. His name is Penwyn, and he is the first cousin of that poor young fellow who was murdered at Eborsham; and by that young man's death he comes into this property. Rather a lucky thing for him, wasn't it, that this cousin was shot from behind a hedge? If such luck had happened to a chap of my quality, a rogue and vagabond bred and born, there'd have been people in the world malicious enough to say that I had a hand in the murder. But who could suspect a gentleman like Mr. Penwyn? No gentleman would shoot his cousin from behind a hedge, even though the cousin stood between him and ever so many thousands a year."

" I don't know what you mean by your sneers," returned Rebecca. " Mr. Penwyn was over two hundred miles away at the time."

" Oh, you know all about him! You occupy a post of confidence here, I see. Pleasant for you. Shall I tell you something more about him? Shall I tell you that he has family plate worth thousands—solid old plate that has been in the family for more than a century; that his wife makes no more account of her diamonds than if they were dog-roses she pulled out of the hedges to stick in her hair? That's what I call good luck, for they were both of 'em as poor as Job until that cousin was murdered. Hard for a chap like me to stand outside their gates and hear about their wealth, and pass on with hungry stomach and blistered feet—pass on to wheedle a few pence out of a peasant wench or steal a barn-door fowl! There's destiny for you."

He emptied the beer-jug, which had held a quart of good home-brewed, took out his pipe, and began to smoke, his mother watching him uneasily all the time. These two were alone in the lodge. The moonlight and balmy air had lured Elspeth far afield, wandering over the dewy moorland, singing her snatches of gypsy song, and happy in her old wild way—happy though she knew she would get a scolding with her supper by and by.

" They've got a party to-night, haven't they ?" asked Paul. " Half a dozen fine carriages passed me an hour or so ago, before I struck out of the road into the foot-path."

" Yes, there's a dinner-party."

The gypsy rose and went to the open window. The lighted windows of the Manor-house shone across the shadowy depth of park and shrubberies. Those dark eyes of his glittered curiously as he surveyed the scene.

" I should like to see them feasting and enjoying themselves," he said, moving toward the door.

" You mustn't go near the house—you mustn't be seen about the place!" cried Rebecca, following him hurriedly.

" Mustn't I ?" sneered the gypsy. " I never learned the meaning of the word mustn't. I'll go and have a peep at your fine ladies and gentlemen—I'm not quite a fool, and I sha'n't let them see me—and then come back here for a night's rest. You needn't be frightened if I'm rather long. It'll amuse me to look on at the high jinks through some half-open window. There, don't look so anxious. I know how to keep myself dark."

CHAPTER XXXI.
"AND SOME TO THE SETTING MOON HAVE GONE, AND SOME TO THE RISING DAY."

THE dinner-party is over, the county families have retired to their several abodes. They are dispersed. like the soft summer mist which has melted from the moorland with the broadening light of the harvest moon.

Madge, Viola, and Lady Cheshunt are assembled in Mrs. Penwyn's dressing-room, a long, low room, with a wide and deep bow-window at one end, and three other old-fashioned windows, with broad cushioned seats therein—a room made for lounging and pleasant idleness, and half hours with the best authors. Every variety of the genus easy-chair is there, chintz-covered, and blossoming with all the flowers of the garden, as they only bloom in chintz, large, gorgeous, and unaffected with aphids or blight of any kind. There are tables here and there—gypsy tables. loaded with new books and other trumpery. There is a large Duchesse dressing table in one of the windows, and an antique ebony wardrobe, with richly carved doors. in a convenient recess; but baths and all the paraphernalia of the toilet are in a small chamber adjoining, this large apartment being rather a morning-room. or boudoir, than dressing-room proper.

There are water-color sketches on the walls, by famous modern masters; a portrait of Churchill Penwyn, in crayon, hanging over the velvet-covered mantel-board; there are dwarf bookcases containing Madge's own particular library—the poets, old and new, Scott, Bulwer, Dickens, Thackeray, Carlyle; altogether the room has just those homely lovable characteristics which make rooms dear to their owners.

To-night the windows are all open to the soft summer coolness. The day has been oppressively warm, and the breath of night brings welcome refreshment to jaded humanity. Madge sits before her dressing-table. slowly unclasping her jewels as she talks. Her maid has been dismissed for the night. Mrs. Penwyn being in no wise dependent on her abigail's help; and the jewel-case, with its dark velvet lining, stands open on the wide marble slab. Lady Cheshunt lies back in the deepest and softest of the easy-chairs, fanning herself with a big black and gold fan, a large and splendid figure in her lustrous amber satin and hereditary point lace—lace which one of the queens of Spain had presented to the dowager's mother when her husband was embassador at Madrid. She looks like a picture by Rubens, large and fair, and glowing with richest color.

"Well, my love, all dinner-parties are more or less heavy, but upon the whole your county people were better than I expected," said the dowager, with her authoritative air. "I have seen duller parties in the home counties. Your people seemed to enjoy themselves, and that is a point gained, however dull their talk of the births, marriages, and deaths of their belongings might be to *nous autres.* They have a placid belief that their conversation is entertaining, which is perhaps the next best thing to being really amusing. In a word, my dear Madge, I was not nearly so much bored as I expected to be. Those diamonds are positively lovely, child; where did you get them?"

Madge had just taken her necklace—a string of large single stones—from her neck, and was laying it in its velvet nest.

"They are heir-looms, some of them, at least," she answered, "and came to Churchill with the estate. They have been locked up in an old tin cash-box at the county bank for a quarter of a century, I believe, and nobody seemed to know anything about them. They are described in the old squire's will as 'sundry jewels in a tin box at the bank.' Churchill had the stones re-set, and bought a good many more to complete the set."

"Well, my dear, they are worthy of a duchess. I hope you are careful of them."

"I don't think it is in Madge's nature to be careful of anything, now she is rich," said Viola. "She was thoughtful and saving enough when we lived with poor papa, and when it was such a hard struggle to keep out of debt. But now she has plenty of money, she scatters it right and left, and is perpetually enjoying the luxury of giving."

"But I am not careless about my diamonds, Viola. Mills will come presently and carry off this box to the iron safe in the plate-room."

"I never believed much in plate-rooms," said Lady Cheshunt. "A plate-room, with its iron door, is a kind of invitation to burglars. It tells them where the riches of the house are concentrated. When I am in other people's houses I generally keep my jewel-case on my dressing-table, but I take care to have it labeled 'gloves,' and that it looks as little like a jewel-case as possible. I wouldn't trust it in anybody's plate-room. There, child, you are yawning. I see, in spite of your efforts to conceal the operation. Come, Viola, your sister is tired after the mental strain she has undergone in pretending to be interested in all these people's innumerable relations."

The ladies kissed and parted, with much affection, and Madge was left alone to sit by her dressing-table in a dreamy attitude, forgetful of the lateness of the hour.

It was a sad thought that kept her musing there while the night deepened, and the broad gold moon sank lower in the placid sky—she thought that all was not well with the husband of her love. She could not forget that look and gesture of his when she had questioned him about his faith as a Christian, nothing fearing his answer to that solemn inquiry when she asked it. That darkening brow, those gloomy eyes turned upon her for a moment in anger or in pain, had haunted her ever since. Not a Christian!—her love, her idolatry, the dearer half of soul and heart and mind. Death assumed new terrors in the thought that in worlds beyond they two must be parted.

"Rather let us endure a mutual purgation," she thought, with a wish that was half a prayer. "Let me carry half the share of his sins."

He had gone to church with her, he had assisted in the service with grave attention, nay, sometimes even with a touch of fervor, but he had never taken the sacrament. That had troubled her not a little, but when she ventured to speak to him upon the subject he had replied with the common argument, "I do not feel my faith strong enough to share in so exalted a mystery."

She had been content to accept this reason, believing that time would strengthen his faith in holy things. But now he had told her in hardest, plainest words that he had no claim to the grand name of Christian.

She sat brooding upon this bitter thought for some time, then rose, changed her dinner dress for a loose white muslin dressing-gown, and went into her bedroom, which opened out of the dressing-room. She had not once thought of those earthly jewels in the open box on the table, or even wondered why Mills had not come to fetch them. The truth being that, distracted by the abnormal gayety which prevailed below stairs, where the servants regaled themselves with a festival supper after the patrician banquet, Miss Mills had forgotten her duties so far as to become for the time being unconscious of the existence of Mrs. Penwyn's diamonds. At this moment she was sleeping comfortably in her chamber in the upper story, and the diamonds were left to their fate.

Lady Cheshunt was accustomed to late hours, and considered midnight the most agreeable part of her day, so on leaving Madge's dressing-room, she took Viola to her own apartment, at the other end of the corridor, for another half hour or so of friendly chat, to which Viola, who was an inveterate gossip, had not the slightest objection. They talked over everybody's dress and appearance, the discussion generally ending in a verdict of "guy," or "fright." They talked over Churchill, Viola praising him enthusiastically, Lady Cheshunt good-naturedly allowing that she had been mistaken in him.

"He used to remind me of Mephistopheles, my dear," said the vivacious matron. "I don't mean that he had a hooked nose, or diagonal eyebrows, or a cock's feather in his hat: but he had a look of secret repressed power that almost frightened me. I fancied he was a man who could do anything, whether great or wicked, by the sovereign force of his intellect and will; but that was before his cousin died. Wealth has improved him wonderfully."

At last a clock in the corridor struck one. Viola gave a little scream of surprise, kissed her dear Lady Cheshunt, for the twentieth time that night, and tripped away. She had gone half way down the corridor when she stopped, startled by a sight that moved her to scream louder than she had done just now at the striking of the clock, had not some instinctive feeling of caution checked her.

A man—a man of the vagabond or burglar species—was in the act of leaving Mrs. Penwyn's dressing-room. His back was turned to Viola; he looked neither to the right nor the left, but crept along the corridor with stealthy yet rapid footsteps. Viola paused not a moment ere she pursued him. Her footfall hardly sounded on the carpeted floor, but the flutter of her dress startled the intruder. He looked at her, and then dashed onward to the head of the staircase, almost throwing himself down the shallow oak stairs, the flying figure in its airy white robe closely pursuing him.

At the head of the stairs Viola essayed to give the alarm, with a cry which rang through the silent house. She was gaining upon the thief. At the bottom of the stairs she had him in her grasp, the two small hands clutching his greasy velveteen collar.

He turned round upon her with a fierce oath, would have struck her to the ground, perhaps, and marred her delicate beauty forever with one blow of his iron fist, had not the billiard-room door opened suddenly and Mr. Penwyn appeared, Sir Lewis Dallas, a visitor staying in the house, at his elbow.

"What is the matter? Who is this man?" cried Churchill, while he and Sir Lewis hastened to Viola's side and drew her away from the ruffian.

"A thief, a burglar!" gasped the excited girl. "I saw him coming out of my sister's dressing-room. He has murdered her, perhaps. Oh, do go and see if she is safe, Churchill."

"Hold him, Lewis," cried Churchill, and ran up-stairs without another word.

Sir Lewis was tall and muscular, an athlete by nature and art. In his grip the marauder waited submissively enough till Churchill returned, breathless, but relived in his mind. Madge was safe—Madge did not even know that there was anything amiss.

"Thanks, Lewis," he said, quietly, taking the intruder from his friend's hand as coolly as if he had been some piece of lumber.

"Go up-stairs to your room, Vio, and sleep soundly for the rest of the night," added Churchill to his sister-in-law. "I'll compliment you on your prowess to-morrow morning."

"I don't think I could go to bed," said Viola, shuddering. "There may be more burglars about the house. I feel as if it was swarming with them, like the beetles Mills talks about in the kitchen."

"Nonsense, child. The fellow has no companions. Perhaps you'd be kind enough to see my sister as far as the end of the corridor, Lewis?"

"Oh, no," cried Viola, quickly. "Indeed, I'm not frightened. I don't want any escort;" and she ran up-stairs so fast that Sir Lewis lost his opportunity of saying something sweet at the end of the corridor. His devotion to the pretty Miss Bellingham was notorious, and Viola apprehended some soft speech, perhaps a gentle pressure of her hand, a fervid assurance that no peril should come near her while he watched beneath that roof. And the portionless daughter of Sir Nugent Bellingham was not wise enough in her generation to encourage this wealthy young baronet.

"Now you, sir, go in there," said Churchill, pushing the gypsy into his study. "You needn't wait, Lewis, I can tackle this fellow single-handed."

"No, I can't let you do that. He may have a knife about him."

"If he has, I don't think he'll try it upon me. I brought this from my dressing-room just now."

He pointed to the polished butt of a revolver lurking in the breast pocket of his smoking-coat.

"Well, I'll smoke a cigar in the billiard-room while you hold your parley with him. I shall be within call."

Sir Lewis retired to enjoy his cigar, and Churchill went into his study. He found that the burglar had availed himself of this momentary delay, and was beginning to unfasten the shutters.

"What? You'd like to get out that way," said the squire. "Not till you and I have had our talk together. Let go that shutter, if you please, while I light the lamp."

He struck a wax match, and lighted a shaded reading-lamp that stood on the table.

"Now," he said, calmly, "be good enough to sit down in that chair while I overhaul your pockets."

"There's nothing in my pockets," growled Paul, prepared for resistance.

"Isn't there? Then you can't object to have them emptied. You'd better not be needlessly objective. I've an argument here that you'll hardly resist"—showing the pistol—"and my friend who grappled you just now is ready to stand by me."

The man made no further resistance. Churchill turned out the greasy linings of his pockets, but produced nothing except loose shreds of tobacco and various scraps of rubbish. He felt inside the vagabond's loose shirt, thinking that he might have hidden his booty in his bosom, but with no result. A cunning smile curled the corners of the scoundrel's lips—a smile that told Churchill to persist in his search.

"Come," he said, "you've some of my wife's diamonds about you. I saw the case open, and half empty. You were not in that room for nothing. You shall strip to your skin, my man. But first, off with that neckerchief of yours."

The man looked at him vengefully, eyed the pistol in his cap-

tor's hand, weighed the forces against him, and then slowly
and sullenly untied the rusty black silk handkerchief which en-
circled his brawny throat, and threw it on the table. Something
inside the handkerchief struck sharply on the wood.

"I thought as much," said Churchill.

He untwisted the greasy whisp of silk, whereupon his wife's
collet necklace and the large single stones she wore in her ears
fell upon the table. Churchill put the gems into his pocket without a word.

"Is that all?" he asked.

"Yes," the man answered, with an oath.

Churchill looked at him keenly. "You will go straight from
here to jail," he said; "so concealment wouldn't serve you much.
You are a gypsy, I think?"

"I am."

"What brought you here to-night?"

"I came to see a relation."

"Here, on these premises?"

"At the lodge. The woman you've chosen for your lodge-
keeper is my mother."

"Rebecca Mason?"

"Yes."

Churchill took a turn or two up and down the room, thoughtfully.

"Since you've been so uncommonly kind to her, perhaps you'll
strain a point in my favor," said the gypsy. "I shouldn't have
tried to rob you if I hadn't been driven to it by starvation. It
goes hard with a man when he has a wolf gnawing his vitals,
and stands outside an open window and sees a lot of women
with thousands of pounds on their necks, in the shape of blessed
gems that do no more real good to any one than the beads our
women bedizen themselves with. And then he sees the blessed
old ivy-roots are thick enough to serve for a ladder, and the window up-stairs left open, and handy for him to walk inside.
That's what I call temptation. Perhaps you were outside the
good things of this world at some time of your life, and can feel
for a poor wretch like me."

"I have known poverty," answered Churchill, wondrously
forbearing toward this vagrant, "and endured it."

"Yes, but you hadn't to endure it forever. Fortune was kind
to you. It isn't often a man drops into such a berth as this by a
fluke. You've got your property, and you may as well let me
off easily for my mother's sake."

"You don't suppose your mother is more to me than any
other servant in my employ?" said Churchill, turning upon him
sharply.

"Yes, I do. You wouldn't go to the gypsy tents for a servant
unless you had your reasons. What should have brought you
to Eborsham to hunt for a lodge-keeper?"

The mention of that fatal city startled Churchill. Seldom
was that name uttered in his hearing. It was among things
tabooed.

"I'm sorry I can't oblige you by condoning a felony," he said,

in his most tranquil manner. "As justice of the peace any sentimentality on my part would be somewhat out of character.
The utmost I can do for you is to get the case heard without delay. You may anticipate the privilege of being committed for
trial at the petty sessions to-morrow at noon."

He left the room without another word, and locked the door
on his prisoner. The lock was good. and in excellent order, the
door one of those ponderous portals only to be found in old
manor-houses and their like.

But Mr. Penwyn seemed to have forgotten the window, which
was only guarded on the inside. He had shut one side of a trap,
ignoring the possibility of escape on the other.

He looked into the billiard-room before he went up-stairs. Sir
Lewis Dallas had finished his cigar and was slumbering peacefully, stretched at full length on one of the divans, like an uninterested member of the House of Commons.

"He's nearly as well off there as in his room, so I won't inter-
rupt his dreams." thought Churchill as he retired.

That shriek of Viola's had awakened several of the household. Mills had heard it, and had descended half-dressed to the
corridor, in time to meet Miss Bellingham on her way up-stairs,
and to hear the history of the gypsy's attempt from that young
lady. Mills had taken the news back to the drowsy house-maids
—had further communicated it to the startled footman, who
looked out of his half-opened door to ask what was the row.
Thus by the time the household began to be astir again, between
five and six next morning, everybody knew more or less about
the attempted robbery.

"What have they done with the robber?" asked the maids
and the odd man and boot-cleaner, who alone among the masculine retainers condescended to rise at this early hour.

"I think he must be shut up in master's study," answered one
of the women, whose duty it was to open the house; "for the
door's locked, and I couldn't get in."

"Did you hear anybody inside?" asked the cook with keen
interest.

"Not a sound. He must be asleep, I suppose."

"The hardened villain! To think that he can sleep, with such
a conscience as his, and the likelihood of being sent to Botany
Bay in a week or two!"

"Botany Bay has been done away with," said the odd man,
who read the newspapers. "They'll send him no further than
Dartmoor."

CHAPTER XXXII.
O HEAVEN! THAT ONE MIGHT READ THE BOOK OF FATE.

CHURCHILL PENWYN looked something the worse for that half
hour's excitement after midnight when the Manor-house party
assembled at breakfast, between eight and nine next morning.
The days began early at Penwyn, and only Lady Cheshunt was
guilty of that social malingering involved in a chronic headache,
which prevented her appearing on the dewy side of noon.

Perhaps Mr. Penwyn's duties as host during the previous evening might have fatigued him a little. He had a weary look in
that bright morning sunshine—a look of unrest, as of one who
had slept hardly at all in the night hours. Madge glanced at
him every now and then with but half-concealed anxiety.
Every change, were it ever so slight, in that one beloved face
was visible to her.

"I hope last night's business has not worried you, love,"
she said tenderly, making some excuse for carrying him his
breakfast cup with her own hands. "The diamonds are safe,
and no doubt the man will be properly punished for his audacity."

Churchill had told her all about the attempted robbery in
his clear, passionless way, but not a word of that interview in
the study between gentleman and vagabond. Madge, merciful
to all innocent sufferers, had no sentimental compassion for
this frustrated burglar, but desired that he should be duly
punished for his crime.

"I am not particularly worried, dear. It was rather an unpleasant ending to a pleasant evening, that is all."

They were still seated at the breakfast-table, and Sir Lewis
Dallas was still listening with rapt attention to Viola's account
of her feelings at sight of the thief, when the butler, who had
left the room a few moments before in compliance with a
whispered request from his subordinate, entered, solemn of aspect, and full of that self-importance common to the craft.

"The man has been taken again, sir, and is in the village
lock-up," he announced to his master.

Churchill rose hastily.

"Taken again! What do you mean? I left him locked up in
my study at two o'clock this morning."

"Yes, sir; but he unfastened the shutters and got out of the
window, and would have got clean off. I dare say, if Tyrrel, the
gamekeeper, and his son, hadn't been about with a couple of
dogs on the lookout for poachers. The dogs smelled him out
just as he was getting over the fence in the pine wood, and the
Tyrrels collared him, and took him off to the lock-up then and
there. He fought hard, Tyrrel says, and would have been almost
a match for the two of 'em, if it hadn't been for the dogs. They
turned the scale," concluded the butler, grandly.

"Imagine the fellow so nearly getting off!" exclaimed Sir
Lewis. "I wonder it didn't strike you that he would get out at
the window, Penwyn. You locked the door and thought you
had him safe. Something like the painter fellow who went in
for the feline species, and cut two holes in his studio door,
a big one for his cat, and a little one for her kitten, forgetting
that the little cat could have got through the big cat's door.
That's the way with you clever men; you're seldom up to trap in
trifles."

"Rather stupid of me, I confess," said Churchill; "but I suppose I was a little obfuscated by the whole business. One hasn't
a burglar on one's hands every night in the week. However,"
he added slowly, "he's safe in the lock-up; that's the grand

point, and I shall have the pleasure of assisting at his official examination at twelve o'clock."

" Are the petty sessions on to-day?" asked Sir Lewis, warmly
interested. " How jolly!"

" You don't mean to say that you take any interest in that sort
of twaddle?" said Churchill.

" Anything in the way of crime is interesting to me," replied
the young man; " and to assist at the examination of the rultian
who frightened Miss Bellingham will be rapture. I only regret
that the old hanging laws are repealed."

" I don't feel quite so unmerciful as that," said Madge, " but
I should like the man to be punished, if it were only as an example. It isn't nice to lose the sense of security in one's own
house, to be afraid to open one's window after dark, and to feel
that there may be a burglar lurking in every corner."

" And to know that your burglar is your undeveloped assassin,"
added Sir Lewis. " I've no doubt that scoundrel would have
tried to murder us both last night if it hadn't been for my biceps
and Churchill's revolver."

The breakfast party slowly dispersed, some to the grounds,
some to the billiard-room. Every one had letters to write, or
some duty to perform, but no one felt in the cue for performance.
Nor could anybody talk of anything except the burglar, Viola's
courage, Churchill's coolness in the hour of peril, and carelessness in the matter of the shutters. Lady Cheshunt required to
have bulletins carried to her periodically, while she sipped orange
Pekoe in the luxurious retirement of an Arabian bed.

Thus the morning wore on, till half-past eleven, at which time
the carriage was ordered to convey Mrs. Penwyn. Miss Bellingham, and Sir Lewis Dallas to the village inn, attached whereto
was the justices' room, where Mr. Penwyn and his brother magistrate, or magistrates, were to meet in solemn assembly.

Viola and Sir Lewis were wanted as witnesses. Mrs. Penwyn
went ostensibly to take care of her sister, but really because she
was acutely anxious to see the result of the morning's work.
That look of secret care in her husband's face had disturbed her.
Looks which for the world at large meant nothing had their language for her. She had studied every line of that face, knew
its lights and shadows by heart.

The day was lovely, another perfect August day. The shining faces of the reapers turned toward them as they drove past
the golden fields, sun-browned and dewy with labor's honorable
sweat. All earth was gay and glad. Madge Penwyn looked at
this fair world sadly, heavy with a vague sense of secret care.
The skylark sang his thrilling notes high up in the blue vault
that arched these golden lands, and the note of rapture jarred
upon the wife's ear.

" I am afraid we have been too happy. Churchill and I," she
thought, and then recalled a line of Hood's, full of sweetest
pathos,

> " For there is e'en a happiness
> That makes the heart afraid."

They had been utterly happy only a little while ago, but since that confession of Churchill's the wife's heart had been burdened with a secret grief. And to-day she felt that hidden care keenly. Something in her husband's manner had suggested concealed anxieties, fears, cares which he could not or would not share with her.

"If he did but know how loyal I could be to him," she thought, "he would hardly shrink from trusting me."

Viola was full of excitement, and quite ferociously disposed toward the burglar.

"I suppose to-day's business is only a kind of rehearsal," she said, gayly, "and that we shall have to go over our evidence again at Bodmin Assizes. And some pert young barrister on the Western Circuit will browbeat me, and try to make me contradict myself, and make fun of me, and ask if I had my hair in papers, or had unplaited my chignon, when I ran down-stairs after the burglar."

"I should like to see him do it," muttered Sir Lewis, in a vengeful tone.

They were in Penwyn village by this time, the old-fashioned straggling village, two rows of cottages scattered apart on the wide high-road, a tiny Methodist chapel in a field, the pound, the lock-up, big enough for one culprit, and the village inn, attached to which there was the justice-room, a long, narrow chamber with a low ceiling.

All the inhabitants of Penwyn had turned out to see the great folks. It was like an Irish crowd—children, old women, and young matrons with infants in their arms. The children had just turned out from the pretty Gothic school-house which Mr. Penwyn had built for them. They bobbed deferentially as their patroness descended from her carriage, and a murmur of praise and love ran through the little crowd—sweetest chorus to a woman's ear.

"We ought to be happy in this fair land," thought Madge, as her heart thrilled at sight of her people. "It is like ingratitude to God to keep one secret care when He has blessed us so richly."

CHAPTER XXXIII.
"QUI PEUT SOUS LE SOLEIL TROMPER SA DESTINEE?"

CHURCHILL was waiting at the inn door to receive his wife. He had ridden across on his favorite horse, Tarpan—a long-necked, raking bay, sixteen hands high, and a great jumper—a horse with a tremendous stride, just such a brute as Lenore's lover might have bestridden in that awful night ride.

"Is the man here, Churchill?" Madge asked, anxiously.

"Yes, love. There is nothing to be uneasy about," answered her husband, replying to her looks rather than to her words.

"Yet you seem anxious, Churchill."

"Only in my magisterial capacity. Tresillian is here. We shall commit this fellow in no time. It will only need a few words from Viola and Sir Lewis."

Not a syllable about the diamond necklace had Mr. Penwyn said to his wife. He had replaced the gems in her dressing-case while she slept peacefully in the adjoining room, and no one but himself and the burglar knew how the attempted robbery had gone.

They all went up the narrow little staircase, Mr. Penwyn lead·ing his wife up the steep stairs, Viola and Sir Lewis following. The justice-room was full of people—or at least that end of it devoted to the public. The other end of it was fenced off; and here at a table sat Mr. Tresillian, J. P., and his clerk—ready for action.

" Look, Churchill," whispered Madge, as her husband put her hand through his arm and led her toward this end of the room, " there is the woman at the lodge. What can have brought her here ?"

Mr. Penwyn's glance followed his wife's for a moment. Yes, there stood Rebecca Mason, of the north lodge, sullen, even threatening of aspect, or seeming so to the eye that looked at her now. What a horrible likeness she bore to the ruffian he had dealt with last night!

Mr. Tresillian shook hands with the two ladies. He was a tall, stout man, with a rather red face, who rode to hounds all the season, and devoted himself to the pleasures of the table for the rest of the year. It was something awful to the crowd to see him shake hands, and smile, and talk about the weather, just like a common mortal: to see him pretend to be so good-natured, too, when it was his function—the very rule of his be-ing—to inflict summary punishment upon his fellow-men, to have no compassion for pleasant social vices, and to be as hard on a drunkard as upon a thief.

There was only one case to be heard this morning, and the thrilling interest of that one case held the spectators breathless. Women stood on tiptoe peering over the shoulders of the men—women who ought to have been at their wash-tubs, or baking homely satisfying pasties for the family supper.

The ruffian was brought in, closely guarded by a couple of rural policemen, and looking considerably the worse for last night's recapture. He had fought like a wild-cat for his free-dom; had given and taken a couple of black eyes; had further-more received a formidable cut across his forehead, and had had his clothes torn in the scuffle.

The two Tyrrels, father and son, also in a damaged condition, were there to relate proudly how they had pounced upon the offender just as he was clambering over a fence. They had told their story already so many times, in an informal manner, to curious friends and acquaintances, that they were prepared to give it with effect presently when they should be put upon oath.

Mr. Tresillian, who went to work in a very slow and ponder-ous way, was still conferring with his clerk in a bass under-tone, which sounded like distant organ music, when Rebecca Mason strode forth from the crowd, and came to that privileged portion of the room where Mr. Penwyn and his wife were sit-ting.

"I want to know if you're going to press this charge, Mr. Pen-wyn," she asked, quietly enough, but hardily.

"Of course he is," answered Madge, with a flash of anger. "Do you suppose we are going to overlook such an attempt— a man breaking into our house after midnight, and frightening my sister nearly out of her wits? We should never feel secure at the Manor if this man were not made an example of. Pray what interest have you in pleading for him?"

"I'll tell you that by and by, madam. I did not ask the question of you, but of my master."

"Your master and I have but one thought in the matter."

"Do you mean to prosecute that man, Mr. Penwyn?" asked Rebecca, looking steadfastly at the squire. Even while addressing Madge she had never taken her eyes from Churchill's face. The brief dialogue had been carried on in an under-tone while Mr. Tresillian and the clerk were still whispering and making notes on a sheet of foolscap.

"The case is out of my hands. I have no power to prevent the man's committal."

"Yes, you have," answered Rebecca, doggedly; "you have power to do anything here. What is law or justice against a great land-owner in a place like this? You are lord and master here."

"Why do you bother me about this burglar?"

"He is my son."

"I am sorry any servant of mine should be related to such a scoundrel."

"I am not proud of the relationship," answered the lodge-keeper, coolly. "Yet there are men capable of worse crimes than entering another man's house—criminals who wear smooth faces and fine broadcloth—and stand high in the world. I'd rather have that vagabond for my son than some of them."

Churchill glanced at his wife, as if to consult her feelings. But Madge, so tender and pitying to the destitute and afflicted, had an inflexible look just now. Rebecca Mason was her particular antipathy, a blot upon the fair face of Penwyn Manor, which she was most anxious to see removed; and now Rebecca appeared in a new and still more disagreeable light as the mother of a burglar. It was hardly strange, therefore, that Mrs. Penwyn should be indisposed to see the law outraged in the cause of mercy.

"I regret that my wish to serve you will not allow me to con-done a felony on behalf of your son," said Churchill, with slow distinctness and meeting that piercing gaze of the gypsy's with as steady a look in his own gray eyes. "The attempt was too daring to be overlooked. A man breaks into my house at mid-night, naturally with some evil intent."

Still not a word about the diamonds which he had recovered from the burglar's person.

"He did not break into your house," argued Rebecca; "you left your windows open, and he walked in. He had been drink-ing, I know, and hardly knew where he was going or what he was doing. If he had had his wits about him he couldn't have allowed himself to be caught by a girl," she added, contemptuously.

"He may have been drunk," said Churchill, witn a thoughtful look; "but that hardly mends the matter. It isn't pleasant to have a drunken vagabond prowling about one's house. What do you say, my queen?" he asked, turning to Madge with a smile; but not quite the smile which was wont to brighten his face when he looked at her. "Will you exercise your prerogative of mercy? Shall I try what I can do to get this vagabond off with a few days in Penwyn lock-up, instead of having him committed for trial?"

"I have no compassion for a man who lifted his hand against my sister," answered Madge, warmly. "Sir Lewis told me all about it, Churchill. He saw that villain raise his [clinched fist to strike Viola's face. He would have disfigured her for life, or killed her, perhaps, if Sir Lewis had not caught his arm. Do you suppose I am going to plead for such a scoundrel as that?"

"Come, Mrs. Penwyn, you are a woman and a mother," pleaded Rebecca, "you ought to be merciful."

"Not at the expense of society. Justice and order would, indeed, be outraged if the law were stretched in favor of such a ruffian as your son."

"You are a hard lady," said the gypsy, "but I think I can say a word that will soften you. Let me speak to you in the next room," looking toward a half open door that communicated with a small parlor adjoining. "Let me speak with you alone for five minutes—you'd better not say no, for his sake," she urged, with a glance at Churchill.

Mr. Penwyn rose suddenly with darkening brow, seizing Madge by the arm, as if he would hold her away from the woman.

"I will not suffer any communication between you and my wife," he exclaimed. "You have said your say and been answered. I will do anything I can for you, grant anything you choose to ask for yourself"—with emphasis—"but your son must take his chance. Tresillian, we are ready."

"Lady, you had better hear me," pleaded the gypsy.

That plea weighed lightly enough with Madge Penwyn. She was watching her husband's face, and it was a look in that which alone influenced her decision.

"I will hear you," she said to the gypsy. "Ask Mr. Tresillian to wait for a few minutes, Churchill."

"Madge, what are you thinking of?" cried her husband. "She can have nothing to say that has not been said already. She has had her answer."

"I will hear her, Churchill, and alone."

That "I will" was accompanied by an imperious look not often seen in Madge Penwyn's face—never before seen by him she looked at now.

"As you will, love," he answered, very quietly, and made way for her to pass into the adjoining room.

Rebecca Mason followed, and shut the door between the two

rooms. There was a faint stir, and then the low hum of the little crowd sunk into silence. Every eye turned to that closed
door; every mind was curious to know what those two women
were saying on the other side of it.

There was a pause of about ten minutes. Churchill sat by the
official table, silent and thoughtful. Mr. Tresillian fidgeted
with the stationery, and yawned once or twice. The ruffian
stood in his place, dogged and imperturbable, looking as if he
were the individual least concerned in the day's proceedings.

At last the door opened, and Madge appeared. She came
slowly into the room—slowly, and like a person who only
walked steadily by an effort. So white and wan was the face
turned appealingly toward Churchill that she looked like one
newly risen from some sickness unto death. Churchill rose to
go to her, but hesitatingly, as if he were doubtful whether to
approach her—almost as if they had been strangers.

"Churchill," she said, faintly, looking at him with pathetic
eyes—a gaze in which the deepest love and despair were mingled.
At that look and word he went to her, put his arm round her,
and led her gently back to her seat. "You must get this man
off, Churchill," she whispered faintly. "You must."

He bent his head, but spoke not a word, only pressed her
hand with a grip strong as pain or death. And then he went to
Mr. Tresillian, who was growing tired of the whole business,
and was at all times plastic as wax in the hands of his brother
magistrate, not being troubled with ideas of his own in a general way. Indeed, he had expended so much brain-power in the
endeavor to outmaneuver the manifold artifices of certain ancient dog-foxes in the district that he could hardly be supposed
to have much intellectual force left for the Bench.

"I find that there has been a good deal of muddle in this
business," said Churchill to him, confidentially. "The man is
the son of my lodgekeeper, and a decent, hard-working fellow
enough, it seems. He had been drinking, and strayed into the
Manor-house in an obfuscated condition last night—my servants
are most to blame for leaving doors open—and Viola saw him,
and was frightened, and made a good deal of unnecessary fuss.
And then my keepers knocked the fellow about more than they
need have done. So I really think if you were to let him off with
a day or two in the lock-up, or even a severe reprimand——"

"Yes—yes—yes—yes—yes," said Mr. Tresillian, keeping up a
running fire of muttered affirmatives throughout Churchill's
speech. "Certainly. Let the fellow off, by all means, if he had
no felonious intention, and Mrs. Penwyn wishes it. Ladies are
so compassionate! Yes, yes, yes, yes."

Mr. Tresillian was thinking rather more about a certain fif-
teen-acre corn-field now ready for the sickle than of the business
in hand. Reapers were scarce in the land just now, and he was
not clear in his mind about getting in that corn.

So instead of swearing in witnesses and holding a ceremon-
ious examination, Mr. Tresillian disappointed the assembled
audience by merely addressing a few sharpish words to the
delinquent, and sending him about his business, with a warning

never more to create trouble in that particular neighborhood,
lest it should be worse for him. The offender was further en-
joined to be grateful to Mr. and Mrs. Penwyn for their kindness in not pressing the charge. And thus the business was
over, and the court rose. The crowd dispersed slowly,
grumbling not a little about Justice's justice, and deeply disappointed at not having seen the strange offender committed
for trial.

" If it had been one of us," a man remarked to a neighbor,
" we shouldn't have got off so easy."

" No," growled another. " If it had been some poor devil
had up for licking his wife, he'd have got it hot."

All was over. Viola and Sir Lewis Dallas, who had been indulging in a little quiet flirtation by an open window, and not attending to the progress of events, were beyond measure surprised at the abrupt close of the proceedings, and not a little
disappointed, for Viola had quite looked forward to appearing
in the witness-box at Bodmin assize court, and being cross-ex-
amined by an impertinent barrister, and then complimented
upon her heroism by the judge, and perhaps cheered by the
multitude. Nothing could be flatter than this ending.

" It's just like Madge!" exclaimed Viola. "She may make
believe to be angry for half an hour or so, but that soft heart of
hers is melted at the first piteous appeal. The horrid woman at
the lodge has begged off her horrid son."

Madge, whiter than summer lilies, did not look in a condition
to be questioned just now.

" See how ill she looks." said Viola to Sir Lewis. " They have
worried her into a nervous state with their goings on. Let us
get her away."

There was no need for Sir Lewis' intervention. Churchill led
her out of the room. Erect, and facing the crowd firmly enough,
both of them, but one pale as death.

" Are you going to ride home, Churchill?" asked Madge, as
her husband handed her into the carriage.

"Yes, love; I may as well go back as I came, on Tarpan."

" I had rather you came with us," she said, with an appealing
look.

" As you like, dear. Sir Lewis, will you ride Tarpan?"

Sir Lewis looked at Viola, and then at his boots. It was an
honor to ride Tarpan, but hardly a pleasant thing to ride him
without straps; and then Sir Lewis would have liked that homeward drive, with Viola for his *vis-a-vis.*

" By all means, if Mrs. Penwyn would rather you went back
in the carriage," he said, good-naturedly, but with a look at
Viola which meant, " You know what a sacrifice I am making."

That drive home was a very silent one. Viola was suffering
from reaction after excitement, and leaned back with a listless
air. Madge looked straight before her, with grave fixed eyes,
gazing into space. And still there was not a cloud in the blue,
bright sky, and the reapers, standing among the tawny corn,
turned their swart faces toward the squire's carriage, and pulled
their moistened forelocks, and thought what a fine thing it was

for the gentry to be driving swiftly through the clear warm air, lolling back upon soft cushions, and with no more exertion than was involved in holding a big white silk umbrella.

" But how white Madam Penwyn looks," said one of the men, a native of the place, to his mate. " She doan't look as if the good things of this life agreed with her. She looks paler and more tired like thau you nor me."

CHAPTER XXXIV.
" THIS IS MORE STRANGE THAN SUCH A MURDER IS."

THEY were in the dressing-room at Penwyn, that spacious, many-windowed chamber, with its closed Venetians, which was cool and shadowy even on a blazing August day like this. They were alone together, husband and wife, face to face—two white faces turned toward each other, blanched by passions stronger and deeper than it is man's common lot to suffer.

They had come here straight from the carriage that brought them back to the Manor-house, and they were alone for the first moment since Madge had heard Rebecca Mason's petition.

" Churchill," she said, slowly, with agonized eyes lifted to his face, " I know all—all that woman could tell; and she showed me——"

She stopped with a shudder, and clasped her hands before her face. Her husband stood like a rock, and made no attempt to draw nearer to her. He stood aloof and waited.

" I know all," she repeated with a passionate sob, and I remember what I said when you asked me to be your wife. You were too poor—we were too poor. I could not marry you because of your poverty. It was my worldliness, my mercenary decision, that influenced you, that urged you to—— Oh, Churchill, half the fault was mine! God give me leave to bear half the burden of His anger!"

She flung herself upon her husband's shoulder, and sobbed there, clinging to him more fondly than in their happiest hour, her arms clasping him round the neck, her face hidden upon his breast, with such love as only such a woman can feel—love which, supreme in itself, rises above every lesser influence.

" What! you touch me, Madge! You come to my arms still! you shed compassionate tears upon my breast! Then I am not wholly lost. Vile as I am, there is comfort still. My love, my fond one, fortune gave me nothing so sweet as you."

" Oh, Churchill, why, why——" she sobbed.

He understood the question involved in that one broken word, hardly audible for the sobs that shook his wife's frame.

" Dearest, Fate was hard upon me, and I wanted you," he said, with a calmness that chilled her soul. " A good man would have trusted in Providence, no doubt, and waited unrepiningly for life's blessings until he was gray and old, and went down to his grave without ever having known earthly bliss, taking with him some vague notion that he was to come into his estate somewhere else. I am not a good man. My passionate love and my scorn of poverty would not let me wait. I knew that by one swift bold act—a wicked deed if you will, but not a cruel one, since every man must die once—I could win all I desired. Fortune had made two men's lots flagitiously unequal. I balanced them."

"Oh, Churchill, it is awful to hear you speak like that. Surely you have repented, surely all your life must be poisoned with regret."

"Yes, I have felt the canker called remorse. I could surrender all good things that earth can give—yes, let you go from these fond arms, beloved—if that which is done could be undone. And now you will loathe me, and we must part."

"Part. Churchill? What, leave you because you are the most miserable of men? No, dearest. I will cling to you, and hold by you to the end of life, come what will. If it was I who tempted you to sin, you shall not bear your burden alone. Loathe you!" she cried, passionately, looking up at him with streaming eyes; "no, Churchill, I cannot think of that hideous secret without horror; I cannot think of the sinner without pity. There is a love that is stronger than the world's favor, stronger than right, or peace, or honor, and such a love I have given you."

"My angel—my comforter. Would to God I had kept my soul spotless for your sake!"

"And for our child, Churchill; for our darling. Oh, dearest, if there can be pardon for such a sin as yours—and Christ spoke words of mercy and promise to the thief on the cross—let us strive for it, strive with tears and prayers and deepest penitence. Oh, my love, believe in a God of mercy, a God who sent His Son to preach repentance to sinners. Love, let us kneel together to that offended God, let us sue for mercy, side by side."

Her husband drew her closer to his breast, kissed the pale lips with unspeakable tenderness, looked into the true, brave eyes which did not shrink from his gaze.

"Even I, who have had you for my wife, did not know the divinity of a woman's love—until this miserable hour. My dearest, even to comfort you, I cannot add deliberate blasphemy to my sins. I cannot kneel or pray to a Power in which my faith is of the weakest. Keep your gentle creed, dearest, adore your God of mercy—but I have hardened my heart against these things too long to find comfort in them now. My one glory, my one consolation, is the thought that, lost as I am, I have not fallen too low for your love. You will love me, and hold by me, knowing my sin; and let my one merit be that in this dark hour I have not lied to you. I have not striven to outweigh that woman's accusation by some fable which your love might accept."

"No, Churchill, you have trusted me, and you shall find me worthy of your trust," she answered, bravely. "No act of mine shall ever betray you. And if you cannot pray, if God withholds the light of truth from you for a little while, my prayers shall ascend to Him like ever-burning incense. My intercession shall never cease. My faith shall never falter."

He kissed her again without a word—too deeply moved for

speech—and then turned away from her and paced the room to and fro, while she went to her dressing-table, and looked wonderingly at the white, wan face which had beamed so brightly on her guests last night. She looked at herself thoughtfully, remembering that henceforward she had a part to act, and a fatal secret to keep—no wan looks, no tell-tale pallor, must betray the horrid truth.

"Madge," said her husband, presently, after two or three thoughtful turns up and down the room, "I have not one word to say to you in self-justification. I stand before you confessed, a sinner of the blackest dye. Yet you must not imagine that my whole life is of a color with that one hideous act. It is not so. Till that hour my life had been blameless enough—more blameless perhaps than the career of one young man in twenty in our modern civilization. Temptation to vulgar sins never assailed me. I was guiltless till that fatal hour in which my evil genius whispered the suggestion of a prize worth the price of crime. Macbeth was a brave and honorable soldier, you know, when the fatal sisters met him on the heath, and hissed their promise into his ear. And in that moment guilty hopes seized upon his soul, and already, in thought, he was a murderer. Dearest, I have never been a profligate, or cheat, or liar, or coward. I have concentrated the wickedness which other men spread over a lifetime of petty sins in one great offense."

"And that shall be forgiven," cried Madge, with a sublime air of conviction. "It shall, if you will but repent."

"If to wish an act undone is repentance, I have repented for more than two years," he answered. "Hark, love, that is the luncheon-bell! We must not alarm our friends by our absence. Or stay, I will go down to the dining-room. You had better remain here and rest. Poor agonized head, tender, faithful heart, what bitter need of rest for both!"

"No, dear; I will go down with you," Madge answered, firmly. "But let me ask one question first, Churchill, and then I will never speak to you more of our secret. That hateful woman—you have pacified her to-day, but how long will she be satisfied? Is there any fear of new danger?"

"I can see none, dearest. The woman was satisfied with her lot, and would never have given me any trouble but for this unlucky accident of her son's attempt last night. I will get the man provided for and sent out of the country where you shall never hear of him again. The woman is harmless enough, and cares little enough for her son; but that brute instinct of kindred, which even savages feel, made her fight for her cub."

"Why did you bring her here, Churchill? Was that wise?"

"I thought it best so. I thought it wise to have her at hand under my eye, where she could only assail me at close quarters, and where she was not likely to find confederates—where she could have all her desires gratified, and could have no motive for tormenting me."

"It is best, perhaps," assented Madge. "But it is horrible to have her here."

"The Egyptians had a skeleton at their feasts lest they should forget to make the most of their brief span of carnal pleasures. It is as well to be reminded of the poison in one's cup of life."

"And now go to our guests, Churchill. Your face tells no tale. Say that I am coming almost immediately."

"My darling, I fear you are exacting too much from your fortitude."

"No, Churchill; I shall begin as I mean to go on. If I were to shut myself up, if I were to give myself time for though to-day—just at first—I should go mad."

He went, half unwillingly. She stood for a few moments fixed to the spot where he had left her, as if lost in some awful dream, and then walked dizzily to the adjoining room, where she tried to wash the ashy pallor from her cheeks with cold spring water. She re-arranged her hair with hands that trembled despite her endeavor to be calm, put on a fresh white muslin dress with infinite flouncings and delicate embroidery, fastened a scarlet *coque* upon her dark coronal of plaited hair, and went down to the dining-room looking a little wan and fatigued, but not less lovely than she was wont to look.

What a mad world it seemed to her when she saw her guests assembled at the oval table, talking and laughing in that easy, unreserved way which seems natural at the midday meal, when servants are banished, and gentlemen perform the onerous office of carver at the loaded sideboard; when hungry people, just returned from long rambles over hills and banks where the wild thyme grows, or from a desperate croquet match, or a gallop across the moorland, devour a heterogeneous meal of sirloin, perigord pie, clouted cream, fruit, cutlets, and pastry, and drink deeper draughts of that sparkling Devonian cider, better a hundred times than champagne, than they would quite care to acknowledge if a reckoning were demanded of them.

Everybody seemed especially noisy to-day—talk, flirtation, laughter, made a Babel-like hubbub: and at the end of the table sat the Squire of Penwyn, calm, inscrutable, and no line upon the expansive forehead, with its scanty border of crisp brown hair, showed the brand of Cain.

CHAPTER XXXV.

"AH, LOVE, THERE IS NO BETTER LIFE THAN THIS."

JUSTINA had made a success at the Royal Albert Theater. The newspapers were tolerably unanimous in their verdict. The more æsthetic and critical journals even gave her their approval, which was a kind of *cachet*. The public, always straightforward and single-minded in their expression of satisfaction, had no doubt about her. She was accepted at once as one of the most popular and promising young actresses of the day—natural yet artistic, free from all trick, unaffected, modest, yet with the impulsive boldness of a true artist, who forgets alike herself and her audience in the unalloyed delight of her art.

A success so unqualified gave the girl extreme pleasure, and elevated Mathew Elgood to a region of bliss which he had never before attained. For the first time in his life he found himself supplied with ample means for the gratification of desires which, at their widest, came within a narrow limit. The manager of the Royal Albert Theater had made haste to be liberal, lest other managers, ever on the watch for rising talent, should attempt to lure Justina to their boards by offers of larger reward. He sprung his terms at once from the weekly three guineas, which Mathew had gladly accepted at the outset, to double that amount, and promised further increase if Miss Elgood's second part were as successful as the first.

" With a very young actress one can never be sure of one's ground," he said, diplomatically. " The part in ' No Cards ' just fits your daughter. I've no idea what she may be in the general run of business. I've seen so many promising first appearances lead to nothing."

" My daughter has had experience and tuition from an experienced actor, sir," replied Mathew, with dignity. " She has a perfect knowledge of her art, and the more you call upon her the better stuff you will get from her. Such a part as that in ' No Cards ' is a mere bagatelle for her. Fits her, indeed! It fits her too well, sir. Her genius has no room to expand in it."

Six guineas—by no means a large income in the eyes of a paterfamilias with a wife, and a servant or two, and a nestful of small children to provide for, to say nothing of the rent of the nest to pay—seemed wealth to Mr. Elgood, whose ideas of luxury were bounded by a Bloomsbury lodging, a hot dinner every day, and his glass of gin-and-water mixed with a liberal hand. He expanded himself in this new sunshine, passed his leisure in spelling through the daily papers, escorting his daughter to and from the theater, and hanging about the green-room, where he told anecdotes of Macready, bragged of Justina's talents when she was out of the room, and made himself generally agreeable.

That Bloomsbury lodging of Mr. Elgood's, though located in the shabbier quarter of that extensive parish, seemed curiously near that highly respectable street where Humphrey Clissold had his handsome first-floor chambers, so little account did Mr. Clissold make of the distance between the two domiciles. He was always dropping in at Mr. Elgood's, bringing Justina fresh flowers from the glades of Covent Garden, or a new book or some new music. She had improved her knowledge of that 'delightful art during the last two years, and now played and sang sweetly, with taste and expression that charmed the poet.

Before Justina had been many weeks at the Albert Theater it became an established fact that Mr. Clissold was to drink tea with Miss Elgood every afternoon. The gentle temptations of the kettle-drum, which he had resisted so bravely in Eton Square, beguiled him here in Bloomsbury, though the simple feast was held on a second floor, with a French mechanic working sedulously at his trade below. Many an hour did Humphrey Clissold waste in careless, happy talk in that second-floor sitting-room, with its odor of stale tobacco, its shabby old-fashioned furniture, its all-pervading air of poverty and commonness. The room was glorified for him somehow, as he sat by

t. sunny window sipping an infusion of· congou and pekoe out of a blue delf tea-cup.

One day it struck him suddenly that Justina ought to have prettier tea-cups, and a few days afterward there arrived a set of curious old dragon-china cups and saucers. He had not gone to a china shop, like a rich man, and ordered the newest and choicest ware that Minton's factory had produced. But he had walked half over London, and peered into all manner of obscure dens in the broker's shop line, till he found something to please him. Old red and blue sprawling monsters of the crocodile species on thinnest opalescent porcelain, cups and saucers that had been hoarded and cherished by ancient housekeepers, only surrendered when all that life can cling to slipped from death's dull hand. The old fragile pottery pleased him beyond measure, and he carried the cups and saucers off to a cab, packed in a basket of paper shavings, and took them himself to Justina.

"I don't suppose they're worth very much nowadays, when Oriental china is at a discount," he said; "and they cost me the merest trifle. But I thought you'd like them."

Justina was enraptured. Those old cups and saucers were the first present that she had ever received—the first actual gift bestowed out of regard for her pleasure which she could count in all her life, except the same donor's offerings of books and music.

"How good of you!" she said, more than once, and with a look worth three times as many words.

Humphrey laughed at her delight.

"It was worth my perambulation of London to see you so pleased." he said.

"What! did you take so much trouble to get them?"

"I walked a good long way. The only merit my offering has is that I took some pains to find it. I am not a rich man, you know, Justina."

He called her by her Christian name always, with a certain brotherly freedom that was not unpleasant to either.

"I am so glad of that!" she exclaimed, naively.

"Glad I'm not rich? Why, that's scarce friendly, Justina."

"Isn't it? But if you were rich you wouldn't come to see us so often, perhaps. Rich people have such hosts of friends."

"Yes, Crœsus has generally a widish circle—not the best people, possibly. but plenty of them. But I don't think all the wealth of the Indies—the peacock-throne of the great Mogul, and so on—would make any difference in my desire to come here. No, Justina, were the chief of the Rothschilds to transfer his balance to my account to-morrow, I should drop in all the same for my afternoon refresher as regularly as five o'clock struck."

They had talked of literature and poetry, and fully discussed that new poet whose book Justina had wept over; but by no word had Humphrey hinted at his identity with the writer. He liked to hear her speculate upon that unknown poet—wondering what he was like—setting up her ideal image of him. One day he made her describe what manner of man she imagined the author of a "Life Picture;" but she found it difficult to reduce her fancies to words.

"I cannot compliment you on the clearness of your delineation," he said. "I haven't yet arrived at the faintest notion of your ideal poet. If you could compare him to any one we know it might help me out. Is he like Mr. Flittergilt, the dramatist?"

"Mr. Flittergilt!" she cried, contemptuously—"Mr. Flittergilt, who is always making bad puns, and talking of his own successes, and telling us that clever remark he made yesterday!"

"Not like Flittergilt? Has he any resemblance to me, for instance?"

Justina laughed and shook her head—a very positive shake.

"No; you are too light-hearted for a poet. You take life too easily. You seem too happy."

"In your presence, Justina. You never see me in my normal condition," remonstrated Humphrey, laughing.

"No, I cannot fancy the author of that poem at all like you. He is a man who has suffered."

Humphrey sighed.

"And you think I have never suffered?"

"He must be a man who has loved a false and foolish woman, and who has been stung to the quick by remorse for his own weakness."

"Ah, we are all of us weak once in our lives, and are apt to be deceived, Justina. Happy the man who knows no second weakness, and is not twice deceived!"

He said this gravely enough for poet and thinker. Justina looked at him with a puzzled expression.

"Now you seem quite a different person," she said. "I could almost fancy you capable of being a poet. I know there are glimpses of poetry in your talk sometimes."

"When I talk to you, Justina. Some people have an influence that is almost inspiration. All manner of bright thoughts come to me when you and I are together."

"That cannot be true," she said. "It is you who bring the bright thoughts to me. Consider how ignorant I am, and how much you know—all the great world of poetry, of which so many doors are barred against me. You read Goethe and Schiller. You go into that solemn temple where the Greek poets live in their strange old world. When you took me to the museum the other day you pointed out all the statues, and talked of them as familiarly as if they had been the statues of your own friends; while I, who have hardly a school-girl's knowledge of French, cannot even read that Alfred de Musset of whom you talk so much."

"You know the language in which Shakespeare wrote. You have all that is noblest and grandest in human literature in your hand when you take up that calf-bound, closely printed, double-columned volume yonder, from the old Chiswick press. I think an English writer who never read anything beyond his Bible and Shakespeare would have a nobler style than the man of widest reading who had not those two books in his heart of hearts. Other poets are poets. That one man was the god of poetry. But we will read some of De Musset's poems together, Justina, and I will teach you something more than a school-girl's French.

After this it became an established thing for Humphrey and Justina to read together for an hour or so, just as it was an es-tablished thing for Humphrey to drop in at tea-time. He made his selections from De Musset discreetly, and then passed on to Victor Hugo; and thus that more valuable part of education which begins when a school-girl has been "finished" was not wanting to Justina. Never was a pupil brighter or more in-telligent, never master more interested in his work.

Mathew Elgood looked on, not unapprovingly. In the first place, he was a man who took life lightly, and always held to the Gospel text about the day and the evil thereof. He had ascertained from good-natured Mr. Flittergilt that Humphrey Clissold had an income of some hundreds per annum, and was, moreover, the scion of a good old family. About the good old family Mathew cared very little; but the income was an im-portant consideration; and, assured of that main fact, he saw no harm in the growing intimacy between Justina and Humph-rey.

It's on the cards for her to do better, of course," reflected Mr. Elgood. "Actresses have married into the peerage before to-day, and no end of them have married bankers and heavy mer-cantile swells. But, after all, Justina isn't the kind of beauty to take the world by storm; and this success of hers may be only a flash in the pan. I haven't much confidence in the duration of this blessed new school of acting, these drawing-room comedies with their how-d'ye-do and won't-you-take-a-chair dialogue. The good old heavy five-act drama will have its turn by and by, when the public is tired of this milk and water. And Justina has hardly physique enough for the five-act drama. It might be a good thing to get her comfortably married, if I was quite clear about my own position."

This was an all-important question. Justina single and on the stage meant at a minimum six guineas a week at Mr. El-good's disposal. The girl handed her salary over to the pa-ternal exchequer without question, and was grateful for an oc-casional pound or two toward the replenishment of her scanty wardrobe.

Mr. Elgood lost no time in trying to arrive at Humphrey's ideas upon this subject.

" It's a hard thing for a man when he outlives his generation," he remarked, plaintively, one Sunday evening, when Humphrey had dropped in and found the comedian alone, Justina not hav-ing yet returned from evening service at St. Pancras. "Here am I, in the prime of life, with all my faculties in full vigor, laid up in port, as useless a creature as if I were a sheer hulk, like poor Tom Bowling, actually dependent upon the industry of a girl! There's something degrading in the idea. If it were not for Justina, I'd accept an engagement for the heavies at the lowest slum in London, roar my vitals out in three pieces a night, rather than eat the bread of dependence. But Justina won't have it. ' I want you to bring me home from the theater of a night, father,' she says. And that's an argument I can't resist. The streets of London are no place for unprotected innocence after dark, and cabs are an expensive luxury. Yet it's a bitter thing to consider that if Justina were to marry I should have to go to the workhouse."

" Hardly, if she married an honest man, Mr. Elgood," replied Humphrey. " No honest man would take your daughter away from you without making some provision for your future."

" Well, I have looked at it in that light." said Mathew reflectively, as if the question had thus dimly presented itself before him. "I think an honest man wouldn't feel it quite the right thing to take away my bread-winner, and leave me to spend my declining days in want and misery. Yet, as Shakespeare has it, ' Age is unnecessary.' 'Superfluous lags the veteran on the stage.' ' *To have done* is to hang

      " ' Quite out of fashion, like a rusty mail,
      In monumental mockery.' ' "

" Be assured, Mr. Elgood, that if your daughter marries a man who really loves her, your age will not be uncared for."

" I do not wish to be a burden upon my child," pursued the actor, tearfully.

His second tumbler of gin-and-water was nearly emptied by this time.

" A hundred and four pounds per annum—two pounds a week—secured to me would give me all I ask of luxury; my lowly lodging, say in May's Court, St. Martin's Lane, or somewhere between Blackfriars Bridge and the Temple, my rasher or my bloater for breakfast, my beefsteak for dinner, and my modest glass of gin-and-water hot, to soothe the tired nerves of age. These, and an occasional ounce of tobacco, are all the old man craves."

" Your desires are very modest, Mr. Elgood."

" They are, my dear boy. I would bear the pangs of severance from my sweet girl if I saw her ascend to a loftier sphere, and keep my lowly place without repining. But I should like the two pounds a week made as certain as the law of the land would make it."

This was a pretty clear declaration of his views, and having thus expressed himself, Mr. Elgood allowed life to slip on pleasantly, enjoying his comfortable little two o'clock dinners and his afternoon glass of gin-and-water, and dozing in his easy chair, while Humphrey and Justina read or talked, only waking at five o'clock, when the dragon tea-cups made a cheerful clatter, and Justina was prettily busy with the task of tea-making.

Even the old common lodging-house sitting-room began by and by to assume a bright home-like air. A vase of choice flowers, a row of books neatly arranged on the old-fashioned side-board, a Bohemian glass ink-stand, clean muslin covers tacked over the faded chintz chair-backs—small embellishments by which a woman makes the best of the humblest materials

The dragon-china tea-service was set out on the *chiffonier* top when not in use, and made the chief ornament of the room. Composition statuettes of Shakespeare and Dante which Humphrey had bought from an itinerant image-seller, adorned the chimney-piece, whence the landlady's shepherd and shepherdess were banished.

In a scene so humble, in a circle so narrow. Humphrey Clissold spent some of the happiest hours of his life. He remembered Cavendish Square sometimes with a pang, the shadowy drawing-room at twilight, the flower-screened balcony, so pleasant a spot to linger in when the lamps were lighted in the square below, and the long vista of Wigmore Street converged to a gittering point, and the moon rose above the gloomy roof of Cavendish House, hours of happiness as unalloyed, dreams that were over, days that were gone. And he asked himself whether this second birth of joy was a delusion and a snare like the first.

CHAPTER XXXVI.
LOVE IS A THING TO WHICH WE SOON CONSENT.

HUMPHREY CLISSOLD had not forgotten that entry in the register at Seacomb Church, and one afternoon, when Mathew, Justina, and he were cozily seated at the clumsy old lodging-house table drinking tea, he took occasion to refer to his rambles in Cornwall, and his exploration of the little out-of-the-way market town.

"I should fancy you children of Thespis must have found life rather difficult at such a place as Seacomb," he said. "Dramatic art must be rather out of the line of those Nonconformist miners. I saw three Dissenting chapels in the small town, one of them being the very building which was once the theater."

"Yes," said Mr. Elgood, with a thoughtful look, "we had a bad time of it at Seacomb. My poor wife was ill, and if it hadn't been for the kindness of the people we lodged with, well —we might have made a closer acquaintance with starvation than any man cares to make. There's no such touch-stone for the human heart as distress, and no man knows the goodness of his fellow-men till he has sounded the lowest deep of misery."

"You lost a child at Seacomb, did you not, Mr. Elgood?" asked Humphrey.

The comedian looked up with a startled expression.

"How did you know that?" he asked.

"I was turning over the parish register, looking for another entry, when I stumbled across that."

"Why, father," exclaimed Justina, "you never told me that you lost a child at Seacomb. I did not even know I ever had a brother or sister. I thought I was your only child."

"The only one to live beyond infancy, my dear. Why should I trouble you with the remembrance of past sorrows? We have had cares enough without raking up dead-and-gone griefs."

"Was your wife a Cornishwoman, Mr. Elgood?" asked Humphrey.

"No; she was born within the sound of Bow-bells, poor soul. Her father was a bookbinder in Clerkenwell. She had a pretty voice, and a wonderful ear for music; and some one told her she would do very well on the stage. Her home was dull and poor, and she felt she ought to earn her living somehow. So she be-gan to act at a little amateur theater near Cold Bath Fields, and, having a bright, pretty way with her, she got a good deal of notice, and was offered an engagement to play small singing parts at Sadler's Wells. I was a member of the stock company there at the time, and her pretty little face and her pretty little ways turned my stupid head somehow, and I told myself that two salaries thrown into one would go further than they would divided, never considering that managers would want to strike a bargain with us—lump us together on the cheap—when we were married, or that when two people are earning no salary it's harder for two to live than one. Well, we married, and lived a hard life afterward; but I was true to my poor girl, and fond of her to the last; and when hunger was staring us in the face we were not all unhappy."

"Justina is like her mother, I suppose," said Humphrey, "as she doesn't at all resemble you."

"No," replied Mathew; "my wife was a pretty woman, but not in Justina's style."

"What made you hit upon such an out-of-the-way name as Justina? Mind, I like the name very much, but it is a very un-common one."

Mr. Elgood looked puzzled.

"I dare say it was a fancy of my wife's," he said. "But I really don't recollect anything about it."

"I'll tell you why I ask the question," pursued Humphrey. "While I was in Cornwall, staying at a farm called Borcel End, I came across the name."

The comedian almost dropped his tea-cup.

"Borcel End!" he exclaimed; "you were at Borcel End?"

"Yes. You know the place, it seems. But that's hardly strange, since you lived so long at Seacomb. Did you know the Trevanards?"

"No; I only knew the farm from having it pointed out to me once when a friend gave me a drive across the moor in his dog-cart. A queer out-of-the-way place. What could have taken you there?"

"It was something in the way of an adventure," replied Humphrey; and then proceeded to relate his experience on that midsummer afternoon among the Cornish hills.

He touched lightly upon his visit to Penwyn Manor-house, knowing that this might be a painful subject for Justina; but she showed a warm interest in his story.

"You saw *his* house," she said, "the old manor-house he told me about that night at Eborsham? Oh, how like the mem-ory of a dream it seems when I think of it! I should like so much to see that place!"

"You shall see it some day, Justina, if—if you will let me show it you," said Humphrey, stumbling a little over the last part of the sentence. "It is strange that you should be twice associated with that remote corner of the land, once in your birth, a second time in poor James Penwyn's devotion to you."

"It is very strange, sir," said the comedian, solemnly, and then with his grand Shakespearean manner continued,

"' There are more things in heaven and earth, Horatio,
Than are dreamt of in your philosophy.' "

"It was at Borcel End I heard the name of Justina," said Humphrey, going back to the subject most interesting to him. "There is an old picture there, the portrait of the present proprietor's grandmother, whose name was Justina."

"Is the old grandmother living still?" asked Matthew, suddenly.

"What, blind old Mrs. Trevanard? Yes, she is still living. But you said you did not know the Trevanards."

"Only by repute. I heard people talk about them. Rather a curious family, I fancy."

"In some respects," answered Humphrey, puzzled by the comedian's manner. It seemed as if he were affecting to know less about the family at Borcel End than he really knew. Yet why should he conceal so simple a circumstance as his acquaintance with the Trevanards?

When Humphrey and Justina were alone together for a short time next day, the girl questioned her companion about his visit to Penwyn Manor.

"I want you to describe the old place," she said. "I cannot think of it without pain. Yet I like to hear of it. Please tell me all about it."

Humphrey obeyed, and gave a detailed description of the grave old mansion as he had seen it that summer afternoon.

"How happy he would have been there!" said Justina. "How bright and fair that young life would have been! I am not thinking of my own loss," she said, as if in answer to an unspoken question of Humphrey's. "I never forgot what you said about unequal marriages that evening at Eborsham, when you came in and found me in my grief, and spoke some hard truths to me. I felt afterward that you were wiser than I, that all you said was just and true. I should have been a basely selfish woman if I had taken advantage of his foolish impulsive offer, if I had let the caprice of a moment give color to a life. But believe me, when I let myself love him I had no thought of his worldly wealth. It was his bright kind nature that drew me to him. No one had ever spoken to me as he spoke. No one had ever praised me before. It was childish love I gave him, perhaps, but it was true love all the same."

"I believe that, Justina. I believed it then when I saw you, little more than a child, so faithfully sorry for my poor friend's fate. If I had known you better in those days I should not have called his love foolish. I should never have opposed his boyish fancy. I look back now at my self-assertive wisdom, and it seems to me a greater folly than James Penwyn's unreasoning love."

"You must not say that," remonstrated Justina, gently; "all

that you said was spoken well and wisely; and if Providence had spared him, and if he had married me, he would have been ashamed of his actress·wife."

"I doubt it, Justina. A man must be hard to please who can be ashamed of you."

"I suppose it is very wicked of me," said Justina, after a brief silence, "but I cannot help grudging those people their happiness in *his* house. It makes me angry when I think of that cousin—Mr. Churchill Penwyn—who gained so much by James' death. I remember his cold, calm face as I saw it at the inquest. There was no sorrow in it."

"He could hardly be supposed to be very sorry. He and James had seen very little of each other; and James' death lifted him at a bound from poverty to wealth."

"Yes, I can never think of him without remembering that. He gains so much. The murderer with his brutal greed of gain little thought that he was helping another man to fortune—a man who in the evil wish may have shared his guilt."

"You have no right to say that, Justina."

"It is unjust, perhaps, but I cannot be temperate when I think of James Penwyn's murder. Nobody thought of interrogating the man who profited so much by his death. You were suspected because you were not at your inn that night; but no one asked where Mr. Churchill Penwyn spent the night of the murder."

"There was no ground for suspecting him."

"There was the one fact that he was the only gainer by the crime. He should have been made to prove himself innocent. And now he is happy, proud of his usurped position."

"So far as one man can judge another man's life, Churchill Penwyn seems to me completely happy. His wife is a woman in a thousand, and devoted to him. But I shall have the pleasure of introducing you to her some day, perhaps, Justina."

"Do not think of such a thing. I could never regard Churchill Penwyn as a friend. I hope never to see him again."

Humphrey Clissold saw that this feeling about James Penwyn's successor was deeply rooted, and he argued the question no further. He was too happy in Justina's society to dwell long upon discordant notes. They had so much to talk about, small as was the actual world in which they had mutual interest! Humphrey had undertaken to show all the glories of London to the girl whose life hitherto had been spent in small provincial towns. Justina had ample leisure for sight-seeing, for Mr. Flittergilt's original comedy proved an honest success, and there was no new piece yet in rehearsal at the Royal Albert Theater. Nor had Mr. Elgood, comedian, any prudish notions about the proprieties, which might have hindered his daughter's enjoyment of picture-galleries and museums, abbeys and parks. He did not care for sight-seeing himself; for his love of art, he confessed honestly, was not strong enough to counterbalance certain gouty symptoms in his feet, which made prolonged standing a fatigue to him.

"Let me enjoy my pipe and my newspaper, and let Justina

see the pictures and crockery," he said, with reference to the South Kensington Museum. So the two young people went about together as freely as if they had been brother and sister, and spent many a happy hour among the national art treasures, or in Hyde Park, in whose deserted alleys autumn's first leaves were falling.

Mr. Clissold went less and less to his clubs, and became, as it were, a dead letter in the minds of his friends.

One man suggested that Clissold must be writing a novel. Another opined that Clissold had fallen in love.

In the meanwhile Clissold was perfectly happy after his own fashion. Never had his mind been more serene; never had his verse flowed clearer in those quiet night hours which he gave to the Muses; never had the notes of his lyre rung out with a fuller melody. He was writing a poem to succeed the "Life Picture," a romance in verse, calculated to be as popular with Mudie's subscribers as his first venture had been. He soared to no empyrean heights of metaphysical speculation, but in strong melodious verse, with honest force and passion, told his story of human joys and human sorrows, human loves and human losses.

It pleased him to hear Justina praise the "Life Picture," pleased him to think that he would be exalted in her eyes were she to know him as its author. But it pleased him still better to keep his secret, to hear her frank expression of opinion, and leave her free to form her ideal fancy of the poet.

"The prize I seek to win must be won by myself alone," he thought. " My literary work is something outside myself. I will not be valued for that."

One Sunday, that being Justina's only disengaged evening, Mr. Clissold persuaded Mr. Elgood to bring his daughter to dine with him in his bachelor quarters.

"I want to show you my books," he said to Justina. "Collecting them has been my favorite amusement for the last five years, and I think it may interest you to see them."

Justina was delighted at the idea. Mr. Elgood foresaw something special in the way of dinner, perhaps a bottle or two of champagne; so the invitation was accepted with pleasure.

The September evenings were shortening by this time. They dined by lamp-light, and the bachelor's room, with its dark crimson curtains and paper, its heterogeneous collection of pictures, prints, bronzes, and china, looked its best in the mellow light of a pair of large Carcel lamps. The inner room was lined from floor to ceiling with books, handsomely bound most of them; for Mr. Clissold devoted all his superfluous cash to books and book-binding. To this study and sanctum the party adjourned for coffee and dessert, and while Mr. Elgood did ample justice to a bottle of old port, Humphrey showed Justina his favorite authors, and expatiated on the beauty of wide margins. Innocent, happy hours! yes, every whit as happy as those days of delusion in Cavendish Square. And all this time there were all manner of distinguished people anxious to be introduced to Miss Elgood, Richmond and Greenwich dinners without number which she might have eaten had she been so minded, diamonds, broughams, seal-skin jackets, pug-dogs, all the glories of existence ready to be laid at her feet.

CHAPTER XXXVII.
SORROW AUGMENTETH THE MALADY.

THIS happy, easy-going life of Humphrey Clissold's was suddenly disturbed by a letter from Martin Trevanard. Some time had elapsed without any communication from the young man, when this letter arrived, but Humphrey, in his new happiness, had been somewhat forgetful of his Cornish friend. He felt a touch of remorse as he read the letter.

"Things have been going altogether wrong here," wrote Martin. "I don't mean in the way of worldly prosperity. We have a first-rate harvest, and a good year in all respects. But I am sorry to say my mother's health has been declining for some time. She has been unable to attend to the house, and things get out of gear without her. My father has grown moody and unhappy, and, I'm afraid, puts a dash of brandy into his cider oftener than is good for him. Muriel is much the same as usual, and the good old grandmother holds out bravely. It is my mother gives me most uneasiness. I feel convinced that she has something on her mind. I have sometimes thought that her trouble is in some way connected with poor Muriel. I only wish you were here. Your clearer mind might understand much that is dark to me. If it were not asking too much from your friendship, I would willingly beg you to come down here for a week or two. It would do me more good than I can express to see you."

Humphrey's answer to this appeal was prompt and brief:

"DEAR MARTIN,—I shall be at Borcel End, all things going well, to-morrow night. Yours always. H. C."

It was a hard thing for him to leave town just now. There was his new poem, which had all the charm and freshness of a composition recently begun. Little chance for him to continue his work at Borcel, with Martin always at his elbow, and the family troubles and family secrets on his shoulders. And then there was Justina—his afternoon cup of tea in the second-floor parlor—all his new hopes and fancies, which had grouped themselves around the young actress, like the Loves and Graces round Venus in an allegorical ceiling by Lely or Kneller. But friendship with Humphrey Clissold being something more than a name, he felt that he could do no otherwise than hasten to his friend's relief. So he took his farewell cup of tea out of the dragon-china, and departed by an early express next morning, after promising Justina to be away as brief a span as possible.

Borcel End looked very much as when he had first seen it, save that the warm glow of summer had faded from the landscape and that the old farm-house had a gloomy look in the autumn dusk. Humphrey had chartered a vehicle at Seacom,

Station, and driven seven miles across country—a wild moorland district, made awful by a yawning open shaft here and there, marking the place of an abandoned mine.

The glow of the great hall fire shining through the latticed windows was the only cheerful thing about the aspect of Borcel. All the rest of the long rambling house was dark.

Martin received his friend at the gate.

" This is good of you, Clissold," he said, as Humphrey alighted. " I feel ashamed of my selfishness in asking you to come to such a dismal place as this; but it will do me a world of good to have you here. I've told my mother you were coming for a fortnight's ramble among the moors. It wouldn't do for her to know the truth."

" Of course not. But as to Borcel being a dismal place, you know that I never found it so."

" Ah, you have never lived here," said Martin, with a sigh ; "and then you've the family up at the ·Manor to enliven the neighborhood for you. There's always plenty of cheerfulness there."

" And how is Mr. Penwyn going on? Is he getting popular ?"

" He ought to be, for he has done a great deal for the neighborhood. You'll hardly recognize the road between here and the Manor when you drive there. But I don't believe the squire will ever be as popular as Mrs. Penwyn. The people idolize her. But they seem to have a notion that whatever the squire does is done more for his own advantage than the welfare of his tenants. And yet, take him for all in all, there never was a more liberal landlord."

Martin was carrying his friend's small portmanteau to the porch as he talked. Having deposited that burden, he ran back and told the driver to take his horse round to the stables, and to go round to the kitchen afterward for his own supper. This hospitable duty performed, Martin opened the door and ushered Humphrey Clissold into the family sitting-room.

There sat the old grandmother in her accustomed corner, knitting the inevitable gray stocking which was always in progress under those swift fingers. There, in an arm-chair by the fire, propped up with pillows, sat the mistress of the homestead, sorely changed since Humphrey had last seen her. The keen dark eyes had all their old brightness; nay, looked brighter from the pallor of the shrunken visage; the high cheek-bones, the square jaw, were more sharply outlined than of old; and the hand which the invalid extended to Humphrey—that honest, hard-working hand which had once been coarse and brown—was now white, and thin, and delicate of texture.

Michael Trevanard sat at the opposite side of the hearth, with a pewter tankard, a newspaper, and a long clay pipe on the square oak table at his elbow. These idle autumn evenings were trying to the somewhat mindless farmer, to whom all the world of letters afforded no further solace than the county paper, or an occasional number of the *Field*.

"I am sorry to see you looking so ill, Mrs. Trevanard," Humphrey said, kindly.

" I've had a bad time of it this year, Mr. Clissold," she answered· " I had an attack of ague and low fever in the spring, and it left a cough that has stuck to me ever since."

" I hope my coming here while you are an invalid will not be troublesome to you."

" No," answered Mrs. Trevanard, with a sigh. " I've got used to the notion of things being in a muddle, and neither Michael nor Martin seems to mind; so it doesn't much matter that the house is neglected. I've been obliged to take a second girl, and the two between them make more dirt than they ever clean up. Your old room's been got ready for you, Mr. Clissold; at least I told Martha to clean it thoroughly early this morning, and light a good fire this afternoon; so I suppose it's all right. But you might as well make up your mind that the wind was always to blow from one quarter as that a girl would do her duty when your eyes are off her. If I had a daughter now, a handy young woman, to look after the house——"

She turned her head upon her pillow with a shuddering sigh. That thought was too bitter.

" My dear Mrs. Trevanard," cried Humphrey, cheerfully, " I feel assured that the room will be—well, not so nice as you would have made it, perhaps, but quite clean and comfortable."

He took his seat by the hearth, and entered into conversation with the master of the house, who seemed cheered by the visitor's arrival.

" And pray, what's doing up in London, Mr. Clissold?" Michael Trevanard asked, as if he took the keenest interest in metropolitan affairs.

Humphrey told him the latest stirring events—wars and rumors of wars, reviews. royal marriages in contemplation—to which the farmer listened with respectful attention, feeling these facts as remote from his life as if they had occurred in the East Indies.

He, on his part, told Humphrey all that had been stirring at Penwyn; among other matters, that curious circumstance of the attempted burglary, and Mr. Penwyn's lenity toward the offender.

" I'm rather surprised to hear that," said Humphrey. " I should not have thought the squire a particularly easy-going person."

" No; he can be stern enough at times," answered the farmer. " That business up at the justice-room caused a good bit of talk. If it had been one of us, folks said, Squire Penwyn wouldn't have let go his grip like that. They couldn't understand why he should have been so lenient just because the man was the son of his lodge-keeper. It would have seemed more natural for him to get rid of the whole lot altogether, for they're a set of vaga·bonds to be about a gentleman's place. That girl Elspeth, who brought you here, is always robbing the orchards and hen-roosts about the neighborhood. She's a regular pest to the farmers' wives."

" That curious-looking woman is still at the lodge, then?" asked Humphrey.

" Yes, she's still there."

" Perhaps it was Mrs. Penwyn who interceded for the son ?"

" Well, it was a curious business altogether," answered the farmer. " Mrs. Penwyn and the woman had a talk together in a room to themselves, and then Mrs. Penwyn comes back to the justice-room looking as white as a corpse, and says a few words to her husband, and on that he talks over Mr. Tresillian, and then Mr. Tresillian lets the vagabond off with a reprimand. Now, why Mrs. Penwyn should intercede for the woman's son I can't understand, for it's well known, through Mrs. Penwyn's own maid having talked about it, that the squire's lady can't endure the woman, and is vexed with her husband for keeping such trash on his premises."

" I dare say there's something more in it than any of us Cornish folks are likely to find out," said Mrs. Trevanard. "The Penwyns were always a secret, underhand lot; smooth on the outside, as fair as whitened sepulchers, and as foul within."

" Come, Bridget, you're prejudiced against them. You always have been, I think. It isn't fair to speak ill of those that have been good landlords to us."

" Haven't we been good tenants ? We're even there, I think."

The maid-servant came in to lay the supper-table, Mrs. Trevanard's watchful eyes following the girl's every movement. A good substantial supper had been prepared for the traveler, but the old air of comfort seemed somehow to have deserted the homestead, Humphrey thought. The sick wife, with that unmistakable prophetic look in her face, the forecast shadow of coming death, gave a melancholy air to the scene. The blind old grandmother sitting apart in her corner, looked like a monument of age and affliction. The farmer himself had the heavy dullness of manner which betokens a too frequent indulgence in alcohol. Martin was spasmodically gay, as if determined to enjoy the society of his friend; but care had set its mark on the bright young face, and he was in no wise the Martin of two years ago.

Humphrey retired to his bedroom soon after supper, conducted by Martin. The apartment was unchanged in its dismal aspect; the dingy old furniture loomed darkly through the dusk. Martin's one candle making only an oasis of light in the desert of gloom.

The memory of his first night at Borcel End was very present to Humphrey Clissold as he seated himself by the hearth, where the fire had burned black and dull.

" Poor Muriel," he thought. " what a dreary chamber for youth and beauty to inhabit! And in a fatal hour the girl's first love dream came to illumine the gloom—sweet delusive dream, bringing pain along with it, and inextinguishable regret."

Martin set down the candle on the dressing-table, and poked the fire vehemently.

" Poor mother's right," he said. " Those girls never do anything properly now she isn't able to follow them about. I told Phœbe to be sure to have a bright fire to light up this cheerless old den, and she has left nothing but a mass of smoldering coal."

"Never mind the fire, Martin. Sit down, like a good fellow, and tell me all your troubles. Your poor mother looks very ill."

"So ill that the doctor gives us no hope of her ever getting better. Poor soul, she's going to leave us. Heaven only knows how soon. She's been a good faithful wife to father, and a tender mother to me, and a good mistress, and a faithful servant in all things, so far as I can tell. Yet I'm afraid there's something on her mind—something that weighs heavy. I've seen many a token of secret care since she's been ill and sitting quietly by the fire, thinking over her past life."

"And you imagine that her trouble is in some way connected with your sister?"

"I don't see what else it can be. That's the only unhappiness we've ever had in our lives. All the rest has been plain sailing enough."

"Have you questioned your mother about her anxieties?" asked Humphrey.

"Many times. But she has always put me off with some impatient answer, She has never denied that she has secret cares, but when I have begged her to trust me or my father, she has turned from me peevishly. 'Neither of you could help me,' she has told me. 'What is the use of talking of old sores, when there's no healing them?'"

"An unanswerable question," said Humphrey.

"You remember what you said to me about poor Muriel the day you left Borcel? Well, those words of yours made a deep impression upon me, not so much at the time as afterward. I thought over all you had said, and it seemed to grow clear to me that there was something sadder about my poor sister's story than had ever come to my knowledge. She had not been quite fairly used, perhaps. Things had been hushed up and hidden for the honor of her family, and she had been the victim of the family respectability. My mother's one fault is pride—pride in the respectability of the Trevanards. She doesn't want to be with her betters, or to be thought anything better than a yeoman's wife, but her strong point has been the family credit. 'There are no people in Cornwall more looked up to than the Trevanards.' I can remember hearing her say that as soon as I can remember anything, and I believe she would make any sacrifice of her own happiness to maintain that position. It is just possible that she may have sacrificed the peace of others."

"I agree with you there, Martin. Whatever wrong has been done, great or small, has been done for the sake of the good old name."

"Now it struck me," continued Martin, earnestly, "that although my mother cannot be persuaded to confide in me, or in my father, who has been a little dull of late, poor soul, she might bring herself to trust you. I know that she respects you as a clever man and a man of the world. You live remote from this little corner of the earth where the Trevanards are of importance. She would feel less pain perhaps in trusting you with a family secret than in telling it to her own kith and kin. You would go away carrying the secret with you; and if there were any wrong to be righted, as I fear there must be, you might right it without giving rise to scandal. This is what I have thought, foolishly, perhaps."

" Indeed, no, Martin, I see no folly in your idea; and if I can persuade your mother to trust me, depend upon it I will."

" She knows you are a gentleman, and might be willing to trust in your honor, where she would doubt any commoner person."

" We'll see what can be done, Martin," answered Humphrey, hopefully. " Your poor sister lives apart from you all, I suppose, in the old way ?"

" Yes," replied the young man, " and I fear it's a bad way. Her wits seem further astray than ever. When I meet her now in the hazel copse, where she is so fond of wandering, she looks scared and runs away from me. She sings to herself sometimes of an evening, as she sits by the fire in grandmother's room. I hear her, now and then, as I pass the window, singing some old song in her sad, sweet voice, just as she used to sing me to sleep years ago. But I think she hardly ever opens her lips to speak."

" Does she ever see her mother ?"

" That's the saddest part of all. For the last year my mother hasn't dared go near her. Muriel took to screaming at the sight of her, as if she was going into a fit; so, since then, mother and she have hardly ever met. It's hard to think of the dying mother, so near her only daughter, and yet completely separated from her."

" It's a sad story altogether, Martin," said Humphrey, "and a heavy burden for your young life. If I can do anything to lighten it, be sure of my uttermost help. I am very glad you sent for me. I am very glad you trust me."

On this the two young men shook hands and parted for the night, Martin much cheered by his friend's coming.

No intrusion disturbed the traveler's rest. He slept soundly after his long journey, and awoke to hear farm-yard cocks crowing in the sunshine, and to remember that he was more than two hundred miles away from Justina.

CHAPTER XXXVIII.

" BUT OH! THE THORNS WE STAND UPON."

MR. CLISSOLD spent the morning sauntering about the farm and lounging in one of the hillside meadows with Martin. The young man was depressed by the sense of approaching calamity, and the thought of parting with his mother, who had been more tender to him than to any one else in the world, was a bitter grief not to be put aside. But he did his best to keep his sorrow to himself, and to be an agreeable companion to his friend; while Humphrey, on his side, tried to beguile Martin to forgetfulness by cheery talk of that wide busy world in which the young Cornishman longed to take his place.

" I shall have my liberty soon enough," said Martin, with a sigh. " I could not leave Borcel during my mother's lifetime, for I knew it would grieve her if I deserted the old homestead.

But when she is gone the tie will be broken. Father can rub on
well enough without me, if I find him an honest bailiff to take
my place. He can afford to sit down and rest now, and take
things easily; for he's a rich man, though he and mother always
made a secret of it. And I can run down here once or twice a
year to see how things are going on. Yes, I shall certainly go
to London after my poor mother's death. Borcel would be hateful to me without her. And if you can get me into a merchant's
office I would try my hand at commerce. I'm pretty quick at
figures."

"I'll do my best to start you fairly, dear boy. though I have
not much influence in the commercial world. I think a year or
two in London would do you good, and perhaps reconcile you to
your country life afterward. A little London goes a long way
with some people. And now I think I'll walk over to Penwyn,
and see how the squire and his wife are getting on. I shall be
back at Borcel by tea-time. Will you come with me, Martin?"

"I should like it of all things, but my mother sets her face
against any intercourse between the two families. She doesn't
even like my father to go to the audit dinner. And just now,
when she's so ill, I don't care to do anything that can vex her.
So I'll loaf about home while you go up yonder."

"So be it, then, Martin. I think you're quite right."

The walk across the moorland was delightful in the late September weather. a fresh breeze blowing off the land, and Atlantic's mighty waves breaking silver-crested upon the rugged
shore.

"If Justina were but here!" thought Humphrey Clissold, with
a longing for that one companion in whose presence he had found
perfect contentment. the companion who always understood,
and always sympathized. who laughed at his smallest jokelet,
for whom his loftiest flight never soared too high. He thought
of Justina mewed up in her Bloomsbury parlor, while he was
gazing on that wide ocean. breathing this ethereal air, and he felt
as if there were selfishness in his enjoyment of the scene without her.

"Will the day ever come when she and I shall be one, and
visit earth's fairest scenes together?" he wondered. "Has she
forgotten her romantic attachment to my poor friend. and can
she give me a whole heart? I think she likes me. I have sometimes ventured to tell myself that she loves me. Yet there is
that old memory. She can never give me a love as pure and
perfect as that early passion—the first-fruits of her innocent,
girlish heart, pure as those vernal offerings which the Romans
gave their god."

He looked back to that summer day at Eborsham when he
had seen the overgrown, shabbily clad girl sitting in the meadow,
with gathered wild flowers in her lap, lifting her pale young
face, and looking up at him with melancholy eyes—eyes which
had beheld so little of earth's brightness. Nothing fairer than
such a meadow as this on a summer afternoon.

"I did not know that was my fate," he said to himself, remembering his critical, philosophical consideration of the group.

Thinking of Justina shortened that moorland walk, the subject being, in a manner, inexhaustible; just that one subject which, in the mind of a lover, has no beginning, middle, or end.

By and by the pedestrian struck into one of Squire Penwyn's new roads, and admired the young trees in the squire's plantations, and the thickets of rhododendron planted here and there among the stems of feathery Norwegian and sturdy Scotch firs. A keeper's or forester's lodge here and there, built of gray stone, gave an air of occupation to the landscape; the neatly kept garden full of autumn's gaudy flowers; a group of rustic children standing at gaze to watch the traveler.

These plantations wonderfully improved the approach to Penwyn Manor-house. They gave an indication of residential estate, as it were, and added importance to the country-seat of the Penwyns, the Manor-house of days gone by having been an isolated mansion set in a wild and barren landscape. Nowadays the traveler surveyed these well-kept plantations on either side of a wide high-road, and knew that a lord of the soil dwelt near.

Humphrey entered the Manor-house grounds by the north lodge. He might have chosen a shorter way, but he had a fancy for taking another look at the woman who had first admitted him to Penwyn, and who had become notorious since then on account of her son's wrong-doing.

The iron gate was shut, but the woman was near at hand, ready to admit visitors. She was sitting on her door-step, basking in the afternoon sunshine. She no longer wore the close white cap in which Humphrey had first seen her. To-day her dark hair, with its rare streaks of gray, was brushed smoothly from her swarthy forehead, and a scarlet handkerchief was tied loosely across her head.

That bit of scarlet had a curious effect upon Humphrey Clissold's memory. Two years ago he had vaguely fancied the face familiar. To-day brought back the memory of time and place, the very moment and spot where he had first seen it.

Yes, he recalled the low water meadows. the tow-path, the picturesque old red-tiled roofs and pointed gables of Eborsham, the solemn towers of the cathedral. the crook-backed willows on the bank, and youth and careless pleasure personified in James Penwyn.

This lodge-keeper was no other than that gypsy who had prophesied evil about Humphrey Clissold's friend. A slight thing, perhaps, and matter for ridicule, that dark saying about the severed line of life on James Penwyn's palm, but circumstances had given a fatal force to the soothsayer's words.

"What," said Humphrey, looking at the woman earnestly, as she unlocked the gate, "you and I have met before, my good woman, and far away from here."

She stared at him with a stolid look.

"I remember your coming here two years ago," she said. "That was the first and last time I ever saw you till to-day."

"Oh, no, it was not—not the first time. Have you forgotten Eborsham and your fortune-telling days, when you told my

friend Mr. Penwyn's fortune, and talked about a cut across his
hand? He was murdered the following day. I should think
that event must have impressed the circumstance upon your
mind."

"I don't know what you're talking about," Rebecca Mason
answered, doggedly. " I never saw you till you came here. I
never was at any place called Eborsham."

"I cannot gainsay so positive an assertion from a lady," said
Humphrey, ironically: " but all I can say is that there is some
one about in the world who bears a most extraordinary likeness
to you. I hope the fact may never get you into trouble."

He passed on toward the house, sorely perplexed by the
presence of this woman at Mr. Penwyn's gates. He had no
shadow of .doubt as to her identity. She was the very woman
he had seen plying her gypsy trade at Eborsham—that woman,
and no other. And what could have brought her here?
Through what influence, by what pretense, had she wormed
her way into a respectable household, and acquired so much
power that her vagabond son might attempt a burglary with
impunity?

The question was a puzzling one, and worried Humphrey not
a little. He remembered what Mrs. Trevanard had said about
there being something in the background—something false and
underhanded in the squire's life. Only the suggestion of a
prejudiced woman, of course; but such suggestions made their
impression even upon the clearest mind. He remembered Justina's prejudice against the man who had been so great a gainer
by James Penwyn's death.

" Heaven help Churchill Penwyn!" he thought. " It is not a
pleasant thing to succeed to a murdered man's heritage. Let
him walk ever so straight, there will be watchful eyes that will
see crookedness in all his ways. It's a curious business about
that gypsy woman, though," he went on, after a pause. " Does
Mr. Penwyn know who she is, I wonder? or has she deceived
him as to her character, and traded upon his benevolence? Although he is not much liked here, he has done a great deal that
indicates a benevolent man and kindly intentions toward his dependents. He may have given that woman her post out of pure
charity. I'll try if I can get to the bottom of this business."

He drew near the house. Everywhere he saw improvement
—everywhere the indication of an'all-pervading taste, which had
turned all things to beauty. The gardens, whose half-neglected
air he remembered, were now in most perfect order.· Additions
had been made to the house, not important in their character,
but in a manner completing the harmony of the picture. And
over all there was a wealth of color, and varied light and shadow,
which would have made most country mansions seem dull and
commonplace in comparison with this one.

" It is Mrs. Penwyn's taste, no doubt, which has made the
place so charming," Humphrey thought. " Happy man to have
such a wife. I will think no ill of him for her sake."

The aspect of the house impressed Humphrey as suggestive of
a happy domestic life. Grandeur was not the character of the

mansion—homelike prettiness rather, a gracious smiling air, which seemed to welcome the stranger.

Humphrey Clissold entered by an Elizabethan porch, which had been added to the old lobby entrance at one end of the house. The lobby had been transformed into the prettiest little armory imaginable; the dark and shining oak walls decorated with weapons and shields of the Middle Ages, all old English. This armory opened into a corridor with a row of doors on either side, a corridor which led straight to the hall, now the favorite family sitting-room, and provided with what was known as the ladies' billiard-table. The billiard-room proper was an apartment at the outer end of the house, lighted from the open Gothic roof, a room which Churchill had added to the family mansion.

Here, in the spacious old hall, Humphrey found the family and guests assembled after luncheon. Lady Cheshunt enthroned in a luxurious arm-chair, drawn close to the bright wood fire, which pleasantly warmed the autumnal atmosphere; Viola Bellingham deeply engaged in the consideration of whether to play for the white or the red, her own ball having been sent into a most uncomfortable corner by her antagonist, Sir Lewis Dallas; Mrs. Penwyn seated on a sofa by the sunniest window, with the infant heir on her knees, a sturdy, fair-haired youngster in a dark blue velvet frock, trying his utmost to demolish a set of Indian chess-men which the indulgent mother had produced for his amusement; Churchill seated near, glancing from an open quarterly to that pleasing picture of mother and child, two or three young ladies and a couple of middle-aged gentlemen engaged in watching the billiard players; and, finally, Sir Lewis Dallas engaged in watching Viola.

No brighter picture of English home life could be imagined.

Churchill threw down his Quarterly, and rose to offer the unexpected guest a hearty welcome, which Madge as heartily seconded.

"This time, of course, you have come to stay with us," said Mr. Penwyn.

"You are too good. No. I have put up at my old quarters at Borcel End. But I dare say I shall give you quite enough of my society. I walked over to spend an hour or two, and perhaps ask for a cup of tea from Mrs. Penwyn."

"You'll stop to dinner, surely?"

"Not this evening, tempting as such an invitation is. I promised Martin Trevanard that I would go back before dark."

"You and that young Martin are fast friends, it seems?"

"Yes. He is a capital young fellow, and I am really attached to him," answered Humphrey, somewhat absently.

Humphrey was looking at Mrs. Penwyn, surprised, nay, shocked, by the change which her beauty had suffered since he had last seen the proud handsome face, only a few months ago. There was the old brightness in her smile, the same grand carriage of the nobly formed head, but her face had aged somehow. The eyes seemed to have grown larger, the once perfect oval of the cheek had sharpened to a less lovely outline, the clear dark complexion had lost its carnation glow, and that warm golden tinge which had reminded Humphrey of one of De Musset's Andalusian beauties had faded to an ivory pallor.

Madge was as kind as ever, and seemed no less gay. Yet Humphrey fancied there was a change even in the tone of her voice. It had lost its old glad ring.

The stranger was presented to the guests of the house. The younger ladies received him with something akin to enthusiasm, there being only one eligible young man at Penwyn Manor, and he being hopelessly entangled in the fair Viola's silken net. Lady Cheshunt asked if Mr. Clissold had come straight from London, and on being answered in the affirmative, ordered him to sit down by her immediately and tell her all the news of the metropolis—about that dreadful murder in the Bow Road, and about the American comedian who had been making people laugh at the Royal Bouffonerie Theater, and about the new French novel which the *Saturday Review* said was so shocking that no respectable woman ought to look at it, and which Lady Cheshunt was dying to read.

Humphrey stayed for afternoon tea, which was served in the hall, Viola officiating at a Sutherland table in the broad recess which had once been the chief entrance.

"So you have abandoned your ancient office, Mrs. Penwyn?" said Humphrey, as he carried the lady of the manor her cup.

"Madge has not been very strong lately, and has been obliged to avoid even small fatigues," answered Churchill, who was standing near his wife's chair.

"There is a cloud on the horizon," thought Humphrey, as he set out on his homeward walk. "Not any bigger than a man's hand, perhaps, but the cloud is there."

CHAPTER XXXIX.

"OH, MUTTER, MUTTER! HIN IST HIN!"

HAVING come to Borcel End to perform a certain duty, Humphrey Clissold gave himself up heart and soul to the task in hand. Pleasant as it might have been to him to spend the greater part of his time in the agreeable society of Mrs. Penwyn and her guests, playing croquet on sunny afternoons, or joining in a match of billiards in the old hall, meeting the best people to be met in that part of the world, and living that smooth smiling life in which care seems to have no part—pleasant as this might have been he gave it up without a sigh, and spent his days and nights strolling about the farm, or sitting by the hearth where the sick woman's presence maintained an unchanging gloom.

Every day showed the swift progress of disease. The malady, which had made its first approaches with insidious slowness, was now advancing upon the sufferer with appalling rapidity. Every day the hectic of the dying woman's cheek took a more feverish brightness, the glassy eye a more awful light. Humphrey felt that there was no time to be lost. His eyes, less accustomed to the aspect of the invalid than the eyes of kindred who had seen her daily throughout the progress of decline, clearly perceived that the end was not far off. Whatever secrets were hidden in that proud heart must be speedily revealed, or would remain buried there till the end of time. Yet how was he, almost a stranger, to win confidence which had been refused to a son?

He tried his uttermost to conciliate Mrs. Trevanard by small attentions. He adjusted the window-curtains so as to temper the light for those weary eyes. He arranged the invalid's pillow as tenderly as Martin could have done. He read to her, sometimes reading passages of Scripture which she herself selected, and which were frequently of an awful and denunciatory character—the cry of prophets and holy men against the iniquities of their age.

Those portions of Holy Writ which he himself chose were of a widely different character. He read all that is most consoling, most tender, in the Gospel. The words he chose were verily messengers of peace. And even that stubborn heart was touched; the woman who had prided herself on her own righteousness felt that she was a sinner.

One afternoon when Humphrey and Mrs. Trevanard were alone by the fireside—Martin and his father being both at Seacomb market, and old Mrs. Trevanard being confined to her own room with a sharp attack of rheumatism—the invalid appeared struck by the young man's kindness in remaining with her.

"I should be dull company for you at the best of times," she said, "and it's worse for you now that I'm so ill. Why don't you go for a ride or a drive, and enjoy the country, instead of sitting in this dull old room with me?"

"I am very glad to keep you company, Mrs. Trevanard," he answered, kindly. "You must find it dull on market days, when there's no one here."

"Yes, the hours seem very long. I make one of the girls sit here at her needle-work. But that's almost worse than loneliness, to hear the click, click, click of the needle, and see the girl sitting there, with no more sense in her than a statue, or not so much, for a statue does no harm. And then one gets thinking of the past, and the things we have done which we ought not to have done, and the things left undone which we ought to have done. It's a dreary thought. When I was well and strong and able to bustle about the house I used to think I had done my duty in that state of life to which it had pleased God to call me. I knew that I had never spared myself or given myself up to the lusts of the flesh, such as eating and drinking and slothfulness. The hardest crust or the poorest bit of the joint was always good enough for me. I was always the first up of a morning, summer and winter, and my hands were never idle. But since I've been ill, and sitting here all day, I've come to think myself a sinner. That's a hard thought, Mr. Clissold, after a life of care and labor."

"Perhaps it is the best thought any of us can have," he answered, "the natural conclusion of every Christian who considers the surpassing merits of his Saviour, and sees how far his highest endeavors fall short of that Divine standard. Remember the story of the publican."

And then he read that sublimely simple record of the two men who went up into the Temple to pray.

He had hardly finished when Mrs. Trevanard burst into tears. the first he had ever seen her shed. The sight shocked him, and yet inspired hope.

"I have been like the Pharisee—I have trusted in my own righteousness," she said at last, drying her tears.

"Dear Mrs. Trevanard," Humphrey began, earnestly, "there are few of us altogether blameless; there are few lives in which some wrong has not been done to others—some mistake made which perhaps has gone far to wreck the happiness of others. The uttermost we can do, the uttermost God will demand from us, is repentance and atonement—such poor atonement, at least, as we may be able to offer for the wrong we have done. But it is a bitter thing to outstand God's hour, and hold by our wrongdoing, to appear before him as obstinate sinners who know their sin, yet cleave to it."

The words moved her, for she turned her face away from him, and buried it on her pillow. He could see the feeble frame shaken by stifled sobs.

"If you have wronged any one, and seek to atone for that wrong now in this eleventh hour——" said Humphrey.

Mrs. Trevanard turned quickly round, interrupting him. "Eleventh hour!" she repeated. "Then they have all made up their minds that I am to die?"

"Indeed, no. Your husband and son, and all about you, most earnestly desire your recovery. But you have been so long suffering from this trying disease, without improvement, that a natural fear has arisen——"

"They are right," she said, with a gloomy look. "I feel that my doom is upon me."

"It will not shorten your days or lessen your chances of recovery if you prepare for the worst, Mrs. Trevanard," said Humphrey, determined to push the question to its ultimate issue. "Many a man defers making his will from a dim notion that to make it is to bring death nearer to him; and then some day death approaches him unawares, and his wishes remain unfulfilled. We must all die; so why should we not live prepared for death?"

"I thought I was prepared," replied Mrs. Trevanard, "because I have clung to the Scriptures."

"The Gospel imposes certain duties upon us, and if those duties are unfulfilled, our holding by the Bible will avail us very little. It isn't reading the Bible, but living according to its teaching, that will make us Christians."

"You talk to me boldly," said the sick woman; "as if you knew I was a sinner."

"I know nothing about you. Mrs. Trevanard—except that you seem to have been a good wife and a good mother."

At that word mother, Bridget Trevanard winced as if an old wound had been touched.

"But I believe that you have some heavy burden on your mind," continued Humphrey, " and that you will know neither rest nor peace until that load has been lightened."

"You are a shrewd judge," said Mrs. Trevanard, bitterly, "And pray how came you to think this of me?"

"The conviction has grown out of various circumstances, which I need not trouble you with. I am a student of mankind, Mrs. Trevanard, a close observer by habit. Pray do not suppose that I have watched you, or played the spy at your fireside. Be assured that I have no feeling but friendship toward you, that my sympathy is ready for your sorrows. And if you can be induced to trust me——"

"If I could trust you!" repeated Mrs. Trevanard. "If there was any one on earth I dared trust, in whose honest friendship I could believe, in whose word I dare confide the honor of a most unhappy household, Heaven knows I would turn to him gladly enough. My husband is weak and helpless, a man who would blab a bitter secret to every acquaintance he has, who would look to others to drag him out of every difficulty, and make his trouble town-talk. My son is hot-headed and impulsive, would take trouble too deeply to heart, and would be betrayed into some act of folly before I was cold in my grave. No, there are none of my own household I dare trust."

"Trust me, Mrs. Trevanard."

She looked at him earnestly with her melancholy eyes—looked as if she would fain have pierced the secrets of his heart.

"You are a man of the world," she said, "and therefore might be able to give help and counsel in a difficult matter. You are a gentleman, and therefore would not betray a family secret. But what reason can you have for interesting yourself in my affairs? Why should you take any trouble about me or mine?"

"First, because I am honestly attached to your son, and secondly because I have felt a profound interest in your afflicted daughter."

At that word the mother started up from her reclining position, and looked at the speaker fixedly.

"Muriel!" she exclaimed. "I did not know you had ever seen her."

"I have seen her and spoken to her. I met her one evening in the copse at the bottom of the garden, and talked to her."

"What did she talk about?"

"You—and—her child."

This was a random shot, but it hit the mark.

"Great Heaven! she spoke to you of that—a secret of years gone by, which it has been the business of my life to hide, which I have thought of through many a wakeful night upon my weary pillow. And she told you—a stranger!"

"I spoke to her about you—but at the word mother she shrank from me with a look of horror. 'Do not speak to me of my mother,' she cried; 'what has she done with my child?' That speech made a profound impression upon me, as you may im-

agine. The remembrance of that speech emboldens me to ask
for your confidence to-day."

"I saved that unhappy girl's good name," said Mrs. Trevanard.·

"There you doubtless did a mother's duty. But was it the
maintenance of her character which occasioned the loss of her
reason?"

"I don't know. It is a miserable story from first to last. But
since you know so much, I may as well trust you with the rest;
and if, when you have heard all, you think there has been a
wrong done that needs redress, you will perhaps help me to
bring about that redress."

"Be assured of my uttermost help, if you will but trust me
fully."

"You shall hear all." said Mrs. Trevanard, decisively. She
took a little of some cooling drink which always stood ready
for her on the table by her easy-chair, and then began the story
of a family sorrow.

"You have seen Muriel," she said, "and you have perceived
in her wasted countenance some faint traces of former beauty.
At eighteen years of age she was a noble creature. She had a
face which pleased and attracted every one who saw her. Her
schoolmistress wrote me letters about the admiration she had excited on the breaking-up day, when the gentry, whose daughters attended the school, met to witness the distribution of
prizes. I was weak enough to shed tears of joy over those letters—weak enough to be proud of the gifts which were destined
to become a snare of the Evil One. Muriel was clever as well
as beautiful. She was always at the top of her class, always
the winner of prizes. Her father and I used to read her letters
again and again, and I think we both worked all the harder,
looking forward to the day when Muriel would marry some
gentleman-farmer, and would require a handsome portion. We
were quite content with our own position as simple working-
people, but we had given Muriel the education of a lady, and we
counted upon her marrying above her station. 'After all, she's
a Trevanard,' her father used to say, 'and the Trevanards come
of as good a stock as any in Cornwall—not even barring the
Penwyn's.' Well, the time came for Muriel to come home for
good. She had not spent much of her holidays at home, for
there'd almost always been some of her fellow-pupils that
wanted her company. and when she was invited to stay at
gentlefolks' houses I didn't like to say no, and her father said it
was a good thing for her to make friends among the gentry.
So most of her holiday time had been spent out visiting, in
spite of old Mrs. Trevanard, who was always grumbling about
it, and saying that no good ever came of people forgetting
their position. But now the time had come for Muriel to take
her place beside the family hearth, and share our plain, quiet
life."

The mother paused, with a bitter sigh, vividly recalling that
by-gone day and her daughter's vanished beauty—the fair young
face which had smiled at her from the other side of the hearth,

the happy girlish laugh, the glad young voice, the atmosphere
of youth and brightness which. Muriel's return had brought to
the grave old homestead.

"Her grandmother had declared that Muriel would be dull
and discontented at home, that we had made a great mistake in
having her educated and brought up among her superiors in
station, spoiling her by putting false notions in her head, and a
good deal more of the same kind. But there was no discontent
about Muriel when she came among us. She took her place as
naturally as possible, wanted to help me with the dairy or about
the house, or to do anything she could to make herself useful.
But I was too proud of her beauty and her cleverness to allow
that. 'No, Muriel,' I said, 'you've been educated as a lady, and
you shall not be the less a lady because you've come home.
Your life here may be very dull; there's no help for that; but it
shall be the life of a lady. You may play the piano, and read
your books, and do fancywork, and no one shall ever call upon
you to soil your fingers in dairy work or housework.' So, when
she found I was determined, she gave way and lived like a lady.
Her father bought her a piano, which still stands in the best
parlor. He gave her money to buy all the books she wanted.
Indeed, there's nothing she could have asked of him that he
would have denied her, he was so proud and fond of his only
daughter.

"She brought you happiness, then, in the beginning?" said
Humphrey.

"Yes; there couldn't have been a better girl than Muriel for
the first year after she left school. She was always the same
sweet smiling creature. full of life, never finding the old house
dull, amusing herself day after day with her books and piano,
roaming about the fields and along the beach for hours together,
sometimes alone, sometimes with her little brother to keep her
company."

"She was very fond of her brother, I understand?"

"Yes, she doted upon Martin. She taught him his letters, and
used to tell him fairy tales of an evening between the lights, sitting in a low chair by the hearth. She sang him to sleep many
a night. In fact, she took all the trouble of him off my hands.
She and her grandmother got on very well together, too, and the
old lady having nothing to do. Muriel and she were often companions. Mrs. Trevanard was not blind at that time, but her
sight was weak, and she was glad to let Muriel read to her. Altogether our home seemed brighter and happier after Muriel
came back to us. Perhaps we were not humble enough or
thankful enough for our happiness. Anyhow trouble now
came."

"How did the evil begin?" asked Humphrey.

"As it almost always does. It stole upon us unawares, like
a thief in the night. The squire's eldest son, Mr. George Penwyn, came home on leave before going on foreign service with
his regiment, and spent a good deal of his leisure time fly-fishing in the streams about here. It was splendid summer weather,
and we weren't surprised at his being about so much, especially as

folks said that he and his father didn't get on well together. Now and again he would come in on a warm afternoon and take a draught of milk, and sit and talk for half an hour or so. He was a perfect gentleman, or had the seeming of one. He was grave and thoughtful in his ways, yet full of kindness and pleasantness. He was just the last kind of man that any father and mother would have thought of shutting their door against. His manner to Muriel was as respectful as if she had been the greatest lady in the land, but he and she naturally found a good deal to say to each other, she having been educated as a lady, and being able to understand and appreciate all he said."

Mrs. Trevanard paused. She was approaching the painful part of her story, and had need to nerve herself for the effort.

" Heaven knows I had neither fear nor thought of fear at the time our sorrow came upon us. I had complete confidence in Muriel. If I had seen her surrounded by a score of admirers I should have felt no anxiety. She was a Trevanard, and the Trevanards had always been noted for beauty and pride. No female of the Trevanard family had ever been known to lower herself or to forfeit her good name. And she came of as good a race on her mother's side. The last thing I would have thought of was that my daughter should degrade herself by listening to a dishonorable proposal. Well, time went on, and one day Muriel brought me a letter she had received from her late school-mistress, asking her to go and stay at the school for a week or two. The school was just outside Seacomb, a handsome house, standing in its own gardens, and there were very few of the pupils that were not gentleman's daughters, or at any rate daughters of the rich farmers in the neighborhood. Altogether Miss Barlow's school stood very high in people's estimation, and I felt flattered by Miss Barlow's asking my daughter to visit her, now that Muriel's schooling days were over, and there was no more money to be expected from us."

Again a pause and a sigh, and a few minutes of thoughtful silence, before Mrs. Trevanard resumed.

" Muriel was very much excited about the invitation. I distinctly remember the bright flush upon her cheeks as she showed me the letter, and her curious, half-breathless way when she asked if I would let her go, and if I thought her father would consent to her going. ' Why, you're very anxious to run away from us, Muriel,' I said, ' but that's only to be expected; Borcel End must be dull for you.' ' No, indeed, mother,' she answered, quickly, ' Borcel End is a dear old place, and I've been very happy here; but I should like to accept Miss Barlow's invitation.' "

" You consented, I suppose ?" said Humphrey.

" Yes, it wouldn't have been easy for us to refuse anything she asked at that time. And I think both her father and I were proud of her being made a friend of by such a superior person as Miss Barlow. So one September morning, at the beginning of the Michaelmas holidays, my husband drove Muriel over to Seacomb in the trap, and left her with Miss Barlow. She was to stay a fortnight, and her father was to fetch her at the end of the visit; but before the fortnight was over we had a letter from Muriel, asking to be allowed to extend her visit to three weeks, and saying that her father needn't trouble about fetching her, as Miss Barlow would arrange for sending her home. This wounded Michael a little, being so proud of his daughter. 'I thought my girl would have been glad to see her father after a fortnight's separation,' he said. 'She always used to be glad when I went over to see her on market-days; and if I missed a week she used to call me unkind, and tell me how she had fretted at not seeing me; but I suppose things are changed now she's a young woman.'"

"Did she come back at the time promised?"

"No, it was two or three days over the three weeks when she returned. She came in a hired fly from Seacomb, and I had never seen her look more beautiful or more a lady than she looked when she stepped out of the carriage in front of the porch. 'Ah,' I thought to myself, 'she looks as if she was born to hold a high position in the country;' and I thought of young Mr. Penwyn, and what a match he would be for her. I did not think he was a bit too good for her. 'There's no knowing what may happen,' I said to myself. Well, from this time forward she had a strange, fitful way with her, sometimes all brightness and happiness, sometimes low-spirited. Her grandmother noticed the change, and said it was the consequence of over-education. 'You've reared up your child to have all kinds of wishes and fancies that you can't understand or satisfy,' she said, 'and have made her unfit for her home.' I wouldn't believe this, yet, as time went on, I could see clearly enough that Muriel was not happy."

Again a heavy sigh, and a brief pause.

"Mr. George Penwyn left Cornwall about this time to join his regiment in Canada, and after he had gone I observed that Muriel's low spirits, which had been fitful before, became continual. She evidently struggled with her grief, tried to amuse herself with her books and piano, tried to interest herself in little Martin, but it was no use. I have often gone into the best parlor, where she sat, and surprised her in tears. I have asked her the cause of her despondency, but she always put me off with some answer. She had been reading a book that affected her, or she had been playing a piece of music which always made her cry; and I noticed that at this time she rarely played any music that was not melancholy. If she began anything bright and gay, she always broke down in it, and her father sometimes asked her what had become of all her lively tunes. All at once it struck me that perhaps she had grown attached to Mr. Penwyn, little as they had seen of each other, and that she was fretting at his absence. Yet I thought this would be too foolish for our Muriel. Or perhaps she had been wounded by his indifference to her. A girl accustomed to so much admiration as she had received might expect to make conquests. I used to puzzle myself about the cause of her sadness for hours together as I went about the house, but in all my thoughts of Muriel I never imagined anything near the horrible truth."

She stopped, clasped her hands before her face, and then went on hurriedly. "One night, when Muriel was sitting by this hearth, with her brother in her arms, singing to him, she broke down suddenly, and began to sob hysterically. Her father was frightened out of his wits, and came fussing about her in a way to make her worse; but I put my arm round her and led her to her own room. When we were together there she flung herself upon my breast, and then the awful truth came out. A child was to be born in this house—a child whose birth must be hidden, whose father's name was never to be spoken."

"Did she tell you all the truth?"

"She told me nothing. There was a secret, she said—a secret she had solemnly sworn to keep, come what might. She asked me to trust her, to believe in her honor, in spite of all that seemed to condemn her. She asked me to send her away somewhere, to some quiet corner of the earth, where no one need know her name or anything about her. But I told her there was no corner of the earth so secret that slander and shame would not follow her, and no hiding-place so safe as her father's house. 'If you were to go away it would set people talking,' I said."

"There may have been a secret marriage," suggested Humphrey.

"I asked her that question, but she refused to answer. I cannot believe that she would have kept back the truth from me, her mother, in that hour of agony. I asked her if George Penwyn was the villain who had brought this misery upon us, but this question also she refused to answer. She had made a promise that sealed her lips, she said. I must think the worst of her, if I could not trust her."

"Would it not have been better and wiser to believe in your daughter's honor, even in the face of circumstances that seemed to condemn?" asked Humphrey, with a touch of reproach.

"Who can be wise when they see all they have most loved and honored suddenly snatched away from them? The discovery of my daughter's dishonor was more bitter to me than her sudden death would have been. When I left her that night my prayer was that she might die, and her sorrow and her blighted name go down unknown to the grave. A wicked prayer, you think, no doubt; but you have never passed through such an agony as I felt that night. I lay awake thinking what was to be done. I had no doubt in my own mind that George Penwyn was the man I had to hate. There was no one else I could suspect. When I rose at daybreak next morning I had my plan, in some measure, settled."

Humphrey listened breathlessly; he felt that he was on the threshold of the household mystery—the sacrifice that had been made to the family's good name.

"Whenever any of us were ill, old Mrs. Trevanard used to doctor us. She has all kinds of recipes for medicines that cure small ailments. It was only when a case was very bad that we sent for a doctor. Now my first precaution was to remove Muriel to the room above her grandmother's—a room cut off from the rest of the house, as you know, and to place her under old Mrs. Trevanard's care, in such a manner that the house-servant (we had only one then) had no chance of approaching her. To do this, of course I had to tell Mrs. Trevanard the secret. You may suppose that went hard with me; but the old lady behaved well throughout my trouble, and never spoke a reproachful word of Muriel. 'Let her come to me, poor lamb,' she said; 'I'll stand by her, come what may.' So we moved Muriel to that out-of-the-way room, and I told her father that she was ill with a slight attack of low fever, and that I thought it wisest to place her in her grandmother's care. He was very anxious and fidgety about her, and a dreadful gloom seemed to fall upon the house. I know that I went about my daily work with a heart that was ready to break."

"It must have been a hard time, indeed," said Humphrey, compassionately.

"It was so hard as to try my faith in God's goodness. My heart rebelled against his decrees; but just when my despair was deepest, Providence seemed to come to my help in a most unlooked-for manner. It was winter at this time, near the end of winter, and very severe weather. The moors were covered with snow, and no one came near Borcel from one week's end to another. One evening about dusk I was leaving the dairy, which is detached from the house, and crossing the yard to go back to the kitchen, when I saw a man and woman looking over the yard gate, the snow beating down upon them—two as miserable objects as you could see. My heart was hardened against others by my own grief, so I called to them to go away, I had nothing to give them.

"'If we go away from here it will be to certain death,' answered the man. 'As you are a Christian, give us a night's shelter. We left Seacomb early this morning to walk to Penwyn Manor, having a letter recommending us to the squire's charity; but the walk was longer and more difficult than we knew, and here we are at dark, just half-way on our journey. I don't ask much from you, only enough to save us from perishing—a night's lodging in one of your empty barns.' This was an appeal I could not resist. There was room enough to have sheltered twenty such wanderers. So I took these two up to a half-empty hay-loft, and gave them a truss of hay for a bed; and I carried them a loaf and a jug of milk with my own hands. I don't know what put it into my head to wait upon them myself instead of sending the servant to them: but I think it pleased me to do this humble office, knowing how low my daughter had fallen, and feeling as if there was some kind of atonement in my humility."

CHAPTER XL.
"LOST TO HER PLACE AND NAME."

"THESE people were not common wanderers," said Mrs. Trevanard, continuing her story. "I soon discovered that they belonged to a very different class from the tramps who came prowling about the place in summer, begging or stealing whenever they had a chance. The woman was a pretty-looking, gentle creature, who seemed deeply grateful for small kindnesses. She had not long recovered from a serious illness, the husband told me, and her delicate looks confirmed his statement. The man spoke well, if not exactly like a gentleman, and his clothes, worn almost to rags, were not the clothes of a working-man. I fancied that he was a lawyer's clerk, or perhaps, from his fluency of speech, a broken-down Methodist parson."

"He spoke like a man accustomed to speaking in public, then, I conclude," said Humphrey.

"Yes, that was the impression he gave me," replied Mrs. Trevanard. "I went back to the house after having made them tolerably comfortable in the loft," she continued, "and all that night I lay awake thinking about these two people. They seemed to have dropped from the skies somehow, so suddenly and unexpectedly had they come upon me in the winter dusk, and it came into my head, in that weary night, that they were instruments of Providence sent to help me in my trouble. I had no clear thought of what they would do for me, but I felt that since I should be compelled to trust some one by and by with some part of our fatal secret, it would be easier and better to trust waifs and strays like these people, who might wander away and carry their knowledge with them, than anybody else. Neighbor or friend I dared not trust. My sole hope lay among strangers."

"Did none of the farm people know of these wanderers' arrival?" asked Humphrey.

"No. The men were at their supper when I took these people to the loft. It was a loft over some empty stables, where Squire Borcel used to keep his hunters over a hundred years ago, and was only used at odd times for a surplus supply of fodder. I knew it was safe enough as a hiding-place so long as the people kept tolerably quiet. I had warned them against making their presence known, as my husband was a hard man— Heaven forgive me for so great a falsehood!—and might object to their being about the place. Well, the snow came down thicker than ever next morning, and to try and find a path across the moor would have been madness. Those most accustomed to the country round would have been helpless in such weather. So I took the people in the loft a warm, comfortable breakfast of coffee and bread and bacon, and I told them that they might stay till the weather changed."

"They were grateful, I suppose."

"They thanked and blessed me with tears. I was ashamed to receive their thanks, knowing my selfish thought had been only of my own trouble, and how little I had cared for their distress. The man told me that his name was Eden, and that he was a broken-down gentleman. I think he said he had been in the army, and had wealthy relations; but they had discarded him, and after trying to earn his living by the use of his talents, he had fallen into extreme poverty. He and his wife had come to

Cornwall, having heard that living was cheap in the west of England. I gathered from him that he had tried to pick up a living by teaching in a gentleman's school, but had failed, and was at last compelled to leave his lodgings, and in his extremity had determined to appeal to Squire Penwyn, whom he had heard of as a wealthy man. For that purpose he had rashly attempted to walk across the moor, the snow having held off for a little, with his weakly wife. 'Heaven help you if you had found your way to the old squire,' I told him; 'he's not the man to do much for you.' I told them both that they might stay until the weather was better, or stay till Mrs. Eden had picked up her strength by means of rest and good plain food, provided they kept themselves quiet in the loft; and they blessed me again as if I had been their good angel."

" It was a welcome boon, no doubt."

" In the course of that day it came out that Mrs. Eden had not long before lost her first baby, and that she had fretted for it a good deal. This confirmed my idea that these people were instruments sent me by Providence, and I laid my plans. and arranged everything clearly in my own mind. A fortnight went by, and the snow began to melt in the valleys, and our men had hard work to keep the place from being flooded. Michael was out all day helping to cut drains to carry the water off the stack-yard. As the weather brightened, Mr. Eden seemed to get uneasy in his mind. 'You'll be wanting to get rid of us, ma'am,' he said. 'The wayfarers must resume their journey through the wilderness of life.' But I told him he could stay till the weather was milder, on account of his sickly wife. I was not ready for them to leave yet awhile."

" And in all this time no one discovered them?" asked Humphrey.

" No; that part of the premises lies out of every one's way. You may go and look at it to-morrow, if you like, and see what a deserted corner it is. They had a fright once or twice— heard the men's voices near—but no one ever approached the loft. I took care to pay my visits to them at meal times, when there was no one about to see me. I always kept my dairy under lock and key, and I used to put the supplies for my pensioners in the dairy. It was easy to carry things from the dairy to the loft without being observed. I fed them well, gave them a few old books to read, and gave Mrs. Eden working materials, and a piece of calico to make under-garments for herself, and a useful gown or two into the bargain. I had ample stores of all kinds hoarded up, and it was easy enough for me to be charitable."

" Your pensioners did not get tired of their retreat?" inquired Humphrey.

" Far from it. They had suffered too much from actual want not to be thankful for food and shelter, which cost them nothing. Mr. Eden told me that he had never been happier than in that loft. I had contrived to take them over blankets, and a few old cushions to sit upon, and many other comforts by degrees. Mrs. Eden's health had wonderfully improved. One day, after she had been talking to me of the child she had lost, I asked her if she could love and cherish a motherless infant confided to her care. She said she could, indeed, with all her heart, and her whole face softened at the thought. It was a kind and gentle face at all times. I asked her no further questions upon the subject, but I felt full confidence in her. A week after that I took her a new-born babe in the dead of the night— a sweet little lily-faced creature, dressed in the baby clothes my own fingers had stitched for my own first-born child, Muriel. Heaven knows what I suffered that night when I laid the innocent lamb in Mrs. Eden's arms—she only half-wakened, and scared and surprised by the suddenness of my coming. I had meant to tell her that the infant was the child of one of my servants, but when the time came I could not utter the lie. I told her only that the child was motherless, and that I confided it to her care from that hour, and that on consideration of Mr. Eden and herself taking the babe in their keeping and bringing it up as their cwn, I would give them a good sum of money to start them in a respectable way of life. But before I did this they must pledge themselves never again to appear at Borcel End, or anywhere in the neighborhood of Borcel End, and never to make any application to me on account of the child. From the hour they left Borcel End the child would belong wholly to them, and there would be no link to connect it with me. I said all this hurriedly, that night, but I repeated it again next day, in a formal manner, and made them take a solemn oath upon my Bible, binding them to perform their part of the bond."

" Did they stay long at Borcel after the child's birth?"

" Only five days, for I dreaded lest the baby's crying should be heard by any one about the place. Mrs. Eden took great care of the helpless little thing, and kept it wonderfully quiet, but the fear of its crying haunted me day and night. I was always fancying I heard it. I used to start up from my pillow in the dead of the night, with the sound of that child's crying in my ears, and used to wonder my husband was not wakened by it, although it would not have been possible for the sound to reach our bedroom if the child had cried its loudest. But, though I knew this. the sound haunted me all the same, and I determined that the Edens should start directly it was reasonably safe for the infant to be moved. The weather was now mild and dry; the mornings were light soon after six o'clock."

" How did you get them away secretly?"

" That was my great difficulty. There was no possibility of going away in any vehicle. They must go on foot, and make their way back to Seacomb. At Seacomb they would take the train and get out of the county. After thinking it over a long time I decided that the safest thing would be for them to leave at half-past six o'clock in the morning, when the men would be all in the fields. I knew exactly what was going forward upon the farm, and could make my plans accordingly. It would be easy for me to take care that the maid-servant was safely employed in-doors, and could see nothing of Mr. and Mrs. Eden's departure."

" Did you give these people much money ?"

" All that I possessed in the world—my secret savings of years. Good as my husband is, and well to do though we were from the beginning, it had pleased me to save a little money that was quite my own, to dispose of as I pleased, unquestioned by Michael. I had wronged no one in saving this money; it was all the result of small economies and of self-denial. My husband had given me a five-pound note for a new gown, and I put the money away, and turned my last new silk gown instead of buying a new one, or I had reared a brood of choice poultry and sold them to a neighboring farmer.. The money was honestly come by, and it amounted to over two hundred pounds, in notes and gold. ৲I gave it to the Edens in a lump. ' Now remember that this is to start you in life,' I said to them, finally,·'and that on consideration of this you take the responsibility of this child's maintenance henceforward, and that she shall be called by your name. and as you thrive, she shall thrive.' This they pledged themselves to most solemnly. Mrs. Eden seemed honestly attached to the desolate baby already, and I had no fear that it would be unkindly treated. Desperate as my necessities were, I do not think I could have intrusted that helpless infant to any one of whose kindness I had not felt confident."

" Was the child christened when it left Borcel End ?" asked Humphrey.

He had a reason for thinking this question of considerable importance.

" No. I might have baptized it myself, had it been in danger of death. But the child was well enough, and seemed in a fair way to live. I told Mr. and Mrs. Eden to have it christened as soon as they had left Cornwall and settled themselves in a new neighborhood."

" Did you tell them what name to call the infant ?"

" No. It was to be their child henceforward. It was their business to choose its name."

" They got safely away, I suppose ?"

" Yes, they left secretly and safely. just as I had planned. I shall never forget that gray morning, in the chilly spring weather, and the last glimpse I had of those two wanderers—the woman with the child nestled to her breast, wrapped in my Muriel's blue cloak—the cloak it had been such pleasure to me to quilt when I was a young woman."

Mrs. Trevanard sighed bitterly.

· "I can remember sitting in this room at work at the beginning of my married life," she said dreamily, "thinking what a grand thing it was to be married, and the mistress of a large house and a prosperous farm. I look back upon my life now—nine-and-thirty years of wedded life—and think how heavily the care of it weighs against the happiness, and what a life of toil it has been. ' Heaping up riches, and ye know not who shall gather them.' "

" Did you never hear any more of Mr. and Mrs. Eden, or the

child ?" asked Humphrey, most anxious to hear all that was to be told by lips that must ere long be silent.

"From that day to this.not a word. They have kept their promise. Whether they prospered or failed I know not. They were young people, and there seemed to me no reason why they should not get on pretty well in some small trade, such as I ad- vised them to try. beginning humbly, with a part of their little capital. Heaven knows what may have become of them. The child may be dead—dead, years ago, taking that quiet rest which I shall soon know."

"Or she may be living. She may have grown up beautiful, good, and clever; such a grandchild as you would be proud to own."

"I should never be proud of a nameless child," answered Mrs. Trevanard, gloomily.

"The child you banished may not have been without a name. Forgive me if I speak plainly. Far be it from me to reproach you. I offer you sympathy and help, if help be possible. But I think you acted precipitately throughout this sad business. What if there were a secret marriage between your daughter and Mr. Penwyn ? Such a marriage might easily have taken place during the three weeks that your daughter was away from home, ostensi- bly on a visit to her late school-mistress. Did you never ques- tion that lady ?"

"It was not possible for me to do so. Miss Barlow retired from business very soon after Muriel's visit, and her school passed into the hands of strangers. She went abroad to live, and I could never find out where to communicate with her. But even if I had known where to address her, I should have feared to write, lest my letter should compromise Muriel. My one all-absorbing desire was to hide the disgrace that Provi- dence had been pleased to inflict upon our family, doubtless as a chastisement for our pride."

"What effect upon your daughter had the loss of her child ?"

"Ah, that was terrible! After the baby's birth Muriel had a fever. It rose from no want of care or good nursing, for old Mrs. Trevanard nursed her with unceasing devotion, and there couldn't be a more skillful nurse than my mother-in-law. But Muriel missed the child, and the loss of it preyed upon her mind, and then, in her feverish delirium, she fancied I had taken the baby away and murdered it. We had a fearful time with her, old Mrs. Trevanard and I, while that delusion lasted, but by care we brought her through it all; and, as the fever passed off, she grew more reasonable, and understood that I had sent away the child to save her good name; but she was different in her man- ner to me from what she had been. She never kissed me or asked me to kiss her, or seemed to care to have me near her. I could see that my only daughter was estranged from me for- ever. She clung to her grandmother, and it was as much as I could do by and by to get her to come down-stairs and sit among us. I was very anxious to do this, if it was only to pacify her father, for he had been anxious and fidgety all the time she was away from us; and after the Edens had taken the baby away I had been obliged to call in a doctor from Seacomb, just to satisfy Michael. The doctor listened to all that Mrs. Trevanard told him about Muriel, and just echoed what she said, and did neither good nor harm by his coming."

" And your daughter resumed her place in the family ?"

"She came among us, and sat by the fire, reading, or sometimes singing to little Martin, but she seemed in all things like the ghost of her former self, and it was heart-breaking to see her poor pale face. She would sit, with her melancholy eyes fixed on the burning logs, sometimes for half an hour at a time, lost in thought. You may judge how I felt toward the wretch who had worked this evil when I saw his victim sitting there joyless and hopeless—she who might have been so bright and glad but for him! Her father was dreadfully cut up by the change in Muriel. He would hang over her sometimes, calling her his poor faded child, and asking her what he could do to make her happy, and to bring the roses back to her cheeks; and sometimes, to please him, she would brighten up a little, and pretend to be her old glad self. But any one could see how hollow her smile was. I never said my prayers, night or morning, without praying God to avenge my daughter's great wrongs, and it never seemed to me that such a prayer was sinful."

" Did your daughter ask you what had become of her child ?"

" I saved her the pain of asking that question. As soon as reason returned after the fever I told her that the child was in safe hands, with kind people, and would be well cared for, and that she need give herself no anxiety about its fate. ' Let that dark interval in your life be forgotten, Muriel,' I said, ' and may God forgive you as freely as I do now.' She made no answer, except to bow her head gently, as in assent."

" How was it that her mind again gave way after this recovery ?"

" I am coming to that presently. That was the heaviest blow of all. Just when I was beginning to hope time would work her cure, just when I fancied I could see a glimmer of the old smile brightening her pale face now and then, the blow fell. We were sitting round this hearth one evening, Muriel and her grandmother and little Martin and I, when Michael came in, looking very much agitated. We asked him what was the matter. ' The saddest thing I've heard of for many a year,' he answered. ' Well, we've all got our troubles. There's been bad news for the squire up at Penwyn.' Muriel started up, with a faint cry, but I caught hold of her, and squeezed her hand tight, to warn her against saying anything that might betray her. ' Dreadful news,' Michael went on: ' Mr. George, the eldest son, the one we know so well, has been murdered by the savages. Lord only knows what those red devils did to him. Scalped him, they say, tied him to a tree, and tortured him——' Muriel gave one long, piercing scream, and dropped upon the stone floor. We lifted her up and carried her to bed, and the doctor was sent for post haste. I was sore afraid she would let out her secret in her father's hearing or the doctor's when she came round out of that death-like swoon; but I need not have feared. Her mind was quite gone, and all her talk was mere disjointed raving. From that day to this she has been the helpless, hopeless creature you have seen her. We have kept her out of a mad-house by keeping her close, under old Mrs. Trevanard's care. We have done all we could think of to soften the misery of her state, but she has never, for the briefest interval, recovered her reason. And now I have told you all, Mr. Clissold, without reserve, confessing the wrong I have done as freely as when I acknowledge my sins to my God."

The sick woman sank back upon the pillows, pale to the lips. The indomitable strength of will which had been ever the distinguishing mark of her character had sustained her throughout this prolonged effort. And, deeply as he compassionated the sufferer's state, Humphrey felt that it was vital to obtain from her at once, and without delay, all the information she could give him.

"I am grateful to you for having honored me with your confidence, Mrs. Trevanard," he said, kindly: "and now that you have so fully trusted me, receive once more my solemn promise to do all that may lie in my power to obtain justice for your daughter and your daughter's child. I am inclined to think that Mr. Penwyn may have been less base than you believe him, and that his unhappy death alone may have prevented him making some atonement, or revealing the fact of a secret marriage between himself and your daughter. I can hardly think that a girl brought up as your daughter was brought up could be so easy a victim as you imagine her to have been. My endeavor shall be to ascertain the truth upon this point of marriage or no marriage. A young London clergyman, a friend of mine, has told me many a curious fact connected with private marriages—stray leaves of family histories which have been a sealed book to him in all other respects—and I see no reason why this George Penwyn, who impressed you as an honorable and a well-meaning man, should not have contracted such a union with your daughter."

"God grant that it was so!" ejaculated Mrs. Trevanard. "I should go down to my grave with an easier mind if I could believe George Penwyn something less of a villain than I have considered him for the last twenty years. When I heard of his dreadful death in the Canadian forest·I said to myself, 'The Almighty Avenger of all wrongs has heard my prayer.'"

"It shall also be my endeavor to find your granddaughter." said Humphrey. "I have a curious fancy upon that point, but perhaps a foolish fancy, and therefore hardly worth speaking about."

"Pray tell me what it is."

"It is really too foolish, and would only mislead you. All I ask is that you will give me any detail which may help me in my attempt to discover the girl you intrusted to Mr. and Mrs. Eden. What kind of a man was this Mr. Eden, for instance?"

The sound of wheels rolling toward the door prevented this question being answered. In another moment the dog-cart drew

up before the porch, father and son alighted, and came into the
room, bringing a fresh gust of moorland air along with them.
The opportunity of obtaining further details from Mrs. Trevanard was gone, for the time being, and it might be long before
Humphrey again found himself alone with her, or found her inclined to speak. He heartily wished that the attractions of Seacomb Market, or of the homely hostelry where the farmers ate
their substantial two o'clock dinner, had detained Michael
Trevanard and his son just a little longer.

The invalid was more cheerful that evening than she had been
for a long time, and something of the old air of domestic comfort seemed to return to the homestead parlor as Humphrey
and the family sat at tea. Both her husband and son noticed
the improvement.

" You must be rare good company," said the farmer, " for
Bridget looks ever so much brighter for spending the afternoon
with you. Cheer up, old lady! we may cheat the doctors after
all," he added, bending over his wife affectionately as he handed
her the cup of strong tea which was the only kind of refreshment she now enjoyed.

" The doctors may have their own way about me, Michael,"
answered Mrs. Trevanard, " if I can only go down to my grave
with my mind pretty easy."

Her son drew his chair beside hers after tea, and sat with his
hands in hers, clinging to her with melancholy fondness, sadly
expectant of the coming day when there would be nothing
on this earth more distant from him than that motherly hand.

Humphrey Clissold had pledged himself to spend the next day
at Penwyn, where there was to be a cottagers' flower show, in
which Mrs. Penwyn and Miss Bellingham were deeply interested.
It was the squire's wife who had organized the annual exhibition, and stimulated the love of floriculture in the peasant mind
by the offer of various useful and attractive prizes—a silver
watch, a handsome rose-wood tea-caddy, a delf dinner-service,
a copper tea-kettle—prizes which were dear to the tastes of the
competing floriculturists, and which were eagerly competed for.
The most gigantic yellow roses, the longest and greenest cucum-
bers, the finest bunches of grapes, the most mathematically correct dahlias, were produced within a ten mile radius of Penwyn;
and by this simple means the cottage gardens and flower-pots in
latticed casements which Mrs. Penwyn beheld in her walks and
drives were things of beauty and a perennial source of joy.

The show was held in a vast circular marquee, erected in the
grounds of the Manor-house. Lady Cheshunt was one of the
lady adjudicators, and sat in state gorgeously attired in a tea-
leaf-colored silk, fearfully and wonderfully made by a Regent
Street *confectionneuse*, who tyrannized over her customers, and
seemed to gratify a malicious disposition by inflicting hideous
combinations of form and color upon a too submissive *clientelle*.

" I really can't say I think it pretty, dear Lady Cheshunt,"
said Madge, when her friend asked her opinion of this tea-leaf-
colored abomination.

" No more do I, my love," replied the dowager, calmly, "but

it's strikingly ugly.   All your county people will be blazing in what they call pretty colors.   This dirty greenish-brown is *chic!*"

After the cottage flower show came a German tea for the gentility, and croquet and archery, and the usual amount of indis·criminate flirtation which accompanies those sports. Humphrey Clissold found himself among pleasant, sunshiny people, and almost enjoyed himself, which seemed, in some wise, treason against Justina.

But even in those piny glades, while the click of the croquet balls was sounding to an accompaniment of silvery laughter, his fancy went back to the Bloomsbury parlor and the happy hours he had wasted there, and he longed to sit in his old corner reading French poetry, or sipping tea out of the dragon china.

It was late when he drove back to Borcel in Michael Trev·anard's dog-cart, which had been placed at his disposal for the day.   When he came down to breakfast next morning, Mrs. Trev·anard's chair was empty.   This startled him, for, ill as she was, she had been rigidly regular in her habits, coming down-stairs at eight o'clock every morning, and only retiring when the rest of the family went to bed.

On questioning Mr. Trevanard he heard that the invalid was much weaker this morning.   She had not been able to rise.

"It is a bad sign when Bridget gives way," added Michael, despondently. "She's not one to knock under while she has strength to bear up against her weakness."

The next day and the next the chair remained empty. Humphrey roamed about the farm, hardly knowing what to do with himself in this time of trouble, yet nowise willing to desert his post.   On the third day he was summoned to Mrs. Trevanard's room.   Phœbe, the housemaid, came in quest of him to an old orchard where he was fond of smoking his cigar.

"Missus is very bad, sir, and I believe she's asked to see you," said the girl, breathless.

Humphrey hurried to the house, and to Mrs. Trevanard's room.   Husband and son were standing near the bed, and the dying woman lay with her hand clasped on Martin's, her eyes looking with a strangely eager expression toward the door.

At sight of Humphrey her wan face brightened, ever so little, and she gave a faint choking cry.

"Want—tell you—something," she gasped, half inarticulately.

He went close to the bed and leaned over her.

"Dear Mrs. Trevanard, I am listening."

"A Bible—gave—family Bible."

That was all.   She spoke no more after this; and before night-fall the windows were darkened at Borcel End, and the careful housewife had gone to that land where there is no thought of sordid things.

CHAPTER XLI.

"THOU HAST ALL SEASONS FOR THINE OWN, O DEATH!"

WHAT was it that Mrs. Trevanard would have told when death sealed her lips forever? This was the question which Humphrey Clissold asked himself many a time in those dismal days at Borcel End, when. the house was darkened, while he and Martin sat together in friendly silence, full of sympathy, and for the most part alone, Mr. Trevanard preferring the solitude of the best parlor in this day of affliction. What was that circumstance or detail which she would have told him, and what clew to the mystery was he to discover from those two words "family Bible"—the only words that he had been able clearly to gather from the dying woman's disjointed speech.

He suffered Martin to give full sway to his grief; stanch in friendship, prompt with sympathy, but never attempting to strangle sorrow with set speeches of consolation: and then one evening, when Michael Trevanard had gone to bed, worn out with grief and confusion of mind, and when Martin was more composed and resigned than he had been since his mother's death, Humphrey approached the subject which absorbed all his thoughts just now. He had told Martin that Mrs. Trevanard had given him her confidence, but he had also told him that the circumstances she had confided to him must remain a profound secret.

"She has intrusted me with a hidden page of your family history, Martin," he said. "If ever I can set right the wrong that has been done—not by your mother, she may have been mistaken in her course of action, but she has deliberately wronged no one—you shall know all; but if I fail, the secret must remain a secret to the end of my life."

"How good you are," said Martin. "Can I ever be grateful enough for your interest in our troubles?"

"My dear Martin, there is less cause for gratitude than you imagine. I have a reason of my own for being eager in this matter. A foolish reason, perhaps. and most certainly a selfish one. So let there be no talk of gratitude on your part."

This evening, finding Martin in a more comfortable frame of mind, Humphrey deemed it safe to question him.

"You heard what your poor mother said to me on her death-bed?" he began.

"Every word. She was wandering, I think; poor dear soul."

"I hardly think that, Martin. There was so much expression in her face, as she looked at me, and she seemed so eager to tell me something. I feel sure that there was some additional circumstance, some previously forgotten detail of the story she had told me which she wanted to communicate in that last hour—something relating to a family Bible. Will you let me see your family Bible, Martin?"

"Certainly. It is kept where all the world can see it—all the world of Borcel End, at least. It is on the side-table in the best parlor. My poor father was reading it this afternoon. I'll go and get it."

Martin took one of the candles and went into the next room, whence he speedily returned, carrying a substantial folio bound in brown leather.

This was the family Bible—a goodly volume, profusely garnished with old-fashioned woodcuts, and printed in a large, fat faced type on thick-ribbed paper, mellowed to a yellowish hue by the passage of years.

On the fly-leaf were recorded the births, marriages, and deaths of the Trevanards for the last hundred and fifty years, but beyond this plain, straightforward catalogue, the page held nothing. There was the first inscription, in ink of a faded, brownish hue, recording the marriage of Stephen Trevanard, of Treworgey, with Hannah Penrose, of St. Austell. July 14, 1773—a marriage from which the Borcel End branch of the Trevanard's had arisen—and the last entry in Michael Trevanard's heavy, sprawling penmanship, recording the death of Bridget, the beloved wife, etc., etc. Humphrey read every line of that family catalogue—Muriel's birth, Martin's—but there was nothing here to suggest the faintest clew to Mrs. Trevanard's dying words.

Then carefully, and leaf by leaf, he went through the volume, looking for any stray document which might lurk between the pages. Here he found a withered flower, with its faint, ghost-like odor of departed perfume, there a scrap of sacred poetry copied in a girlish hand—such a pretty, graceful penmanship, which he surmised to be Muriel's. Yes, here was one-half sheet of note-paper, with an extract from Milton's "Hymn," signed Muriel Trevanard, Christmas, 1851.

" May I keep this scrap of paper, Martin ?" he asked.

It struck him that it might at some future time be well for him to possess a specimen of Muriel Trevanard's writing—ready to be compared with any other document.

" By all means," answered Martin. " Poor girl! She used to be so fond of poetry. Many a quaint old Scotch ballad has she repeated to me, learned out of some old books my father had picked up for her at a stall in Seacomb Market."

Beyond those loose leaves of manuscript poetry and those stray flowerets, Humphrey's most careful search could discover nothing between the pages of the family Bible. He began to think that Martin was right, and that those last words of Mrs. Trevanard were but the meaningless babble of a mind astray, with no more significance than Falstaff's dying talk of fair green fields familiar to his boyhood, before ever he had learned to find pleasure in midnight carouses or the company of Mistress Tearsheet.

" By the bye," said Martin, suddenly, while his friend sat with his arms folded on the sacred volume, deep in thought, " there's a Bible somewhere that belonged to my great-grandmother—a Bible I can just remember when I was a little chap, before Muriel's wits went astray—a Bible with queer old pictures in it, which I was very fond of looking at—not a big folio like this, but a thick dumpy volume, bound in black leather, with a brass clasp. My mother generally used it when she read the Scriptures of a Sunday evening, and it was called Mother's Bible."

" Was there anything written in it ?" asked Humphrey.

" Yes, there was writing upon the first page, I believe."

" How long is it since you saw that Bible, Martin ?"

" How long ?" echoed Martin, meditatively. " Oh, ever so many years. Why, I don't remember having seen that book since I was quite a little lad."

" Did you ever see it after your sister's mind went wrong?"

" That's asking too much. I can't remember so closely as that; and yet, on reflection, I don't think I ever did see it after Muriel's long illness, for I was sent to Helston Grammar School just at that time, and I certainly don't remember ever having seen that Bible after I went to school. However, I dare say it's somewhere about the house. Nothing is ever lost at Borcel. That Bible is among my poor mother's stores most likely. She was always a great hand for keeping old things."

" I should like very much to see it, if you could find it for me, by and by, Martin."

By and by meant when that solemn presence of the dead, which set its seal upon all things at Borcel, had been removed from the old farmhouse.

" I'll look for it among mother's books next week," said Martin. " There are a good many books upon the old walnut-wood chest of drawers in her bedroom."

*   *   *   *   *   *   *

Humphrey stayed at Borcel all through that dismal week, though he received a very kind letter from Mrs. Penwyn begging him to take up his abode at the Manor-house for the rest of his stay in Cornwall. He felt that it would be a hard thing to leave Martin in that house of gloom, and he knew that his presence there was some kind of comfort, even to Michael Trevanard, who had given way to complete despondency since his wife's death. The look of the place was so strange to him without Bridget, he complained. For five-and-thirty years she had been the chief person in that house—the prop and stay of all things—the axis upon which the wheel of life turned. The farmer knew that he owed her the maintenance and increase of his fortune. It was Bridget's help, Bridget's indefatigable spirit guiding and sustaining him, which had made him rich enough to buy Borcel, had the squire been disposed to sell it. She had taught him to hoard his money—she had held him back from all share in the boisterous pleasures of his class, but she had kept his table liberally, provided assiduously for all his creature comforts, and, in a drowsy, monotonous way, had made life very easy to him. He looked round him now, and, seeing her vacant chair, wondered what he was to do with the remnant of his days.

The silent horror of the house stupefied him. He went in and out of the rooms in a wandering, purposeless manner; he looked into the kitchen where the two girls sat stitching away at their

black gowns, and looked forward to the funeral as a solemn ceremonial in which it was rather a grand thing to be concerned.
He went into old Mrs. Trevanard's bedroom, to which apartment
the old lady was still confined by that chronic rheumatic gout
which at times crippled her.

Here he sat himself down by the fireside, drearily, with his
elbows on his knees, looking at the fire, silent for the most of
his time, and shaking his head despondingly when his mother
essayed some feeble attempt at consolation—some Scriptural
phrase, which had been aired at all deaths in the family for the
last sixty years.

"I never thought that she would have gone before me,"
crooned the old lady, "but the Lord's ways are wonderful, and
His paths past finding out. It's a sad thing to think that Muriel
can't follow to-morrow. It will be the first time in our family
that a daughter has been absent at her mother's funeral."

"Ah, poor Muriel," said the father, hopelessly. "*That* trouble seems harder to bear now. It would have comforted me in
my loss if I had had a daughter to take my dead wife's place,
some one to look after the servants and pour my tea out of a
morning, some one to sit opposite me at table, and help me off
with my coat when I came in of a wet evening."

"There's Martin," said old Mrs. Trevanard; "he ought to be a
comfort to you."

"Martin's a good fellow, but he can't be what a daughter
might have been. A daughter would put her arms round my
neck, and cling to me, and shed tears upon my breast; and in
trying to comfort her I should almost forget my own sorrow. A
daughter could fill her mother's empty place in the house, which
Martin can never do. He'll be wanting to run away from home,
fast enough, you'll see, now his mother's gone. She had a great
deal more influence over him than I ever had. Who hadn't she
influence over, I wonder? Why, the very cow-boys thought
more of her than of me. Ah, she was a wonderful woman!"

"Yes, Michael," answered his mother with a sigh. "She
was a good and faithful servant, and in such the Lord is well
pleased. She never missed morning and afternoon service, let
the weather be what it might, on Sundays. She read her Bible
diligently, and she did her duty to the best of her knowledge.
If ever she was mistaken——"

"She never was mistaken," interrupted the widower, testily;
"Bridget was always right. When Martin bought those Kerry
cows, and I scolded him for buying such small, mean-looking
cattle, Bridget stood by him and said she'd warrant they were
good milch cows. And so they were. I never knew Bridget out
of her reckoning."

The grandmother sighed. She had been thinking of something wide apart from the sordid cares of farm or homestead.

Humphrey Clissold attended the funeral, which took place
on a chilly September afternoon, when autumn's biting blast
swept across the broad moorland and over the quiet valleys, and
stripped the yellowing leaves from the orchard trees. The leaves

were falling earlier than usual this year, after the long droughts and heat of the summer.

There were three mourning coaches, in the first of which Michael Trevanard and his son sat in solemn state. The second was occupied by Humphrey, the doctor, and a neighboring farmer; the third by three other farmers, long-standing acquaintances of the Borcel End family. These people and their households had constituted Mr. Trevanard's little world. It was for the maintenance of her respectability in their eyes she had toiled and striven; to be deemed wealthy and honorable and upright above all other women of her class had been her desire, and she had been gratified. They followed her to the little churchyard on the brown hillside, discoursing of her virtues as they went, and declaring her the paragon of wives.

They laid her in the family grave of the Trevanards, and left her there just as the sun declined, and an air of evening solitude crept over the scene. And then they went back to Borcel End, where the blinds were all drawn up, and the house had put on a factitious aspect of cheerfulness. The table was plenteously spread with sirloin and chine, fowls and ham, decanters of port and sherry, shining tea-tray and silver teapot, all the best things in the house brought out to do honor to Mrs. Trevanard's obsequies. The four farmers and the doctor sat down to this feast with appetites sharpened by the autumn breezes, and poor Michael took his place at the head of the table, and did his best to perform the duties of hospitality; and the funeral guests enjoyed themselves not a little during the next hour or so, though they studiously preserved the solemnity of their countenances, and threw in a sigh now and then, midway between fowl and ham, or murmured some pious commonplace upon the brevity of life, as they held their plates for a second slice of beef.

"Ah!" said the fattest and wealthiest of the farmers, "she was a respectable woman. There's not her equal within twenty miles of Seacomb."

And this was the praise for which Mrs. Trevanard had toiled —this was the highest honor she had ever desired.

CHAPTER XLII.

FIRE THAT IS CLOSEST KEPT BURNS MOST OF ALL.

HUMPHREY CLISSOLD did not leave Borcel End for some days after the funeral. He saw how Martin clung to him in this dark hour, when the sense of bereavement was still a new and strange pain to the young heart, and, anxious though he was to return to his library and Justina, he lingered, loath to leave, since departure might seem unkind. When he told Martin that he had literary work to do—that young man being aware that his friend was some manner of author, though not in the least suspecting him to be capable of poetry—Martin argued that it was just as easy to write at Borcel End as in London—easier, indeed, since there was so small a chance of interruption.

"I've heard you say myself that the great beauty of your

trade is that it requires no ' plant,' except a ream of paper and a bundle of pens," said Martin.

" Did I say that? Ah, I forgot one important item, the library of the British Museum, some millions of books, more or less. I may not want to refer to them very often, perhaps, but I like to have them at my elbow."

" The book you're writing is something prodigiously learned, then. I conclude," said Martin.

" Not at all; but it is nice to be able to verify a quotation. But I'll tell what I'll do with you, Martin; I'll stop at Borcel a week if you'll promise to go to London with me when I leave. You told me that your poor mother's death would set you free."

" So it will, by and by; but not just yet. It would be un-kind to leave father while his grief is fresh. He's so completely down."

" Upon my word, Martin, I'm afraid you're right," answered Humphrey. " But remember, you must come to me directly you feel at liberty to leave Borcel—come to me and share my home,'just as you would if I were your elder brother."

Martin employed the day after the funeral in looking over his dead mother's hoards, a painful task, but not a difficult one. Bridget Trevanard's possessions had been kept with the most perfect neatness, every scrap of lace or ribbon folded and laid in its place, all the old-fashioned trinkets of her girlhood treas-ured in their various boxes, the desk and work-box of her school-days in perfect order. Strange that these trifles should be so much less perishable than their owner.

But despite his careful examination of his mother's drawers and boxes. Martin failed to find the object of his search, that old family Bible with the clasps, which he had described to Mr. Clissold. The book was nowhere to be found. Martin dis-tributed his mother's clothes, the best to old Mrs. Trevanard, to do what she liked with. the rest to the two handmaidens. both tolerably faithful after their manner, and honestly regretful of a mistress who, though sharp and exacting, had been just in her dealings with them, and careful of their comfort. The trinkets and work-box and desk, and little collection of gift-books, chiefly of a devotional character, Martin Trevanard put away, under lock and key, in the old bureau opposite his mother's bed. He kept them for Muriel. with the faint idea that some day the light of reason might return, if only in some small measure, to that clouded brain.

" No one else had so good a right to them," he said to him-self, as he put away these homely treasures, " and no one else shall have them while I live."

" I suppose my dear mother must have given that Bible away," he said to Humphrey, after describing his unsuccessful search. " And yet it was hardly like her to give away an old family Bible. She was one who set so much store by old things, and above all by her religious books."

At that moment there flashed across Humphrey's recollection

one hitherto forgotten word in the dying woman's broken sentence.

"Gave—family Bible———"

That word "gave" confirmed Martin's idea. The Bible had been given away, but to whom? and why did it concern Humphrey, in his endeavor to right the wrongs of the past, to know that fact? Why, indeed, unless the Bible had been given to Mr. and Mrs. Eden, the people who took Muriel's infant.

He went over in his note-book the story which Mrs. Trevanard had told him. He had been careful to write down all the facts, recording every detail as closely as possible, upon the night of that day on which he received that story of the past from the invalid's lips. Going over it carefully in the silence of his own room on the second night after the funeral, he came to this passage: "I made them take a solemn oath upon my Bible, binding them to perform their part of the bond."

It was clear, then, that Mrs. Trevanard had carried her Bible to the loft—that the oath had been sworn upon her own Bible. Was it not likely that on so solemn an occasion as her parting with these people, who were to carry the last of her race—the nameless child she discarded—away with them, she, a woman of deep religious convictions, might have given them her Bible, the most sacred gift she could bestow, symbol of good faith between them?

Now if this Bible had been given, and the name of Martin's great-grandmother, Justina Trevanard, was written in it, the fact would add one more link to that chain of evidence which Humphrey Clissold had been putting together lately.

It had entered into his mind that Justina Elgood was Muriel's daughter—the child given into the keeping of strangers, perhaps—ah, too bitter thought—the child of shame!

The facts in support of this notion were not many, would have made very little impression perhaps in a court of justice, yet, though he struggled against a notion which appeared to his sober reason absurd and groundless, his fancy was taken captive, and dwelt upon the idea with a tormenting persistence.

In the first place he was a poet, and there seemed to him a curious fatality in all the circumstances connected with his presence at Borcel End. He had gone there by the merest accident, guided by that Will-o'-the-wisp of a child, tramping miles across a barren moor, intruding himself on an unwilling hostess. Then on the very first night of his habitation beneath that lonely roof he had been visited by one who, if not a wanderer from the shadow-world, was at least a ghost of the past—one who had outlived life's joy and hopes, almost its cares and sorrows. This appearance of Muriel's had at once awakened his interest in her. But for this midnight visit, and the chance meeting in the hazel copse, he might have come and gone a dozen times without being aware of Muriel Trevanard's existence.

This idea of Destiny was, of course, a mere fanciful reason.

To-night, in the silence, having gone over every word of Mrs. Trevanard's story in his note-book, he placed on record those other circumstances which had impressed him in relation to this question.

1. The fact that Justina Elgood was said to have been born at Seacomb, a curiously out-of-the-way corner of the earth.

2. Her age exactly corresponded with the age of Muriel's daughter, were she living.

3. The particularly uncommon name of Justina, a family name of the Trevanard's.

4. The description of the man who had called himself Eden; a fluent speaker, a man who seemed accustomed to public speaking.

5. Mathew Elgood had lost an infant daughter at Seacomb. The fact stood recorded in the register. These Edens had also lost a child.

Very little, certainly, all this, when set down formally upon paper, but the idea floating in Humphrey's mind seemed to have a stronger foundation than these meager facts. Whence the fancy came he knew not, yet it seemed to him that for a long time he had been skeptical as to Justina's relationship to Mathew Elgood. There was so evident a superiority in the daughter to the supposed father. They were creatures of a different clay.

"It is just as if some clumsy delf pitcher were to pretend to be made of the same paste as Justina's dragon-china tea-service," he said to himself.

He remembered how reticent Mr. Elgood had always been upon the subject of the past—how the little that had been told had been told somewhat reluctantly, extorted, in a manner, by Humphrey's questioning. He remembered Mr. Elgood's startled look when he, Humphrey, had spoken for the first time of Borcel End.

"I dare say, after all. the fancy is groundless," he said to himself. as he closed his pocket-book, ·"and that the circumstances which have impressed me so strongly could be explained in quite a different manner. A provincial actor's wandering life may bring him to any corner of the earth, and the name Justina may have been chosen out of some novel of the day by Mrs. Elgood. But since I have promised to do my uttermost to see Muriel Trevanard righted. I am bound to sift this matter thoroughly. And again, it would be hard if I were not allowed to investigate the pedigree of the woman I hope to win for my wife. Heaven knows that the worst or the best that I can learn of my darling's parentage will make no difference in my love for her true self."

For three or four days after the funeral Humphrey gave himself up almost entirely to friendship, and spent his time strolling about the farm with Martin, philosophizing. consoling, talking hopefully of the future, when the young man was to come to London and carve out some kind of career for himself. But the last two days of his stay in Cornwall Mr. Clissold had apportioned to his own business. One day for a farewell visit to Penwyn Manor, another day for Seacomb, where he had certain inquiries and researches to make. He had arranged to leave

Borcel the morning after his visit to the Manor-house, and to spend the following night at a hotel in Seacomb. This would give him the whole of the day and evening in that somewhat melancholy town.

He had written to Mrs. Penwyn, gratefully acknowledging her kind invitation to make the Manor-house his headquarters, and explaining how it was that his friendship for Martin obliged him to decline her hospitality. But in his heart of hearts there was another reason why he did not care to stay at Penwyn Manor, or increase his intimacy with Churchill Penwyn. Justina had expressed her antipathy to that gentleman, and Humphrey felt as if it were in some manner treasonable to cultivate the friendship of any gentleman whom Justina disliked. That large madness, Love, is a conglomeration of small follies.

Courtesy, however, demanded that he should pay his respects to the Penwyn family before leaving Cornwall, and he had a lurking curiosity about that household, a somewhat morbid interest perhaps, with which Justina's vague suspicions, far as they were from any thought of his own, may have had something to do.

That change in Madge Penwyn, hardly to be described, yet to his eye very palpable, had puzzled him not a little. Was it possible that the husband and wife, so devoted to each other a little while ago, had undergone some change of feeling, that one or the other had looked back upon the sun-lit path of love and perceived that the rose-bloom was fading from life's garden? No, Humphrey could not for a moment believe in any lessening of Madge Penwyn's love of her husband or Churchill's devotion to her. He had seen "that little look across the crowd" which the poet has sung of—the look of utter trust and sympathy which passes between a husband and wife now and then in some busy hour of the day, amidst some friendly circle, a sudden interchange of thought or feeling, stolen from the throng. And in Madge's case he had seen a look of devotion curiously pathetic, love fraught with pity, a look of deepest melancholy. This dwelt in his memory and influenced his thoughts of Churchill Penwyn and his wife.

There was some hitch, some dissonant interval in the harmony of their lives; yet what the jarring notes could be it was hard for the student of humanity to discover. No life could seem outwardly more perfect. Churchill's position was of all positions most enviable, with just sufficient wealth for all the joys of life, an estate just large enough to give him importance in his neighborhood, without the weighty responsibility of a large landowner, ambition gratified by his Parliamentary success, the fairest wife that man could desire to adorn his home. And yet there were shadows on the face of husband and wife that denoted a secret trouble. In this house which held all things the skeleton was not wanting.

"Can there be any ground for Justina's suspicion?" Humphrey asked himself. "And is a clear conscience the one thing missing in Churchill Penwyn's sum of happiness?"

CHAPTER XLIII.
FOR HERE'S NO SAFETY IN THE REALM FOR ME.

It was a dull autumnal afternoon when Humphrey Clissold paid his final visit to the Manor-house. That brilliant summer, which had lasted in all its heat and glory to the end of August, and even extended to September, had vanished all at once, and had given place to a bleak and early autumn. Stormy winds by night and dull gray skies by day, had prevailed of late: sad stories of disaster at sea filled many a column in the newspapers —to the relief of editors, who must needs have had recourse to gigantic gooseberries, or revived the sea-serpent, but for these catastrophes.

Even the Manor-house had a gloomy look under this leaden sky. Pyramids of scarlet geraniums, thickets of many-colored dahlias, lent their gaudy hues to the scene: but the lack of sun-light made all dull. The gilded vane pointed persistently north-east. Gardeners and underlings had labored in vain to keep the paths and lawns clear of dead leaves. Down they came, in a crackling shower, with every gust, emblems of decay and death. Humphrey Clissold, sensitive, as the poet must ever be, to external influences, felt depressed by the altered aspect of the place.

Within, however, all was mirth and brightness. There was the usual family group in the hall, where a mighty wood fire blazed in the wide modern-antique grate, with its massive iron-work, and two burnished brazen globes, on iron standards—golden orbs that reflected the ruddy glow of the fire. The bill-iard players were at work. A party of young ladies played pool industriously, under the leadership of Mr. Tresillian, J. P., who was in great force in feminine circles where there was not much strain upon a man's intellect. Lady Cheshunt was in her pet chair by the fire—her complexion guarded by a tapestry banner-screen—deeply absorbed in that very French novel, the iniquity whereof she had seen denounced in that modern censor, the *Saturday Review*. Viola Bellingham was working point lace at a little table by the central window, and listening with rather a listless, uninterested air to Sir Lewis Dallas' discourse. Neither Madge nor her husband was present.

Lady Cheshunt closed her novel with a faint sigh, leaving a finger between the pages. Mr. Clissold was not so interesting as a French novelist who was worth a page and a quarter of de-nunciation in the *Saturday*, yet she felt called upon to be civil to him.

" How is Mrs. Penwyn?" he asked, when he had shaken hands with and duly informed himself as to the health of the dis-tinguished dowager.

"That poor child is not very well," replied her ladyship. "East wind, I suppose. I don't think we were created for a world in which the wind is perpetually in the east. On such a day as this I always wish myself in the torrid zone, the center of Africa, anywhere where one could feel the sun. To look at that gray sky and those falling leaves is enough to give one the horrors. It's as bad as reading Young's ' Night Thoughts,' or staying at a country-house with goody people who insist upon reading one of Blair's sermons aloud on a wet Sunday afternoon."

" I hope it is nothing serious," said Humphrey, meaning Mrs. Penwyn's indisposition.

" Oh, dear, no; not in the least. She is only a little out of spirits, and has been spending the morning in her own room with the baby. I dare say she will come down presently. I think she worked a little too hard last season, giving dinners to all the people Mr. Penwyn wanted to conciliate, and going everywhere he wished. She would make an admirable cabinet minister's wife, I tell her, so devoted and self-sacrificing; and. I suppose, at the rate Mr. Penwyn is going on, he is sure to be in the cabinet sooner or later. A very wonderful man—so serious and self-contained—a man who never wasted a minute of his life, I should think." ·

Madge entered at this moment, a little paler than in the days of old, but very beautiful. Her flowing gray silk dress, with broad sash, and gimps and fringes of richest violet, became her admirably. Not a jewel or ornament, except the single amethyst stud which fastened her plain linen collar, and the triple band of diamonds on her wedding finger. The glorious dark hair wound, coronet fashion, round the small head. A woman for a new Velasquez to paint, just as she stood before Humphrey Clissold to-day in the soft gray light.

" I am so sorry to hear you have been ill," he said, as they shook hands.

" But you must not be sorry, for I was not ill. I was a little tired, perhaps a little idle, too, and I wanted a morning alone with my boy. What have you done with Churchill, Lady Cheshunt?" with a little anxious look round the room—empty for her, lacking but one occupant.

" What have I done with him?" ejaculated the dowager. " Do you suppose your husband is a man to be kept in-doors by any fascinations of mine? I should as soon expect to see Brutus or Cassius, or any of those dreadful Shakespearean persons, in togas, playing the tame cat. I asked your husband to read aloud to us, thinking that might please him—most men are proud of their elocution—but you should have seen his look of quiet contempt. ' I am so sorry I am too busy to allow myself the pleasure of amusing you,' he said, and then went off to superintend some new plantation of Norwegian firs. Wonderful man!"

" You have come to spend the rest of the day with us, of course, Mr. Clissold?" said Madge, with that pleasant, cordial manner which was one of her charms, and in nowise out of harmony with her somewhat queenly bearing. Who more delightful than a queenly woman when she desires to please?

" I shall be only too happy if I may, and if you will excuse my appearing at dinner in a frock-coat. I reserved this day for my visit here. It is my last day but one in the west."

" I am so sorry," said Madge. " Well, since we have you for

so short a time we must do our best to amuse you. Perhaps "—
with a happy thought—" you would like to go and see Churchill's new plantation. We might go for a drive and join
him."

Humphrey understood the wife's desire to be near her husband, a new proof of that love which had an element of pathos
in its quiet intensity.

" I should like it of all things," he answered.

" But are you sure you have lunched?" It was between three
and four in the afternoon.

" Quite sure. I joined Mr. Trevanard at his early dinner."

" Clara—Laura—which of you will come for a drive?" asked
Madge, indiscriminately, of the pool players. " I know it would
be useless to ask you, dear Lady Cheshunt."

" My love, I would as soon drive across the Neva in a sledge
for pleasure. I never stir from my fireside, except to go out to'
dinner, when the wind's in the east. Setting aside the discom-
fort, I can't see why one should make a horror of one's self by
exposing one's complexion to be rasped as the bakers rasp their
rolls."

The pool players were too deeply involved in their game to
care about leaving it, unless dear Mrs. Penwyn particularly
wished them to go out.

" Let me come, Madge," said Viola, " and let us take Nugent.
You won't mind, will you, Mr. Clissold ?"

" Do you think I am such a barbarian as to object to that
small individual's society?" asked Humphrey. " He shall sit on
my knee, and pull my beard as hard as he likes."

Sir Lewis Dallas asked to be allowed to join the party, so the
sociable was ordered, and Mrs. Penwyn and her sister retired to
put on their hats.

" She is not looking well," said Humphrey.

" No, she is not," answered Lady Cheshunt, with more earnestness than was common to that somewhat frivolous dowager.
" She has never been quite the same since that burglar business."

" Indeed! The alarm caused her a great shock, I suppose ?"

" Well, she knew nothing about the attempt till it was all
over; but I suppose the worry and excitement afterward were
too much for her. The man turned out to be a son of the lodge-
keeper's, and the woman came whining to Mrs. Penwyn to let
him off easily, and Madge, who is the most tender-hearted
creature in the world, persuaded Churchill to use his influence
with that good-natured Mr. Tresillian, whom he can wind round
his finger," in a whisper, " and the man got off. It was particularly good of Mrs. Penwyn, for I know she detests that lodge
woman."

" Really," said Humphrey, affecting ignorance. " Then I
wonder Mr. Penwyn keeps her on his premises, now that he
knows her son to be such a dangerous character."

" Yes, it's just one of those absurd things men do for the sake
of having their own way. I've talked to Mr. Penwyn about it
myself ever so many times. 'Why do you annoy your poor

wife by keeping a horrid creature like that?' I have asked him.
'Suppose I know your horrid creature to be deserving of protection and shelter, Lady Cheshunt? Should I not be unmanly
if I were to sacrifice her to a foolish prejudice of Madge's?' he
retorts. So both Madge and I have left off talking about the
creature; but I must say that it always makes me feel uncomfortable to see her squatting on the threshold in the sunshine,
like an overgrown toad. I think there's something like it in
some Greek play; but I don't know where, or which," added
Lady Cheshunt, vaguely.

"Perhaps I could tell Mr. Penwyn something about his *protegee's* antecedents that would make him change his opinion."

"Then pray do. But is it anything very dreadful—murder,
or anything of that kind?" asked Lady Cheshunt, with a scared
look. "You make me feel as if we were all going to have our
throats cut."

"It is nothing very dreadful. Perhaps hardly enough to
cause any change in Mr. Penwyn's opinion. I remember that
woman plying her trade as a gypsy fortune-teller at Eborsham
the day before my poor friend, James Penwyn, was murdered.
She, in a manner—by the merest accident, of course—foretold
James' early death."

"Dear me, what an extraordinary thing! And you find her,
two years afterward, in Churchill Penwyn's service. That is
very curious."

"The whirligig of time brings many curious things to pass,
Lady Cheshunt. But here are the ladies."

They went to the porch, where the sociable was waiting for
them, with a pair of fine bays, impatient to be gone. It was
not an inviting day for open-air excursions, but just one of
those gray afternoons which have a kind of poetry—a sentiment
all their own. The somber expanse of moorland, dun color
against the gray, had a fine effect.

They took a longish drive, made a circuit, and came round to
the new plantation, where Churchill was superintending the
work, seated on his favorite Tarpan, an animal which had of
late shown himself unmanageable by any one except his master,
and had been the cause of more than one groom's retirement
from a service which was in every other respect admirable.
Churchill seemed to have a peculiar fancy for the somewhat ill-
conditioned brute, though he did not often ride him, on account
of Mrs. Penwyn's nervous apprehensions.

"My dear love, he will never throw *me*," Churchill said in
answer to his wife's request that Tarpan should be disposed of.
"If I were not thoroughly convinced of that, I would part with
him. The brute understands me, and I understand him, which
neither of those fellows did. And I like his pace and action
better than those of any other horse in the stable. Nothing re-
vives me like a gallop on Tarpan."

Wonderful to see the influence of Madge Penwyn's presence
on her husband as Humphrey Clissold saw it to-day. The moody
brow relaxed its contemplative frown, the thoughtful eye bright-

ened, while a gentle pressure of the hand and fondly whispered sentence welcomed the wife.

" This is an unexpected pleasure, Madge," he said. " I did not think you would drive to-day."

" I want to show Mr. Clissold your new plantation, Churchill."

They all alighted, and Churchill showed them his newly-planted groves, the graceful feathery Norwegian saplings (a ship-load of them brought from Norway for his special benefit), rhododendrons planted in between, and here and there a mountain ash, or a copper beech to give color and variety.

While they were walking in the plantation, Humphrey and Churchill side by side, the former seized the opportunity of speaking of the gypsy woman whose presence at Penwyn Manor was a perplexity to him. It might possibly be an impertinence on his part to call in question Mr. Penwyn's domestic arrangements, but Humphrey Clissold felt that there were circumstances in this case which fully justified a breach of manners.

" Do you know that I have made a curious discovery about a person in your employment, Mr. Penwyn ?" he began.

" Indeed! And pray who and what is the person ?" asked Churchill, with the slightest possible change of manner, from cordiality to reserve.

" Your lodge-keeper," returned Humphrey; and then he proceeded to relate the circumstances of his first meeting with Rebecca Mason.

Mr. Penwyn received the information with supreme indifference.

" Curious," he said, carelessly; " but I have long since discovered that life is made up of curious coincidences, and I have lost the faculty of astonishment. Multitudinous as the inhabitants of this globe are, we seem to be perpetually moving in circles, and knocking our heads against some one or other connected with our past lives. If I had wronged a man in Otaheite twenty years ago, it would not in the least surprise me to meet him at Seacomb Corn Exchange to-morrow. With regard to the woman Mason, I found her in circumstances of extreme distress, and offered her a home. It was one of those rare occasions on which I have indulged in the luxury of doing good," with an ironical laugh. " I knew when I did this that Rebecca had gypsy blood in her veins, and had led a roving life. But I had reason to believe her an honest woman then, and I have never found any cause for thinking her otherwise since. And this being so, I have made up my mind to keep her, in spite of the vulgar prejudice against her tawny skin, in spite even of my wife's dislike."

" You are not alarmed by the idea of her relationship to a burglar ?"

" No. First and foremost, I am not prepared to admit that the man is a burglar; and secondly, if he be, I am as well able to defend the Manor-house from him as from any other member of his profession."

"Except that he would have the advantage of his mother's lodge as a base of operations, and his mother's knowledge of your domestic arrangements," remonstrated Humphrey, determined to push the question.

"I have told you that I know her to be an honest woman, whatever the son may be. Come, Mr. Clissold, we may as well drop this subject. You are not likely to influence me upon a point which I have maintained against the wish of my wife."

"So be it," said Humphrey, closing the discussion, with the conviction that there was some hidden link between the gypsy and the Squire of Penwyn, some influence stronger than philanthropy which secured the wanderer's home. The fact that it should be so, that there should be some secret alliance between the woman who had foretold James Penwyn's death and the man who had been so large a gainer by that early death, impressed him strangely. He was thoughtful and silent throughout the homeward drive—so thoughtful and so silent as to arouse Madge Penwyn's curiosity.

"I can hardly compliment you upon being the most amusing of companions, Mr. Clissold," she said, with a forced smile, as they approached the Manor-house. "There was a time when your conversation used to be amusing enough to enliven the dullest drive, but to-day you have been the image of gloom."

"Black care sits behind us all at odd times, Mrs. Penwyn," he answered, gravely. "Be assured I must have cause for serious thought when the charm of your presence does not put me in spirits."

"Thanks for the compliment; but you talk rather too much like a Greek oracle," retorted Madge, lightly, but with an uneasy look, which did not escape Humphrey's observation.

"There is a cloud hanging over this house," he said to himself. "A trouble in which husband and wife share. But it can be no such dark secret as Justina's suspicions point to, or Mrs. Penwyn would know nothing about it. No husband would reveal such guilt as *that* to his wife."

CHAPTER XLIV.

"FOR THOU WERT STILL THE POOR MAN'S STAY."

DINNER at Penwyn Manor went off gayly enough. Lady Cheshunt, inspirited by various light wines, a good deal of maraschino in the ice pudding, and a glass of curacoa as a corrective afterward, was a host in herself, and talked loud enough, fast enough, recklessly enough, to keep the dullest dinner going. Mr. Penwyn was an excellent host, starting fresh subjects of conversation with such admirable tact that no one knew who changed the current of ideas when interest was just beginning to flag—never taking the lion's share of the talk, or drifting into monologue, listening to every one, encouraging the timid, sustaining the weak, and proving himself a living encyclopedia whenever dates, names, or facts were wanted.

The gentlemen left the dining-room about ten minutes after the ladies had quitted it, to the delight of Sir Lewis Dallas, and the secret disgust of Mr. Tresillian. who liked to prose about stable and kennel for an hour or so over his claret.

The assembly being merely a household party, people scattered themselves in a free and easy manner through the rooms, the ivory balls clicking in hall and billiard-room, as usual, a little group of ladies round the piano trying that sweet bit of Schumann's, chiefly remarkable for cinquepation, and little jerky chords. up and down the piano, and demanding no small skill in the executant.

Humphrey found himself in the deep embrasure of one of the hall windows, talking literature with Miss Bellingham, who evidently preferred his society to that of the devoted Sir Lewis.

" A good opportunity to find out a little more about George Penwyn," thought Humphrey. " Miss Bellingham must be acquainted with all the traditions of the house. If I could but discover what manner of man he was, I should be better able to arrive at a just conclusion about his relations with Muriel Trevanard."

A little later when they were talking of libraries and book collecting. Viola said: " There were hardly fifty books altogether at Penwyn, I think. when my brother-in-law came into the property. The library here is entirely Churchill's collection. The squire and his predecessors must have been strangely deficient in literary taste. Even the few books there were had most of them belonged to Mr. George Penwyn, the poor young man who was killed in Canada."

"Ah, poor fellow! I heard of his sad fate from the housekeeper here, when I came to see the Manor-house last summer. A tragical end like that gives a melancholy interest to a man's history, however commonplace it may be in other respects. I suppose you have heard a good deal of gossip about this George Penwyn?"

" Yes, our old housekeeper is fond of talking about him. He seems to have been a favorite with people, especially with cottagers and small tenants on the estate. I have heard old people regret that he never came to his own. even in my presence, though the speech was hardly civil to my brother-in-law. I know that by some of the people we are looked upon as intruders on George Penwyn's account. He seems to have been constantly doing kindnesses."

" And you have never heard anything against his character— that he was dissipated—wild, as the world calls it ?"

" Never so much as a word. On the contrary, Mrs. Darvis has often told me that he was particularly steady—that he was never known to take too much wine, or anything of that kind. In fact, she talks as if he had been a paragon."

"Ah," thought Humphrey, "these paragons are sometimes viler at the bottom than your open profligate. Few men ever knew the human heart better than he who gave us Charles and Joseph Surface."

" I have an inward conviction that George Penwyn must have been nice," said Viola.

" Indeed! On what ground is that conviction based?"

"On various grounds. First, there are the praises of people who cannot flatter, since there is nothing to be gained by speaking well of the dead. Secondly, there is that shelf full of books with George Penwyn's name in them, all nice books, the choice of a man of culture and good feeling. Thirdly, there is his portrait, and I like his face. Are those reasons strong enough, do you think?"

"Quite, for a woman. His portrait—ah, by the bye, I should like to have another look at that."

"Come and see it at once, then," replied Viola, good-naturedly. "It is in the little study yonder, the old squire's room. The books are there too."

The study was a little room off the hall. Humphrey remembered it well, though he had never entered it since Mrs. Darvis showed him George Penwyn's portrait, on his first visit to the Manor-house.

Viola took a wax candle from the mantel-shelf and led the way to the study, a room which was still used for business interviews with stewards or tenants, a second door opening into a passage communicating with the offices and obscure passages by which such inferior beings were admitted to the squire's presence.

Humphrey took the candle from Miss Bellingham's hand, and held it up before the picture over the mantelpiece.

His grip tightened on the bronze candlestick, and his breath came stronger and quicker as he looked, but he said never a word.

That picture was to him a stronger confirmation of his idea about Justina's parentage than all the circumstantial evidence in the world. There, in those pictured lineaments, he saw the very lines of Justina's face—lines modified in her countenance, it is true, and softened to feminine beauty, but characteristics too striking to be mistaken even by a casual observer.

"Strange that the likeness did not occur to me when I saw that picture first," he thought. "But then at that time I had only looked at Justina with the eye of indifference. I did not know her face by heart as I do now. And I remember that even then the picture struck me as like some one I knew. Memory only failed to recall the individual."

Those placid blue eyes, with their somewhat melancholy expression, were so like the eyes he had seen looking at him mournfully only three weeks ago, when Justina bade him good-bye. The eyes which he faintly remembered looking up at him for the first time in the buttercup meadow near Eborsham.

Humphrey Clissold put down the candle without a word.

"I hope you have stared long enough at that picture," said Viola, laughing. "You appear to find it remarkably interesting."

"It is a very interesting portrait—to me."

"Why to you in particular?"

"Because it resembles some one very dear to me."

"Oh, I understand," said Viola, gently.   "Your poor friend, James Penwyn."

Humphrey did not attempt to set her right.

"Now let us look at the books," he said, going to the *secretaire*, the upper shelves of which held about thirty volumes, all well bound.   They were Valpy's Shakespeare, in green morocco, Wordsworth, Coleridge, Byron and Shelley, Keats and Hood, and a few other volumes, chiefly Oxford classics, which Mr. Penwyn had brought from the university, not by any means the books of a man wanting in refinement or culture.   That they had been well read was evident, and many a verse underlined in pencil marked the reader's approbation.

In a volume of Byron, containing "Manfred" and some of the minor poems, Humphrey found a penciled note here and there in a woman's hand, which he recognized as Muriel Trevanard's.   Words of praise or of criticism, but in all cases denoting a cultivated mind and a sound judgment.   A girl who coul l write thus was hardly likely to have been fooled by the first seducer who came across her path.

"I wonder who wrote in that book," said Viola.   "George Penwyn had no sister, and his mother died while he was very young. Perhaps they were written by Miss Morgrave, the young lady his father wanted him to marry."

"I should hardly have thought they were on intimate terms enough for that kind of thing."

"True.   One must be very sure of a person's friendship before one can venture to scribble one's opinions in their books," returned Viola.

An hour later Humphrey Clissold left the Manor-house.   Glad to be alone, and free to think over the day's work.

The idea which had hitherto seemed little better than a baseless fancy, the filmy weaving of his own romantic dreams, was now conviction.   He held it as a certain fact that Justina was George Penwyn's daughter, and that it must be his work to discover the missing link in Muriel Trevanard's story, and the nature of that fatal union which had ended in shattered wits and a broken heart.

"God grant that I may find evidence to confirm my own belief in the girl's purity and the man's honor," he said to himself, as he drove the dog-cart back to Borcel End.   "If the popular idea of George Penwyn is correct, he must have been too good a man to play so base a part as that of betrayer, too kind to leave his victim to face the storm of parental wrath unprotected. But he was in his father's power, and it is possible that he might have had recourse to a secret marriage rather than forfeit the old man's favor and the Penwyn estate.   Yet, if this were the case, it is strange that he should have left England without endeavoring to secure his wife's safety—that he should have made no provision for his child's birth—an event the possibility of which he ought to have foreseen."

This was a puzzling point.   Indeed, the whole story was involved in mystery.   Either George Penwyn must have deceived everybody who knew him as to his moral character, or he must have acted honestly toward Muriel.

"There is only one person I can think of as likely to know the truth of the story," Humphrey said to himself, "and that person is Miss Barlow, the school-mistress at Seacomb. My first endeavor must be to find Miss Barlow, if she is still an inhabitant of this lower world."

He had a good deal to do in Seacomb, yet was anxious, with a lover's foolish yearning, to get back to London; so he got Martin to drive him over to the quiet old market-town early next morning, and took care to put up at the oldest inn in the place—a rambling old house with a quadrangular yard—a relic of the good old coaching days.

"There's no better place than an old inn in which to learn the traditions of a town," Humphrey told himself. "I dare say I shall find some ancient waiter here who remembers everything that has happened at Seacomb for the last fifty years."

CHAPTER XLV.

I FOUND HIM GARRULOUSLY GIVEN.

THE oldest inn in Seacomb was the New London Inn, built upon the site of a still more ancient hostelry, but itself well-nigh two hundred years old. The quadrangular yard, in which the coaches were wont to stand, was now embellished with a glazed roof, and served for the assembling of farmers on market-days. Here was held the corn exchange, and samples of grain were exhibited and bargains made amidst a lively hubbub, while the odor of roast beef and pastry pervaded the atmosphere.

Here Humphrey and Martin parted, the former telling his friend that he had business to transact in Seacomb, the young Cornishman bidding his companion a reluctant farewell.

As soon as the dog-cart had driven off, Humphrey strolled into the bar, called for soda-water and sherry, and surveyed his ground. On the other side of the shining counter a comfortable-looking elderly matron, in a black silk gown and a cap with rose-colored ribbons, was engaged in conversation with a stalwart gray-coated farmer, who had been admitted to the privileged sanctorum within. "The landlady, evidently," thought Humphrey.

He sipped his sherry and soda, and asked if he could be accommodated with an airy bedroom.

"Certainly, sir. You'd like a room on the first floor, perhaps, overlooking the street. Chamber-maid, show No. 10."

"I won't trouble to look at the room, thank you, ma'am. I've no doubt it's all that's comfortable."

"There's not much fear about that, sir. I look after my bedrooms myself, and always have done so for the last thirty years. I go into every room in the house every morning, after the chamber-maids have done their sweeping and dusting; and that's neither more nor less than a housekeeper's duty, in my opinion."

"Just so, ma'am. It's a pity that kind of housekeeping should ever go out of fashion."

"It is, indeed, sir. You intend staying for some days at Seacomb, perhaps? There are a good many objects of interest in the neighborhood."

"I am sorry to say that I shall have to leave to-morrow."

"Well, good-morning, Mrs. Chadwick," said the farmer, having drained a deep glass of sparkling cider, and wiped his lips with an air of satisfaction.

Mrs. Chadwick opened the half door of the bar for him to go out, and then holding it open politely invited Mr. Clissold to enter.

"You may as well sit down, sir, and take your soda and sherry," she said, nothing averse to a little gossip with the stranger.

"I shall be very glad to do so," answered Humphrey. "The fact is, I want a little friendly chat with some one who knows Seacomb, and I dare say you know pretty well as much as any one else about the town and its inhabitants."

The landlady smiled, as with inward satisfaction.

"It's my native town, sir. I was born here, and brought up here, and educated here, and I could count the months I've spent away from Seacomb on my fingers. It isn't everybody can say as much."

"You were educated at Seacomb," said Humphrey. "Then perhaps you may remember Miss Barlow's school for young ladies?"

"Yes, sir. I remember Miss Barlow well; but her school flourished after my schooling days, and it was above my father's station. No Seacomb trades-people ever went to Miss Barlow's. Their money might be good enough for most people, but Miss Barlow wouldn't have it. She set her face against anything under a rich farmer's daughter. She had a good deal of pride—stuckupishness some people went so far as to call it—had Miss Barlow. And a very pretty show she used to make with her young ladies at the parish church, in the south gallery on the left of the organ."

"Do you happen to remember a daughter of a Mr. Trevanard, of Borcel End?"

"Remember Miss Trevanard! I should think I did. She was about the prettiest girl I ever saw, and the Seacomb gentlemen would go out of their way to get a look at her. I've seen them hanging about the church door to watch Miss Barlow's young ladies come out, and heard them whisper, 'That's the beauty! That's Trevanard's daughter!' I thought she'd have made a rare good match when she left school, but she never married, and I believe she went a little queer in her head, or was bedridden, or some affliction of that kind, while she was quite young. I haven't heard anybody mention her name for the last twenty years—not her own father, even, though he dines here every market-day. That was young Mr. Trevanard drove you here, wasn't it? I just caught a glimpse of him in the hall."

"Yes; Martin and I are great friends."

"A very nice young man he is, too, and nice looking, but not a patch upon his sister."

"Do you know what became of Miss Barlow when she left Seacomb?"

"Well, I've heard say that she went to the Continent to cultivate music. She had a fine finger for the piano, and took a great deal of pride in her playing; and after she'd lived abroad some years, studying in a conservatory—I suppose they teach them that way on account of the climate—I heard that she came back to England, and settled somewhere near London, and gave lessons to the nobility and gentry, and stood very high in that way. She made a nice little fortune at Seacomb before she retired, so she had no call to work unless she liked. But Miss Barlow wasn't the woman to be idle. She had a vast amount of energy."

A musical professor, and residing in the neighborhood of London. It seemed to Humphrey that, knowing this much, he ought to be able to find Miss Barlow. There was only the question of time.

"How long is it, do you imagine, since you last heard of this lady?" he asked, in a purely conversational tone.

" Well, I can't take upon myself to say very particularly for a year or so. But I think it might be about eight or nine years since I heard Dr. Dorlick, our organist, say that a friend of his in London had told him Miss Barlow was residing in the neighborhood of the parks, and doing wonderfully well."

"Could I see Dr. Dorlick, do you think?" asked Humphrey, eagerly.

"Dr. Dorlick is in heaven," replied Mrs. Chadwick, with solemnity.

"I'm sorry for that," said Humphrey, with reference to his own disappointment rather than Dr. Dorlick's elevation.

He passed on to another subject, also an important one in his mind.

"How is it that you managed to do away with your theater in Seacomb?" he asked.

"Well, you see, sir," returned Mrs. Chadwick, musingly, "I don't think the theater ever fairly took with the Seacomb people. Ours is a serious town, and though there's plenty of spare room in our old parish church—a very fine old church, as you may have seen with your own eyes, but rather in want of repair—there's always a run upon oui chapels, evening services, and tea-meetings, and love-feasts, and what not. People must have excitement of some sort, no doubt, and the Seacomb people like chapel-going better than play-going, besides which it costs them less. I've no prejudices myself, and I know that a theatrical is a human being like myself; but I can't say that I've ever cared to see theatricals inside my doors."

"But I suppose you used to go to the theater sometimes, when there was one?"

"Once in a way I have gone to our theater, when there was a bespeak night, or a London star performing, more to please my husband, who was fond of anything in the way of an entertainment, than for my own pleasure."

"Do you remember the names of the actors whom you saw there?"

"No, I can't call to mind one of them. But if you take any interest in theatricals, go and see Mr. Clipcome, our hairdresser. He'll talk to you for the hour together of our theater, and the people who've acted there. He never cut my hair in his life that he didn't tell me how he once curled and powdered a wig for the celebrated Miss Foote to act Lady Teazle in. It's his 'obby."

"Indeed! Then I shall certainly look in upon Mr. Clipcome. Where does he live?"

"In a little court, by the side of Bethlehem Chapel, which was the theater."

"Thanks, Mrs. Chadwick," said Humphrey. rising. "I'll step round to Mr. Clipcome at once, and get him to give me the county crop. I've been running to seed lately. Perhaps you'll be kind enough to order me a little bit of dinner in the coffee-room at half-past six."

"With pleasure, sir. Any choice?"

"None whatever. I shall walk about your town for a few hours, and get an appetite for anything you like to set before me."

"A very agreeable gentleman," thought Mrs. Chadwick, as Humphrey strolled out of the bar; "so chatty and friendly. Doesn't give himself half the airs of your commercial gents, yet any one can see he's altogether superior to them."

Humphrey Clissold strolled through the quiet old town, with its long straggling high street, graced here and there by a picturesque gable or an ancient lattice, but, for the most part, somewhat commonplace. At one point there was a kind of square, from which two lateral streets diverged, a square with a pump and a police office in the center. and a Methodist chapel on each side. One of these chapels, the newest and smartest, was Bethlehem. as an inscription over its portal made known to the world at large—Bethlehem, 1853—and at the side of Bethlehem, once the Temple of Thespis. there was a clean paved alley leading to another street—an alley with a public-house at one corner, and a few decent shops on one side facing the blank wall of the chapel. One of these shops was the emporium of Mr. Clipcome, who was at once tobacconist, hair-dresser, and dealer in fancy and miscellaneous articles too numerous to mention.

Humphrey found Mr. Clipcome standing upon his threshold, contemplating life as exhibited in Play-house Court, where a small child in a go-cart and a woman cheapening bloaters at the green-grocer's were the only objects that presented themselves at this particular time to the student of humanity. But then Mr. Clipcome had an oblique view of the square, town-pump, and police-station, and in a general way could see anything that was going on from the vantage-ground of his door-step.

He was an elderly man, stout, and comfortable-looking, but

balder than he ought to be, considering the resources of his art, and that he was himself the inventor of an infallible cure for baldness. But he may have preferred that smooth and shining surface as cooler and more comfortable than capillary embellishment. He wore a clean linen apron, with a comb or two stuck in the pocket thereof—an apron that was in itself an invitation to the passing pedestrian to have his hair cut. On seeing Mr. Clissold making for his door, Mr. Clipcome stepped aside with a smile and a bow, and made way for the stranger to enter his abode.

It was a very small abode, consisting of a shop and a little slip of a parlor behind it, both the pink of neatness, and both agreeably perfumed with hair-oil and lavender-water. There was a shining arm-chair with a high back, whereon the patient sat enthroned during the hair-cutting process. A looking-glass squeezed into an angle of the parlor reflected patient and operator. A pincushion hung beside it, balanced by a smart chintz bag containing a variety of implements. But the object which most struck Humphrey's eye was an old play-bill, smaller than modern play-bills, and yellow with age, framed and glazed, and hanging against the wall as if it had been some choice work of art.

It was the programme of a performance of "Othello" that had taken place early in the century. "Othello, the Moor of Venice, Mr. Kean."

"You remember the great Kean?" said Humphrey.

"Yes, sir," answered Mr. Clipcome, with pride. "I remember Edmund Kean, and I remember Charles Young, and Miss O'Neil, and Miss Foote, and Mrs. Nesbitt, and Mr. Macready, and a good deal more talent such as you're not likely to see in these days. Seacomb Theater was worth going to in my boyhood."

"And you were an enthusiastic patron of the drama, I imagine?"

"If spending every sixpence of my pocket-money upon admission to the pit is a proof of enthusiasm, I was an enthusiast, sir," replied Mr. Clipcome. "The sixpences which boys—well, I will venture to say boys of inferior mind—would have laid out upon cakes and apples, peg-tops, and such-like, I spent upon the drama. There's hardly a line of Shakespeare you could quote that I couldn't cap with another line. I used to go to the pit of that theater twice a week while I was a youngster, and three or four times a week after my father's death, when I was in business for myself and my own master, and used to get a weekly order for exhibiting the bills. And though there were a good many opposed to the closing of the theater forever, I don't believe there was any one in all Seacomb took it to heart as keenly as I did. 'Othello's occupation was gone.'"

"Why did they do away with your theater at last?" asked Humphrey.

"Well, you see, sir, the town had grown serious-minded, and for some years before they turned it into a chapel, the theater had been going down. The great actors and actresses were dead and gone, and the stars that were left didn't care about coming to Seacomb. Managers had been doing worse and worse year after year, business dwindling down to next to nothing, half salaries or no salaries toward the end of every season, and it became a recognized fact in the theatrical profession that Seacomb was no go. The actors and actresses that came here were sticks, or if not, they made up in rant what they wanted in talent. The county families left off coming to the place; there were no bespeaks, and the poor old theater got to have a dilapidated, woe-begone look, so that it gave one the horrors to sit out a play. The actors looked hungry and out at elbows. It made one uncomfortable to see them. Many a time I asked one of them in to share my one o'clock dinner, if it was but a potato pasty or a squab pie made with scrag of mutton. The stage-door used to be just opposite my shop. It's walled up now, but you may see the outline of it in the brickwork. The actors used to be always lounging about that doorway of a morning, on and off, and while the rehearsal was going on inside. And they were very fond of coming into my shop for a gossip or a peep at a newspaper. Papers were dear in those days. No *Standard* or *Telegraph* with all the news of the world for a penny. And the poor chaps couldn't afford to lay out fivepence."

"You must have been on friendly terms with a good many of them," said Humphrey, feeling that from this loquacious barber, if from any one in Seacomb, he was likely to obtain the information he sought. "Do you happen to remember a man called Elgood?"

"Elgood! Mat Elgood!" cried the operator, dropping his scissors in the vehemence of his exclamation; "I should think I did, indeed! He was one who hung on to our Theater Royal to the very last—stuck to it like a barnacle, poor fellow, when there was not enough sustenance to be got out of it to keep body and soul together. He lodged in this very court, the last house on the other side, next door but one to the theater—a tailor's it was then—and a good little man the tailor was, and a kind friend to Mat Elgood, as long as he had a crust to share with him or a garret to shelter him. But one day, about a month after the theater shut up shop altogether, the manager having bolted, the brokers walked into poor Jones' little place and took possession of everything, and Jones went to prison; so Mat Elgood and his wife, a poor weak thing that had lost her baby only a few weeks before that time, were cast loose upon the world, and what became of them from that hour to this I never heard. If I'd had an empty room in my house I'd have given it them, but I hadn't, and my wife is a prudent woman, who never forgot to remind me that my first duty was to her and my children; or, in other words, that charity begins at home."

"Do you remember the date of this occurrence—the year and month in which Mathew Elgood left Seacomb? I may as well tell you that I do not ask these questions out of idle curiosity. I am personally interested in knowing all about this Mr. Elgood."

"My dear sir," exclaimed the barber, swelling with importance at the idea of giving valuable information, "you could not have come to a better source. If I fail to remember the dates you require, I can produce documentary evidence which will place the fact beyond doubt. For a period of ten years or upward I made it a rule to keep a copy of every play-bill issued in our town. They were delivered at my door gratis for exhibition in my window, and instead of throwing them aside as waste paper, I filed them as interesting records for reperusal in the leisure of my later life. I am rather proud of that collection. It contains the name of many a brilliant light in the dramatic hemisphere, and, indeed, I look upon it as a history of dramatic art in little. My impression is that Elgood and his wife left Seacomb nineteen years ago last winter, but the bills will make matters certain. Mathew Elgood was among that diminished band which trod the boards of our poor little theater on that final night when the green curtain descended on the Seacomb stage never to rise again. The theater remained in abeyance for some two or three years after that last performance, dismantled, shut up, a refuge for rats and mice and such small deer."

"Nineteen years ago, you say?"

"Nor more nor less," returned Mr. Clipcome, who was wont to wax Shakespearean. "I remember it was an extraordinary severe winter. We had frost and snow, a great deal of snow, as late as the end of February, and even into March. Some of the roads between Seacomb and neighboring villages were impassable, and there was a good deal of trouble generally. I felt all the more for those unfortunate Elgoods on this account. It was a hard winter in which to be cast adrift."

"Thanks, Mr. Clipcome; you have given me really valuable information. I should be glad to refer to that file of bills, so as to get the exact date of the closing of the theater."

The hair-dresser produced his collection, roughly bound in a ponderous marble-paper covered tome of his own manufacture, a triumph in amateur book-binding.

Here Humphrey Clissold saw the last play-bill that had ever been issued by the manager of the Seacomb theater.

Its date was January 10, 1849.

"And Mr. Elgood staid at the tailor's for a month after the closing of the theater?" interrogated Humphrey.

"About a month."

Having jotted down dates and facts in his note-book, and reiterated his thanks to the good-natured barber, Humphrey felt that his business in Play-house Alley was concluded. He bought some trifles in the shop on his way out, an attention peculiarly pleasing to Mr. Clipcome from the rarity of the event, his trade being chiefly confined to two-pennyworths of hair-oil, or three-half-penny cakes of brown Windsor.

CHAPTER XLVI.
" FULL COLD MY GREETING WAS AND DRY."

A QUIET evening at the New London Inn, and another confidential chat with its proprietress, convinced Humphrey Clissold

that there was nothing more to be learned in Seacomb. He led
Mrs. Chadwick on to talk of the family at Penwyn Manor house,
the old squire and his sons, who, sanctified by the shadows of
the past, beautified by old memories and associations—just as a
ruin is beautified by the ivies and lichens that cling to its
crumbling arches—were dearer to the hearts of the elderly Sea-
combites than the reigning squire and his lovely wife.

"I don't say but what the present gentleman is better for
trade, and has done more good to the neighborhood in two years
than the old squire would have done in ten," said Mrs. Chadwick. "But the old squire was more one of ourselves, as you
may say. He'd take his glass of cider—a very temperate man
was the squire—in my bar parlor, and chat with me as friendly
and familiar as you could do, and it was quite a pleasant thing
to see him in his Lincoln-green coat and brass basket buttons
and mahogany tops."

Of George Penwyn Mrs. Chadwick said nothing that was not
praise. He had been everybody's favorite, she told Humphrey,
and his death had been felt like a personal loss throughout the
neighborhood.

Was this a man to betray an innocent girl, and bring disgrace
upon an honest yeoman's household?

Before leaving Seacomb next morning Mr. Clissold went to
the parish church, looked once more at the register in which he
had seen the burial of Mathew Elgood's daughter. There was
the entry: "Emily Jane, daughter of Mathew Elgood, comedian,
and Jane Elgood, his wife, aged five weeks. January 4, 1849."
Just six days before the closing of Seacomb Theater.

Humphrey distinctly remembered Justina having told him
once in the course of their somewhat discursive talk that her
birthday was in March, and that she had completed her nine-
teenth year on her last anniversary. Now if Mrs. Elgood had
had a daughter born in the December of '48, it was not possible
for her to have been the mother of Justina, if Justina was born
in the March of '49.

He had now no shadow of doubt that Mathew Elgood, who
had left Seacomb in February in the midst of frost and snow,
was the same man who had sought shelter at Borcel End, and
who had called himself Eden. A false pride had doubtless induced the penniless stroller to hide his poverty under an assumed
name.

"The plainest, most straightforward way of doing things will
be to tax Elgood himself with the fact," thought Humphrey.
"Once sure of my darling's identity with Muriel's daughter,
my next duty shall be to discover the evidence of her mother's
marriage. And if I succeed in doing that—— Well, I suppose
the next thing will be for some clever lawyers to prove her
right to the Penwyn estate, and Churchill Penwyn and his wife
will be ruined, and Justina will be a great heiress, and I shall
retire into the background. Hardly a pleasant picture of the
future that. Perhaps it would have been wiser, from a purely
selfish point of view, to have left my dear girl Justina Elgood
to the end of the chapter—or at least till I persuaded her to ex-

change that spurious surname for the good old name of Clissold. But now, having gone so far, won the confidence of a dying woman, sworn to set right an old wrong, I am in honor bound to go on, not to the ultimate issue perhaps, but at any rate to the assertion of my darling girl's legitimacy."

He rejoiced in the swiftness of the express which carried him homeward by stubbly fields and yellowing woods, rejoiced at the thought that he should be in time to see Justina, were it only one half hour before she went to the theater. He took a hansom and drove straight to Mr. Elgood's lodgings, told the man to wait, and left his portmanteau and traveling-bag in the cab while he ran up-stairs to the second-floor sitting-room.

Mathew Elgood was enjoying his afternoon siesta, his amiable countenance shrouded from the autumnal fly by a crimson silk handkerchief. Justina was sitting at a little table by the window, reading.

She looked a shade paler than when he had seen her last, the lover thought, fondly hoping that she had missed him, but as she started up from her chair, recognizing him with a little cry of gladness, the warm blood rushed to cheek and brow, and he had no ground for compassionating her pallor.

For a moment she tried to speak, but could not, and in that moment Humphrey Clissold knew that he was beloved.

He would have given worlds to take her to his heart then and there, to have kissed the blushes into a deeper glow, to have told her how supremely dear she was to him, how infinitely deeper and holier and sweeter than his first foolish passion this second love of his had become. But he put the curb on impulse, remembering the task he had to accomplish. To woo her now, to win her promise now, knowing what he knew, would have seemed to him a meanness.

"To-day I am her superior in fortune," he said to himself, "a year hence I may be her inferior—a very pauper compared with the mistress of Penwyn Manor. I will not win her unawares. If change of fortune does come to pass, I shall not be too proud to share her wealth, so long as I have all her heart; but if she should change with change of fortune, she shall be free to follow where her fancy leads, and no old promise, made in her day of obscurity, shall bind her to me. Free and unfettered she shall enter upon her new life—and, if I am the means of her exaltation, she shall not even know that she owes wealth and station to my efforts."

So instead of taking her to his heart of hearts, and pouring out his tale of love in a tender whisper—too low to penetrate the crimson handkerchief which veiled the ears of the sleeper, Humphrey greeted Justina with hearty loudness, talked about his journey, asked how the new piece at the Albert worked out at rehearsal, inquired about his friend Flittergilt, the dramatist, and behaved altogether in a commonplace fashion. There was just time for a cup of tea before Justina started for the theater —and a very pleasant tea-drinking it was. Humphrey was touched by Justina's pretty joyous ways this evening, her bright looks, the silvery little laugh gushing out at the slightest provocation—laughter which told of a soul that was gladdened by his presence.

"I think I shall come to the theater to-night," he said, as they parted.

"What, to see ' No Cards?' You must be dreadfully tired of it."

"No. I believe I have seen it seven times, but I could see it seven more," answered Humphrey; and this was the only compliment he paid Justina that evening.

Before parting with Mr. Elgood he asked that gentleman to dine with him the next evening, at eight, *en garcon.*

"We can go to the theater afterward to escort Miss Elgood home," he added.

"My dear Clissold," exclaimed the comedian, with effusion. "After the bottle of port you gave me that Sunday evening Justina and I enjoyed your hospitality, I should be an ass to refuse such an invitation."

CHAPTER XLVII.
"WHEN TIME SHALL SERVE, BE THOU NOT SLACK."

NOTHING could be more inviting than the aspect of Humphrey Clissold's rooms at eight o'clock on the following evening, when their proprietor stood on his hearth, waiting the arrival of his expected guest. The weather was by no means warm, and the glass and silver on the friendly-looking circular table sparkled in the glow of a brightly burning fire. The spotless damask, the dainty arrangement of the table, with its old Chelsea-ware dessert dishes filled with amber-tinted Jersey pears and dusky-hued filberts, agreeably suggestive of good old port, indicated a careful landlady and well-trained servants. The dumb-waiter, with its reserve of glasses and cruets, guaranteed that luxurious ease which is not dependent on external service.

Mr. Elgood, arriving on the scene as the clocks of Bloomsbury struck the hour, surveyed these preparations with an eye that glistened with content—nay, almost brightened to rapture as it wandered'from the table to the fender, where, in a shadowy corner, reposed the expected bottle of port, cobweb-wreathed, chalk-marked liquid rubies, clouded here and there by a bee's-wing, as an emerald by its feather.

The savory odor of fried fish, mingled with the appetizing fumes of roasting meat, had greeted the visitor's nostrils as he ascended the stairs. Even his nice judgment had failed to divine whether the joint were beef or mutton, but he opined mutton. No one but a barbarian would load his table with sirloin for a *tete-a-tete* dinner when Providence had created the Welsh hills, doubtless with a view to the necessities of the dinner-table.

"Glad to see you so punctual," said Humphrey, cheerily.

"My dear Mr. Clissold, to be unpunctual is to insult one's host and injure one's self. What can atone for the ruin of an excellent dinner? You may remember what Dean Swift said to his cook when she had roasted the joint to rags, and was fain to confess she could not undo the evil: 'Beware, wench, how you commit a fault which cannot be remedied.' A dinner spoiled is an irremediable loss."

The soup had been put upon the table while Mr. Elgood thus philosophized, so the two gentlemen sat down without further delay, and the comedian gazed blandly upon the amber sherry and the garnet-hued claret, while Humphrey invoked a blessing on the feast, and then the business of dinner began in good earnest.

The joint was mutton, and Welsh, whereby Mr. Elgood's soul was at ease, and he gave himself up to the enjoyment of the table with unaffected singleness of purpose. A brace of partridges and a Parmesan *fondu* followed the haunch, and when these had been dispatched the comedian flung himself back in his chair with a sigh of repletion.

"Well, my dear Mr. Clissold," he said, "you are a very accomplished gentleman in many ways, but this I will say, that I never met the man yet who was your match in giving a snug little dinner. Brilsby Savory, or whatever his name was, couldn't have beat you."

"I am glad-you have enjoyed your dinner. Mr. Elgood. I am of opinion that a good dinner is the best prelude to serious conversation; and I want to have a little quiet and confidential talk with you this evening upon a very serious matter."

"Behold me at your service—your slave to command," answered Mathew, whose enthusiasm was not easily to be damped. "I bare my bosom to your view," he added, with a dramatic gesture, indicative of throwing open his waistcoat.

They were alone by this time. The servant had carried away the dinner things, and only the decanters and fruit dishes remained on the table.

"You speak boldly, Mr. Elgood," said Humphrey, with sudden gravity, "yet, perhaps, if I were to ask you some questions about your past life you would draw back a little."

"My past life, although full of vicissitude, has been honest," answered the comedian. "I fear no man's scrutiny."

"Good. Then you will not be angry if I question you quite closely upon one period of your checkered career. It is in the interest of your—of Justina that I do so."

"Proceed, sir," said Mathew, a troubled look overclouding the countenance which had just now beamed with serenity.

"Did you ever hear the name of Eden?"

Mr. Elgood started, more violently than he had done on a previous occasion at the mention of Borcel End. The silver dessert-knife with which he was peeling a Jersey pear dropped from between his fingers.

"I see you do know that name," said Humphrey, passing from interrogation to affirmation. "You bore it once at Borcel End, the old farm-house on the Cornish moors, where you took shelter in the bitter winter weather, just nineteen years ago last February."

The glow which the good things of this life had kindled in Mr. Elgood's visage faded slowly out, and left him very pale.

"How did you know that?" he gasped.

"I had it from the lips of a dying woman—Mrs. Trevanard."

"What! is Mrs. Trevanard dead?"

"Yes; she died a fortnight ago."

"And she told you——"

"All. The birth of the child she intrusted to your care. The old family Bible she gave you, from which you took the name of Justina."

The shrewd guess, stated as a fact, passed uncontradicted. Humphrey's speculative assertion had hit the truth.

"The supposed daughter who has borne your name all these years, the girl who has worked for you, who now maintains you, who has been faithful, obedient, and devoted to you, has not one drop of your blood in her veins. She is Muriel Trevanard's child."

"You choose to make a statement," said Mathew Elgood, who had somewhat recovered his self-possession by this time, "which I do not feel myself called upon either to deny or admit. I am willing to acknowledge that in a time of severe misfortune I took shelter upon Mrs. Trevanard's premises; that I called myself by a name that was not my own, rather than expose my destitution to the world's contumely. But whatever passed between Mrs. Trevanard and myself at that period is sacred. I swore to keep the secret confided to me to my dying day, and it will descend with me to the tomb of my ancestors," added Mr. Elwood, grandly, as if, for the moment at least, he really believed that he had a family vault at his disposal.

"You may consider yourself absolved of your oath," said Humphrey. "Mrs. Trevanard confided in me during the last days of her life, and I pledged myself to see her grandchild righted."

"Mrs. Trevanard must have changed very much at the last, if she expressed any interest in the fate of her grandchild," returned Mathew, forgetting that he had refused to make any admission. "When she gave the child to me and my wife she resigned all concern in its future; it was to fare as we fared, to sink or swim with us."

"In that wretched hour she thought the child nameless and fatherless. I did my best to persuade her that she had been too hasty in her conclusion. It shall be my business to prove Justina's legitimacy."

"That is to say, you mean to take my daughter away from me," exclaimed the comedian, wrathfully. "Little did I know what a snake in the grass I had been cherishing, warming the adder in my bosom, sheltering the scorpion on my domestic hearth. This is what your kettle-drums and snug little dinners and port and filberts are to end in. You would rob a poor old man of the staff and comfort of his declining years; six pounds a week, and a certainty of a rise to ten if the next part she plays is a success."

"You are hasty, Mr. Elgood, and unjust. Heaven knows if it were a question of my own happiness, I would leave the dear girl you have brought up, Justina Elgood, till I had the Archbishop of Canterbury's permission to give her my own name. But, having promised to perform a certain duty, I should be a scoundrel if I left it undone. What if I tell you that I have reason to believe Justina entitled to a large estate, an estate of six or seven thousand a year?"

Mr. Elgood sank back in his chair aghast. He had drunk a good many glasses of wine in the course of that comfortable little dinner, and there was some slight haziness in his brain. Six thousand a year, six pounds a week. Six pounds a week, six thousand a year—over a hundred pounds a week. There was a wide margin for spending in the difference between the lesser and the greater sum. But of the six pounds a week, while Justina supposed herself his daughter, he was certain. Would she share her annual six thousand as freely when she knew that he had no claim upon her filial piety?

He pondered the question for a few moments, and then answered in the affirmative. Generous, good, loving, she had ever been. If good fortune befell her she would not grudge the old man his share of the sunshine. He had not been a bad father to her, he told himself, take him for all in all—not overpatient or considerate, perhaps, in those early days before he had discovered any dramatic talent in her, a little prone to think of his own comfort before hers, but, upon the whole, as fathers go, not a bad kind of parent. And he felt very sure she would stand by him. Yes, he felt sure of Justina. But he must be on his guard against this scheming fellow, Clissold, who had contrived to get hold of a secret that had been kept for nineteen years, and doubtless meant to work it for his own advantage. It would be Mathew Elgood's duty to countermarch him there.

"So, Mr. Clissold," he began, after about five minutes' reverie. "You are a pretty deep fellow, you are, in spite of your easy, open handed, open-hearted, free-spoken ways. You think you can establish my Justina's claim to a fine fortune, do you? And, I suppose, when the claim is established, and the girl I have brought up from babyhood, and toiled for and struggled for many a long year, comes into her six thousand per annum, you'll expect to get her for your wife, with the six or seven thousand at her back. Rather a good stroke of business for you."

"I expect nothing," answered Humphrey, gravely. "I love Justina with all my heart, as truly as ever an honest man loved a fair and noble woman; but I have refrained from any expression of my heart's desire, lest I should bind her by a promise while her position is thus uncertain. Let her win the station to which I believe she is entitled; and if, when it is won, she cares to reward my honest affection, I will take her and be proud of her, but not one whit prouder than I should be to take her for my wife to-morrow, knowing her to be your daughter."

"Spoken like a man and a gentleman," exclaimed the comedian. "Come, Mr. Clissold, I couldn't think badly of you if I tried. I'll trust you; and it shall be no fault of mine if Justina is not yours, rich or poor. She's worthy of you, and you're worthy of her, and I believe she has a sneaking kindness for you."

Humphrey smiled, happy in a conviction which needed no support from Mathew Elgood's opinion. That little look of Justina's yesterday, that tender look of greeting, that sweet expression, had been worth volumes of common eloquence. He knew himself beloved.

"And now tell me what your ideas are, and how Mrs. Trevanard—the strangest woman, and the closest, that I ever met—came to confide in you, and how it has entered into your mind that our Justina has any legal right to either name or fortune."

"I'll tell you," said Humphrey, and forthwith proceeded to relate all that he had learned at Borcel, a great deal of which was new to Mathew Elgood, who had been told nothing about the parentage of the child committed to his care. It was essential to Justina's interests that her adopted father should know all, since he was the only witness who could prove her identity with the child born at Borcel End.

"It seems tolerably clear that this George Penwyn must have been the father," said Mr. Elgood. "But who is to prove a marriage?"

"If a marriage took place the proof must exist somewhere, and it must be for one of us to find it," answered Humphrey. "The first person to apply to is Miss Barlow. Muriel's schoolmistress, supposing her to be still living. The only period of Muriel's absence from the farm after she left school was the time she spent with Miss Barlow—three weeks—so that if any marriage took place, it must have happened during that visit. I have searched the registers of both churches at Seacomb without result. But it is not likely that George Penwyn would contract a secret marriage within twelve miles of his father's house. Whatever occurred in those three weeks Miss Barlow must have been in some measure familiar with. My first business, therefore, must be to find her. When last heard of, she was established as a teacher of music in the neighborhood of London. A directory ought to help us to her address if she is still living within the postal radius."

"True," said Mathew, glancing at the shelves which lined the room from floor to ceiling. "I suppose among all these books you have the Post-Office Directory?"

"No; strange to say, it is a branch of literature I am deficient in. I must wait till to-morrow to look for Miss Barlow's address."

"How did it occur to you that my daughter Justina and that castaway child were one and the same?"

"Well, I hardly know how the idea first took possession of me. It was a kind of instinct. The circumstances that led me to think it seem insignificant enough when spoken of, but to my mind they assumed exaggerated importance; perhaps it was your look of surprise when I mentioned Borcel End that first awakened my suspicions, not of the actual truth, but of some mysterious connection between yourself and the Trevanards."

"I certainly was astonished when you spoke of that out-of-the-way farm-house."

"Then the name Justina, which I heard of as a family name at Borcel End, set me thinking; the fact that your daughter was said to have been born at Seacomb, within a few miles of that remote farm-house, the fact that her age tallied with the age of Muriel's child. Never mind how I came by the conviction, since I happily, or unhappily, stumbled on the truth. But tell me how you fared when you left Borcel End that bleak spring morning."

"Well, it wasn't the most comfortable kind of departure, certainly—seven miles on foot on a cold March morning, and an infant to carry into the bargain. But my poor wife and I had gone through too much to be particular about trifles, and we were both of us sustained by the thought of a snug little fortune in my breast pocket; for you may suppose that to us two hundred pounds odd seemed the capital of a future Rothschild. Mrs. Trevanard had given us some substantial clothing into the bargain, and my poor Nell wore a good cloth cloak, under which the baby was kept warm and snug. She was stronger, too, my poor girl, for the month's rest and plentiful food that we had enjoyed at Borcel; indeed, though our lodging there was but a deserted hay-loft, I don't think either of us were ever happier than when Nell sat at her needlework and I lay luxuriously reposing on a truss of hay while I read an old magazine aloud to her. We were shut out from the world; but we had peace and rest and plenty; and I think we were pretty much like the birds of the air as to thought of the morrow, in those days. But now that I had Mrs. Trevanard's savings in my breast pocket I began to take a serious view of life and throughout that walk to Seacomb I was scheming and contriving, till at last, just as we came in sight of the town, I cried out in a burst of enthusiasm, 'Yes, Nell, I've hit it.' 'Hit what?' asked my wife. 'Hit upon the surest way to make our fortunes, my girl,' I answered, all of a glow with the thought. 'We'll take a theater.' 'Lor', Mat.' said my wife, with a gasp, 'and I can play the leading business!' Managers had been putting other women over her head in the Juliets and Rosalinds, and she felt it, poor soul. 'But, Mathew,' she went on, growing suddenly serious, 'we haven't seen much good come of taking theaters. Look at Seacomb, for instance.' 'Seacomb isn't a case in point,' I answered, quite put out by her narrow way of looking at things. 'A psalm-singing place like that was never likely to support the drama. When I take a theater it will be in a very different town from Seacomb.' 'But,' remonstrated poor Nell, 'don't you think it would be breaking faith with Mrs. Trevanard? She gave us the money to set us up in some nice little business. We were to start with a part of the capital, and keep the rest in reserve against a rainy day.' 'Well, isn't the theatrical management a business,' I retorted, 'and the only business that I am fit for? Do you suppose that I can blossom into a full blown grocer, or break out all at once into a skillful butcher, because Mrs. Trevanard wishes it? Why, I shouldn't know one end of

an ox from the other when his head was off. And as for Mrs.
Trevanard,' I went on, ' you ought to have sense enough to know
that she cares precious little what becomes of us now we've
taken this unfortunate child off her hands." 'I don't believe
that, Mathew,' answered my wife. 'She's a Christian, and she
wouldn't like us to starve on the child's account.' 'Who's going
to starve?' I cried, savagely, for I felt it was in me to make
money as a manager. There never was an actor yet that hadn't
the same fancy, and many a man has brought ruin upon himself
and his family by the delusion."

" You had your own way, of course," said Humphrey.

" I had, sir. First and foremost, my poor little wife never
obstinately opposed me in anything; and. secondly, her foolish
heart was longing for the leading business, and to be a manager-
ess, and cast all the pieces, and get herself in for the best parts.
So we went straight to the Seacomb station, where we found we
should have to wait upward of an hour for a train, and I thought
I could not make better use of my time than by buying an *Era*,
and finding out what theaters were to let. There were about
half a dozen advertisements of this class, and one of them struck
me as the exact thing. 'The Theater Royal, Slowberry, in
Somersetshire, to let for the summer season. Rent moderate.
Can be worked with a small company. Scenery in good condition. Market-town; population twelve thousand.' I made a
calculation on the spot, demonstrating that ten per cent. of those
twelve thousand inhabitants—allowing a wide margin for infants. the aged and infirm—were bound to come to the theater
nightly. Now a nightly audience of twelve hundred was safe to
pay. I found that we could get straight to Slowberry by
the Great Western, and accordingly took tickets for that
station, third class; for prudence was to be the order of the day.
Well, Mr. Clissold, I need not 'trouble you with details. We
went to Slowberry, and established ourselves in humble and in-
expensive lodgings, apartments which I felt were hardly
worthy of my managerial position; but prudence prevailed. I
became lessee of the Slowberry theater, which I am fain to admit was in architectural pretensions even below the Temple of
the Drama at Seacomb. I engaged my company, cheap and
useful. My old man combined the heavy business and second
low comedy; my first chamber-maid—second I need hardly say
there was none—danced or sang between the pieces, and acted
in male attire when we ran short of gentlemen. My wife and I
played all the best parts. Nothing could have been organized upon more rigid principles of economy, yet the financial
result was ruin. For a considerable part of the season I only
paid half salaries; for the concluding portion we became a
commonwealth. Yet Mrs. Trevanard's savings dribbled away;
and when my poor wife and I left Slowberry, with Justina,
then a fine child of seven months old, we had not twenty pounds
left out of a capital which had appeared to my mind to be almost inexhaustible.

" The child was christened at Slowberry, I suppose?"

" Yes, we lost no time in having the baptismal rite performed, lest she should go off with croup, or red-gum, or vaccination, or any of the perils which beset the infant traveler on life's thorny road. The Bible which Mrs. Trevanard had given to my wife contained in the fly-leaf the name of Justina Trevanard, doubtless its original possessor. That name caught my wife's fancy. Is struck me, also, as euphonious and arristocratic, a name that would look well in the bills, by and by, when our daughter was old enough to make her first juvenile efforts in the profession, as the child in 'Pizarro' or little William in 'The Stranger.' We were fond of her already, and soon grew to forget that there was no tie of kindred between us. My wife, indeed, passionately adored this nameless orphan, and was never tired of weaving romantic fancies about her future: how she would turn out to be the daughter of a nobleman, and we should see her by and by with a coronet on her head, and owe comfort and wealth to her affection when we grew old. It would be a curious thing if if one of poor Nell's romantic dreams were to be realized. How proud that loving heart would have been!—but it lies under the grass and daisies in a Berkshire churchyard, and neither joy nor sorrow can touch it any more."

Mr. Elgood checked a rising sigh, and helped himself to another glass of port.

" You fared ill, I fear, after your managerial experiment," said Humphrey.

" Our life from that point was a series of struggles. If the efforts of the honest man battling with adversity form a spectacle which the gods delight in—a fact which I vaguely remember having seen stated somewhere—my career must have afforded considerable entertainment in Olympus. We had our brief intervals of sunshine, but cloud prevailed; and in the course of years my poor wife sank beneath the burden, and Justina and I were left to jog on together, just as you saw us in the town of Eborsham two years ago. So far as a struggler can do his duty to his daughter I believe I did mine to Justina. I gave her what little education I could afford, and luckily she was bright enough to make the most of that little. There never was such a girl for picking up knowledge. Clever people always seemed to take to her and she to them, though for a long time we thought her stupid on the stage. Her talent for the profession came out all at once. Heaven knows she has been a good girl to me, through good and evil fortune, and I love her as well as if she were twenty times my daughter. It would be a hard thing if any change of circumstances were to part us."

"Have no fear of that," said Humphrey. " Justina is too true a woman to be changed by changing fortune. I do not hesitate to leave my fate in her hands. You, who have an older claim upon her love, have even less cause for fear."

The little black marble clock on the mantel-piece chimed the half hour after ten—time to repair to the theater. Mr. Flittergilt's piece ended at a quarter before eleven, and at a few minutes past the hour Justina appeared at the stage-door, ready to be escorted home.

Humphrey and Mr. Elgood went together to the dark little

side street in which the stage-door of the Royal Albert was situated, dingy and repellent of aspect, after the manner of stage-doors.

It was a clear starlight autumn night, and that walk back to Bloomsbury, with Justina's little hand resting on his own arm, was very pleasant to Humphrey Clissold. They chose the quietest streets, without reference to distance, and the walk lasted about a quarter of an hour longer than it need have done had they gratified Mr. Elgood's desire for certain short-cuts, by Wych Street and Drury Lane. But throughout that homeward walk not one whispered word of Humphrey's betrayed the lover, and when he and Justina parted at the door of her lodgings, the girl thought wonderingly of that summer night in Eborsham, more than two years ago, when James Penwyn told her of his love in the shadow of the old minster.

"Shall I ever have a second lover as generous and devoted?" she mused. "That was only boy and girl love, I suppose, yet it seemed truer and brighter than anything that will ever come my way again."

She had been thinking of Humphrey not a little of late, and had decided that he did not care for her in the least.

CHAPTER XLVIII.
"THE DAYS HAVE VANISHED, TONE AND TINT."

HUMPHREY CLISSOLD lost no time in setting about his search for Miss Barlow, the quondam schoolmistress of Seacomb. But the first result of his endeavors was failure. The London "Post-office Directory" for the current year knew not Miss Barlow. Barlows there were in its pages, but they were trading Barlows, Barlows who baked or Barlows who brewed, Barlows who dealt in upholstery, Barlows who purveyed butcher's-meat, or professional Barlows who wrote Rev. before their names or M.R.C.S. after their names. A spinster of the musical profession was not to be found among the London Barlows.

In the face of this disappointment Humphrey paused to consider his next effort. Advertising in the *Times* he looked upon as a last resource, and a means of inquiry which he hoped to dispense with. So many spurious Miss Barlows, eager to hear of something to their advantage, would be conjured into being by any appeal published in the second column of the *Times*.

There remained to him the detective medium, but Mr. Clissold cherished a prejudice against private inquiry offices, and would not for all the wealth of the realm have revealed Justina's name and story to a professional detective. He was resolved to succeed or fail in this business single-handed.

"If Miss Barlow is above ground her existence must be known to somebody," he reasoned, "to musical people more particularly. I'll go down to the Albert Theater and have a chat with the leader of the orchestra. Your musical director is generally a man of the world, with a little more than the average amount of brains. And I have heard Justina speak very highly of Her

Fisfiz. Flittergilt's new comedy is in rehearsal, so I have an excuse for going behind the scenes."

It was about noon on the day after his little entertainment to Mr. Elgood that Humphrey arrived at this decision. He went straight from his club, where he had explored the Court Guide and Postal Directory, to the snug little theater in the Strand, where, after some parley with the stage-door keeper, he obtained admittance, and groped his way through subterranean regions of outer darkness, and by some break-neck stairs to the side-scenes, where, in a dim glimmer of cold daylight and flaring gas, he beheld the stage on one side of him, and the open door of the green-room on the other.

Justina was on the stage rehearsing. Mr. Flittergilt, in a state of mental fever, sat by the stage manager's little table, manuscript and pencil in hand, underlining here, erasing there, now altering an exit, now suggesting the proper emphasis to give point to a sparkling sentence, evidently delighted with his own work, yet as evidently painfully anxious about the result.

" I sha'n't be satisfied with a moderate success," he told Humphrey. " I want this piece to make a greater hit than ' No Cards.' You remember what was said of Sheridan when he hung back from writing a new comedy. He was afraid of the author of ' The Rivals.' Now I don't want that to be said of *me*."

" No fear, dear boy." remarked Humphrey. But Mr. Flittergilt's exalted mind ignored the interjection.

" I want the public to see that I have not emptied my sack; that '·No Cards ' was not my ace of trumps, but only my knave. I've queen, king, and ace to follow. Did you hear the last scene ?" asked the author, with a self-satisfied smile. " It's rather sparkling, I think, and Elgood hits the character to the life."

Mr. Clissold did not approve this familiar allusion to the girl of his choice.

" I've only just this moment come in," he said. " I'm glad Miss Elgood likes her new *role*."

" Likes it!" cried Flittergilt, with an injured look. " It wouldn't be easy for any actress on the boards not to like such a part. ' No Cards ' made Miss Elgood; but this piece will place her a step higher on the ladder."

" Don't you think there may be people weak-minded enough to believe that Miss Elgood's acting made ' No Cards ?' " asked Humphrey, quietly.

" I can't help people's weak-mindedness," answered Mr. Flittergilt, with dignity; " but I know this for a fact, that no acting —not of a Macready or a Fawcet—ever made a bad piece run over a hundred nights." And with this assertion of himself Mr. Flittergilt went back to his table and his manuscript, and began to badger the actors—being possessed by the idea that because he was able to construct a play from the various foreign materials at his command, he must necessarily be able to teach experienced comedians their art.

Justina looked up from her book presently and espied Mr,

Clissold. Her blush betrayed surprise; her eyes revealed that
the surprise was not unpleasant.

"Have you come to criticize the new comedy?" she asked.
"That's hardly fair, though, for a piece loses so much at rehearsal. Mr. Flittergilt is always calling us back to give us his
own peculiar reading of a line. I never saw such an excitable
little man. But I suppose he'll take things more coolly when
he has written a few more plays."

"Yes, he is new to the work as yet. I am glad to hear you
have such a good part."

"It is a wonderfully good part, if I can only act it as it ought
to be played."

"Is your leader, Herr Fisfiz, here this morning?" asked
Humphrey, carelessly.

"He is coming presently. There's a gavotte in the third act."

"You dance?"

"Yes, Mr. Mortimer and I. Herr Fisfiz has written original
music for it—so quaint and pretty. You should stay to hear it,
now you are here."

"I mean to stay till the rehearsal is over. I should like you
to introduce me to Mr. Fisfiz. I want to ask him a question or
two about some musical people."

"I shall be pleased to introduce you to each other. He is a
very clever man, not in music only, but in all kinds of things,
and I think you would like him."

Humphrey seated himself in a dark corner, near the prompter's box, and awaited Mr. Fisfiz, amusing himself by listening
to the comedy, and beholding his friend Flittergilt's frantic exertions in the meanwhile. He had been thus occupied nearly an
hour when Mr. Fisfiz appeared, attended by his *ame damnee* in
the person of the *repetiteur*. The director was a little man, with a
small, delicate face, and a Shakespearean brow; spoke English
perfectly, though with a German accent, and had no dislike to
hearing himself talk, or to wasting a stray half hour in the society of a pretty actress, or even bestowing the sunshine of his
presence for a few leisure minutes on a group of giggling—or,
as he called them, gikklink—ballet girls. He was evidently a
great admirer of Miss Elgood, and inclined to be gracious to any
one she introduced to him.

"I think you'll like the gafotte," he said, playing little pizzi-
cato passages on his violin, with a satisfied smile. "It sounds
like Bach."

Justina told him it was charming. The dance began presently,
and though she only walked through it, the grace of her movements charmed that silent lover of hers, who sat in his corner
and made no sign, lest in uttering the most commonplace compliment he should betray that secret which he had pledged himself to keep.

When the gavotte was finished Justina brought Herr Fisfiz to
the dark corner, and left him there with Humphrey while she
went on with her rehearsal.

Mr. Clissold gave the gavotte its meed of praise, said a few

words about things in general, and then came to the question
he wanted to ask.

"There is a lady connected with the musical profession I am
trying to find, Herr Fisfiz," he said, "and it struck me this
morning that you might be able to assist me."

"I know most people in the musical world," answered Herr
Fisfiz. "What is the lady's name?"

"Miss Barlow."

"Miss Barlow. How do you spell the name?"

Humphrey spelled it. and the director shook his head.

"I know no one of that name. No Miss B-a-r-l-o-w," he said.
"I never heard of any one so called in the musical profession.
Is your Miss Barlow a concert singer? Young—an amateur,
perhaps, who has not yet made herself known?"

"She is not a concert singer, and she must be middle-aged—
probably elderly. The last account I have of her goes back to
ten years ago. She may be dead and gone for anything I know
to the contrary; but I have heard that she was living in or near
London ten years ago, giving lessons in music, and that she was
doing well. She was a retired school-mistress, and had made
money, therefore was not likely to go in for ill-paid drudgery.
She must have had some standing in her profession, I fancy."

"I know of a Madame Balo—B-a-l-o—who might answer to
that description," said the leader thoughtfully, "an elderly
lady, a very fine pianiste. She still receives a few pupils—
chiefly girls studying for concert playing; but I believe she does
so more from love of her art than from any necessity to earn
money. She lives in considerable comfort, and appears to be
very well off."

"She is a foreigner. I suppose, from the name. The lady I
mean is—or was—an Englishwoman."

"Madame Balo is as British as you are. She may have married a foreigner, perhaps. But I really don't know whether she
is a widow or a spinster. She lives alone, in a nice little house
in Maida Vale."

"I wonder whether she can be the lady I want to find. The
description seems to answer. She may have Italianized the
spelling of her name to make it more attractive to her patrons."

"Yes, you English seem to have a small belief in your own
musical abilities, since you prefer to intrust the cultivation of
them to a foreigner."

"Do you know this lady well enough to give me a note of introduction to her?" asked Humphrey; "if I may venture to ask
such a favor at the beginning of our acquaintance."

"Delighted to oblige a friend of Miss Elgood's," answered
Herr Fisfiz, politely. "Yes, I know Madame Balo well enough
to scribble a note of introduction to her. She is a very clever
woman, with a passion for clever people. And I believe you
belong to the world of letters. Mr. Clissold."

"I have written for the quarterlies," answered Humphrey.

"Just the very man to delight Madame Balo. She is a woman
of mind. When do you want the letter?"

"As soon as ever you can oblige me with it. I dare say a line on one of your cards would do as well. I merely wish to ask Madame Balo a few questions about a young lady who was once a member of her establishment at Seacomb; supposing that she is identical with the Miss Barlow I have spoken of."

"I'll do what you want at once," said Herr Fisfiz.

He seated himself at the prompter's table, and wrote on the back of a card, in a neat and minute penmanship:

"DEAR MADAME,—Mr. Clissold, the bearer of this card, is a literary gentleman of some standing, who wishes to make your acquaintance. Any favor you accord him will also oblige yours very truly, R. F."

"I think that will be quite enough for Madame Balo," he said.

Half an hour later Humphrey was in a hansom, bowling along the Edgeware Road toward Maida Vale.

Here on the banks of the canal, in a somewhat retired and even picturesque spot, he found the abode of Madame Balo, stuccoed and classical as to its external aspect, with a Corinthian portico, which almost extinguished the house to which it belonged.

A neat maid-servant opened the iron gate of the small parterre in front of the portico, and admitted him without question. She ushered him into a drawing-room handsomely furnished, and much ornamented with divers specimens of feminine handicraft; water-colored landscapes on the walls; Berlin-work chair-covers; a tapestry screen whereon industrious hands had imitated Landseer's famous Bolton Abbey; fluffy and beady mats on the tables and chiffoniers; and alabaster baskets of wax fruit and flowers carefully preserved under glass shades.

A glance at these things told Humphrey that he was on the track of the original Miss Barlow. Such a collection of fancy-work could only belong to a retired school-mistress.

A grand piano, open, with a well-filled music stand beside it, occupied an important position in the room. Early as it was in the autumn, a bright little fire burned in the shining steel grate.

Mr. Clissold had ample leisure to study the characteristics of the apartment before Madame Balo made her appearance: but after examining all the works of art, and roaming about the room somewhat impatiently for some time, Humphrey heard an approaching rustle of silk, and Madame Balo entered, radiant in black moire antique, profusely bugled and fringed, and a delicate structure of pink crape and watered ribbon, which no doubt was meant for a cap.

She was a smiling, pleasant-looking little woman, short and stout, with a somewhat rubicund visage and a mellow voice—nothing prim or scholastic about her appearance, her distinguishing quality being rather friendliness and an easy geniality.

"Delighted to see any friend of Herr Fisfiz," she said, with a gushing little manner that had something fresh and youthful about it in spite of her sixty years—not affected juvenility, but the real thing. "Charming man, Herr Fisfiz, one of the finest quartette players I know. We have some pleasant evenings here now and then, when his theater is shut. I should be happy to see you at my little parties, Mr. Clissold, if you are fond of chamber music."

"You are very kind. I should be pleased to make one of your audience, however limited my powers of appreciation might be. But my call to-day is on a matter of business rather than of pleasure, and I fear I am likely to bore you by asking a good many questions."

"Not at all," said Madame Balo, with a gracious bend of the pink structure.

"First and foremost, then, may I venture to ask if you always spelled your name as it is inscribed on the brass plate on your gate, or whether its present orthography, the circumflex accent included, is not rather fanciful than correct? Pray pardon any seeming impertinence in my inquiry. The lady I am in quest of was proprietress of a school at Seacomb, in Cornwall, eminently respected by all who knew her. It struck me that you might be that very Miss Barlow."

The lady blushed, coughed dubiously, and after a little hesitation, answered frankly:

"Upon my word, Mr. Clissold, I don't know why I should be ashamed of the matter," she said, smiling. "It is a free country, and we are always taught that we may do as we like with our own. Now nothing can be more one's own property than one's name."

"Certainly not."

"When I came back to England after a lengthened sojourn in romantic Italy—the dream of my life through many a year of toil—I found that I was still too young and of far too energetic a temperament to settle down to idleness and retirement. I am speaking now of fifteen years ago. In Italy I had cultivated and improved my powers as an instrumentalist, and I had made myself mistress of the mellifluous language to which a Dante and a Tasso have lent renown. In Italy I had been known as the Signora Balo, the odious *r* and *w* being unacceptable to southern orthography. Gradually I had fallen into the way of writing my name as my Italian friends preferred to write it: and ultimately, when I established myself in this modest dwelling, and issued my circulars, I preferred to appeal to a patrician and fashionable public under the Italianized name of Balo, and with the prefix Madame."

"Your explanation is perfect, madame," replied Humphrey, "and I thank you sincerely for your candor. And now may I inquire if you remember among your pupils at Seacomb a young lady of the name of Trevanard?"

Madame Balo looked agitated even at the mention of the name.

"Remember Muriel Trevanard!" she exclaimed. "I do indeed remember her. She was my favorite pupil, a lovely girl, full of talent—a charming creature."

"Have you any idea of her fate in after-life?"

"No," returned the school-mistress with a troubled look.

"It ought to have been brilliant; but I fear it was a blighted life."

"It was indeed," said Humphrey; and then, as briefly as he could, told Madame Balo the story of her pupil's after life.

Madame Balo heard him with undisguised agitation. A little cry of horrified surprise broke from her more than once during his narrative.

" Now, after considering this case from every point of view, I arrived at a certain conclusion," said Humphrey.

" And that was——"

"That George Penwyn and Muriel Trevanard were man and wife, and that you were aware of their marriage."

It was some moments before Madame Balo recovered herself sufficiently to reply. She sat looking straight before her, with a troubled countenance, then suddenly rose and walked up and down the room once or twice, made as if she would have spoken, yet was dumb, and then suddenly sat down again.

" Mr. Clissold," she said, abruptly, after these various evidences of a perturbed spirit, "you have made me a very miserable woman."

"I am sorry to hear that, Madame Balo."

" That poor ill-used girl—that martyred girl—condemned by her own mother—disgraced and exiled in her own home—tortured till her brain gave way—was as honest a woman as I am —a true and loyal wife, bound to George Penwyn legally and with my knowledge. Yes, there was a marriage, and I was present at the ceremony. I foolishly permitted myself to be drawn into George Penwyn's boyish scheme of a secret marriage. It was to be the mere legal marriage, only a tie to bind them forever; but no more than a tie until George should have won his father's consent or been released by his father's death, and they should be free to complete their union. A foolish business, you will say, in the bud, but I was a foolish woman, and I thought it such a grand thing for my pet pupil—my bright and beautiful Muriel, whom I loved as if she had been my own daughter—to win the young Squire of Penwyn."

Madame Balo said all this in little half-incoherent gushes, not strictly calculated to make things clear.

" If you would kindly give me a direct and succinct account of this matter, so far as you were concerned in it or privy to it, you would be doing me an extreme kindness, Madame Balo," said Humphrey, earnestly. " Much wrong has been done that can never be repaired upon this earth; but there is some part of the wrong that may perhaps be set right if you will give me your uttermost aid."

" It is yours, Mr. Clissold. Command me. You have no idea how fond I was of that poor girl—how proud of the talents which it had been my privilege to develop."

" Tell me everything: straightly, simply, fully."

" I will," replied Madame Balo, " and if I appear to blame in this unhappy story, you must remember I erred from want of thought. I believed I was acting for the best."

" Most of our mistakes in this life are made under that delusion," said Mr. Clissold, with his grave smile.

" You want to know how I came to be mixed up in Muriel's love affair. First you must know that before he went to Eton George Penwyn came to me to be prepared for a public school. I was a mere girl, and had only just set up my establishment for young ladies in those days, and I was very glad to give two hours every morning to the squire's little boy, who used to ride over to Seacomb on his Exmoor pony in the charge of a groom. A very dear little fellow he was at nine years old. I grounded him in French and Latin, and even taught him the rudiments of Greek during the year and a half in which I had him for a pupil, my own dear father having given me a thorough classical education; and, without vanity, I didn't think many little lads went to Eton that year better prepared than George Penwyn. He was a grateful, warm-hearted boy, and he never forgot his old friend, or the old-fashioned garden with the big yellow egg-plums on the western wall. He came to see me many a time in his summer holidays, and afterward when he was in the army. I never knew him to be three days at home without spending a morning with me. He was about the only young man I ever let come in and out of my house without restraint, for I knew he was the soul of honor."

" Did he first see Muriel Trevanard in your house ?"

" No; he was abroad at the time Muriel was with me. My first knowledge of his acquaintance with Muriel and of his love for her came from his own lips, and came to me as a surprise."

CHAPTER XLIX.

" OH, LOVE, WHAT HOURS WERE THINE AND MINE!"

MADAME BALO paused, with a sigh, and then continued her story.

"George Penwyn came to me one day, just before the Michaelmas holidays—it was about a year after Muriel had gone home for good—and asked me for half an hour's private talk. Well do I remember that calm September afternoon, and his bright, eager face as we walked up and down together in the garden at Seacomb, by the sunny wall, where the last of the figs and plums were ripening. He told me he was madly in love with Muriel Trevanard, deeper in love than he had ever been in his life—in fact, it was the one true passion of his life. 'I may have fancied myself in love before,' he said, ' but this is reality.' I tried to laugh him out of his fancy; reminded him of the difference in station between himself and a tenant-farmer's daughter; asked him what his father would say to such an infatuation. ' That's what I'm here to talk about,' said George. ' You know what my father is, and that I might just as well try to turn the course of those two rivers we used to read about when you were grinding me as to turn my father from his purpose. He has made up his mind that I am to marry land—he dreams of land, sleeping and waking—and spends half his time in calculating the number of his acres. If I refuse to marry land, he will disinherit me, and one of my younger brothers will get Penwyn. Now you know how fond I am of Penwyn, and how fond all the people round Penwyn are of me; and you may imagine that it would be rather a hard blow for me to lose an estate which I have always looked upon as my birth-right.'

" 'I should think so, indeed,' said I.

" ' But I love Muriel Trevanard better than house or land,' replied he. ' and I would rather lose all than lose her.' "

" What did you say to this?" asked Humphrey.

" I told him that he was simply mad to think about Muriel, except as he might of a beautiful picture which he had seen in a gallery. But I might as well have reasoned with the wind. He had made up his mind that life without Muriel wasn't worth having. If ever I saw passionate, reckless, all-absorbing love in my life, I saw it in him. Nothing would content him but that Muriel and he should be married before he went abroad with his regiment. He only wanted the tie, the certainty that nothing less than death could part them. He would ask no more than that she should be legally his wife, and would wait a fitting time to take her away from her father's house, and proclaim his marriage to the world. Nothing would be gained by my repeating the arguments I used. They were of no avail. He held to his foolish, romantic purpose of calling Muriel his wife before he left England. ' I shall only be away a year or two,' he said, ' and who knows but I may gain a shred of reputation before I come back—return full major, perhaps, and be able to soften my father's flinty heart?' He told me that he wanted my help, but if I refused it, the marriage would take place all the same. He would not leave England until he had made Muriel his own."

" And you consented to help him?"

" He talked me out of my better reason. Mr. Clissold, I must confess to a romantic temperament, and that reason is not my strong point. I was touched by the intensity of his love, the romance of the situation; and after a long argument, and doing my uttermost to dissuade George from the step he contemplated, I ultimately promised him my aid, and, above all, the strictest secrecy. Muriel was to be asked to spend the Michaelmas holidays with me, and then we were to go quietly to a little watering-place in Devonshire, where no one would know anything about us or about George Penwyn. George was to slip up to London by the morning express and come back by the mail, bringing the license with him, and everything was to be managed in such a way as to prevent the possibility of suspicion on the part of the squire."

" Did Muriel consent readily to such a plan ?"

" I think not. But, however unwillingly, her consent had been given before she came to me, and when I, as woman to woman, asked her if she really wished this marriage to take place, she told me yes, she wished all that George wished. He had a foolish idea that her father and mother would oblige her to marry some one else if he left her unfettered, she told me, and nothing would satisfy him but that indissoluble bond,

Well, he went to Didmouth, the quietest little sea-port town you can well imagine, and here Muriel and I lived in lodgings for a fortnight, while George had his quarters at the hotel. I think those were happy days for both of them. The country round Didmouth is lovely, and they used to wander about together all day long on the hills, and in the lanes where the blackberries were ripening, and the ferns beginning to change their tint. I never saw such innocent, happy lovers. The simplest things pleased and interested them. They were full of hope for the future, when the old squire should relent. I don't know how they supposed he would be brought to change his ideas, but they had some vague notion that he would come round to George's way of thinking in a year or two. As the wedding-day drew near their spirits drooped a little, for it was an understood thing that they were to part at the church door, and meet no more until the squire's consent had been won, lest by any imprudent meeting they should betray the secret of their union, and bring about George's disinheritance. I made them both promise most solemnly that they would not meet after the wedding until George had told his father all, and settled his future fate for good or evil. I stood beside Muriel at the altar; I signed my name in the parish register. I saw bride and bridegroom kiss with their parting kiss, and then I took my old pupil off to the Didmouth coach—there was no rail to Didmouth in those days—and by nightfall we were back in Seacomb, worn out both of us by the emotions of that curious wedding-day. A few days later Muriel went back to Borcel End, and I saw no more of her until the following Christmas, when I drove over to the farm one afternoon to say good-bye to my old pupil, after having advantageously disposed of my school, and on the eve of my departure for the Continent. I could only see Muriel in the presence of her mother and father, who received me with old-fashioned ceremoniousness, and gave me no opportunity of being alone with my pupil. And thus I left Cornwall ignorant of any need that Muriel might have of my friendship, counsel, or aid. I looked upon George Penwyn's marriage as a foolish whim of a headstrong young man passionately in love; but I had no thought that peril or ruin could come of that act; and I looked forward hopefully to the time when Captain Penwyn would return and claim his wife before all the world. Whether the old squire did or did not forego his threat of an unjust will, it would be no bad thing for Muriel to be a captain's or a major's wife, I thought, even if her husband were landless or fortuneless. Better than marrying trade or agriculture, I told myself. Very foolish, no doubt; but my dear old father, who taught me the classics, taught me a good many prejudices into the bargain, and though I had to get my living as a school-mistress, I always looked down upon trade. It pleased me to think that the girl whose mind I had formed had a gentleman for her husband, and a gentleman descended from one of the oldest families in Cornwall. And now, Mr. Clissold, that is the whole of my story. From the time I left Seacomb I never heard from Muriel Penwyn, though I had given her my London agent's address when we parted, an address from which letters would always be forwarded to me."

" You heard of her husband's death, I suppose?"

" Not till nearly six months after it happened, when I saw an account of the poor fellow's melancholy fate in an Italian newspaper, a paragraph copied from *Galignani*. You may imagine that my heart bled for Muriel, yet I dared not write to express my sympathy, fearing to betray a secret which she might prefer to keep forever hidden from her parents. The foolish marriage was now no more than a dream, I thought; a shadow which had passed across the sunshine of her bright young life, leaving grief and pain in its track, but exercising no serious influence on her future. 'She will get over her sorrow in a year or so, and marry some good-looking farmer or Seacomb shopkeeper, after all,' I thought, bitterly disappointed at this sad ending of my pretty little romance. I wrote to a friend at Seacomb soon after to inquire about my old pupil, putting my questions with assumed carelessness. My friend replied that Miss Trevanard was still unmarried and with her parents—a dull life for the poor girl, she feared—but she understood that Miss Trevanard was well. That was all I could hear."

" The breaking of a heart is a quiet transaction," said Humphrey, " hardly noticeable to the outward world. Small-pox is a far more obvious calamity."

Madame Balo sighed. She felt that she had some cause for remorse on the subject of Muriel Trevanard; that she had taken too little trouble about the young wife's after-fate; had been too much absorbed by her own musical studies, her continental friends, and her own interests generally.

" What was the name of the church at Didmouth where the marriage took place?" asked Humphrey.

" The parish church, St. John's."

" And the date of the marriage?"

" September 30, 1847."

This was all that Madame Balo could tell him, and all that he wanted to know. It seemed to him that his course was tolerably clear. He had to prove first the marriage, then the birth of the infant, and finally Justina's identity with that infant.

His three witness would be:

1. Miss Balo, to prove the marriage.
2. Old Mrs. Trevanard, who could testify to the birth of the child.
3. Matthew Elgood, in whose custody Justina had been from the day of her birth, and whose evidence, if held worthy of credence, must needs establish her identity with the child born at Borcel End.

On leaving Madame Balo, with whom he parted on excellent terms, Humphrey went straight to his solicitors, Messrs. Willgross & Harding, of Old Square, good old family solicitors—substantial, reliable, sagacious. Before the younger partner, his especial friend and counselor, he laid his case.

Mr. Harding heard him with a thoughtful countenance, and was in no haste to commit himself to an opinion.

" Rather difficult to dispossess such a man as this Mr. Church ill Penwyn on the testimony of a strolling player," he said. "It's a pity you haven't witnesses with better standing in the world. It might look like a got-up case."

" There is the evidence of the parish register at Didmouth church."

" To prove the marriage. Yes, but only an old blind woman to prove the birth of an heiress, and only this Elgood to show that the infant was intrusted to him. And on the strength of his evidence you want to claim an estate worth seven thousand a year for a young actress at the Albert Theater. The story is very pretty, very romantic, but, upon my word, Clissold, between friends, if I were you, I would not take much trouble about it."

" I will take whatever trouble may be needful to prove Justina's legitimacy," replied Humphrey, with decision. "The estate is a secondary consideration."

" Of course. A mere bagatelle. Well, one of our clerks shall go down to Didmouth to make a copy of the entry in the register."

" I'll go with him," said Humphrey.

CHAPTER L.
"THE SADDEST LOVE HAS SOME SWEET MEMORY."

MR. CLISSOLD left London for Didmouth by the mail, accompanied by Mr. Pointer, a confidential clerk of Messrs, Willgross & Harding. Didmouth was still off the main line, and they had to drive seven or eight miles in a jolting little omnibus, very low in the roof, and by no means luxurious within. They reached Didmouth too late for anything except supper and bed, but they were at the sexton's cottage before eight o'clock next morning, and thence repaired to the church, with the elderly custodian and his keys in their company.

The registers were produced, and the entry of the marriage found under the date supplied by Miss Barlow. A duly testified copy of this entry being taken by Mr. Pointer, in duplicate, Humphrey's mission at Didmouth was concluded.

He parted from Mr. Pointer at the railway-station, after having endured another hour of the jolting omnibus; and while the clerk hastened back to London with one of the two documents, Humphrey went down the line to Seacomb with the other.

He had not been away a week, and yet he had established the one fact he most desired to prove—Justina's right to bear her father's name. He could now venture to confide Muriel's story to Martin, or at least so much of it as might be told without reflecting on his dead mother.

He walked into the old farm-house at breakfast-time next morning, after having spent the night at Seacomb, and crossed the moors in the autumnal mists of earliest morning, not without some hazard of losing his way.

Martin was surprised and delighted.

" What good wind blows you here, dear old fellow ?" he cried, his brow, gloomy enough a moment before, now all sunshine.

" The best wind that ever blew, I think," answered Humphrey.

Mr. Trevanard had gone about his day's work; he had taken to working harder than ever of late, Martin said; so the two young men had the old hall to themselves.

Here Humphrey told his story, Martin listened with profound emotion, and shedding no unmanly tears at the record of his sister's sorrows.

" My poor mother," he sobbed out at last. " She acted for the best—to save the honor of our family; but it was hard on Muriel; and she was sinless all the time—a wife, free from taint or wrong-doing, except the fatal concealment of her marriage."

Then, when the first shock was over, the young man inquired eagerly about his niece, his beloved sister's only child, the babe that had been exiled from its birth-place, robbed of its name.

" How nobly, how wisely, how ably you have acted from first to last, Clissold!" he exclaimed. " Without your help this tangled web could never have been unraveled. But how did it ever occur to you that Miss Elgood and my sister's daughter could be one and the same person ?"

" Perhaps it was because I have thought so much more of Justina Elgood lately than any one else," answered Humphrey; and then he went on to confess that his old wound was healed, and that he loved Justina with a deeper and truer love than he had given the doctor's daughter. Martin was delighted. This would make a new link between himself and his friend.

Humphrey's next anxiety was for an interview with old Mrs. Trevanard. He wanted to test that aged memory, to discover how far the blind grandmother might be relied upon when the time came for laying this family secret before the world.

Mrs. Trevanard still kept her room. She was able to move about a little, able to keep watch and ward upon Muriel, but she preferred the retirement of her own chamber to her old corner in the family sitting-room.

" The place would seem strange to me without Bridget," she told Humphrey, when he expressed his regret at finding her still in her own room. " It's not so much of the rheumatics that keep me here as the thought of that. Bridget was all in all in this house. The old room would seem desolate without her. So I just keep my own bit of fire, and knit my stocking, and think of old times."

" I dare say your memory is a better one than many young people can boast of," said Humphrey, who had taken the empty chair by the fire-place, opposite Mrs. Trevanard.

" Well, I haven't much to complain of in that respect," answered the old woman, with a sigh. " I have sometimes thought that it is better for old people when their memories are not quite so strong as mine. But then, perhaps, that's owing to my blindness. I have nothing left me but memory. I can't see to read, not even my Bible, and I haven't many about me that care to read to me. So the past is my book, and I'm reading the saddest chapters in it. It's a pity Providence has made us so that our minds dwell longest on sorrowful things."

Humphrey related his discovery gently and with some preparation to Muriel's grandmother. When she heard that Muriel was sinless, that her marriage with George Penwyn was an established fact, the blind woman lifted up her voice in thanksgiving to her God.

"I always thought as much," she said, after the first gush of prayer and praise. "I always thought my poor lamb was innocent, but Bridget would not have it so. Bridget hugged the notion of our wrong. She always was talking of God's vengeance on the wrong-doer, and when he met with that cruel death, she declared that it was a judgment, forgetting that the judgment fell heaviest on our poor Muriel."

They talked long and earnestly of the hapless daughter of the house, Humphrey confiding unreservedly in Mrs. Trevanard, who evinced a shrewd sense that filled him with hope. Old and blind though she was, this was not a witness to be browbeaten by a cross-examining counsel, should the issue ever be tried in a court of justice.

"Now, from what we know, and from what happened to me on the first night I ever spent in this house," said Humphrey, "it is clear to my mind that your granddaughter and her husband were in the habit of meeting secretly in the room at the end of the corridor, at night, when the rest of the household was wrapped in sleep."

He went on to describe the scene of his first night at Borcel End—Muriel watching at the open window, entreating her lover to come back to her. Did not this conduct indicate that he had been in the habit of entering the house secretly by that window? Its height was little over eight feet from the ground, and the ivy-clad wall would have been easy enough for any active young man to climb, to say nothing of the ledge and projecting masonry of the lower window, which made the ascent still easier.

"My idea is this," said Humphrey. "Your poor granddaughter's instinct takes her to that room whenever she is free to ramble about the house at night, when all is still, and she has no fear of interruption. For her that room is haunted by sad and sweet memories. What more likely than that, if free to go there nightly, she would in the self-communion of a wandering mind, reveal more of the past than we have yet learned, act over again her meetings with her lover, say over again the old words? Will you leave her free to wander to-night if the fancy seizes her? I will lie down in my clothes and keep watch, ready to listen, or to follow her if need be. The moon is nearly at the full, and the night will be bright enough to tempt her to wander. Will you let it be so, Mrs. Trevanard?"

"I don't see that any harm could come of it," answered the old woman, dubiously. "She is reasonable enough in her way, and I have never known her attempt to do herself a mischief. But as to what she can reveal in her wild wandering talk, I don't see myself how that can be of any good."

"Perhaps not. It is only a fancy of mine at best, but I shall be pleased if you will indulge it. I shall not be here more than two or three nights, at most."

"I will leave my door unlocked on those nights," said Mrs. Trevanard. "But I shall not have much rest while that poor child is wandering about."

To the grandmother, to whom the past was more real than the present, Muriel was still the girl of eighteen newly returned from school.

The rest of the day was spent quietly enough by Humphrey and Martin in a ramble by the sea-shore. At dinner Mr. Trevanard appeared, but although he was surprised to see Humphrey so soon after his departure, he evinced no curiosity as to the motive of his return. The master of Borcel Farm seemed to have lost all interest in life in losing the partner of his days and cares. He went about his work with a mechanical air, talked very little, drank more than he ate; and seemed altogether in a bad way.

Humphrey observed him with concern.

"If we could but kindle a glimmer of reason in his daughter's breast, she might be a comfort to him in the decline of his life," speculated the poet, "and it is just possible that a father's love might exercise some healing influence upon that disordered mind. The isolation to which her mother condemned her was the surest method of deadening mind and memory."

He would have given much had he been free to summon Justina to Borcel, and test the power of a daughter's love upon Muriel's brain. But to summon Justina away from London would be to imperil the prosperity of the Albert Theater, and doubtless to incur legal penalties. Nor did he wish to draw Justina into the business till his chain of evidence was too complete for the possibility of failure in the establishment of her rights.

"No," he told himself; "for some time to come I must act without Justina."

Martin could talk of nothing but his newly-discovered niece, and was full of impatience to see her. It was only by promising to take him to London in a few days and introduce him to Justina that Humphrey succeeded in keeping this young man quiet during his first day at Borcel End. And thus the day wore itself out, and night, with the full autumn moonlight, descended upon the old farm-house.

CHAPTER LI.

"STABBED THROUGH THE HEART'S AFFECTIONS TO THE HEART."

IT was a clear autumn night, still and cloudless. The mists of evening had rolled away from moorland and meadow, from the dark brown field where the plow had been busy, and the long line of rippling water in the distance. The moon was as bright and full as on that first night of Humphrey Clissold's sojourn at Borcel. He had been told that on such a night as this Muriel was wont to be restless.

"Now if that poor ghost of days departed will but haunt my room to-night, I may gather some shred of information from her disjointed talk," he said to himself.

But the night wore away while he lay awake and watchful, and there was no sound of slippered footfalls in the corridor, no opening of the creaking old door. Mr. Clissold fell asleep at last, when the moon had vanished, and did not wake till ever so long after the Borcel End breakfast hour.

This was disappointing, but he waited another day, and watched another night, with the same result.

"If she doesn't come to-night I give it up," he said to himself. "After all, there can be but little for me to gather from her rambling self-communion."

He slept for an hour or two on the third afternoon, and thus on the third night of his watch was more wakeful than before: The nights were moonlight still, but the moon rose later, and had lost her full brightness.

He lay awake for three hours on this particular night, and heard not a sound, save the occasional scufflings, patterings, and squealings of mice behind the wainscot. But a few minutes after the eight-day clock in the hall had struck two the watcher heard the sound that had startled him at his first coming—the slipshod footfall—the slow, ghost-like tread on the uncarpeted floor of the corridor.

Muriel was approaching.

She entered slowly—quietly—as before, and went straight to the window, which she opened noiselessly, taking infinite pains to avoid all sound. Then, kneeling on the window-seat, she put her head out of the window, and looked downward, as if she were watching some one below.

"Be careful, love," she exclaimed, in a whisper just loud enough for Humphrey's attentive ear to catch, "that root of ivy is loose. I'm afraid your foot will slip. Be careful."

For some time she remained thus, holding imaginary communion with some one below. Then all at once she awoke to a sense of her solitude, and knew that she had been talking to a phantom. She drew back into the room, and began to walk up and down rapidly, with a distracted air, her hands clasped upon her head, as if by that pressure upon her temples she would have stilled the trouble within her brain.

"They told me he was dead," she said to herself; "murdered, barbarously murdered. But there was no truth in it. They have told me other lies as well as that. They are all false, all cruel. My mother has made them so. She has taken away my husband. She has taken away my child. She has left me nothing but memory. Why did she not take that away? I should be happy—yes, quite happy, sitting by the fire and singing all day long, or roaming about among the hazel bushes and the old apple trees in the wilderness, if I did not remember. But I look down at my empty arms and remember that my blessed child ought to be lying in them, and then I hate her. Yes, I hate the mother that bore me."

All this was said in disjointed gushes of quick, eager speech, divided by intervals of silence.

Suddenly she burst into a shrill laugh.

"Who says he is dead?" she cried. "Don't I see him every moonlight night when I can come here? They shut me up mostly, lock all the doors, and keep me prisoner. Cruel—cruel —cruel. But he is standing under the window all the same, whenever the moon shines. He is there, waiting for me to open my window, like Romeo. Yes, that's what he said, 'like Romeo.'"

Then, with an entire change of tone, a change to deepest tenderness, mingled with a remorseful fear, she went on, as if speaking to her lover:

"Love, it was very wrong of us to break our promise. I fear that harm will come of it. My mind is full of fear."

After this came a long silence. She went back to the window, knelt upon the broad wooden seat, and laid her head upon the sill, and remained motionless, speechless.

Humphrey fancied she was weeping.

This continued for nearly an hour; then, with a sudden move- ment—all her movements were sudden—she started up and looked about the room as if in quest of something.

Humphrey had left his extinguished candle on the dressing- table, with a box of matches in the candlestick. Quick as thought Muriel seized the box, struck a match, and lighted the candle, and then hurried from the room.

The watcher sprung from the bed where he had been lying hidden by the shadow of the curtains, and followed that retiring figure, full of apprehension.

A confirmed lunatic rushing about an old timber house with a lighted candle was not the safest of people, and Humphrey held himself responsible for any harm that might happen in conse- quence of Muriel's liberty.

When he emerged from his room the corridor was empty, but the gleam of the candle in the distance guided his hurried steps. At the end of the corridor there was a winding stair—a stair which he had never ascended—but which he understood to lead to certain disused garrets in the roof.

It was from this narrow stair that the glimmer of light came, and hither Humphrey Clissold hastened. He was just in time to see the edge of Muriel's white drapery flutter for an instant on the topmost stair before it vanished, and the light with it.

He rushed up the stairs, knocking his head against a heavy cross-beam in the course of his swift ascent, and almost stun- ning himself; but even that blow did not make him pause. He staggered on to the last step, and found himself in a curious chaos, which, in the dim light of the waning moon, looked to him like the hold of a ship turned upside down. Ponderous beams crossed each other in every direction, the faint moon- shine streamed through a broken skylight, cobwebs and dust hung all around, and in one corner of this deserted loft a few articles of furniture were crowded together, shrouded from the dust by some old patchwork coverlets. Even this loft had doubtless been kept in good order so long as that vigilant house-wife, Bridget Trevanard, had been able to attend to her domestic duties.

Muriel was kneeling near this shrouded heap of discarded furniture—kneeling by an old-fashioned basket-work cradle. She held the candlestick in one hand, and seemed to be searching for something in the cradle with the other hand. Her head was bent, her brow contracted, and she was muttering to herself as she groped among the tumbled blankets and discolored linen which had once made the warm nest of some idolized infant. Her own nest most likely.

Humphrey stopped short. To startle her in such a moment might be dangerous. Better for him to hold his peace and keep a watch upon her movements, ready to rush to the rescue should there be peril.

Presently she seemed to have found what she wanted. It was a letter, in a sealed envelope, which she looked at and kissed, but made no attempt to open. She replaced this presently in the cradle, and took out more letters, two or three together, open, and these she kissed, looking long and fixedly at the written lines, as if she were trying to read them, but could not.

" My love, my love," she murmured. " Your own true words —nothing but death could part us. Death has parted us. Yes, death! They told me you were dead. And yet that can't be true. The dead are spirits. If you were dead, you would hover near me. I should see your blessed shade. I should——"

Her eyes, wandering slowly from the letter, penetrated that dusky corner where Humphrey stood watching her. She saw him—gave one long wild shriek—and sprung toward him.

To her excited imagination that dark and silent form seemed the ghost of her dead lover.

She had thrown the candlestick from her as she sprung to her feet. The candle rolled from its socket and fell upon her long white night-dress. A moment, and she stood before Humphrey's affrighted sight a pillar of flame.

He flew to her, clasped her in his arms, and trampled on the candle, dragged one of the loose coverings from the furniture, and rolled her in it, tightly, firmly, extinguishing the flames in his vigorous grasp. The peril, the horror, had been but momentary, yet he feared the shock might be fatal. The frail form shivered in his arms. The tender flesh had been scorched.

Even in that moment of terror she still believed him to be her lover.

" Not a spirit," she murmured. " Not the shadow of the dead, but living, and returned to me to rescue, to cherish. Oh, George, is it really you?"

It was the first time he had heard her utter George Penwyn's name.

" It is one who will protect and cherish you," Humphrey said, tenderly. " One whom you may trust and cling to in all confidence, one who will restore your daughter to you."

" My daughter, my baby girl," she cried. " No, you can never do that on earth; in heaven we shall meet again, perhaps, and know each other, but never in this life. She was taken away from me, and they murdered her.''

" No, she was given into safe hands; she was loved and cared for. Years have passed since then, and she has grown up into a beautiful young woman. You shall see her again, live with her, and she will love and honor you."

" I don't want her; I want my lovely baby, the little child they took away from me. The baby that lay in my arms, and clung to my breast for one short hour before it was taken away." She shuddered, and a faint moan broke from her lips.

" You are in pain," said Humphrey.

" Yes, the fire is burning still. It scorches me to the heart."

He took her in his arms with infinite tenderness and carried her slowly across the loft and down the narrow stair, making his way amidst those massive cross-beams and by those steep steps with extreme caution, lighted only by the pale glimmer of the fading moon.

Once at the bottom of the stairs and in the broad corridor, his way was easy enough. He carried his light burden through the silent house across the empty hall, and to the open door of old Mrs. Trevanard's room. Here he laid her gently on the sofa before awakening the blind grandmother. He found a candle on the table, and a match-box on the mantelpiece, and was soon provided with a light.

His first look was at Muriel. She had fainted, and lay motionless where he had placed her—white and deathlike.

He went to Mrs. Trevanard's bed ide, and woke her gently.

" Dear Mrs. Trevanard, there has been an accident. Your granddaughter is hurt; not seriously, I trust, but the shock has made her faint. Will you give her some kind of restorative while I go and call the servants?"

He left the room for this purpose, hurried to the end of the house where he had been told the servants slept in a room over the kitchen, knocked at the door of this room, and told one of the girls to get up and dress herself as fast as she could and come to Mrs. Trevanard's room without a moment's loss of time. This done, he hastened back to Muriel, and found the blind grandmother administering to her—holding a glass containing some cordial of her own concoction to the white lips of the sufferer.

" Why did you persuade me to leave my door open?" exclaimed Mrs. Trevanard, reproachfully. "See what harm has come of it."

" Not much harm, I trust in Providence. There has been a shock, but I hope no real injury."

" What was it? Did she fall?"

" No, it was worse than a fall."

He told how the flame had caught Muriel's thin night-gear, and how rapidly it had been extinguished.

" If you will tell me where to find your doctor, I will saddle one of the farm horses and ride over to fetch him, however far it may be," said Humphrey.

" You ride," cried Mrs. Trevanard, contemptuously, "and

how are you to find your way from here to Seacomb before day-break?"

"I am not afraid. I have driven the road of+en with Martin."

"Let Martin go. He has known the way from childhood."

This seemed a reasonable suggestion, and Humphrey hurried off to wake Martin just as Phœbe the house-maid arrived on the scene, sleepy, but sympathetic. She had expected to find old Mrs. Trevanard ill; in fact, had made up her mind that the old lady had had "a stroke," and was at her last gasp. She was there-fore surprised to find the blind woman keen and active, only needing the aid of some one with eyes to carry out her instruc-tions.

Humphrey was not sorry to remain on the spot while Martin went for the doctor, feeling that coolness and nerve might be needful.

Martin was up and dressed in the briefest possible space of time, and ran out to the stables to saddle the useful hack which was kept for the dog cart. Day was beginning to show faint and pale in the east as he galloped away by the road that led to Seacomb, the same road by which Mathew Elgood and his wife had gone in the chill March morning, twenty years ago, with Muriel's child in their custody.

Humphrey walked up and down the hall, listening for any sound from that inner room, and in half an hour had the satis-faction of hearing that she was sleeping tranquilly, and that she had been very little burned.

"Thank God," he ejaculated, fervently. "If this acci-dent had been fatal, I should have deemed myself her mur-derer."

At seven o'clock the doctor arrived, an old man, with a wise, kind face. He had assisted at Muriel's birth, and had been in some measure familiar with the various stages of her life, though never intrusted with the fatal family secret.

"A shock to the system, undoubtedly," he said; "but I trust not involving any danger. Indeed, I am not without hope that it may have a beneficial effect in subduing that restlessness which Mrs. Trevanard tells me is the worst feature of the case. Anything which would induce repose would be favorable, and, by and by, perhaps, change of air and scene—a total change of surroundings—might do good in weaning the mind from old im-pressions, introducing, if I may say so, a new color into the patient's life. I have often suggested this to our worthy friend, the late Mrs. Trevanard, but without effect. She had her prej-udices, good soul, and she thought her daughter could only be properly cared for at home."

"And do you think your patient might soon be moved?" asked Humphrey, who had a scheme for bringing mother and daughter together.

"Well, not immediately. Under present circumstances rest is most to be desired; but when strength returns I feel assured that change would be advantageous."

When he had heard all the doctor had to say, and eaten a hearty breakfast, Humphrey went quietly up-stairs, and, having reconnoitered the corridor and assured himself that there was nobody about to watch his movements, ascended that upper staircase leading to the loft.

It was broad daylight now in that chaotic cavern formed by the roof of the old house. The sunshine streamed in through the broken skylight, revealing every cobweb which festooned the old oak rafters. Humphrey stepped cautiously across the creaking timbers which roughly floored the chamber, and approached the pile of disused furniture in front of which stood the little wicker cradle, where Muriel had hidden her letters.

Were they actual letters, Humphrey wondered, or only scraps of worthless paper which her distraught fancy had invested with meaning and importance. Had she hidden her lover's letters here in the days when her mind was bright and clear, or had she strayed hither in the cunning of madness to secrete the maniac's treasures of straws and shreds and discarded scraps of paper?

He knelt beside the cradle as she had knelt, and turned out the little sheets and blankets, the small down pillows. Yes, there were letters under the mattress, a small packet of letters written in rusty ink on discolored paper, tied with a faded ribbon.

"These may be worth something in the way of evidence," he said to himself.

He read them one after another as he knelt there. They told the old story of deathless love, doomed to die, of bright hopes never to blossom into reality. They all began "My beloved wife," they were all signed " Your devoted husband, George Penwyn." They were all addressed on the cover, which was an integral part of each letter, "Miss Muriel Trevanard, Borcel End, near Seacomb."

There could be no doubt as to the identity of the person to whom the letters had been written. There could be no doubt as to the writer's recognition of that person as his lawful life. " My Muriel, my darling wife," occurred many times in the letters. Nor was this all; in these letters, written in love and confidence, George Penwyn made frequent allusion to the motives which had led to his secret marriage. His whole mind was here laid bare, his hope of the squire's relenting in time to come, his plans for the future, his intention to declare his marriage for weal or woe immediately upon his return to England, his willingness to face poverty, if need were, with Muriel.

" But I am not without the hope," he wrote, in one of the later letters, " that my absence from England for two or three years will have a good effect upon my father's feelings toward me. He is sore now on account of my having neglected what he was pleased to consider a grand opportunity of enlarging and consolidating the Penwyn estate. But I know that in his heart he loves me best of all his sons, and that it would lacerate that heart to disinherit me. Time will blunt the edge of his angry feelings, and when I come back, perhaps with some little distinction as a soldier, he will be inclined to look leniently upon my choice."

In another letter he hinted at the possible arising of circumstances which would oblige Muriel to leave her home.

"I could not go away without being assured that you have a friend and counselor ready to aid you in any difficulty," he wrote. "I have a stanch friend in Mr. Tomlin, the lawyer of Seacomb, and I herewith inclose a letter which I have written to him, informing him of our marriage, and enlisting his sympathy and assistance for you, should you need them. He will do all that friendship and discretion can inspire, both to secure your comfort and happiness, your safety and respectability of surroundings, *under all circumstances,* and also to assure the preservation of our secret. Give your mind no trouble, darling, whatever may happen, but trust implicitly in Mr. Tomlin's wisdom and kindness, and believe that, distant as I may be in the body, there is no hour of the day or night in which I am not near you in the spirit."

The letter addressed to William Tomlin, Esq., Solicitor, Seacomb, was here—the seal unbroken.

Humphrey had no doubt that the possible difficulty foreseen by the young husband, before he left England, was the difficulty which had actually arisen in the birth of Justina. But why had this letter been left undelivered? How came it that this unhappy wife—finding herself in the most miserable position a woman could be placed in—her honor doubted even by her own mother—should have refrained from applying to her friend and adviser to whom her husband had recommended her, and to whose allegiance he had confided her future?

Had she deliberately chosen to endure shame and outrage at home rather than avail herself of Mr. Tomlin's aid, or had her brain already begun to fail at the time when her trouble fell upon her, rendering her incapable of taking the most obvious as well as the most rational course?

This question sorely puzzled Humphrey, and was for the time unanswerable. He put the letters in his breast pocket, feeling that with this documentary evidence to strengthen Justina's case there must be little doubt as to the issue. The only question open to dispute in the face of the marriage register and of these letters would be the identity of Justina. He went downstairs and out of the house, and took a long ramble across the upland fields with the Atlantic before him—his favorite walk at all times, these bleak fields of turnip or mangel, high above the roaring waves, and wild romantic coast, with its jagged peaks and natural arches and obelisks of serpentine.

There were a family of cormorants disporting themselves among the rocks, one solitary herring boat bobbing up and down in the distance, a man shoveling up sea-weed into a cart on the beach, and this, save for the flash of a sea-gull's silver wing now and-then, was all the life visible from the turnip field on the cliff. Here Martin came presently, refreshed by a couple of hours' sleep after his long ride.

"I thought I should find you here," he said, "when I missed you in the house. Poor Muriel is going on very comfortably,

I was with ner just now when she awoke. She knew me, for a wonder, and was more gentle than I have found her for a long time, but the shock seems to have weakened her very much."

"One could hardly expect it would be otherwise. A few days' rest will restore her, I trust. Believe me, Martin, no one could be more anxious about her than I."

"I am sure of that, dear fellow."

"And now answer me a question. Did you ever hear the name of Tomlin?"

"Yes; there is a solicitor of that name at Seacomb."

"An old man?"

"No; middle-aged at most. I should think him barely forty."

"Then he is not the man I want. He had a father before him, I suppose."

"Yes, old Mr. Tomlin was a wonderful fellow, I believe, universally respected. I never saw him to my knowledge, for he died when I was a youngster, but I have often heard my father talk of him."

Half an hour afterward, when they were seated at the farmer's early dinner, Humphrey took occasion to question Michael Trevanard on the same subject.

"Old Mr. Tomlin," said the farmer. "Yes, I remember him well, though he never did any business for me. A very worthy man, everybody liked him, a lawyer in a thousand, a thoroughly honest man. He died suddenly, poor fellow. Left his house one morning in excellent health to attend the petty sessions, and was seized with a stroke of apoplexy in the court, and never spoke again. His funeral was one of the grandest I ever saw in Seacomb."

"Do you happen to remember the year of his death?"

"Yes, I remember it well, for it occurred in the autumn before Muriel's long illness. He died in October, 1848."

This explained Muriel's conduct. Death had snatched away the one friend to whom she could have made her appeal.

CHAPTER LII.

"'IT IS TIME, O PASSIONATE HEART!' SAID I."

THE reason of Muriel's conduct was fully explained by the fact of Mr. Tomlin's death. The one friend whom her husband's forethought had provided for her had been snatched away before the hour of her need, and she had found herself alone, without help, counsel, or shelter. Doubtless an overstrained respect for her promise—perhaps a latent fear of Bridget Trevanard's severe nature—had withheld her from revealing the fact of her marriage and the manner of it. She had borne the deep agony of shame rather than endanger her husband's future. She had perhaps argued that if her mother and father had been told the truth, nothing would have prevented their communicating it to the squire, and then George would have been disinherited through her broken promise. Woman-like, she had deemed her own peace—her own fair fame even—a lighter sacrifice than her husband's welfare, and she had kept silence.

With this additional evidence of George Penwyn's letters, fully acknowledging Muriel as his wife, Humphrey Clissold felt that there was no further cause for delay. The law could not be too soon set in motion, if the law were needed to secure Muriel and Justina their rights. But before appealing to the law he resolved upon submitting the whole case to Churchill Penwyn and to Justina, in order to discover the possibility of compromise. It would be a hard thing to reduce Churchill and his fair young wife to beggary. They had spent their money wisely, and done good in the land. An equitable division of the estate would be better pleasing to Mr. Clissold's idea of justice than a strict exaction of legal rights, and he had little doubt that Justina would think with him.

His first duty was to go to her and tell her all the truth, and he lost no time in performing that duty. It was on Saturday morning that he found the letters in the loft, and on Saturday evening he was in London, with the quiet of Sunday before him in which to make his revelation.

He left a note for Justina at her lodgings.

"DEAR MISS ELGOOD.—Please do not go to church to-morrow morning, as I want to have a long talk with you on a serious business matter, and will call at eleven for that purpose.

" Yours always,
" HUMPHREY CLISSOLD.

"Saturday evening."

He found her ready to receive him next morning at eleven, fresh and fair in her simple autumn dress of fawn-colored cashmere, with neat linen collar and cuffs, a blue ribbon and silver locket her sole ornaments.

His letter had filled her with vague apprehensions, which Mathew Elgood's arguments had not been able to dispel.

"What business can you have to talk about with me?" she asked, nervously, as she and Humphrey shook hands. "I hope it is nothing very awful. Your letter has kept me in a fever ever since I received it."

" I am so sorry to hear that. I ought to have said less, or more. It is a serious business, but I hope not one that need give you pain, except so far as your tenderness and compassion may be concerned for others. The story I am going to tell you is a sad one, and has to do with your own infancy."

" I can't understand," she said, with a perplexed look.

" Don't try to understand until I have told you more. I shall make everything very clear to you in due time."

" Papa may hear, I suppose," said she, with a glance at the comedian, who had laid down his after-breakfast pipe and was looking far from comfortable.

" Yes, I see no reason why Mr. Elgood should not hear all I have to say. He will be able to confirm some of my statements."

Mathew Elgood moved uneasily in his chair, emptied the

ashes from his pipe with a shaking hand, wiped his forehead
with an enormous bandana, and then burst out suddenly:

"Justina, Mr. Clissold is about to make a revelation. I know
enough of its nature to know that it will be startling. I think
I've done my duty by you, my girl; urged you on in your profession; taught you how to walk the stage, how to make a
point; taught you Miss Farren's orignal business in Lady
Teazle. We've shared and shared alike, through good and foul
weather. Lear and his Fool couldn't have stuck better by each
other. We've tramped the barren heath of life through storm
and tempest, and if you've had to wear leaky shoes sometimes,
why, so have I. And if you discover from Mr. Clissold "—
pointing his pipe at Humphrey with tremulous hand—"that I
am not so much your father as I might have been had nature
intended me for that position, I hope your heart will speak for
me, and confess that I have done a father's duty."

With this closing appeal Mr. Elgood laid down his pipe, buried his face in his big bandana, and sobbed aloud.

Justina was on her knees at his feet in a moment, her arms
round him, his grizzled head drawn down upon her shoulder,
soothing, caressing him.

"Dear papa, what can you mean? Not my father?"

"No, my love," sobbed the comedian. "Legally, actually, as
a matter of fact, I have no claim to that title. Morally, it is
another pair of shoes. I held you at the baptismal font; I have
fed you many a time when your sole refreshment was alike insipid and sloppy; these hands have guided your infantile steps;
yet I am not your father. Legally, I have no authority over
you or your salary."

"You are my father all the same," answered Justina, emphat-
ically. "What other father have I?"

"Your legal parent has certainly been conspicuous by his absence, my love. You were placed in my wife's arms on the day
of your birth—an abandoned child—and from that hour to her
death she honestly performed a mother's part."

"And shall never have less than a mother's love!" cried Justina. "Do not fear, dear papa, that anything I may hear to-day
can ever lessen my affection for you. We have borne too much
misfortune together not to love each other dearly," she added,
with a touch of sadness.

"Say on, sir," exclaimed the actor, with an oratorical flourish
of his bandana; "she is stanch, and I fear not the issue."

Humphrey told his story in plainest words—the story of
Muriel's marriage and Muriel's sorrow. Justina heard him with
tears of tenderness and pity.

"Now, Justina," he said, after having explained everything,
"you understand that you have a legal claim to the Penwyn
estate. Your grandfather's will bequeathed the property to
George Penwyn, your father, or his issue, male or female. If a
daughter inherited, her husband, whomsoever she married, was
to assume the name of Penwyn. I have taken the trouble to
read the will, and I have no doubt as to your position. You can
file a bill in chancery—or your next friend for you—to-morrow,

and you can oust Churchill Penwyn from house and land, wealth and social status. It will be rather hard upon his wife, who is a very sweet woman, and has done much good in her neighborhood."

"Do you think I want his money or his land?" cried Justina, indignantly. "Not a sixpence—not a rood. I only want the name you say I have a right to bear—James Penwyn's name. To think that we were cousins! Poor James!"

"You dislike Churchill Penwyn. This would be a grand revenge for you."

"I dislike him because I have never been able to rid myself of the idea that he had some hand in his cousin's death. But I do not wish to injure him. I leave him to God and his own conscience. If he has sinned, as I believe he has, life must be bitter to him—in spite of wealth and position."

"Are you not intoxicated by the notion of being Lady of Penwyn Manor?" asked Humphrey.

"No. I am content to be what I am—to earn my own bread, and live happily with poor old papa," laying her hand lovingly on the comedian's shoulder.

A welcome hearing this for Humphrey Clissold, who had feared lest change of fortune should work a fatal change in the girl he loved. But he suppressed all appearance of emotion, and went on in his business-like tone.

"Well, Justina, since you seem to regard your right to the Penwyn estate with supreme indifference, you will be the more likely to fall into my way of thinking. Looking at the case from an equitable standpoint, it does certainly appear to me that, although by the old squire's will you are entitled to the whole of the property, it would be not the less an injustice were you to claim all. It would seem a hard thing to deprive Churchill Penwyn altogether of an estate which he has administered with judgment and benevolence. My idea, therefore, is that I, your next friend, if you will allow me the privilege of that position, should state the case to Mr. Penwyn and propose a compromise, namely, that he should mortgage the estate for a sum of money amounting to half its value, and should deliver that money to you. His income would in this manner be reduced one-half, and it would be at his discretion to save money, even with that smaller income, and lessen the amount of the mortgage out of his accumulations, as the years went on. I think this would be at once a fair and liberal proposal, making his change of fortune as light as possible."

"I do not want any of his money," said Justina, impetuously.

"My love, this is simply childish," exclaimed Mr. Elgood.

"Let me act for you, Justina; trust me to deal generously with the squire and his wife."

"I will trust you," she answered, looking up at him with perfect faith and love.

"Trust me in this and in all things. You shall not find me unworthy of your confidence."

And this was all that was said about the Penwyn estate. Humphrey spent the rest of the day with Justina, went to Westminster Abbey with her in the afternoon to hear a great preacher, and walked with her afterward in the misty groves of St. James' Park, and then and there, feeling that he was now free to open his heart to her, told her in truest, tenderest words how the happiness of his future life was bound up in her; how, rich or poor, she was dearer to him than all the world beside.

And so, in the London fog and gloom, under the smoky metropolitan trees, they plighted their troth—Justina ineffably happy.

"I thought you did not care an atom for me," she said, when all had been told.

"I thought you only cared for James Penwyn's memory."

"Poor James! That love was like a midsummer night's dream."

"And this is reality?"

"Yes."

He holds her to his beating heart under the autumnal trees, and kisses her with the kiss of betrothal.

"My love, my dearest, my truest, my best, what is wealth, or position, or all this bitter world can give and take away, measured against love like ours?" And after this homily, which Justina remembered a great deal better than the great preacher's sermon, they turn their faces homeward, and arrive just in time to prevent the utter ruin of the dinner, which their tardiness had imperiled.

"You wouldn't have liked to see a pretty little bit of beef like that reduced to the condition of a deal board, now would you?" asked Mr. Elgood, pointing to the miniature sirloin.

Humphrey and Justina interchanged smiles. They were thinking that they would be content to dine upon deal boards henceforward so long as they dined together.

CHAPTER LIII.
"NOT AS A CHILD SHALL WE AGAIN BEHOLD HER."

HUMPHREY CLISSOLD went back to Cornwall next day, with full powers, so far as Justina's interests were concerned. Her greatest anxiety was to see the unhappy mother from whom she had been severed since the hour of her birth; but to bring about a meeting between these two was not the easiest thing in the world. Other interests were at stake. The Albert Theater could not get on without Justina, or so the manager affirmed; and Justina's engagement was for the entire season. No breaking it, save by forfeiture of reputation with the public, and at the hazard of a lawsuit.

The only thing to be done was to bring Muriel nearer London, so soon as she should be strong enough to bear the journey. Humphrey hoped much from the daughter's influence upon the mother's disordered brain. He was at Borcel End by eight o'clock in the evening—neither Mr. Trevanard nor his son suspecting that their erratic guest had been further than Seacomb—and found the aspect of things improving. Muriel was calmer. the burns had proved of the slightest, and all was going on favorably. He went in and sat by her bedside for a few minutes and talked to her. The wan eyes looked at him calmly enough, but with a curious wonder. He found that she remembered nothing of the fire, and had no idea why she had been ill and in pain. But she did remember the promise he had made her about her daughter.

" Some one told me I should see my baby again," she said. " I don't know who it was, but some one told me so, and I know that I shall see her — when we meet our friends in heaven."

" You shall see her here, on this earth," said Humphrey.

" Is that true?"

" Quite true."

" Then let me go to sleep till she comes; lay her here beside me, and let me find her here when I open my eyes—my sweet baby."

" Consider how many years have come and gone since you saw her. She is an infant no longer, but a beautiful young woman."

Muriel stared at him with a puzzled look.

" I don't want to see any young woman; I want my baby again—the little baby my mother stole from me."

This made things difficult. Humphrey saw in this a fond clinging to the past, memory strong enough to make the lapse of years as nothing. He made no attempt to argue the point, but left Muriel to the devoted grandmother's care.

The blind woman sat in her easy-chair by the bed, knitting industriously, and murmuring a soothing word now and then. No voice had such power to comfort Muriel.

" When shall I see my niece, and when will you tell father?" Martin asked, eagerly, directly he and Humphrey were alone together.

" You shall see your niece as soon as your sister is strong enough to bear a journey, when you can bring her up to some quiet little place in the neighborhood of London. As for your father, I think my chain of evidence is now so complete that I cannot tell him too soon. I will get a quiet hour with him to-morrow after breakfast, if I can. Later I am going to the Manor-house to examine my ground and discover if there is any chance of a friendly compromise."

" I hope you'll be able to settle things pleasantly," said Martin. " I can't bear the idea of those poor young ladies—Mrs. Pen-wyn and Miss Bellingham—being turned out of house and home."

" It shall not be so bad as that, depend upon it," replied Humphrey.

He was down early next morning, and asked Mr. Trevanard for half an hour's conversation after breakfast.

" An hour if you like," answered Michael, in his listless way. " There's not much for me to do upon the farm. I only potter about; the men would go on quite as well without me, I dare say."

" I can't believe that, Mr. Trevanard," said Humphrey, cheer
ily. " The master's eye—you know the old adage."

" Bridget was the ruling mind, sir. Bridget was worth twent;
of me."

It was a cold and blustering morning, the dead leaves fallin;
fast from the few trees about Borcel, but Michael and his con
panion were fond of the open air, so they went into the neg
lected garden, a wilderness where Muriel had been wont t
range alone and at liberty for the last twenty years.

⁻ Here in a narrow path, screened by hazel bushes, the farme
and Humphrey Clissoid paced up and down while Humphre;
told his story, taking care to soften Bridget Trevanard'
part in the domestic tragedy, and to demonstrate that, whe:
erring most, she had been actuated only by regard for the famil
honor, and a mistaken family pride.

Michael heard him with deepest emotion.

" My poor girl—my beautiful Muriel. You don't know ho\
proud I was of her—how I doted on her, and to think that
should never have suspected that all was not well, that my poo
child was being ill-used in her own house."

" Not ill-used," remonstrated Humphrey, pleading for the dea
wife who had trusted him with her secret. "There was no ur
kindness."

" No unkindness! They made her suffer shame; they refuse
to believe in her purity; was that no unkindness? They robbe
her of her child! For what? The world's good word. I woul
have stood between my darling and the world. None shoul
have dared to slander her while I was near. What right ha
my wife to take this matter into her own hands, to hoodwinl
me with her secrecies and suppressions? I would have stood b
my child. Muriel would have trusted me. Yes, she would hav
trusted her indulgent old father even if she feared to confide i
her mother. Bridget was always too severe."   ⁄

" Remember that your wife erred in her anxiety for your goo
name."

" Yes, yes, I know that. God knows it goes hard with me t
speak against her in her grave, poor faithful soul. She wa
faithful according to her notion of right. But she took to
much heed of the world—her world—half a dozen familie
within five miles of Borcel. The sun and moon and heaven an
all God's angels were not so much account to her. Poor soul
She must have suffered. I've seen the lines of trouble growin;
deeper in her face, and never knew why they came there. M;
poor trampled-upon Muriel! It was a cruel thing to send awa;
the child. I could have loved it dearly!"

" You will love her dearly still, when I bring her to you."

" Yes, but not as I could have loved her twenty years ago
when she was a helpless infant. My first-born grandchild."

The idea that this grandchild of his was the rightful owner o
the Penwyn estate, Borcel End included, moved Michael Trev
anard but slightly. He was not calm enough to consider thi
business from a worldly point of view. He could only think o
the grandchild that was born under his roof, and spirited awa;

while he lay in bed, unsuspecting of the evil that was being wrought for love of his good name. He could only think of the persecuted daughter whose life had been made so bitter—of the husband who had never lived to acknowledge his wife—the father who had never known of his child's birth. The thought of these things altogether absorbed his mind, and he scarcely realized the fact of his grandchild's claim to wealth and position.

"And where is she? What is she doing now? Muriel's daughter, my grandchild?" he asked.

Humphrey explained Justina's position.

"What?" cried the old man, with a wry face, "a play-actress? Raddled red and white, and in short petticoats all over tinsel stars, capering outside a show." His only notion of actresses was founded on his experiences at Seacomb cattle fair. "Do you mean to say that my flesh and blood has come to that?"

Humphrey hastened to correct the farmer's idea of the dramatic profession, and to assure him that his granddaughter was to all intents and purposes a lady; modest, refined in feeling and in manner, beautiful in mind and person, a grandchild of whom he might have ample reason to be proud.

"A London theater is not in the least like those itinerant playhouses you have seen at Seacomb fair," he said.

"Humph! They don't dance outside, I suppose, or play the Pandean pipes, and beat a gong?"

"Nothing approaching it. You might mistake a London theater for a church, looking at its outside."

"And they don't raddle their faces, eh?"

"Oh, dear, no," Humphrey replied, with a faint twinge in that region of his censorium which phrenologists appropriate to conscientiousness. "Not in the least. In short, acting in London is a high art."

"And no short petticoats and tinsel stars, eh?"

"No tinsel stars. Nor does your daughter ever appear in short petticoats. She is a most refined and elegant actress, and I know that whether you see her on or off the stage, you will be equally charmed with her."

"I shall love her for Muriel's sake," answered Michael Trevanard, tenderly. "Yes, I should love her dearly, even if she raddled her cheeks and danced outside a show at a fair."

CHAPTER LIV.

"A SOUL AS WHITE AS HEAVEN."

Two hours later Humphrey Clissold was at the gate of Penwyn Manor. The girl Elspeth admitted him. She had bound up her coarse black hair, which had been rough and wild as a mustang's mane when he last saw her, and wore a neat stuff-gown and a clean white muslin cap, instead of the picturesque half-gypsy costume she had worn on that former occasion. This at least was a concession to Mrs. Penwyn's tastes, and argued that even

Elspeth's impish nature had been at last brought under Madge's softening influence.

"Anything amiss with your grandmother?" asked Humphrey, surprised at not seeing that specimen of the Meg Merrilies tribe.

"Yes, sir, she's very ill."

"What is the matter with her?"

"Bilious fever," answered the girl, curtly, and Humphrey passed on. He had no leisure now to concern himself about Rebecca Mason, though he had in no wise forgotten those curious facts which made her presence at Penwyn Manor a mystery.

There were more dead leaves drifting about than on his last visit, and the advance of autumn had made itself obvious in decay which all the industry of gardeners could not conceal. The pine groves were strewn with fallen cones. The chestnuts were dropping their green balls, the chrysanthemums and China asters had a ragged look; the glory of the geranium tribe was over; and even those combinations of color which modern gardeners contrive from flowerless plants seemed to lose all glow and brightness under the dull gray sky. To Humphrey's mind, knowing that he was a messenger of trouble, the Manor-house had a gloomy look.

He asked to see the squire, and was ushered at once into the library, a large room which Churchill had built. It was lighted from the top by a large ground-glass dome, and was lined from floor to ceiling with bookcases of ebonized wood, relieved with narrow lines of gold. In each of the four angles stood a pedestal of dark green serpentine, surmounted by a marble bust—Dante, Shakespeare, Voltaire, Goethe, the four great representatives of European literature. A noble room, filled with noblest books. Such a room as a man, having made for himself, would love as if it were a sentient thing. These books, looking down upon him on every side, were as the souls of the mighty dead. Here, shut in from the outer world, he could never be companionless.

Churchill was seated at a table reading. He started up at Humphrey's entrance, and received him courteously, cordially even, so far as words may express cordiality, but with a sudden, troubled look, which did not escape Humphrey, transient as it was.

"Glad to see you here again, Clissold; but why didn't you go straight to the ladies? You'll find them in the hall. Most of our friends have left us, so you'll be quite an acquisition this dull weather."

"You are very good, but I regret to say that the business which brings me here to-day denies me the right to approach Mrs. Penwyn. I come as a harbinger of trouble."

Churchill's face whitened to the lips, and his thin nervous hand fastened with a tight grip upon the edge of the table against which he stood, as if he could scarcely have held himself erect without that support.

"How frightened he looks!" thought Humphrey. "Strange want of courage in a man of his type!"

"And pray what is the nature of your evil tidings?" Churchill

asked, recovering self-control. His resolute nature speedily
asserted itself. A faint tinge of color came back to his sunken
cheeks. His eyes lost their look of sudden horror, and assumed
a hard, defiant expression.

"This property—the Penwyn estate—is very dear to you, I
think?" interrogated Humphrey.

"It is as dear to me as a man's birthright should naturally be
to him, and it has been the happy home of my married life."
This with a touch of tenderness. In no moment of his existence, however troubled, could he speak of Madge without tenderness.

"Yet Penwyn can hardly be called your birthright, since you
inherit it by an accident," said Humphrey, nervously anxious to
take the edge off his unpleasant communication.

"What is the drift of these remarks, Mr. Clissold? They seem
to me most purposeless, and, pardon me if I add, somewhat impertinent."

"Mr. Penwyn, I am here to inform you that there is a member of your family in existence who possesses a prior claim to
this estate."

"You are dreaming, sir, or you are deceived by some impostor. I and my child are the sole representatives of the Penwyn
family."

"There are secrets in every family, Mr. Penwyn. There has
been a secret in your family, religiously kept for more than
twenty years, but lately brought to light, in some part by my
agency."

"What, sir, you have come into this house as a spy while you
have been secretly assailing my position as inheritor of my
cousin's estate?"

"I have not entered your house since I made the discovery I
am here to inform you of."

"Your discovery has come about with marvelous rapidity,
then, for it is not long since you were my guest."

"My discovery has been arrived at quickly."

"Pray acquaint me with the nature of this mare's nest."

"I have to inform you that your uncle, George Penwyn, before leaving England for the last time, privately married the
daughter of his father's tenant, Michael Trevanard, of Borcel
End."

Churchill Penwyn laughed contemptuously.

"I congratulate you upon having hit upon about the most
improbable story I ever heard of," he said. "My uncle, George
Penwyn, married to old Trevanard's daughter, and nobody upon
earth aware of the fact till you, a stranger, unearthed it? A
likely story, Mr. Clissold!"

"Likely or unlikely, it is true, and I have sufficient evidence
to prove it, or I should not have broached the subject to you. I
have in my possession a certified copy of the entry in the marriage
register at St. John's Church, Didmouth, Devonshire, and five
letters in your uncle's hand, acknowledging Muriel Trevanard as
his wife; also a sealed letter from the same, committing her to
the care of the late Mr. Tomlin, solicitor, of Seacomb, in the

event of her needing that gentleman's protection during her husband's absence. Nor do I rely upon documentary evidence alone. The Vicar of Didmouth, who married your uncle to Miss Trevanard, is still alive; and the principal witness of the marriage, Muriel's friend and confidant, is ready to support the claim of Muriel's daughter, should you force her to appeal to the law, instead of seeing, as I hope you will see, the advisability of an equitable compromise. Miss Penwyn has no desire to exact her legal rights. She has empowered me to suggest a fair and honorable alternative."

Humphrey proceeded to give a brief outline of Justina's case, and to suggest his own idea of an equitable settlement.

Churchill sat with folded arms, and gloomy face bent downward, listening. This story of Humphrey Clissold's seemed to him, so far, hardly worth serious thought. It was so wildly improbable, so like the dream of a fevered brain, that any claimant should come forward to dispute his hold of wealth and station. Yet he told himself that this Clissold was no fool, and would hardly talk of documentary evidence which he was unprepared to produce. On the other hand, this Clissold might be a villain, and the whole business a conspiracy.

"Let me see your copy of the register, sir," Churchill said, authoritatively.

Humphrey took a paper from his breast pocket and laid it on Mr. Penwyn's desk. Yes. It was formal enough.

"George Penwyn, gentleman, of Penwyn Manor, to Muriel Trevanard, daughter of Michael Trevanard, farmer, of Borcel End. The witnesses, Maria Barlow, spinster, school-mistress, of Seacomb, and James Pope, clerk, Didmouth." If this were a genuine copy of an existing entry, there would be no doubt as to the fact of George Penwyn's marriage.

Both gentlemen were too much engrossed at this moment—Churchill pondering the significance of the document in his hand, Humphrey watching his countenance as he meditated—to be aware of the opening of a door near the fireplace, a door which fitted into the book-case, and was masked with dummy books. This door was gently opened, a woman's face looked in for an instant, and was quickly withdrawn. But the door, although apparently closed, was not shut again.

"And you pretend that there was issue to this marriage?" said Churchill.

"The lady whose claim I am here to assert is the daughter of Mr. George Penwyn by that marriage."

"And pray where has this young lady been hiding herself all her life, and how is it that she has suffered her rights to be in abeyance all this time?"

"She was brought up in ignorance of her parentage."

"Oh! I understand," cried Churchill, scornfully. "Some Miss Jones or Smith who has taken it into her wise young head —inspired, doubtless, by some astute friend—that she may as well prove herself a Penwyn if she can. And you come to me with this liberal offer of a compromise, to take half my estate in the most off-hand way. Upon my word, Mr. Clissold, you and this scheme of yours are a little too absurd. I can't even allow myself to be angry with you. That would be taking the thing too seriously."

"Remember, Mr. Penwyn, if I leave this house without arriving at some kind of understanding with you, I shall place the matter in the hands of my lawyers without delay, and the law must take its course. However protracted or costly the process by which Miss Penwyn may obtain her rights, I have no doubt as to the ultimate issue. She would have been contented with half your fortune. The law, if it give her anything, will give her all."

"So be it. I will fight her to the bitter end. First and foremost, this marriage," bringing down his clinched fist upon the paper, and with an evil upward look at Humphrey, "is no marriage!"

"What do you mean?"

"A marriage with a person of unsound mind is no marriage; it is void in law. There is Blackstone to refer to if you doubt me," pointing to a set of volumes in dark brown Russia. "Now Muriel, the daughter of Michael Trevanard, has been deranged for the last twenty years. It is a notorious fact to everybody in the neighborhood."

"When that marriage took place, and for a year after the marriage, Muriel was as sane as you or I. Her brain was turned by the shock she experienced upon being informed suddenly of her husband's awful death. I can bring forward sufficient witnesses to prove the state of her mind up to that time."

"And you are prepared to prove that this young woman—this waif and stray, brought up without the knowledge of her name or parentage—is the legitimate daughter of my uncle, George Penwyn, and Muriel his wife! Go your ways, Mr. Clissold, and make the best use of your evidence, documentary and otherwise. I will stand by my rights against you, and would stand by them against a stronger cause than yours."

He touched a spring bell which stood on his desk—a summons answered with extreme promptitude.

"The door," said the squire, resuming his book without so much as a parting glance at his visitor.

Humphrey was conducted to the porch, and left the house without having seen Mrs. Penwyn or her sister. He was bitterly disappointed by the result of his morning's work, which had proved compromise impossible, and left no course open to him save the letter of the law.

* * * * * * *

Scarcely had the library door closed on Humphrey Clissold when the other door, which had been left ajar during the latter part of the interview, was quietly opened, and Madge Penwyn stole to her husband's side, and knelt down by him, and wound her arms around his neck. He had been sitting with his face buried in his hands, trying to think out his position, when he found her arms about him, his head drawn gently against her shoulder.

"Dearest, I have heard all," she said, quietly.

" You heard, Madge?" he exclaimed, with a startled look. " Well, my love, it matters very little. It is all the merest folly. There is no possibility of what this man threatens."

" Churchill—husband—my beloved," she began, with deepest feeling. " You do not mean to oppose this claim?"

" To the death."

" What? Surely you will accept the truth—if it is the truth —and surrender fortune, and estate. Oh, welcome change of fortune, love, that brings some measure of atonement. I have never told you how hateful, how horrible, all our wealth and luxury have been to me since I have known——"

" Hush, Madge! You know so much that you should know enough to be wise. Do you think I am going to surrender these things? Do you think I am the kind of man to sit down tamely and let a rogue hatch a conspiracy to rob me of wealth and status? They have cost me too dear."

" They have cost you so dear that you can never have joy or peace with them, Churchill. God shows us this way of getting rid of our burden. If you have any hope of mercy, any desire to be forgiven, resign this fortune. It is the price of iniquity. You can know no true repentance while you retain it. If I had seen any way of your surrendering this estate before now without exciting suspicion of the dreadful truth, I should have urged the sacrifice upon you. I urge it now with all the strength of my love."

" It is useless, Madge. I could not go back to poverty, laborious days and nights, the struggle for daily bread. I could not lead that kind of life again."

" Not with me, Churchill? We could go away to the other end of the world—to Australia, where life is simpler and easier than in England. We could know peace again; for you might dare to hope, if your sacrifice were freely made, that God had accepted it as an atonement."

" Can I atone to the dead? Will James Penwyn, in his untimely grave, be any better off because some impostor riots in the wealth that ought to have been his? A left-handed atonement that!"

" But if you find that this girl is no impostor?"

" The lawyers will have to decide that. If she can establish her right, you and I and our boy will have to say good-bye to Penwyn."

" Happy loss if it lighten the burden of your sin! Do you think that I shall be sorry to leave this place, Churchill? I have never known peace here since—— "

She threw herself upon his breast with a shuddering sigh.

" Madge, my dearest, my angel of love and compassion, be content to abide the issue of events. Leave all to me."

" No, Churchill," she answered, raising her head and looking at him with grave and earnest eyes, " I am not content. You know that since that bitter day I have left you in peace. I have not wearied you with my tears. I have suffered in secret, and have made it the chief duty of my life to lighten your burden so far as in me lay. But I can be content no longer. The wealth

that has weighed upon my soul can now be given up with honor.
The world can find no subject for slander in your quiet surrender of an estate for which a new claimant has arisen. And
we can begin life afresh together, love, your soul purified by
sacrifice, your conscience lightened, your peace made with God.
We can begin life anew in some distant land, humbly, toilfully;
so far away from all past cares that your wrong-doing may seem
no more than the memory of an evil dream, and all the future
open for manifold good deeds that shall weigh against that one
dreadful sin."

She seemed like an angel pleading with him for the salvation
of his soul, yet he resisted her.

"It is useless, Madge. You do not know what you are talking
about. I could not live a life of obscurity. It would be moral
suicide."

"Will you choose between me and fortune, Churchill?"

"What do you mean?"

"That unless you give up this estate you must give up me.
I will live here no longer, share your ill-gotten wealth no
longer!"

"Think of your boy."

"I do think of him. God forbid that my son should ever inherit Penwyn! There is the curse of blood upon every rood of
land. Let it pass into other hands—guiltless hands!"

"Give me time to think, Madge; you bewilder me by this sudden attack."

"Think as long as you like, dearest, only decide rightly at
last." And with one long kiss upon his pale forehead, she left
him.

Once alone, he set himself to think out his position, to face
this new aspect of things.

Could this alleged heiress, impostor or not, rob him of his estate? Was it possible for George Penwyn's marriage and the
identity of George Penwyn's child to be proved in a court of
law—proved so indisputably as to dislodge him from his position
as possessor of the estate?

"No," he told himself; "the strength will be all on my side.
The law does not encourage claimants of this stamp. If it did,
no man's estate would be secure, no real property would be
worth ten years' purchase."

He had taken a high tone with Humphrey Clissold, had affected to regard the whole matter as an absurdity; but now,
face to face with the facts that had been put before him, he felt
that the question was serious, and that he could not be too
prompt in action.

He looked at a railway time-table, and found that he would
have just time enough to catch the next train up from Seacomb
—a slowish train, not reaching London till late in the evening.

"I will go up to town and see Pergament," he said to himself,
as he touched the bell.

"Tell them to bring round the dog-cart at once. I shall want
Hunter."

"Any particular horse, sir?"

" Yes, Wallace."

Wallace was the fastest horse in the stable, always excepting the squire's favorite, Tarpan, which had never been degraded by harness.

While the dog-cart was being got ready, Churchill wrote two lines to his wife:

" MY DEAREST,—I am going to London to inquire into this business. Be calm, be brave, as befits my noble wife. Your own till death,　　　　　　　　　　　　　　C. P."

This brief note addressed and sealed, the squire went up stairs to his dressing-room, crammed a few things into his traveling-bag, and went down to the porch with the bag in his hand just as the dog-cart drove up—Wallace, a big, deep-chested bay, in admirable condition, fresh and eager for the start, the groom breathless, having dressed himself against time.

Churchill took the reins, and the light vehicle was soon spinning along that well-made road with which the Squire of Penwyn had improved his property. Less than an hour, and Mr. Penwyn was seated in a railway carriage on his way to London.

He was at Mr. Pergament's office early next morning; indeed, more than half an hour before the arrival of that gentleman, who came in at ten o'clock, fresh and sleek of aspect, with a late tea-rose bud in the button-hole of his glossy blue coat.

Great was the solicitor's astonishment at beholding Churchill.

" My dear Mr. Penwyn, this *is* a surprise. One does not expect to see a man of your standing in town in the dead season. Indeed, even I, a humble working bee in the great hive, have been thinking of getting as far as Aix-les-Bains or Spa. But you are not looking well. You look careworn and fagged."

" I have reason to look so,"' answered Churchill; and then explained the motive for his journey.

He told Mr. Pergament all that Clissold had told him, without reserve, with a wonderful precision and clearness. The lawyer listened intently, and with gravest concern.

But before he said a word in reply, Mr. Pergament unlocked a tin case inscribed " Penwyn Estate," took out a document, and read it from the first line to the last.

" What is that?" asked Churchill.

" A copy of your grandfather's will. I want to be quite sure how you stand as regards this claimant."

" Well?"

" I am sorry to say that the will is dead against you. If this person can be proved to be the daughter of George Penwyn, she would take the estate under your grandfather's will. There is no doubt of that."

" But how is she to prove her identity with the child said to be born at Borcel End, and whose birth was made such a secret?"

" Difficult, perhaps; but if she has been in the charge of the same people all her life, and those people are credible witnesses——"

" Credible witnesses!" cried Churchill, contemptuously. " The man who has brought up this girl belongs to the dregs of society.

and if by a little hard swearing he can foist this stray adoption of his upon society as the rightful owner of the Penwyn estate, do you suppose he will shrink from a little more or less perjury? Credible witnesses! No man's property in the land is secure if claimants such as this can arise ' to push us from our stools.'"

"This Mr. Clissold is a gentleman and a man of good family, is he not?"

"He belongs to decent people, I believe, but that is no reason why he should not be an adventurer. There are plenty of well-born adventurers in the world."

"No doubt, no doubt," replied Mr. Pergament, blandly. In his private capacity, as a Christian and a gentleman, he was benevolently sympathetic; but the idea of a contested estate was not altogether unpleasing to his professional mind.

"Who are Mr. Clissold's lawyers?"

Churchill named them.

"A highly respectable firm—old established—in every way reputable. I do not think they would take up a speculative case."

"I do not feel sure that they will take up this case, though Mr. Clissold appeared to think so," answered Churchill. "However, your business is to be prepared. Remember, I shall fight this to the bitter end. Let them prove the marriage if they can. It will be for our side to deny that there was ever any issue of that marriage."

"Humph!" mused the lawyer. "There, assuredly, lies the weakness of their case. Yes, we will fight, Mr. Penwyn. Pray keep your mind easy. I will get counsel's opinion without delay if you desire it, and I suppose in a case so nearly affecting your interests, you would prefer an unprejudiced opinion to being your own adviser. The best men shall be secured for our side."

"Which do you call the best men?"

Mr. Pergament named three of the most illustrious lights of the equity bar.

"Very good men in their own way, no doubt," said Churchill, "but I would rather have Shinebarr, Shandrish, and say, M'Stinger."

Mr. Pergament looked horrified.

"My dear sir, clever men, but unscrupulous—notoriously unscrupulous."

"My dear Pergament, when a gang of swindlers hatch a conspiracy to deprive me of house and home, I don't want my rights defended by scrupulous men."

"But, really, Shandrish—a man I never gave a brief to in my life!" remonstrated the solicitor.

"What does that signify? It is my battle we have to fight, and you must let me choose my weapons."

CHAPTER LV.
"ENID, THE PILOT STAR OF MY LONE LIFE."

HAVING seen the chief representative of Pergament & Pergament, placed his interests in the hands of that respectable house, and chosen the advocates who were to defend his cause, should this pretended cousin of his dare to assert her rights in a court of law, Churchill Penwyn felt himself free to go back to Cornwall by the midday train. He had an uneasy feeling in being away from home at this juncture—a vague sense of impending peril on all sides—a passionate desire to be near his wife and child.

He had ample time for thought during that long journey westward; time to contemplate his position in all its bearings, to wonder whether his wisdom might not, after all, be folly beside Madge's clear-sighted sense of right.

"She spoke the bitter truth," he thought. "Wealth and estate have not brought me happiness. They have gratified my self-esteem, satisfied my ambition, but they have not given me restful nights or peaceful dreams. Would it be better for me to please Madge, throw up the sponge, and go to the other end of the world, to begin life afresh, far, even, from the memory of the past?"

"No," he told himself, after a pause. "There is no new life for me. I am too old for beginning again."

He thought of his triumphs of last session, those bursts of fervid eloquence which had startled the House into the admission that a new orator had arisen, as when the younger Pitt first demonstrated to the doubtful senate that he was a worthy son of the great commoner.

He was just at the beginning of a brilliant parliamentary career, and with him ambition was an all-powerful passion. To let these things go, even for Madge's sake, would be too great a sacrifice. And his boy—was he to bequeath nothing to that beloved son, neither fortune nor name?

"I could more easily surrender Penwyn than my chances of personal distinction," he said to himself.

It was nine o'clock in the evening when he arrived at Seacomb. He had telegraphed for his groom to meet him with the dog-cart; and as the train steamed slowly into the station he saw the lamps of that well-appointed vehicle shining across the low rail which divided the platform from the road. A dark night for a drive by that wild moorland way.

"Shall I drive, sir?" asked the groom.

"No," Churchill answered, shortly; and the next minute they were flying through the darkness, the light vehicle swaying from side to side on the stony road.

"It would be a short cut out of all my difficulties if I were to come to grief somewhere between this and the Manor-house," thought Churchill. "A sudden fall upon a heap of stones, a splintered skull, an inquest, and all over. Poor Madge! It would be bad for her, but a relief, perhaps—who can tell? She has owned that her life has been bitterness since that fatal day. Her very love for me is a kind of martyrdom. Poor Madge! If it were not a cowardly thing to give up all at the first alarm, I verily believe I could bring myself to turn my back upon Penwyn Manor, and take my wife and child out to Sydney, and try my luck as a barrister in a colonial court. For her sake—for her sake! Would not the humblest life be happiness with her?"

Things seemed to take a new shape to him during that swift homeward drive. He passed the shadowy plantations—the trees of his planting—bowled smoothly along the well-made road that crossed his own estate, and thought with a curious wonder how little actual happiness his possessions had given him—how small a matter it would be, after all, to lose them.

The lighted windows of the north lodge shone out upon him as he mounted the crest of the last hill, and saw Manor-house and gardens, pine groves and shrubberies, before him.

"Mrs. Mason is keeping later hours than usual, isn't she?" he asked.

"She's very ill, sir—at death's door, they do say," answered the groom; "but that queer young granddaughter of hers has kept it dark as long as she could, on account of the drink being at the bottom of it—begging your pardon, sir."

"Do you mean that Mason drinks?"

"Well, yes, sir, on the quiet: I believe she have always been inclined that way. Excuse me for mentioning it, sir; but, you see, a master is always the last to hear of these things."

They were at the gates by this time. Elspeth came out of the lodge as they drove up.

"Take the dog-cart round to the stables. Hunter," said Churchill, alighting. "I am going in to see Mrs. Mason."

"Oh, sir, your dear lady is here—with grandmother," said Elspeth.

"My wife?"

"Yes, sir. She came down this afternoon, hearing grandmother was so bad. And Mrs. Penwyn wouldn't have any one else to nurse her, though she's been raving and going on awful."

Churchill answered not a word, but snatched the candle from the girl's hand, and went up the narrow staircase. A wild, hoarse scream told him where the sick woman was lying. He opened the door, and there, in a close room, whose fever-tainted atmosphere seemed stifling and poisonous after the fresh night air, he saw his wife kneeling by a narrow iron bedstead, holding the gypsy's bony frame in her arms. He flung open the casement as wide as it would go. The cold night breeze rushed into the little room, almost extinguishing the candle.

"Madge, are you mad? Do you know the danger of being in this fever-poisoned room?"

"I know that there would have been danger for you had I not been here, Churchill," his wife answered, gently. "I have been able to keep others out, which nothing less than my influence would have done. Half the gossips of Penwyn village would have been round this wretched creature's bed but for me. And her ravings have been dreadful," with a shudder.

" What has she talked about ?"

" All that happened—at Eborsham—that night. She has forgotten no detail. Again and again, again and again, she has repeated the same words. But Mr. Price says she cannot last many hours—life is ebbing fast."

" Did Price hear her raving ?"

" Not much. She was quieter while he was here, and I was trying to engage his attention, to prevent his taking much notice of her wild talk."

" Oh, Madge, Madge, what have you not borne for me ? And now you expose yourself to the risk of typhoid fever for my sake.

" There is no risk of typhoid. This poor creature is dying of delirium tremens. Mr. Price assured me. She has lived on brandy for ever so long, and brain and body are alike exhausted."

A wild scream broke from Rebecca's pale lips, and then, with an awful distinctness, Churchill heard her tell the story of his crime.

" Drunk, was I," cried the gypsy, with a wild laugh. " Not so drunk but I could see—not so drunk but I could hear. I heard him fire the shot. I saw him creep out from behind the hedge. I saw him wipe his blood-stained hands, and I have the handkerchief still. It's worth more to me than a love-token— it's helped me to a comfortable home. Brandy—give me some brandy; my throat is like a limekiln!"

Madge took a glass of weak brandy-and-water from the table, and held it to the tremulous lips. The gypsy drank eagerly but frowningly, and then struggled to free herself from Madge Penwyn's hands.

" Let me get the bottle," she gasped. " I don't want the cat-lap you give me."

" Let me hold her," said Churchill. " Go home, dearest; I will stop to the end."

" No, Churchill; you would be less patient than I. And if you nursed her it would set people talking, while it is only natural for me to be with her."

Elspeth opened the door a little way and peeped in, asking if she could be useful.

" No, Elspeth, there is nothing for you to do. I have done all Mr. Price directed. Go to bed, child, and sleep if you can. There is nothing more to be done."

" And she'll die before the night is out, perhaps." said the girl, with a horror-stricken look at the emaciated figure on the bed. " Mr. Price told me there was no hope."

" You should not have let her drink so much, Elspeth," said Madge, gently.

" How could I help it? If I'd refused to fetch her the brandy, she'd have turned me out of doors and I should have had to go on the tramp, and I'd got used to sleeping in a house, and having my victuals regular. I daren't refuse to do anything she asked me for fear of the strap. She wouldn't hesitate about laying on to me."

"Poor unhappy child. There, go to your room and lie down. I will take care of you henceforward, Elspeth."

The girl said not a word, but came gently into the room, and kneeled down by Mrs. Penwyn, and took up the hem of her dress and kissed it, an almost Oriental expression of gratitude and submission.

"I've heard tell about angels, but I never believed in 'em till I came to know you," she said, tearfully, and then left the room.

Rebecca had sunk back upon the pillow exhausted. Madge sat beside her, prepared for the next interval of delirium. Churchill stood by the window looking out at the pine grove and the dark sea behind.

And thus the night wore on, and at daybreak, just when the slate-colored sea looked coldest, and the east wind blew sharp and chill, and the shrill cry of chanticleer rang loud from the distant farmyard, Rebecca Mason's troubled spirit passed to the land of rest, and Churchill Penwyn knew that the one voice which could denounce him was silenced forever.

Before breath had departed from that wasted frame the squire had examined all boxes and drawers in the room—they were not many—lest any record of his secret should lurk among the gypsy's few possessions. He had gone down-stairs to the sitting-room for the same purpose, and had found nothing. Afterward, when all was over, he found a little bundle rolled up in a worn and greasy bird's-eye neckerchief under the dead woman's pillow. It contained a few odd coins and the handkerchief with which James Penwyn's murderer had wiped his ensanguined hand. All Churchill's influence had been too little to extort this hideous memento from the gypsy while life remained to her. Madge was kneeling by the open window, her face hidden, absorbed in silent prayer, when her husband discovered this hoarded treasure. He took it down to the room below, thrust it among the smoldering ashes of the wood fire, watched it burn to a gray scrap of tinder which fluttered away from the hearth.

A little after daybreak Elspeth was up and dressed, and had sped off to the village in search of a friendly gossip who was wont to perform the last offices for poor humanity. To this woman Madge resigned her charge.

"Lord bless you, ma'am," said the village dame, lost in admiration, "to think that a sweet young creature like you should leave your beautiful home to nurse a poor old woman."

Madge and her husband went home in the cold autumn dawn —grave and silent both—with faces that looked wan and worn in the clear, gray light. Some of the household had sat up all night; Churchill's body servant, Mrs. Penwyn's maid, and an underling to wait upon those important personages.

"There is a fire in your dressing-room, ma'am," said the maid. "Shall I get you tea or coffee?"

"You can bring me some tea, presently." And to the dressing-room Mr. and Mrs. Penwyn went.

"Madge," said Churchill, when the maid had brought the tea-tray and been told she would be rung for when her services were required, and husband and wife were alone together, "if I had needed to be assured of your devotion, to-night would have proved it to me.   But I had no need of such assurance, and to-night is but one more act of self-sacrificing love—one more bond between us.   It shall be as you wish, dearest.   I will resign fortune and status, and lead the life you bid me lead.   If I sinned for your sake—and I at least believed that I so sinned— I will repent for your sake, and whatever atonement there may be in the sacrifice of this estate, it shall be made."

"Churchill, my own true husband!"

She was on her knees by his side, her head lying against his breast, her eyes looking up at him with love unspeakable.

"Will this sacrifice set your heart at rest, Madge?"

"It will, dear love, for I believe that Heaven will accept your atonement."

"Remember, it is my option, however strong those people's case may be, to compromise matters.   To retain the estate, and only surrender half the income; to hold my place in the county; to be to all effects and purposes Squire of Penwyn; to have the estate and something over three thousand a year to live upon. That course is left open to me.   These people will take half our fortune and be content.   If I surrender what they are willing to leave me, it is tantamount to throwing three thousand a year into the gutter.   Shall I do that, Madge?"

"If you wish me to know rest and peace, love.   I can know neither while we retain one sixpence of James Penwyn's money."

"It shall be done, then, my dearest.   But remember that in making this sacrifice, you perhaps doom your son to a life of poverty.   And poverty is bitter, Madge; we have both felt its sting."

"Providence will take care of my son."

"So be it, Madge.   You have chosen."

She put her arm round his neck and kissed him.

"My dearest, now I am sure that you love me," she said, gently.

"Madge, you are shivering.   The morning air has chilled you," exclaimed her husband, anxiously.   And then turning her face toward him, he looked at her long and earnestly.

The vivid morning light, clear and cold, showed him every line in that expressive face.   He scrutinized it with sharpest pain.   Never till this moment had he been fully aware of the change which secret anguish had wrought in his wife's beauty, the gradual decay which had been going on before his eyes, unobserved in the preoccupation of his mind.

"My love, how ill you are looking!" he said, anxiously.

"I am not ill, Churchill.   I have been unhappy, but that is all past now.   That woman's presence at our gates was a perpetual horror to me.   She is gone, and I seem to breathe more freely; and this sacrifice of yours will bring peace to us both. I feel assured of that.   In a new world, among new faces, we shall forget, and God will be good to us.   He will forgive——"

A burst of hysterical sobs interrupted her words, and for once in her life Madge Penwyn lost all power of self-control. Her weakness did not last long. Before Churchill could summon her maid his wife had recovered herself, and smiled at him, even, with a pale wan smile.

"I am a little tired, dear, that is all. I will go to bed for an hour or two."

"Rest as long as you can, dear. I will write to Pergament while you are sleeping and ask him to make immediate arrangements for our voyage to Sydney. That Wilson seems a faithful girl," speaking of his wife's maid; "she might go with us as Nugent's nurse."

"No, dear. I shall take no nurse. I am quite able to wait upon my pet. We must begin life in a very humble way, and I am not going to burden you with a servant."

"It shall be as you please, dear. Perhaps after all I may not do so badly in the new country. I shall take my parliamentary reputation as a recommendation."

Madge left him. She looked white and weak as some pale flower that had been beaten down by wind and rain. Churchill went to his dressing-room, refreshed his energies with a shower-bath, dressed in his usual careful style, and went down to the dining-room at the sound of the breakfast-bell. Viola was there when he entered, playing with Nugent, which small personage was the unfailing resource of the ladies of the household in all intervals of *ennui.*

The little fellow screamed with delight at sight of his father. Churchill took him in his arms, and kissed him fondly, while Viola rang for the nurse.

"Good-morning, Churchill. I did not know you had come back. What a rapid piece of business your London expedition must have been."

"Yes, I did not care about wasting much time. What were you doing yesterday, Viola?"

"I spent the day with the Vyvyans, at the hall. They had a wind-up croquet match. It was great fun."

"And you were not home till late, I suppose?"

"Not so very late. It was only half-past nine o'clock, but Madge had retired. What makes her so late this morning?"

Viola evidently knew nothing of her sister's visit to the lodge.

"She was engaged in a work of charity last night, and is worn out with fatigue."

He told Viola how Madge had nursed the dying woman.

"That woman she disliked so much! Was there ever such a noble heart as my sister's?" cried Viola.

The form of breakfast gone through, and appearances thus maintained, Churchill went up to his dressing-room, where he had a neat, business-like oak Davenport, and a small iron safe let into the wall, in which he kept his banker's book and all important papers.

He had been spending very nearly up to his income during his reign at Penwyn. His improvements had absorbed a good deal of money, and he had spared nothing that would embellish or substantially improve the estate. The half year's rents had not long been got in, however, and he had a balance of over two thousand pounds at his banker's. This, which he could draw out at once, would make a decent beginning for his new life. His wife's jewels were worth at least two thousand more, exclusive of those gems which he had inherited under the old squire's will, and which would naturally be transferred with the estate. It was a hard thing for Churchill to write to Mr. Pergament, formally surrendering the estate, and leaving it to the lawyer to investigate the claim of Justina Penwyn, *alias* Elgood, and, if that claim were a just one, to effect the transfer of the property to that lady, without any litigation whatsoever.

"Pergament will think me mad," he said to himself, as he signed this letter. ",However, I have kept my promise to Madge. My poor girl! I did not know till I looked in her face this morning what hard lines the stylus of care had engraven there."

He wrote a second letter to his bankers, directing them to invest sixteen hundred in Grand Trunk of Canada First Preference Bonds, a security of which the interest was not always immediately to be relied upon, but which could be realized without trouble at any moment. He told them to send him four hundred in ten, twenty, and fifty pound notes.

His third letter was to the agents of a famous Australian line, telling them to reserve a state cabin for himself and wife in the Merlin, which was to sail in a week, and inclosing a check for fifty pounds on account of the passage-money.

"I have left no time for repentance or change of plans," he said to himself.

His letters dispatched by the messenger who was wont to carry the post-bag to Penwyn village, Churchill went to his wife's room. The blinds were closely drawn, shutting out the sunlight. Madge was sleeping soundly but heavily, and the anxious husband fancied that her breathing was more labored than usual.

He went down-stairs and out to the stables, where he told Hunter, the groom, to put Wallace in the dog-cart and drive over to Seacomb to fetch Dr. Hillyard, the most distinguished medical man in that quiet little town.

"Wallace is not so fresh as he might be, sir; you drove him rather fast last night."

"Take Tarpan, then."

This was a wonderful concession on the squire's part. But Tarpan was the fastest horse in the stable, and Churchill was nervously anxious for the coming of the doctor. That heavy breathing might mean nothing, or it might—— He dared not think of coming ill—now—when he had built his life on new lines—content to accept a future shorn of all that glorifies life in the minds of worldlings, so that he kept Madge, and Madge's fond and faithful heart.

Tarpan was brought out, a fine upstanding horse, as Hunter called him, head and neck full of power, eye a trifle more fiery than a timid horseman might have cared to see it.

" He's likely to go rather wild in harness, isn't he, sir?" asked Hunter, contemplating the bay dubiously.

" Not if you know how to drive," answered the squire. " The man I bought him from used to drive him tandem. Ask Dr. Hillyard to come back with you at once. You can say that I am anxious about Mrs. Penwyn."

" Yes, sir. Very sorry to hear your lady is not well, sir. Nothing serious, I hope."

" I hope not, but you can tell Dr. Hillyard I am anxious!"

" Yes, sir."

Churchill saw the man drive away, the bright harness and Tarpan's shining coat glancing gayly between the pine trees as the dog-cart spun along the avenue, and then went back to his wife's room and sat by the bedside, and never left his post till Dr. Hillyard arrived, three hours later. Madge had slept all the time, but still with that heavy, labored breathing which had alarmed her husband.

Dr. Hillyard came quietly into the room, a small, gray-headed old man whose opinion had weight in Seacomb and for twenty miles round. He sat by the bed, felt the patient's wrist, lifted the heavy eye-lids, prolonged his examination, with a serious aspect.

" There has been mental disturbance, has there not?" he asked.

" My wife has been anxious and over-fatigued, I fear, attending a dying servant."

" There is a good deal of fever. I fear the attack may be somewhat serious. You must get an experienced nurse without delay. It will be a case for good nursing. I don't want to alarm you needlessly," added the doctor, seeing Churchill's ghastly pallor. " Mrs. Penwyn's youth and fine constitution are strong points in our favor; but from indications I perceive, I imagine that her health must have been impaired for some time past. There has been a gradual decay. An attack so sudden as this of to-day would not account for the care-worn look of the countenance or for this attenuation "—gently raising the sleeper's arm, from which the cambric sleeve had fallen back, the wasted wrist, which Churchill remembered so round and plump.

" Tell me the truth," said Churchill, in accents strangely unlike his customary clear and measured tones. " You think there is danger?"

" There is always some danger in a case of this kind."

" What is the matter with my wife?"

" I fear it is the beginning of brain-fever."

CHAPTER LVI.

" FOR ALL IS DARK WHERE THOU ART NOT."

BEFORE the week was out Muriel was so far recovered as to be able to bear a long journey, and so tranquil as to render that journey possible. Her couch had been wheeled into a corner of the family sitting-room—she had been brought back into the household life, and her father had devoted himself to her with a quiet tenderness which went far to soothe her troubled mind.

The old hallucinations still remained. She spoke of George Penwyn as living and she could not be brought to understand that the child who had been taken from her an infant was now a woman. She had little memory—no thought of the past or of the future—but she clung to her father affectionately, and was grateful for his love.

Humphrey had made all arrangements for Muriel's journey before leaving Cornwall, after his interview with Churchill. It had been settled that Martin should bring his sister to the neighborhood of London, accompanied by Phœbe, as her attendant. This Phœbe was a bright, active girl, quite able to manage Muriel. Humphrey was to find pleasant apartments in the suburbs, where Muriel might be comfortably lodged. In less than twenty-four hours after his departure from Borcel he had telegraphed Martin to the effect that he had found pleasant lodgings in a house between Kentish Town and Highgate, where there was a good garden.

Three days later Muriel came to take possession of them, worn out with the long journey, but very tranquil. Her daughter was waiting to receive her on the threshold of this new home.

Very sad, very strange was that meeting. The mother could not be made to comprehend that this noble-looking girl who held her in her arms, and sustained her feeble steps, was verily the child she had been robbed of years ago. Her darling was to her mind still an infant. If they had placed some feeble wailing babe in her arms and called it hers, she would have believed them, and hugged the impostor to her breast and been happy; but she did not believe in Justina.

"You are very kind to me," she said, gently, "and I like you; but it is foolish of them to say you are my child. I am a little wrong in my head, I know, but not so silly as to believe that."

On one occasion she was suddenly struck by Justina's likeness to her father.

"You are like George," she said. "Are you his sister?"

Humphrey brought a famous doctor from Cavendish Square, one of the kindest of men, to see Muriel. He talked to her for some time, inquired into the history of her malady, and considered her attentively. His verdict was that her case was hopeless.

"I do not fear that ever she will be otherwise than gentle," he said. "nor do I recommend any more restraint than she has been accustomed to; but I have no hope of cure. The shock which broke her heart shattered her mind forever."

Justina heard this with deepest sorrow. All that filial love could offer to this gentle sufferer she freely gave, devoting her days to her mother, while her nights were given to the public. None could have guessed how the brilliant actress—all sparkle and vivacity, living in the character her art had created—spent the quiet hours of her daily life. But she had Humphrey always near her, and his presence brightened every hour.

He had laid his case before his lawyers, and even the cautious

family solicitor had been compelled to own that it was not altogether a bad case. What was his astonishment, however,
when, three days later, he was told that Messrs. Pergament &
Pergament had met his solicitors, examined documents, discussed
the merits of Justina's claim, and finally pronounced their client's
willingness to surrender the estate, in its entirety, without litigation.

" But I told Mr. Penwyn of his cousin's willingness to accept
a compromise, to take half the value of the estate, and leave him
in possession of the land," said Humphrey.

" Mr. Penwyn elects to surrender the estate altogether. An
eccentric gentleman, evidently."

" Then the whole business is settled—there will be no lawsuit?"

" Apparently not," said the solicitor, dryly. Lawyers could
hardly live if people were in the habit of surrendering their possessions so quickly.

Humphrey called on Messrs. Pergament & Pergament, and
explained to the head of that firm that the young lady for whom
he was acting had no desire to exact her full claim under Squire
Penwyn's will; that she would prefer a compromise to depriving
Mr. Penwyn and his wife of house and home.

" Very generous, very proper," replied Mr. Pergament. " I
will communicate that desire to my client."

Justina was horrified at the idea of Churchill Penwyn's re-
nunciation. All her old distrust of him vanished out of her
mind; she thought of him as generous, disinterested; abandoning estate and position from an exalted sense of justice.

" But it is no justice," she argued, " though it may be right according to my grandfather's will. It is not just that the child
of the elder born should take all. Humphrey, you must make
some one explain my wishes to Mr. Penwyn. I will not rob
him and his wife of house and means. I cannot have such a sin
upon my head."

" My dearest, I fully explained your views to Mr. Penwyn.
He treated me with scornful indifference, and declared that he
would fight for his rights to the last. He has chosen to see
things in a new light since then. His line of conduct is beyond
my comprehension."

" There must be some mistake, some misapprehension on his
part. You must see him again, Humphrey, for my sake."

" My dear love, I would not mind oscillating between London
and Penwyn Manor for the next six weeks if my so doing could
in the smallest degree enhance your happiness, but I do not believe I can make your views any clearer to Mr. Penwyn than I
made them at our last interview."

" My dear Justina," interposed Mr. Elgood, pompously, " the
estate is yours, and why should you hesitate to take possession
of it? Think of the proud position you will hold in the county;
your brilliant table, at which the humble comedian may occupy
his unobtrusive corner. And I think," he added, with a con-
ciliatory glance at Humphrey, " there is some consideration due
to your future husband in this matter."

"Her future husband would be as well pleased to take her without a shilling as with Penwyn Manor," said Humphrey, with his arm round Justina.

"Of course, my dear boy,

> "'Love is not love
> When it is mingled with respect that stands
> Aloof from the entire point.'

Shakespeare. You would take your Cordelia without a rood of her fathers kingdom; but that is no reason why she should not have all she can get. And if this Mr. Churchill Penwyn chooses to be Quixotic, let him have his way."

"I will write to him," said Justina. "I am his kinswoman, and I will write to him from my heart, as cousin to cousin. He shall not be reduced to beggary because my grandfather's will gave me power to claim his estate. God's right and man's right are wide apart."

CHAPTER LVII.
"BUT IN SOMEWISE ALL THINGS WEAR ROUND BETIMES."

FOR fifteen days and nights Churchill Penwyn watched beside his wife's bed, with but such brief intervals of rest as exhausted nature demanded—an occasional hour, when prostrate on a sofa, he allowed himself to fall into a troubled slumber, from which he would start into sudden wakefulness unrefreshed, but with no power to sleep longer. Even in sleep he did not lose consciousness. One awful idea forever pursued him, the expectation of an inevitable end. She, for whom he could have been content to sacrifice all that earth can give of fame or fortune—she with whom it would have been sweet to him to begin a life of care and toil, his idolized wife—was to be taken from him.

London physicians had been summoned, two of the greatest. There had been solemn consultations in Madge's pretty dressing-room, the room where she had been so utterly happy in the first bright years of her wedded life; and after each council of medical authorities Churchill had gone in to hear their verdict, gravely, vaguely delivered—a verdict which left him at sea, tempest-tossed by the alternate waves of hope and fear.

There had come one awful morning, after a fortnight's uncertainty, when the great London physician and Dr. Hillyard received him in absolute silence. The little gray-haired Seacomb doctor turned away his face, and shuffled over to the window; the London physician grasped Churchill's hand without a word.

"I understand you," said Churchill. "All is over."

His calm tone surprised the two medical men, but the man of wider experience was not deceived by it. He had seen that quiet manner, heard that cold expressionless tone too often before.

"All has been done that could be done," he said, kindly. "It may be a comfort for you to remember that in days to come, however little it lessens your loss now."

"Comfort!" echoed Churchill, drearily. "There is no comfort for me without her. I thank you for having done your uttermost, Dr. Woolcomb, and you too, Dr. Hillyard. I will go back to her."

He left them without another word, and returned to the darkened room where Madge Penwyn's brief life was drifting fast to its untimely close under the despairing eyes of her sister Viola, who from first to last had shared Churchill's watch.

But seldom had either of those two won a recognizing glance from those clouded eyes, a word of greeting from those parched lips. Only in delirium had Madge called her husband by his name, but in all her wanderings his name was ever on her lips, her broken thoughts were of him.

At the last, some hours after the doctors had spoken their final sentence and departed, those tender eyes were raised to Churchill's face with one long, penetrating look, love ineffable in death. The wasted arms were feebly raised. He understood the unexpressed desire, and drew them gently round his neck. The lovely head sank upon his breast, the lips parted in a happy smile, and with one long sigh of contentment, bade farewell to earthly care.

Tearless, and with his calm every-day manner, Churchill Penwyn made all arrangements for his wife's funeral. The smallest details were not too insignificant for his attention. He opened all letters of condolence, arranged who, of the many who had loved his wife, should be permitted to accompany her in that last solemn journey. He chose the grave where she was to lie—not in the stony vault of the Penwyns, but on the sunny slope of the hill, where summer breezes and summer birds should flit across her grave, and all the varying lights and colors of sky and cloud glorify and adorn it. Yet, in those few solemn days between death and burial, he contrived to spend the greater part of his time near that beloved clay. His only rest, or pretense of rest, was taken on a sofa in his wife's dressing-room, adjoining the spacious chamber, where, amidst whitest draperies, strewn with late roses and autumn violets, lay that marble form.

In the dead of night he spent long hours alone in that taper-lit death-chamber, kneeling beside the snowy bed—kneeling, and holding such commune as he might with that dear spirit hovering near him, and wondering dimly whether the dreams of philosophers, the pious hope of Christians, were true, and there were verily a world where they two might see and know each other again.

Sir Nugent Bellingham had been telegraphed to at divers places, but having wandered into inaccessible regions on the borders of Hungary to shoot big game with a Hungarian noble of vast wealth and almost regal surroundings, the only message that reached him had arrived on the very day of his daughter's death. He came to Penwyn Manor, after traveling with all possible speed, in time for the funeral, altogether broken down by the shock which greeted him on his arrival. It had been a pleasant thing for him to lapse back into his old easy-going bachelor life—to feel himself a young man again—when his two daughters were safely provided for; but it was not the less a grief to lose the noble girl he had been at once proud and fond of.

The funeral train was longer than Churchill had planned, for his arrangements had included only the elect of the neighborhood. All the poor whom Madge had cared for—strong men and matrons, feeble old men and women, and little children—came to swell the ranks of her mourners, dressed in rusty black, decent, tearful, reverent as at the shrine of a saint.

"We have lost a friend such as we never had before and shall never see again." That was the cry which went up from Penwyn village, and many a hamlet far afield, whither Madge's bounty had penetrated, where the sound of her carriage wheels had been the harbinger of joy.

Churchill had a strange pleasure, so near akin to sharpest pain, as he stood in his place by the open grave on a sunless autumn morning, and saw the churchyard filled with that mournful crowd. She was honored and beloved. It was something to have won this for her—for her who had died for love of him. Yes, of that he had no doubt. His own sin had slain her. Care for him, remorse for his crime, had snapped that young life.

A curious smile, cool as winter, flitted across Churchill's face as he turned away from the grave, after dropping a shower of violets on the coffin. Some among the crowd noticed that faint smile, and wondered at it.

"Before another week has come I shall be lying in my darling's grave."

That was what the smile meant.

When he went back to the Manor-house, Viola, deeply compassionating his quiet grief, brought his son to him, thinking there might be some consolation in the little one's love. Churchill kissed the boy gently, but somewhat coldly, and gave him back to his aunt.

"My dear," he said, "you meant kindly by bringing him to me, but it only pains me to see him."

"Dear Churchill, I understand," answered Viola, pityingly, "but it will be different by and by."

"Yes," said Churchill, with that wintry smile, "it will be different by and by."

He had received Justina's letter—a noble letter, assuring him of her unwillingness to impoverish him, or to lessen his position as lord of the manor.

"Give me any share of your fortune which you think right and just," she wrote. "I have no desire for wealth or social importance. The duties of a large estate would be a burden to me; give me just sufficient to secure an independent future for myself and the gentleman who is to be my husband, and keep all the rest."

Churchill re-read this letter to-day, calmly, deliberately. It had reached him at a time when Madge's life still trembled in the balance, when there was still hope in his heart. He had not been able to give the letter a thought. To-day he answered it. He wrote briefly but firmly:

" Your letter convinces me that you are good and generous," he began, " and though I ask and can accept nothing for myself, it emboldens me to commit the future of my only son to your care. I surrender Penwyn Manor to you freely. Be as generous as you choose to my boy. He is the last male representative of the family to which you claim to belong, and he has good blood on both sides. Give him the portion of a younger son if you like, but give him enough to secure him the status of a gentleman. His grandfather. Sir Nugent Bellingham, and his aunt, Miss Bellingham, will be his natural guardians."

This was all. It was growing dusk as Churchill sealed this letter in its black bordered envelope—soft gray autumn dusk. He went down to the hall, put the letter in the post-bag, and went out into the shrubbery which screened the stables from the house.

There had been gentle showers in the afternoon, and arbutus and laurel were shining with rain-drops. The balmy odor of the pines perfumed the cool evening air. Those showers had fallen upon her grave, he thought—that grave which should soon be re-opened.

He opened a little gate leading into the stable-yard. The place had a deserted look. The men were all in the house eating and drinking, and taking their dismal enjoyment out of this time of mourning. No one expected horses or carriages to be wanted on the day of a funeral. A solitary underling was lolling across the half-door of the harness-room, smoking the pipe of discontent. He recognized Churchill and came over to him.

" Shall I call Hunter, sir ?"

" No, I want to get a mouthful of fresh air on the moor, that's all. You can saddle Tarpan."

A gallop across the moor was known to be the squire's favorite recreation, as Tarpan was his favorite steed.

" He's very fresh, sir. You haven't ridden him for a good bit, you see, sir," remonstrated the underling, apologetically.

" I don't think he'll be too fresh for me. He has been exercised, I suppose."

" Oh, yes, sir," replied the underling, sacrificing his love of truth to his fidelity as a subordinate.

" You can saddle him, then. You know my saddle ?"

" Yes, sir. There's the label hangs over it."

Churchill went into the harness-room, and while the man was bringing out Tarpan, put on a pair of hunting spurs, an unnecessary proceeding, it would seem, with such a horse as Tarpan, which was more prone to need a heavy hand on the curb than the stimulus of the spur. The bay came out of his loose box looking slightly mischievous, ears vibrating, head restless, and a disposition to take objection to the pavement of the yard, made manifest by his legs. The squire paid no attention to these small indications of temper, but swung himself into the saddle and

rode out of the yard, after divers attempts on Tarpan's side to
back into one of the coach-houses, or do himself a mischief
against the pump.

"I never see such a beast for trying to spile his money value,"
mused the underling when horse and rider had vanished from
his ken. "He seems as if he'd take a spiteful pleasure in laming
hisself, or taking the bark off to the tune of a pony."

Away over the broad free stretch of the gray moorland rode
Churchill Penwyn. There had been plenty of rain of late, and
the short turf was soft and springy. The horse's rapture burst
forth in a series of joyful snorts as he felt the fresh breeze from
the broad salt sea, and stretched his strong limbs to a thundering gallop.

Past the trees that he had planted, far away from the roads
that he had made, went the squire of Penwyn up to the open
moorland above the sea, the wide gray waters facing him with
their fringe of surf, the darkening evening sky above him, and
just one narrow line of palest saffron yonder where the sun had
gone down.

Even at that wild pace, earth and sea flying past him like the
shadows of a magic lantern, Churchill Penwyn had time for
thought.

He surveyed his life, and wondered what he would have made
of it had he been wiser. Yes, for the crime by which he had
leaped at once into possession of his heart's desires seemed to
him now an act of folly, like one of those moves at chess which,
lightly considered, point the way to speedy triumph, and whereby
the rash player wrecks his game.

He had won wife, fortune, position, and lo! in little more
than two years the knowledge of his crime had slain that idolized wife, and an undreamed-of claimant had arisen to dispute
his fortune.

The things he had grasped at were shadows, and like shadows had departed.

"After all," he said to himself, summing up the experience
of his days, "a man has but one power over his destiny—
power to make an end of the struggle at his own time."

He had ridden within a few yards of the cliff. His horse
turned and pulled landward desperately, as if not relishing the
position.

"Very well, Tarpan, we'll have another stretch upon the
turf."

Another gallop, wilder than the last, across the undulating
moor, a sudden turn seaward again, and a plunge of the spurs
deep into the quivering sides, and Tarpan is thundering over the
turf like a mad thing, heedless where he goes, unconscious of
the precipice before him, the rough rock-bound shore below,
the wild breath of the air that meets his own panting breath
and almost strangles him. He flies like a creature possessed
of devils, furiously as those swine that were driven down into
the sea.

Sir Nugent Bellingham waited dinner for his son-in-law,
sorely indifferent whether he ate or fasted, but making a feeble

show of customary hours and household observances. Eight
o'clock, nine o'clock, ten o'clock, and no sign of Churchill
Penwyn. Sir Nugent went up to Viola's room. It was empty,
but he found his daughter in the room which had so lately
been tenanted by the dead, found her weeping upon the pillow
where that pale, still face had lain.

"My dear, it is so wrong of you to give way like this."

A stifled sob, and a kiss upon the father's trembling lips.

"Dear papa, you can never know how I loved her."

"Every one loved her, my dear. Do you think I do not feel
her loss? I have seen so little of her since her marriage. If I
had but known. I'm afraid I've been a bad father."

"No, no, dear. You were always kind, and she loved you
dearly. She liked to think that you were happy among pleasant
people. She never had a selfish thought."

"I know it, Viola. And she was happy with her husband?
You are quite sure of that?"

"I never saw two people so utterly united, so happy in each
other's devotion."

"Yet he seemed to take his loss very quietly."

"His grief is all the deeper for being undemonstrative."

"Well, I suppose so," sighed Sir Nugent. "Yet I should have
expected to see him more cut up. Oh, by the way, I came to
ask you about him. Have you any idea where he has gone? He
may have told you, perhaps?"

"Where has he gone, papa? Isn't he at home?"

"No. I waited dinner for an hour and a half, and went in
alone. learning that you were too ill to come down, and ate a cut-
let. It was not very polite of him to walk off without leaving
any information as to his intentions."

"I can't understand it, papa. He may have gone to town on
business, perhaps. He went away suddenly just before—before my dearest was taken ill—went one day and came back the
next."

"Humph!" muttered Sir Nugent; "rather unmannerly."

There was wonderment in the house that night as the hours
wore on and the master was still absent—wonderment most of
all in the stables, where Tarpan's various vices were commented
upon.

Scouts were sent across the moors, but the night was dark,
the moors wide, and the scouts discovered no trace of horse or
rider.

Sir Nugent rose early next morning, and was not a little
alarmed at hearing that his son-in-law had not returned, and had
gone out the previous evening for a ride on the moor.

The one possibility remained that he had changed his mind,
ridden into Seacomb, and left Tarpan at one of the hotels while
he went by the train which left Seacomb for Exeter at seven
o'clock in the evening. He might have taken it into his head
to sleep at Exeter, and go on to London next morning. A man
distraught with grief might be pardoned for eccentricity or restlessness.

The day wore on as the night had done, slowly. Viola

roamed about the silent house, full of dreariest thoughts, going to the nursery about once every half hour to smother little Nugent with tearful kisses.

Sir Nugent telegraphed to his son-in-law at three clubs thinking to catch him at one of the three if he were in London.

The day wore on to dusk, and it was just about the time when Churchill had gone to the stables in quest of Tarpan. Viola was standing at one of the nursery windows looking idly down the drive, when she saw a group of men come round the curve of the road, carrying a burden in their midst. That one glance was enough. She had heard of the bringing home of such burdens—from the hunting-field, or from some pleasure jaunt on sea or river.

There was no doubt in her mind, only a dreadful certainty. She rushed from the room without a word, and down to the hall, where her father appeared at the same moment, summoned by the loud peal of the bell.

Some farm laborers, collecting sea-weed on the beach, had found the Squire of Penwyn crushed to death among the jagged rocks, his horse above him.

The trampled and broken ground above showed the force of the shock when the horse and rider went down over the sharp edge of the cliff.

A fate so obvious required no explanation. Mr. Penwyn had gone for his gallop across the moor, as he had announced his intention of doing, and, betrayed by the thickening mists of an autumnal evening, his brain more or less enfeebled by the grief and agitation he had undergone, he had lost ken of that familiar ground, and had galloped straight at the cliff. The only curious circumstance in the whole business was the squire's use of his spur, a punishment he had never been known to inflict upon Tarpan before that fatal ride. This was commented upon in the stable, and formed the subject of various nods and significant shoulder shrugs, finally resulting in the dictum that the squire had been off his head, poor chap, after losing his pretty wife.

So, after an inquest and verdict of accidental death, Madge Penwyn's early grave was opened, and he who had loved her with an unmeasured love was laid beside her in that last resting-place.

* * * * * * *

Justina did not deprive little Nugent of his too early inherited estate. A compromise was effected between the infant's next friend, Sir Nugent Bellingham, and Justina's next friend, Mr. Clissold, and the baby squire kept his land and state, while Justina became proprietress of the mines, the royalties from which, according to Messrs. Pergament, were worth three thousand a year. Great was the excitement in the Royal Albert Theater when the young lady who had made so successful a *debut* in "No Cards" left the stage forever, on her inheritance of a fortune.

There was a quiet wedding one November morning, in a quiet Bloomsbury church—a wedding at which Mathew Elgood gave the bride away, and Martin Trevanard was best man—a quiet but not less enjoyable wedding-breakfast in the Bloomsbury lodging, and then a parting at which Mr. Elgood, affected at once by grief and Moselle, wept copiously.

"It's the first time you've been parted from your adopted father, my love," he sobbed, "and he'll find it a hard thing to live without you. Take her, Clissold; there never was a better daughter—and as the daughter, so the wife. She's a girl in a thousand. 'Ay, the most peerless piece of earth. I think, that e'er the sun shone on.' God bless you both. Excuse an old man's tears. They won't hurt you."

And so, with much tenderness on Justina's side they parted. The bride and bridegroom drove away to the Charing Cross station, on the first stage of their journey to Rome, where they were to stay till the end of January. There had been a still sadder parting for Justina that morning with the invalid at Hampstead, where the bride had spent the hour before her wedding. Muriel had kissed her and blessed her. and admired her in her pretty white dress, and so they parted, between smiles and tears.

When they were comfortably seated in the railway carriage, traveling express to Dover, Humphrey took an oblong parcel out of his pocket, and put it into Justina's lap.

"Your wedding present, love."

"Not jewels, I hope, Humphrey."

"Jewels!" he cried, with a laugh. "How should a pauper give jewels to the proprietress of flourishing tin mines! That would be taking diamonds to Golconda. 'I give thee all, I can no more,' etc., etc. 'If not my lute. I offer you my lyre.'"

She tore open the package, with a puzzled look.

It was a small octave volume, bound in ivory, with an antique silver clasp, and Justina's monogram in silver set with rubies—a perfect gem in the way of book-binding.

"Do not suppose that I esteem the contents worthy the cover," said Humphrey, laughing. "The cover is a tribute to you."

"What is it, Humphrey?" asked Justina, turning the book over and over, too fascinated with its outward seeming to open it hastily. "A church service?"

"When one wants to know the contents of a book one generally looks inside."

She opened it eagerly.

"A Life Picture!"

"Oh, how good of you to remember that I liked this poem!" cried Justina.

"It would be strange if I forgot your liking for it, dearest. Do you remember your speculations about the poet?"

"Yes, dear, I remember wondering what he was like."

"Would you be very much surprised if you knew he was the image of me?"

"Humphrey!"

"I have given you the only wedding gift I had to offer, love -the first fruits of my pen."

"Oh, Humphrey, is it really true? Have I married a poet?"

"You have married something better, dear, an honest man, who loves you with all his strength, his heart, and mind."

* * * * * * *

Three years later and Humphrey's fame as a poet is an established fact, a fact that grows and widens with time. Humphrey and Justina have made themselves a summer home, a house of the Swiss *chalet* order, near Borcel End, in which ancient homestead Muriel lives her quiet life, her father's placid companion, harmless, tranquil, only what Phœbe the house-maid calls "a little odd in her ways."

Justina and Viola Bellingham are fast friends, much to the delight of Martin Trevanard, who contrives somehow to be always at hand during Viola's visits to the *chalet*—who breaks in a pair of Iceland ponies for that lady's phaeton, and makes himself generally useful. Mr. and Mrs. Clissold have set up their nursery by this time—an institution people set up with far less consideration than they give to the establishment of a carriage and pair, but which is the more costly luxury of the two —and nurses and babies at the *chalet* are sworn allies with the young squire and his nurse from the Manor-house, where Viola is mistress, Sir Nugent Bellingham coming to Cornwall once in three months for a week or so, yawning tremendously all the time, looking at accounts which he doesn't in the least understand, and going back to his clubs and the stony-hearted streets with infinite relief.

Happy summer-tides for the young married people, for the children, for the lovers! Sweet time of youth and love and deep content, when the glory and the freshness of a dream shineth verily upon this work-a-day world.

[THE END.]

ImTheStory.com

Personalized Classic Books in many genre's

Unique gift for kids, partners, friends, colleagues

Customize:

- Character Names
- Upload your own front/back cover images (optional)
- Inscribe a personal message/dedication on the
  inside page (optional)

Customize many titles Including
- Alice in Wonderland
- Romeo and Juliet
- The Wizard of Oz
- A Christmas Carol
- Dracula
- Dr. Jekyll & Mr. Hyde
- And more...